James Hervey

The Works of the Late Reverend James Hervey, A.M.

Rector of Westen-Favell in Northamptonshire

James Hervey

The Works of the Late Reverend James Hervey, A.M.
Rector of Westen-Favell in Northamptonshire

ISBN/EAN: 9783743408067

Manufactured in Europe, USA, Canada, Australia, Japa

Cover: Foto ©Thomas Meinert / pixelio.de

Manufactured and distributed by brebook publishing software (www.brebook.com)

James Hervey

The Works of the Late Reverend James Hervey, A.M.

THE WORKS

OF

The late Reverend

JAMES HERVEY, A. M.

Rector of Weston-Favell, in Northamptonshire.

VOLUME IV.

CONTAINING

ASPASIO VINDICATED,

In ELEVEN LETTERS from Mr HERVEY to Mr JOHN WESLEY, in answer to that Gentleman's Remarks on THERON and ASPASIO. With Mr WESLEY'S LETTER prefixed.

TO WHICH IS ANNEXED,

A DEFENCE of THERON and ASPASIO, against the Objections contained in Mr SANDEMAN'S *Letters on Theron and Aspasio.* With Mr HERVEY'S Letters to the Author prefixed.

I marvel, that ye are so soon removed from him that called you into the grace of Christ, unto another gospel: which is not another; but there be some that trouble you, and would pervert the gospel of Christ. Gal. i. 6, 7.

EDINBURGH:
Printed for P. WHYTE, and J. ROCH, the Publishers, and sold by them, at their Shop, Luckenbooths, and by the principal Booksellers in Great Britain.

M DCC LXXIX.

ASPASIO VINDICATED.

PREFACE.

THE following letters were written by my late brother, in anſwer to a *piece*, which was firſt ſent him from the Rev. Mr *John Weſley*, by way of private letter, containing ſome remarks which that gentleman had made on reading *Theron* and *Aſpaſio*. When my brother had read it over, he thought it beſt to be ſilent, as it contained nothing which could materially affect his judgment in regard to the work it cenſured: for this reaſon, as well as for peace ſake, he laid it by him unanſwered.—Mr *Weſley* then publiſhed a pamphlet, which he entitled *A preſervative againſt unſettled notions in religion;* in which he printed the above-mentioned letter.

This my brother looked upon as a ſummons to the bar of the Public; and upon this occaſion, in a letter to a friend, dated *June* 23. 1758, writes as follows:

[" My dear friend,

" I little thought, when I put Mr *Weſley*'s manu-
" ſcript into your hand, that I ſhould ſee it in print ſo
" ſoon. I took very little notice of it, and let it lie
" by me ſeveral months, without giving it an attentive
" conſideration‡. It ſeemed to me ſo palpably weak,
" dealing

---

‡ Afterwards he read it again, and gave it, what he calls in the beginning of the firſt letter, " *a careful peruſal.*"

"dealing only in positive assertions and positive deni-
"als, that I could not imagine he would adventure it
"into the world, without very great alterations. But
"it is now come abroad, just as you received it, in a
"two shillings pamphlet, entitled, *A preservative a-
"gainst unsettled notions in religion*. Of this pamphlet
"what he has wrote against me, makes only a small
"part. Now then the question is, Whether I shall
"attempt to answer it ? Give me your opinion, as
"you have given me your assistance ; and may the
"Father of mercies give you increase of knowledge
"and utterance, of peace and joy in the Holy Ghost."]

Between this and the *October* following, my brother began the letters contained in this volume, of which he thus speaks in another letter to his friend, dated *October* 24. 1758.

["My dear friend,
"Let me repeat my thanks for the trouble you
"have taken, and for the assistance you have given
"me, in relation to my controversy with Mr *Wesley*.
"He is so unfair in his quotations, and so magisterial
"in his manner, th t I find it no small difficulty, to
"preserve the decency of the gentleman, and the
"meekness of the Christian, in my intended answer.
"May our divine Master aid me in both these instan-
"ces, or else not suffer me to write at all."]

When, in the *December* following, I was sent for to *Weston*, in the very last period of my brother's long ill-
ness,—I asked him (the evening before he died) "what
"he would have done with the letters to Mr *Wesley*,
"whether he would have them published after his
"death?"— He answered—"By no means, because he
"had only transcribed about half of them fair for the
"press ; but as the corrections and alterations of the
"latter part were mostly in short-hand, it would be
"difficult to understand them, especially as some of
"the short-hand was entirely his own, and others
"could not make it out ; therefore," he said, "as it is
"not

"not a finished piece, I desire you will think no more about it."

As these were his last orders concerning these letters, I thought it right to obey them; and therefore I withstood the repeated solicitations of many of his friends, who wanted to have them printed; alledging the service they might be of to allay the groundless prejudices, which the *Preservative* might occasion in the minds of many, against my brother's other writings, as well as the utility of them in general, as they contained so masterly a defence of " *the truth as it is in JESUS.*"

But, notwithstanding the regard I had for the persons who solicited the publication, I could not be persuaded to print the letters; and they never had appeared in public with my consent, had not a surreptitious edition of them lately made its way from the press, and was I not under a firm persuasion *that* will be followed by *more*.

As this is the case, I think it my duty to the memory of my late brother, to send forth as correct an edition as I possibly can; for as to *that* which has appeared (from what editor I know not,) it is so faulty and incorrect, that but little judgment can be formed from it, of the propriety and force of my brother's answers to Mr *Wesley*.

As to the unfairness of publishing my brother's letters without my consent, and the injustice to his memory, in sending so mangled a performance out under his name, they are too apparent to need any proof: and though the editor, as I have been informed, gave away the whole impression, so that it is plain, lucre was not the motive of his proceeding, and I would charitably hope he did it with a view of benefiting his readers; yet it is so like *doing evil that good may come*, as, in my opinion, to be quite unjustifiable.

However, as the only way now left to remedy in some sort what has been done, and to prevent a further imposition on the public, from worse motives than

than actuated this publisher, I have called a friend to my assistance; and, by this means, present the reader with as perfect a copy of these letters, as can possibly be made out from the original manuscript now in my hands.

That the reader may judge more clearly of the state of the controversy between my late brother and Mr *Wesley*, I have thought it right to subjoin Mr *Wesley*'s letter, word for word, as it stands in the *Preservative*.

A LETTER to the *Rev. Mr* ———

DEAR SIR, Oct. 15. 1756.

A Considerable time since I sent you a few hasty thoughts which occurred to me on reading the dialogues between *Theron* and *Aspasio*. I have not been favoured with any answer. Yet, upon another and a more careful perusal of them, I could not but set down some obvious reflections, which I would rather have communicated, before those dialogues were published.

In the first dialogue there are several just and strong observations, which may be of use to every serious reader. In the second, is not the description often too laboured, the language too stiff, and affected? Yet the reflections on the creation (in the 52d and following pages, vol. I.) make abundant amends for this. (I cite the pages according to the *Dublin* edition, having wrote the rough draught of what follows, in *Ireland* *.)

---

* The pages in this edition refer to the second and third volumes of our author's works; vol. I. denoting the first volume of THERON and ASPASIO, and vol. II. denoting the second volume of that work. The reader will easily see, that Mr *Wesley* has, in most cases, quoted very unfairly.

P. 61.

P. 62. Is *justification* more or less, than GOD's pardoning and accepting a sinner thro' the merits of *Christ?* That GOD herein " reckons the righteousness and obedience which *Christ* performed *as our own* ;" I allow, if by that ambiguous expression, you mean only, as you here explain it yourself, " they are as effectual for obtaining our salvation, *as if they were our own* personal qualifications." P. 63.

P. 66. " WE are not solicitous, as to any *particular* set of *phrases*. Only let men be humbled, as repenting criminals, at *Christ's* feet; let them rely, as devoted pensioners, on his merits ; and they are undoubtedly in the way to a blissful immortality." Then for *Christ's* sake, and for the sake of the immortal souls which he has purchased with his blood, do not dispute for that *particular phrase*, *the imputed righteousness of* Christ. It is not scriptural; it is not necessary. Men who scruple to use, men who never heard the expression, may yet " be humbled, as *repenting criminals*, at his feet, and rely, as *devoted pensioners*, on his merits." But it has done immense hurt. I have had abundant proof, that the frequent use of this unnecessary phrase, instead of " furthering men's progress in vital holiness," has made them satisfied without any holiness at all ; yea, and encouraged them to work all uncleanness with greediness.

P. 68. " To ascribe pardon to *Christ's passive*, eternal life to his *active* righteousness, is fanciful rather than judicious. His universal obedience, from his birth to his death, is the one foundation of my hope."

THIS is unquestionably right. But if it be, there is no manner of need, to make the imputation of his *active* righteousness, a separate and laboured head of discourse. O that you had been content with this plain scriptural account, and spared some of the *dialogues* and *letters* that follow !

THE third and fourth dialogues contain an admirable illustration and confirmation of the great doctrine

of

of *Chrift*'s fatisfaction. Yet even here I obferve a few paffages, which are liable to fome exception.

P. 77. " SATISFACTION was made to the divine law." I do not remember any fuch expreffion in fcripture. This way of fpeaking of the law as a *perfon injured* and to be *fatisfied*, feems hardly defenfible.

P. 100. " THE death of *Chrift* procured the *pardon* and *acceptance* of believers, even before he came in the flefh." Yea, and ever fince. In this we all agree. And why fhould we contend for any thing more?

P. 154. " ALL the benefits of the new covenant are the *purchafe of his blood*." Surely they are. And after this has been fully proved, where is the need, where is the ufe, of contending fo ftrenuoufly, for the *imputation of his righteoufnefs*, as is done in the fifth and fixth dialogues?

P. 169. " IF he was our fubftitute as to *penal fufferings*, why not as to *juftifying obedience*?"

THE former is exprefsly afferted in fcripture. The latter is not exprefsly afferted there.

P. 181. " As fin and mifery have *abounded* thro' the firft *Adam*, mercy and grace have *much more abounded* through the fecond. So that none can have any reafon to complain." No, not if the fecond *Adam* died for all. Otherwife, all for whom he did not die, have great reafon to complain. For they inevitably *fall* by the firft *Adam*, without any *help* from the fecond.

P. 184. " THE whole world of believers" is an expreffion which never occurs in fcripture; nor has it any countenance there: the world in the infpired writings being conftantly taken either in an univerfal or in a bad fenfe; either for the whole of mankind, or for that part of them who know not GOD.

P. 186. " IN *the* LORD *fhall all the houfe of* Ifrael *be juftified*." It ought unqueftionably to be rendered, " by or *through the* LORD:" this argument therefore proves nothing. " *Ye are complete in him*." The words

literally

literally rendered are, *Ye are filled with him.* And the whole paſſage, as any unprejudiſed reader may obſerve, relates to ſanctification, not juſtification.

P. 186. " THEY are accepted *for* Chriſt'*s ſake;* this is juſtification thro' *imputed righteouſneſs.*" That remains to be proved. Many allow the former, who cannot allow the latter.

P. 187. *Theron.* " I SEE no occaſion for ſuch *nice diſtinctions and metaphyſical ſubtilties.*

Aſp. You oblige us to make uſe of them, by confounding theſe very different ideas, that is, *Chriſt*'s active and paſſive righteouſneſs."

I ANSWER, We do not *confound* theſe: but neither do we *ſeparate* them. Nor have we any authority from ſcripture, for either thinking or ſpeaking of one ſeparate from the other. And this whole debate on one of them ſeparate from the other, is a mere *metaphyſical ſubtilty.*

P. 188. " THE righteouſneſs which juſtifies us, is already *wrought out.*"—A crude, unſcriptural expreſſion! " It was *ſet on foot, carried on, completed.*"— O vain philoſophy! The plain truth is, *Chriſt* lived and *taſted death for every man;* and thro' the merits of his life and death, every believer is juſtified.

P. 189. " WHOEVER perverts ſo glorious a doctrine, ſhews he never believed." Not ſo. They who *turn back as a dog to the vomit,* had once *eſcaped the pollutions of the world by the knowledge of* Chriſt.

P. 189, 90. " THE goodneſs of GOD leadeth to repentance." This is unqueſtionably true. But the *nice, metaphyſical* doctrine of *imputed righteouſneſs,* leads not to repentance, but to licentiouſneſs.

P. 190. " THE believer *cannot but* add to his faith, works of righteouſneſs." During his firſt love, this is often true. But it is not true afterwards, as we know and feel by melancholy experience.

P. 192. " WE no longer obey, *in order* to lay the foundation for our final acceptance." No; that foundation

dation is already laid in the merits of *Christ*. Yet we obey, *in order* to our final acceptance through his merits. And in this sense, by obeying we *lay a good foundation, that we may attain eternal life*.

P. 192. " WE *establish the law* : we provide for its honour, by the perfect obedience of *Christ*." Can you possibly think, St *Paul* meant this? that such a thought ever entered into his mind? The plain meaning is, We establish both the true sense, and the effectual practice of it : we provide for its being both understood and practised in its full extent.

P. 193. " On those who reject the atonement, just severity." Was it ever possible for them, not to reject it? If not, how is it just, to cast them into a lake of fire, for not doing what it was impossible they should do? Would it be just (make it your own case) to cast *you* into hell, for not touching heaven with your hand?

P. 196. " JUSTIFICATION is *complete* the first moment we believe, and is incapable of *augmentation*."

NOT so : there may be as many *degrees* in the *favour* as in the *image* of GOD.

P. 231. " ST PAUL often mentions *a righteousness imputed:* (Not *a* righteousness ; never once ; but simply *righteousness*.) " What can this be, but *the righteousness of* Christ ?" He tells you himself, *Rom.* iv. 6. *To him that believeth on him that justifieth the ungodly*, faith *is imputed for righteousness*. " Why is *Christ* styled *Jehovah our righteousness?*" Because we are both justified and sanctified through him.

P. 232. " My death, the cause of their forgiveness ; my righteousness, the ground of their acceptance."

How does this agree with P. 68. " To ascribe pardon to *Christ's passive*, eternal life to his *active* righteousness, is fanciful rather than judicious ?"

P. 236. " HE commends such kinds of beneficence *only*, as were exercised to a disciple as such." Is not this a slip of the pen ? Will not our LORD then commend,

mend, and reward eternally, all kinds of beneficence, provided they flowed from a principle of loving faith? Yea, that which was exercifed to a Samaritan, a Jew, a Turk, or an Heathen? Even thefe, I would not term " tranfient bubbles," though they do not *procure* our juftification.

P. 238. " How muft our righteoufnefs exceed that of the fcribes and Pharifees? Not only in being fincere, but in poffefling a *complete* righteoufnefs, even that of *Chrift.*" Did our LORD mean this? Nothing lefs. He fpecifies, in the following parts of his fermon, the very inftances wherein the righteoufnefs of a Chriftian exceeds that of the fcribes and Pharifees.

P. 240. " HE brings this fpecious *hypocrite* to the teft." How does it appear, that he was an *hypocrite?* Our LORD gives not the leaft intimation of it. Surely he *loved him*, not for his hypocrify, but his fincerity!

YET he loved the world, and therefore could not keep any of the commandments in their fpiritual meaning. And the keeping of thefe is undoubtedly the *way* to, though not the *caufe* of, eternal life.

P. 242. " By *works his faith was made perfect;* appeared to be true." No: the natural fenfe of the word is, *By* the grace fuperadded while he wrought thofe *works, his faith was* literally *made perfect.*

Ibid. " HE *that doth righteoufnefs is righteous,—* manifefts the truth of his converfion." Nay; the plain meaning is, *He* alone *is* truly *righteous,* whofe faith worketh by love.

Ibid. " ST JAMES fpeaks of the *juftification of our faith.*" Not unlefs you mean by that odd expreffion, our *faith* being *made perfect:* for fo the apoftle explains his own meaning. Perhaps the word *juftified* is once ufed by St *Paul* for *manifefted.*—But that does not prove, it is to be fo underftood here.

P. 244. " WHOSO *doth thefe things fhall never fall* into total apoftafy." How pleafing is this to flefh and blood!

blood! But *David* says no such thing. His meaning is; *Whoso doth these things* to the end, *shall never fall* into hell.

THE seventh dialogue is full of important truths, Yet some expressions in it I can't commend.

P. 260. ONE *thing thou lackest*, the imputed righteousness of *Christ*." You cannot think this is the meaning of the text. Certainly the *one thing* our LORD meant was, the love of GOD. This was the thing he lacked.

P. 267. " Is the *obedience* of *Christ* insufficient to *accomplish* our justification?" Rather I would ask, Is the *death* of *Christ* insufficient to *purchase* it?

271. " THE saints in glory ascribe *the whole* of their salvation to the *blood* of the Lamb." So do I: and yet I believe he " obtained for all a *possibility* of " salvation."

P. 272. " THE terms of acceptance for *fallen* man were a *full satisfaction* to the divine justice, and a *complete conformity* to the divine law." This you take for granted; but I cannot allow.

THE *terms* of acceptance for fallen man are *repentance* and *faith. Repent ye, and believe the gospel.*

Ibid. " THERE are but two methods whereby any can be justified, either by a *perfect obedience* to the law, or because *Christ* hath kept the law in our stead." You should say, " or by *faith* in *Christ*." I then answer, This is true. And fallen man is justified, not by *perfect obedience*, but by *faith*. What *Christ* has done is the *foundation* of our justification, not the *term* or *condition* of it.

IN the eighth dialogue likewise there are many great truths, and yet some things liable to exception.

P. 300. " DAVID GOD himself dignifies with the *most exalted* of all characters." Far, very far from it. We have more exalted characters than *David's*, both in the Old Testament and the New. Such are those of *Samuel, Daniel*, yea and *Job*, in the former; of *St. Paul* and *St. John* in the latter.

" BUT

"BUT GOD 'ſtyles him *a man after his own heart.*" This is the text which has cauſed many to miſtake: for want of conſidering, firſt, that this is ſaid of *David* in a particular reſpect, not with regard to his *whole character:* Secondly, the time, at which it was ſpoken. When was *David a man after* GOD's *own heart? When* GOD found him *following the ewes great with young*, when he took him *from the ſheep-folds*, Pſal. lxxviii. 71. It was in the 2d or 3d year of *Saul's* reign, that *Samuel* ſaid to him *The* LORD *hath ſought him a man after his own heart, and hath commanded him to be captain over his people*, 1 *Sam.* xiii. 14. But was he *a man after* GOD's *own heart* all his life? or in all particulars? So far from it, that we have few more exceptionable characters, among all the men of GOD recorded in ſcripture.

P. 309. "THERE *is not a juſt man upon earth that ſinneth not."* Solomon might truly ſay ſo, before *Chriſt* came. And St *John* might, after he came, ſay as truly, *Whoſoever is born of* GOD *ſinneth not.* " But *in many things we offend all."* That St *James* does not ſpeak this of himſelf, or of real *Chriſtians*, will clearly appear, to all who impartially conſider the context.

THE ninth dialogue proves excellently well, that we cannot be *juſtified by* our *works.*

BUT have you thoroughly conſidered the words which occur in the 318th page?

"O CHILDREN of *Adam*, you are *no longer* obliged, to love GOD with all your ſtrength, nor your neighbour as yourſelves. *Once* indeed I inſiſted upon abſolute purity of heart: *now* I can diſpenſe with ſome degrees of evil deſire. Since *Chriſt"*—has fulfilled the law *for you*, " you need not fulfill it; I will *connive* at, yea accommodate my demands to your weakneſs."

I AGREE with you, that " this doctrine makes the holy One of GOD a miniſter of ſin." And is it not your own? Is not this the very doctrine which you eſpouſe throughout your book?

I cannot but except to several passages also in the tenth dialogue. I ask, first,

P. 341. " Does the *righteousness of* God ever mean" (as you affirm) " *the merits of* Christ?" I believe not once in all the scripture. It often means, and particularly in the epistle to the *Romans*, God's *method of justifying* sinners. When therefore you say,

P. 342. " The righteousness of God means, such a righteousness as may justly challenge his acceptance," I cannot allow it at all: and this capital mistake must needs lead you into many others. But I follow you step by step.

P. 343. " In order to entitle us to a reward, there must be an imputation of righteousness." There must be an interest in *Christ*. And then *every man shall receive his own reward, according to his own labour.*

P. 344. " A rebel may be *forgiven*, without being restored to the dignity of a *son*." A rebel against an earthly king may; but not a rebel against God. In the very same moment that God forgives, we are the sons of God. Therefore this is an idle dispute. For *pardon* and *acceptance*, tho' they may be *distinguished*, cannot be *divided*. The words of *Job* which you cite are wide of the question. Those of *Solomon* prove no more than this, (and who denies it?), that justification implies both *pardon* and *acceptance*.

P. 345. " Grace *reigneth through righteousness unto eternal life ;*"—that is, The free love of God brings us, thro' justification and sanctification, to glory. P. 346. " *That they may receive forgiveness, and a lot among the sanctified:*" that is, that they may receive pardon, holiness, heaven.

Ibid. " Is not the satisfaction made by the death of *Christ*, sufficient to obtain both our full pardon and final happiness?" Unquestionably it is, and neither of the texts you cite proves the contrary.

P. 347. " If it was requisite for *Christ* to be baptized, much more to fulfil the moral law."

I CANNOT prove that either the one or the other was requisite *in order* to his *purchasing* redemption for us.

P. 348, " By *Christ's* sufferings alone, the law was not satisfied." Yes it was ; for it required only the alternative, Obey or die. It required no man to obey and die too. If any man had perfectly obeyed, he would not have died. *Ibid.* " Where scripture ascribes *the whole* of our salvation to the death of *Christ,* a *part* of his humiliation is put for the *whole."* I cannot allow this without some proof. *He was obedient unto death* is no proof at all ; as it does not necessarily imply any more, than that *he died in obedience* to the Father. In some texts there is a *necessity* of taking a part for the whole. But in these there is no such *necessity.*

P. 351. " CHRIST *undertook* to do every thing necessary for our redemption;" namely, in a *covenant* made with the Father. 'Tis sure, he *did* every thing necessary : but how does it appear, that he *undertook* this, before the foundation of the world, and that by a positive *covenant* between him and the Father ?

You think this appears from four texts. 1. From that, *Thou gavest them to me.* Nay, when any believe, *the Father gave them* to *Christ.* But this proves no such previous contract. 2. GOD *hath laid upon him the iniquities of us all.* Neither does this prove any such thing. 3. That expression, *The counsel of peace shall be between them,* does not necessarily imply any more, than that both the Father and the Son would concur in the redemption of man. 4. *According to the counsel of his will,*—that is, in the way or method he had chosen. Therefore neither any of these texts, nor all of them, prove what they were brought to prove. They do by no means prove, that there ever was any such covenant made between the Father and the Son.

P. 353. " THE *conditions* of the covenant are recorded. *Lo, I come to do thy will."* Nay, here is no mention

mention of any *covenant*, nor any thing from which it can be inferred. " The recompense stipulated in this glorious *treaty*."—But I see not one word of the treaty itself. Nor can I possibly allow the existence of it without far other proof than this. *Ibid.* " Another copy of this grand *treaty* is recorded *Isaiah* xlix. from the first to the sixth verse." I have read them, but cannot find a word about it, in all those verses. They contain neither more nor less than a prediction of the salvation of the *Gentiles*.

P. 354. " BY the covenant of works, man was bound to obey *in his own person*." And so he is under the covenant of grace; tho' not in order to his justification. " The obedience of *our Surety* is accepted instead of *our own*." This is neither a safe nor a scriptural way of speaking. I would simply say, *We are accepted thro' the Beloved. We have redemption thro' his blood.*

P. 354. " THE second covenant was not made with *Adam*, or any of his posterity, but with *Christ*, in those words, *The seed of the woman shall bruise the serpent's head.*" For any authority you have from these words, you might as well have said, it was made with the Holy Ghost. These words were not spoken *to Christ*, but *of* him, and give not the least intimation of any such *covenant* as you plead for. They manifestly contain, if not a covenant made with, a promise made to *Adam* and all his posterity.

- P. 355. " CHRIST, we see, *undertook* to execute the conditions." We see no such thing in this text. We see here only a promise of a Saviour, made by GOD to man.

Ibid. " 'Tis true, I cannot fulfil the conditions." 'Tis not true. The conditions of the new covenant are, *Repent* and *believe*. And these you can fulfil, thro' *Christ* strengthening you. " 'Tis equally true this is not required at my hands." It is *equally* true, that is, absolutely false, and most dangerously false. If we allow this, Antinomianism comes in with a full tide.

tide.. "*Chrift* has performed all that was *condition-ary for me.*" Has he *repented* and *believed for you?* You endeavour to evade this by faying, " He performed all that was *conditionary* in the *covenant of works.*" This is nothing to the purpofe; for we are not talking of that, but of the *covenant of grace.* Now he did not perform all that was *conditionary* in this covenant, unlefs he repented and believed. " But he did unfpeakably more." It may be fo. But he did not do this.

P. 360. " But if *Chrift's perfect obedience* be ours, we have no more need of pardon than *Chrift* himfelf." The confequence is good. You have ftarted an objection which you cannot anfwer. You fay indeed, " Yes, we do need pardon; for *in many things we offend all.*" What then? If his *obedience* be *ours*, we ftill *perfectly obey in him.*

P. 361. " Both the branches of the law, the *pre-ceptive* and the *penal*, in the cafe of guilt contracted, muft be fatisfied." Not fo. " *Chrift* by his death alone, (fo our church teaches) fully fatisfied for the fins of the whole world." The fame great truth is manifeftly taught in the 31ft article. Is it therefore fair, is it honeft, for any one to plead the articles of our church in defence of abfolute predeftination? Seeing the 17th article barely *defines* the term, without either affirming or denying the thing: whereas the 31ft totally overthrows and razes it from the foundation.

P. 362. " Believers who are notorious tranf-greffors *in themfelves*, have a finlefs obedience *in Chrift.*" O firen fong! pleafing found, to *James Wheatly!* *Thomas Williams!* *James Reiley!*

I know not one fentence in the eleventh dialogue, which is liable to exception: but that grand doctrine of Chriftianity, original fin, is therein proved by irrefragable arguments.

The twelfth likewife is unexceptionable, and contains fuch an illuftration of the wifdom of God, in the

ftructure

structure of the human body, as I believe cannot be paralleled, in either ancient or modern writers.

The former part of the thirteenth dialogue is admirable. To the latter I have some objection.

P. 518, 19. "*Elijah* failed in his resignation, and even *Moses* spake unadvisedly with his lips." It is true: but if you could likewise fix some blot upon venerable *Samuel* and beloved *Daniel*, it would prove nothing. For no scripture teaches, that the holiness of *Christians* is to be measured by that of any *Jew*.

P. 521. "Do not the best of men frequently feel disorder in their affections? Do not they often complain, *When I would do good, evil is present with me?*" I believe not. You and I are only able to answer for ourselves. "Do not they say, *We groan being burthened,*—with the workings of inbred corruption?" You know, this is not the meaning of the text. The whole context shews, the cause of that groaning was their longing *to be with* Christ.

Ibid. "The cure" of sin "will be perfected in heaven." Nay surely, in paradise, if no sooner. "This is a noble prerogative of the beatific vision." No: it would then come too late. If sin remains in us till the day of judgment, it will remain for ever. "Our present blessedness does not consist in being *free from sin.*" I really think it does. But whether it does or no, if we are not *free from sin*, we are not Christian believers. For to all these the apostle declares, *Being made free from sin, ye are become the servants of righteousness*, Rom. vi. 18.

P. 522. If we were perfect in piety (St *John*'s word is, *perfect in love*,) *Christ*'s priestly office would be superseded." No: we should still need his Spirit (and consequently his intercession) for the continuance of that love from moment to moment. Beside, we should still be encompassed with infirmities, and liable to mistakes; from which words or actions might follow, even though the heart was all love, which were not

exactly

exactly right. Therefore, in all these respects, we should still have need of *Christ*'s priestly office: and therefore as long as he remains in the body, the greatest saint may say,

> Every moment, LORD, I need
> The merit of thy death.

The text cited from *Exodus* asserts nothing less than, that *iniquity* " cleaves to all *our holy things* till death."

Ibid. " SIN remains, that the righteousness of faith may have its due honour." And will the righteousness of faith have its due honour no longer than sin remains in us ? Then it must remain, not only on earth and in paradise, but in heaven also—" And the sanctification of the Spirit its proper esteem." Would it not have more esteem, if it were a perfect work ?

Ibid. " It (sin) will make us lowly in our own eyes." What, will pride make us lowly ? Surely the utter destruction of pride would do this more effectually. P. 523. " It will make us compassionate." Would not an entire renewal in the image of GOD make us much more so ? " It will teach us to admire the riches of grace." Yea, but a fuller experience of it, by a thorough sanctification of spirit, soul, and body, will make us admire it more. " It will reconcile us to death." Indeed it will not ; nor will any thing do this, like perfect love.

P. 524. " IT will endear the blood and intercession of *Christ*." Nay, these can never be so dear to any, as to those who experience their full virtue, who are *filled with the fulness of* GOD. Nor can any " feel their continual need" of *Christ*, or " rely on him," in the manner which these do.

VOL. II. DIALOGUE 14. P. 9. " THE claims of the law are all answered." If so, Count *Zinzendorf* is absolutely in the right: neither GOD nor man can claim my obedience to it. Is not this Antinomianism without a mask ?

P. 11. " YOUR sins are expiated through the death

death of *Chrift*, and *a righteoufnefs given you*, by which you have free accefs to GOD." This is not fcriptural language. I would fimply fay, *By him we have accefs to the Father*.

THERE are many other expreffions in this dialogue, to which I have the fame objection, namely, 1. That they are unfcriptural ; 2. That they directly lead to Antinomianifm.

THE firft letter contains fome very ufeful heads of felf-examination. In the fecond,

P. 44. I READ, " There is *a righteoufnefs* which fupplies all that the creature needs. To prove this *momentous* point, is the defign of the following fheets."

I HAVE feen fuch terrible effects of this unfcriptural way of fpeaking, even on thofe *who had once clean efcaped from the pollutions of the world*, that I cannot but earneftly wifh, you would fpeak no otherwife than do the oracles of GOD. Certainly this *mode of expreffion* is not *momentous*. It is always *dangerous*, often *fatal*.

LETTER III. p. 47. " *Where fin abounded, grace did much more abound: that as fin had reigned unto death, fo might grace*—the free love of GOD—*reign thro' righteoufnefs*, thro' our juftification and fanctification, *unto eternal life*, Rom. v. 20, 21. This is the plain natural meaning of the words. It does not appear, that one word is fpoken here about *imputed righteoufnefs*: neither in the paffages cited in the next page, from the common-prayer and the article. In the homily likewife that phrafe is not found at all, and the main ftrefs is laid on *Chrift's fhedding his blood*. Nor is the *phrafe* (concerning the *thing* there is no queftion) found in any part of the homilies.

P. 54. " IF the fathers are not explicit with regard to the imputation of *active* righteoufnefs, they abound in paffages which evince the *fubftitution* of *Chrift* in our ftead: paffages which difclaim all dependence on any duties of our own, and fix our hopes wholly on

the

the *merits* of our Saviour. When this is the case, I am very little solicitous about any *particular forms of expression.*" O lay aside then those questionable, dangerous forms, and keep closely to the scriptural.

LETTER IV. p. 58. "The authority of our church and of those eminent divines," does not touch those *particular forms of expression:* neither do any of the texts which you afterwards cite. As to the doctrine we are agreed.

P. 59. "THE *righteousness of* GOD signifies, the righteousness which God-man wrought out." No. It signifies GOD's method of justifying sinners.

P. 60. "THE victims figured the *expiation* by *Christ*'s death, the cloathing with skins, the *imputation of* his righteousness." That does not appear. Did not the one rather figure our justification, the other, our sanctification?

P. 62. ALMOST every text quoted in this and the following letter, in support of that *particular form of expression,* is distorted above measure from the plain, obvious meaning, which is pointed out by the context. I shall instance in a few, and just set down their true meaning, without any farther remarks.

P. 63. *To shew unto man his uprightness.* To convince him of GOD's justice, in so punishing him.

P. 66. HE *shall receive the blessing*—pardon—*from the* LORD, *and righteousness*—holiness—*from the* GOD *of his salvation,*—the GOD who saveth him both from the guilt and from the power of sin.

Ibid, I WILL *make mention of thy righteousness only.*—Of thy *mercy.* So the word frequently means in the Old Testament. So it unquestionably means in that text, *In* (or by) *thy righteousness shall they be exalted.*

P. 68. ZION *shall be redeemed with judgment*—after severe punishment—*and her converts with righteousness*—with the tender mercy of GOD, following that punishment.

Ibid. IN (or *thro'*) *the* LORD *I have righteousness*

and strength, justification and sanctification. P. 69. *He hath clothed me with the garments of salvation,*—saved me from the guilt and power of sin: both of which are again expressed by, *He hath covered me with the robe of righteousness.*

P. 70. MY *righteousness*—my mercy—*shall not be abolished.*

P. 72. *To make reconciliation for iniquity*—to atone for all our sins,—*and to bring in everlasting righteousness*, spotless holiness into our souls. And this righteousness is not *human*, but *divine*. It is the gift and the work of GOD.

P. 73. THE LORD *our righteousness*—The author both of our justification and sanctification.

P. 84. "WHAT righteousness shall give us peace at the last day, inherent or imputed?" Both. *Christ* died for us and lives in us, *that we may have boldness in the day of judgment.*

LETTER V. p. 89. *That have obtained like precious faith thro' the righteousness*—the mercy—*of our* LORD. *Seek ye the kingdom of* GOD *and his righteousness*—the holiness which springs from GOD reigning in you.

P. 91. THEREIN *is revealed the righteousness of* GOD—GOD's method of justifying sinners.

P. 92. 93. "WE *establish the law*, as we expect no salvation without a perfect conformity to it—namely, by *Christ*." Is not this a mere quibble? and a quibble, which, after all the laboured evasions of *Witsius* and a thousand more, does totally *make void the law?* But not so does St *Paul* teach. According to him, *Without holiness*, personal holiness, *no man shall see the* LORD. None, who is not *himself* conformed to the law of GOD here, *shall see the* LORD in glory.

THIS is the grand, palpable objection to that whole scheme. It directly *makes void the law*. It makes thousands content to live and die *transgressors of the law*, because *Christ* fulfilled it *for them.* Therefore, though

though I believe, he hath *lived* and *died* for me, yet I would speak very tenderly and sparingly of the former, (and *never*, separately from the latter,) even as sparingly as do the scriptures, for fear of this dreadful consequence.

P. 96. " THE *gift of righteousness* must signify a righteousness not their own." Yes, it signifies the righteousness or holiness, which GOD gives to and works in them.

P. 97. " THE *obedience of one* is *Christ*'s actual performance of the whole law." So here his passion is fairly left out ! Whereas his *becoming obedient unto death*, that is, dying for man, is certainly the chief part, if not the whole which is meant by that expression.

Ibid. " THAT *the righteousness of the law might be fulfilled in us.*—That is, by our representative in our nature. Amazing ! but this, you say, " agrees with the tenor of the apostle's arguing. For he is demonstrating we cannot be justified by our own conformity to the law." No : not here. He is not speaking here of the *cause* of our justification, but the *fruits* of it. Therefore that unnatural sense of his words does not at all " agree with the tenor of his arguing."

P. 98. " I TOTALLY deny the criticism on δικαιουν and δικαιωμα, and cannot conceive on what authority it is founded. O how deep an aversion to inward holiness does this scheme naturally create ?

P. 100. " THE righteousness they attained could not be any personal righteousness." Certainly it was. It was *implanted* as well as *imputed*.

P. 104. " FOR *instruction in righteousness*, in the righteousness of *Christ*." Was there ever such a comment before ? The plain meaning is, For training up in *holiness* of heart and of life.

P. 105. *He shall convince the world of righteousness.*—That I am not a sinner, but innocent and holy.

P. 107. " THAT *we might be made the righteousness of* GOD *in him*. Not intrinsically, but imputatively."

Beth

Both the one and the other. GOD *through him*, first *accounts* and then *makes* us *righteous*. Accordingly,

P. 111. THE *righteousness which is of* GOD *by faith*, is both *imputed and inherent*.

P. 112. " MY faith fixes on both the *meritorious life* and *atoning death* of *Christ*." Here we clearly agree. Hold then to this, and never talk of the former without the latter. If you do, you cannot say, " Here we are exposed to no hazard." Yes, you are to an exceeding great one; even the hazard of living and dying without holiness. And then we are lost for ever.

THE sixth letter contains an admirable account of the earth and its atmosphere, and comprizes abundance of sense in a narrow compass, and expressed in beautiful language.

P. 138. GEMS have " a seat on the virtuous fair one's breast." I cannot reconcile this with St *Paul*. He says, *Not with pearls :* by a parity of reason, not with diamonds. But in all things I perceive, you are too favourable, both to *the desire of the flesh* and *the desire of the eye.* You are a gentle casuist as to every self-indulgence which a plentiful fortune can furnish.

P. 144. " OUR Saviour's obedience."—O say, with the good old Puritans, our Saviour's *death* or *merits*. We swarm with Antinomians on every side. Why are you at such pains to increase their number?

P. 157. My *mouth shall shew forth thy righteousness and thy salvation.*—Thy mercy which brings my salvation.

THE eighth letter is an excellent description of the supreme greatness of *Christ*. I do not observe one sentence it it, which I cannot chearfully subscribe to.

THE ninth letter, containing a description of the sea, with various inferences deduced therefrom, is likewise a master-piece, for justness of sentiment, as well as beauty of language. But I doubt whether " mere *shrimps*," P. 214. be not too low an expression; and whether you might not as well have said nothing of

" cod,

"cod, the standing repast of *Lent;*" or concerning
"the exquisite relish of *turbot*, or the deliciousness of
"*sturgeon*," p. 218. Are not such observations beneath
the dignity of a minister of *Christ?* I have the same
doubt concerning what is said (p. 236.) of "delicate-
ly-flavoured *tea*, finely-scented *coffee;* the *friendly
bowl*, the pyramid of *Italian* figs, and the *pistacia*-nut
of *Aleppo.*" Beside that the mentioning these in such
a manner is a strong encouragement of luxury and sen-
suality. And does the world need this? the *English* in
particular?—*Si non insaniunt satis sua sponte, instiga.*

LETTER 10. P. 246. " Those treasures which
spring from the imputation of *Christ's righteousness.*"
Not a word of his *atoning blood?* Why do so many
men love to speak of his righteousness, rather than
his atonement? I fear, because it affords a fairer ex-
cuse for their own unrighteousness. To cut off this,
is it not better to mention both together? at least
never to name the former without the latter?

P. 261. " FAITH is a persuasion that *Christ* has shed
his blood *for me*, and fulfilled all righteousness *in my
stead.*" I can by no means subscribe to this definition.
There are hundreds, yea thousands of true believers,
who never once thought, one way or the other, of
Christ's fulfilling all righteousness *in their stead*. I per-
sonally know many who to this very hour have no idea
of it; and yet have each of them a divine evidence
and conviction, *Christ loved me, and gave himself for
me*. This is St *Paul*'s account of faith: and it is suf-
ficient. He that *thus* believes, is justified.

P. 263. " IT is a *sure* means of purifying the heart,
and *never fails* to work by love." It *surely* purifies
the heart—if we *abide in it;* but not if we *draw back
to perdition*. It *never fails* to work by love, while it
continues; but if itself fail, farewell both love and
good works.

" FAITH is the hand which receives all that is laid
up in *Christ.*" Consequently, if we *make shipwreck of
the*

the faith, how much so ever is laid up in *Christ,* from that hour we receive nothing.

LETTER II. P. 265. " FAITH in *the imputed righteousness* of *Christ,* is a fundamental principle in the gospel." If so, what becomes of all those who think nothing about *imputed righteousness?* How many who are full of faith and love, if this is true, must perish everlastingly?

P. 276. " Thy hands must urge the way of the deadly weapon, through the shivering flesh, till it be plunged in the throbbing heart." Are not these descriptions far too strong? May they not occasion unprofitable reasonings in many readers?

Ne puerum coram populam Medea trucidet.

Ibid. " How can he *justify* it to the world?" Not at all. Can this then *justify his faith* to the world?

P. 285. " YOU take the certain way to obtain comfort; the righteousness of *Jesus Christ.*" What, without the atonement? Strange fondness for an unscriptural, dangerous *mode of expression!*

P. 286. " So the merits of *Christ* are derived to all the faithful." Rather the fruits of the Spirit: which are likewise plainly typified by the oil in *Zecharia*'s vision.

P. 291. " HAS the law any demand? It must go to him for satisfaction. Suppose, " Thou shalt love thy neighbour as thyself." Then *I* am not obliged to love my neighbour. *Christ* has satisfied the demand of the law *for me.* Is not this the very quintessence of Antinomianism?

P. 292. " THE righteousness wrought out by *Jesus Christ,* is wrought out for *all his people,* to be *the cause* of *their* justification, and *the purchase* of their salvation. *The righteousness* is the cause, the purchase." So the *death* of *Christ* is not so much as named! " For all his people." But what becomes of *all other people?* They *must inevitably* perish for ever. The die was cast, or ever they were in being. The doctrine to *pass them by,* has

> Consign'd their unborn souls to hell,
> And damn'd them from their mother's womb!

I could sooner be a Turk, a Deist, yea an Atheist, than I could believe this. It is less absurd to deny the very being of GOD, than to make him an almighty tyrant.

P. 300. "THE whole world and all its seasons, are rich with our Creator's goodness. His tender mercies are over all his works." Are they over the bulk of mankind? Where is his goodness to the non-elect? How are his tender mercies over *them?* "His temporal blessings are given *to them.*" But are they to them blessings at all? Are they not all curses? Does not GOD *know* they are? that they will only increase their damnation? Does not he *design* they should? And this you call *goodness!* this is *tender mercy!*

P. 303. "MAY we not discern pregnant proofs of goodness, in each individual object?" No; on your scheme, not a spark of it, in this world or the next, to the far greater part of the work of his own hands!

P. 317, 18. "Is GOD a generous benefactor to the meanest animals, to the lowest reptiles? And will he deny my friend what is necessary to his present comfort, and his final acceptance?" Yea, will he deny it to any soul that he has made? Would you deny it to any, if it were in your power?

> But if you *lov'd* whom GOD abhorr'd,
> The servant were above his LORD.

P. 321. THE *wedding-garment* here means holiness.

P. 324. "THIS is his tender complaint, They *will not come* unto me!" Nay, that is not the case; they *cannot.* He himself has *decreed,* not to give them that grace without which their coming is impossible!

P. 325. "THE grand end which GOD proposes in all his favourable dispensations to fallen man, is to

demonſtrate the ſovereignty of his grace." Not ſo:
to impart happineſs to his creatures, is his grand end
herein. "Barely to demonſtrate his ſovereignty,"
is a principle of action fit for the great Turk, not the
moſt high God.

P. 326. "God hath pleaſure in the profperity of his
ſervants. He is a boundleſs ocean of good." Nay,
that ocean is far from boundleſs, if it wholly paſſes by
nine-tenths of mankind.

P. 327. "You cannot ſuppoſe God would enter
into a freſh covenant with a rebel." I both ſuppoſe and
know he did. "God made the new covenant with
Chriſt, and charged him with the performance of the
conditions." I deny both theſe aſſertions, which are
the central point wherein Calviniſm and Antinomia-
niſm meet. "*I have made a covenant with my choſen.*"
—Namely, with *David my ſervant.* So God himſelf
explains it.

P. 351. "He will waſh you in the blood which a-
tones, and inveſt you with the righteouſneſs which
juſtifies." Why ſhould you thus continually put a-
ſunder what God has joined?

P. 463. "God himſelf at the laſt day pronounces
them righteous, becauſe they are intereſted in the o-
bedience of the Redeemer." Rather, becauſe they
are waſhed in his blood, and renewed by his Spirit.

Upon the whole, I cannot but wiſh, that the plan
of theſe dialogues had been executed in a different
manner. Moſt of the grand truths of Chriſtianity are
herein both explained and proved with great ſtrength
and clearneſs. Why was any thing intermixed, which
could prevent any ſerious Chriſtian's recommending
them to all mankind? any thing which muſt neceſſari-
ly render them exceptionable, to ſo many thouſands of
the children of God? In practical writings I ſtudiouſ-
ly abſtain from the very ſhadow of controverſy. Nay,
even in controverſial, I do not knowingly write one
line, to which any but my opponent would object. For

opinions

opinions shall I destroy the work of GOD? then am I a bigot indeed. Much more, if I would not drop any *mode of expression*, rather than offend either Jew or Gentile, or the church of GOD. I am,
With great sincerity,
Dear Sir,
Your affectionate brother and servant,

J. W.

I have but one thing more to add, which is, concerning the *seasonableness* of the following publication. It may, perhaps, be thought a needless revival of a dispute, which happened long ago, and which is now probably forgotten. In answer to which, I can assure the reader, that the above is printed from an edition of the *Preservative*, now on sale at the *Foundery*. The *seasonableness* of this publication is therefore apparent; for though my brother died *December* 25. 1758, the controversy did by no means die with him, but still subsists in the daily publication and sale of the *Preservative*, which also comes with a special * recommendation from Mr *Wesley*, into the hands of all his preachers, to be by them first " *carefully read, then to be recommended and explained to the several societies where they labour.*" So that the controversy is, in the most effectual manner, daily and hourly kept alive by Mr *Wesley* himself. This proves very sufficiently the *seasonableness*, and, as things have happened, the *expediency*, of the present appearance of the following letters in public. How pertinent an answer they contain to Mr *Wesley*'s objections, is now to be left to the consideration of the candid reader.

Miles's-Lane,
December 5. 1764.

W. HERVEY.

* See the last paragraph of a tract, entitled, *Reasons against a separation from the church of* England. Printed also in the *Preservative*, p. 237.

LETTERS

TO THE

Reverend Mr JOHN WESLEY.

LETTER I.

REV. SIR,

I RECEIVED the letter you mention, containing remarks on the dialogues between *Theron* and *Aspasio*. As, after a careful perusal, I saw very little reason to alter my sentiments, I laid aside your epistle without returning an answer, in hopes that my silence (which it seems you mistook for obstinacy) would most emphatically speak my advice; which, had it been expressed more plainly, would have been delivered in the apostle's words, *That ye study,* or make it your ambition, *to be quiet* *.

Since you have, by printing these remarks, summoned me, though reluctant, to the bar of the Public, it should seem, that I ought not to discredit *the truth*

---

* 1 Thess. iv. 11. Φιλοτιμεισθαι, a beautiful word, rich with meaning, and not adequately translated by *Make it your ambition,* still more inadequately by our common version.

truth once delivered to the saints, by a timid silence; and I am the more willing to answer for myself, as I have now the privilege of an unprejudised judge, and an impartial jury.—If my defence should be lost on my opponent, it may possibly make some useful impressions on the court, and candid audience. However, I will not absolutely despair of convincing Mr *Wesley* himself, because it is written, *Give admonition to a wise man, and he will yet be wiser* *. On some very momentous and interesting points, I may probably be a little more copious than the strict laws of argument demand, in order to exhibit some of the great truths of the gospel, in so *clear* a light, that *he may run who readeth them;* in so *amiable* and *inviting* a light, that the believer may rejoice in them, and the sinner may long for them. For such digressions, I promise myself an easy pardon, both from yourself and the reader.

Thus you open the debate; " In the second dia-
" logue, is not the description often too laboured, the
" language too stiff and affected?" I must confess, Sir, this animadversion seems to be as just, as the praise which you have here and elsewhere bestowed, appears to be lavish: the former, if not more pleasing, may be no less serviceable than the latter. For both I acknowledge myself your debtor; and if ever I attempt any thing more in the capacity of an author, I will be sure to keep my eye fixed on the caution you have given.

I am sorry that the next words bring on a complaint, so close to my acknowledgment. " You cite the pages
" according to the *Dublin* edition, having wrote the
" rough draught of what follows in *Ireland*." But should you not, in complaisance to your readers on this side the water, have referred to the pages of the *English* edition? For want of such reference, there is
hardly

---

* Prov. ix. 9. The original phrase is only in *Give*, which may signify, *Give admonition*, as well as (what our version has supposed) *instruction*.

hardly diſtinction enough, in ſome places, to know which are your words, and which are *Aſpaſio*'s.— Should you not alſo, in juſtice to the author, before you tranſcribed the rough draught for the preſs, have conſulted the *laſt* edition of his work? Which you well knew was not the copy, from which the *Iriſh* impreſſion was taken, yet might reaſonably ſuppoſe to be the leaſt inaccurate.

When I read your next paragraph, I am ſtruck with reverence, I am aſhamed and almoſt aſtoniſhed, at the littleneſs of the preceding obſervations. Stiffneſs of ſtyle, and a thouſand ſuch trifles, what are they all compared with *juſtification* before the infinite and immortal GOD? This is a ſubject that commands our moſt awful regard, a bleſſing that ſhould engage our whole attention. As this is the grand article to come under our conſideration, I would deſire to maintain an inceſſant dependence on the divine SPIRIT, that my thoughts may be influenced, and my pen guided by the wiſdom which cometh from above; that I may neither pervert the truth, by any erroneous repreſentations, nor diſhonour it by an unchriſtian temper. It would be eaſy to make uſe of bitter ſatire, and diſdainful irony, the contemptuous ſneer, or the indignant frown.—And indeed, Sir, you have laid yourſelf open to every attack of this kind: but theſe are not the weapons of a Chriſtian's warfare.

— — *Non defenſoribus iſtis.*

We are to give a reaſon of the hope that is in us, *with meekneſs and fear ; meekneſs*, with regard to thoſe who interrogate or oppoſe us; *fear*, with regard to HIM, whoſe cauſe we plead, and whoſe eye is ever upon us. " Is juſtification," you ſay, " more or leſs, " than GOD's pardoning and accepting a ſinner, thro' " the merits of *CHRIST?*" I ſomewhat wonder, Sir, that you ſhould aſk this queſtion, when it is proffeſſedly anſwered by *Aſpaſio*, who has preſented you with a

very

very circumftantial definition of juftification, explaining it, eftablifhing it, and obviating feveral objections advanced againft it. If you would animadvert with fpirit and force, or indeed to any confiderable purpofe, fhould you not lay open the impropriety of this definition, fhewing from reafon and fcripture, that it is neither accurate nor orthodox?

At pages 61. 62. the reader may fee *Afpafio*'s account of juftification, and find the words imputation and righteoufnefs of *CHRIST*, particularly explained: the latter denoting, " all the various inftances of his " active and paffive obedience ;" accordingly it is affirmed (page 62.) " The punifhment we deferved, " he endures; the obedience which we owed, he ful-" fils."—What *Afpafio* here profeffes to underftand by the righteonfnefs of *CHRIST*, the reader is particularly requefted to bear in his memory, that he be not mifled by Mr *Wefley*, who often forgets it, and complains when the righteoufnefs of *CHRIST* is mentioned, that his penal fufferings are quite omitted. I would not wifh, Sir, to have a plainer proof, that you do not difcard the active, than *Afpafio* has hereby given, that he never excludes the paffive.

By your queftion, you hint a diflike, yet without informing us what it is, or wherein *Afpafio*'s illuftrations and proofs are deficient. You propofe, and *only* propofe, another definition. Well then, to differ from you as little as poffible, nay, to agree with you, as far as truth will permit, fince you are fo loath to admit of our reprefentation, we will accede to yours; efpecially if it be fomewhat explained, and a little improved. For indeed the words, in their prefent form, are rather too vague to conftitute any definition. *Pardoning* and *accepting* may happen to be only diverfified expreffions of the fame idea. The *merits of CHRIST* will certainly comport, either with *Popifh* or *Socinian* notions. It abounds in writers of the former fort, and it is to be found in the latter. Therefore, to be

more

more explicit,—by *pardoning*, I mean, GOD's acquitting a sinner from guilt of every kind, and of every degree. By *accepting*, I mean still more, GOD's receiving him into full favour, considering and treating him as righteous, yea perfectly and gloriously righteous.—By the *merits of CHRIST*, I would always be supposed to signify, his active and passive obedience, all that he wrought, and all that he suffered, for the salvation of mankind *. Interested in all this, the believer enters into the divine presence, and stands before the divine MAJESTY.—Not like *David's* ambassadors, stealing themselves into *Jericho;* safe indeed, but with the marks of *Ammonitish* insults on their persons : he rather enters like that illustrious exile, *Joseph*, into the presence of *Pharaoh*, when his prison-garments were taken from him, and he was arrayed in *vestures of fine linen*, meet for the shoulders of those who appear before kings. With this explication I am content that *your* definition take place of mine †. I would farther observe, that you have dropt the word *imputed*, which inclines me to suspect, you would cashier the thing. But let me ask, Sir, how can we be
justified

---

* The *merits of CHRIST* is certainly an ambiguous phrase, and what I can by no means admire; but as it occurs in Mr. *Wesley's* letter, and in many valuable writers, I have, led by their example, used it in the following debate, still understanding it, and still using it, in the sense explained above.

† To gratify Mr *Wesley*, I have admitted his phrase, " the " *merits of CHRIST*," though, as it is a phrase of dubious import, and what almost any sect or heresy will subscribe, I should much sooner chuse to abide by *Aspasio's* language. And why should we not all speak with the scriptures? Why should we not use the expressions of the apostle? He says, *justified by the blood of CHRIST*; he says, made righteous *by the obedience of CHRIST*. When therefore we say, Sinners are pardoned and accepted through the blood, and through the obedience of *CHRIST*, we have a warrant for our doctrine, which is indisputable; and a precedent for our language, which is unexceptionable.

justified by the merits of *CHRIST*, unless they are imputed to us? Would the payment made by a surety, procure a discharge for the debtor, unless it was placed to his account? It is certain, the sacrifices of old could not make an atonement, unless they were imputed to each offerer respectively. This was an ordinance settled by JEHOVAH himself *. And were not the sacrifices, was not their imputation typical of *CHRIST*, and things pertaining to *CHRIST?* the former prefiguring his all-sufficient expiation, the latter shadowing forth the way whereby we are partakers of its efficacy. The righteousness (not the righteousness and obedience, *Aspasio* speaks otherwise) which *CHRIST* performed is reckoned by GOD as our own. This you call an ambiguous expression; but, if considered in conjunction with the foregoing and following enlargements, I should think it can hardly deserve the charge. *Aspasio* all along labours to be understood. In this place he more fully opens his meaning, by giving another view of the nature, and by specifying the effects of imputation. The *nature*, —it being the same as placing to our account something not our own †. The *effects*,—*CHRIST*'s righteousness, thus placed to our account, being as effectual for obtaining our salvation, as if it was our own personal qualification ‡. To the latter you expressly agree, to the former you make no objection: to the whole doctrine, thus explained, you elsewhere declare your assent.

If in all this we may depend upon you, Sir, must

we

---

* *Lev.* vii. 18. *If any of the flesh of the sacrifice of his peace-offerings be eaten at all on the third day, it shall not be accepted, neither shall it be imputed unto him that offereth it. It shall not be accepted.* Why? for this reason, because it shall not be *imputed*. A plain indication, that the latter is the cause of the former. That without *imputation*, whether it be of the typical or real sacrifice, the blood of the beast, or the death of *CHRIST*, there is no acceptance.

† *Theron* and *Aspasio*, p. 61.   ‡ Ibid. p. 64.

we not feel an alarming shock at your adjuration in the next paragraph?

"For CHRIST's sake do not." What? surely nothing less can excite or justify this vehement exclamation, but the obtrusion of some doctrine, that is most glaringly false and absolutely damnable. Shall we have such a solemn firing, such a thunder of explosion, only to silence a particular phrase? In another person this would look like profane levity; in Mr *Wesley*, the softest appellation we can give it, is idle pomp.—All this clamour merely against words! words too, the explication of which, and the doctrine contained in them, yourself allow. Dear Sir, what is a word or a phrase? Can it do either good or harm, but as conveying right or wrong sentiments? Will the mere pronouncing or hearing of a word (be it *abbracadabra*, or *higgajon selah*, or *imputed*) without its idea, poison the principles of men, and induce them to work *all uncleanness with greediness?* As you have been firing without an enemy, (*Aspasio* is owned for an ally,) so you seem to be triumphing without a victory. *Aspasio*'s charity for those who are disgusted at the expression, and have no explicit knowledge of the doctrine, is guarded by the words immediately following—" yet live under the belief of the truth, " and in the exercise of the duty," as well as by the annexed description of the persons, and their temper; who are far enough from fancying, that if they may but be pardoned for the sake of CHRIST, they can obtain the divine favour, and a title to future happiness, by their own good behaviour. Hence it will appear, that he has been too cautious, to part with the very thing for which he is contending. And this is more abundantly evident from the close of his charitable paragraph, wherein, though he allows such people to be safe; yet he laments their embarrass, and their deficiency in light, strength, and consolation. " The phrase is not scriptural." Suppose it were not, this would afford but a flight reason, for so passionate an outcry: however, this is certain, St *Paul* uses the phrase, *GOD imputeth* †, and *that righteousness might be imputed* ‡. Now, is it possible, that there should be righteousness imputed, yet not an imputed righteousness? To assert this must argue either a wonderful subtil refinement, or an exceeding strong prejudice. " It is not necessary."—Perhaps so. But is it not necessary Mr *Wesley* should either inform us, what sense of the phrase it is, which he apprehends so likely to mislead men, or else, instead of exclaiming against *Aspasio*, should join all his force with him, in defending that sense which they both espouse? " It has " done immense hurt."—When we are made sensible of the immense, or indeed of any real, hurt done by the phrase, *imputed;* when we see those who dislike it, cordially warm for the sentiment expressed in other words, we will then consent to resign it for its equivalent, *reckoned as our own,—placed to our account,— as effectual as if our own personal qualification.* Till then we must guard the casket for the sake of the jewel. We prefer the word *imputed*, because it says more at once, than any other term we know; and because we are aware of a common practice used in all ages, by the opposers of sound doctrine. They pretend a zeal only against the phrase, that by bringing *this* into disuse, they may cause *that* to be forgotten. Shall we not then dispute for *imputed* righteousness? Yes, Sir, we must dispute, both for the doctrine and for the phrase, since there are persons who openly strike at the one, and we fear with a view to supplant the other. Shall we not dispute for *imputed* righteousness,—tho' the words are a grand peculiarity of the scriptures, and the thing the very spirit and essence of the gospel? Not dispute for that which is better to us sinners than all worlds, better than our hearts could wish, or our thoughts conceive; which in short is the best, the noblest,

† Rom. iv. 6.   ‡ Rom. iv. 11.

blest, the completest gift, that GOD himself can bestow.

When such a gift, and such a righteousness is the subject of disputation, we must not give place, no, *not for an hour;* we must maintain its matchless excellency, so long as we have any breath, or any being. We must say, in direct opposition to your fervent but unadvised zeal, " *For* CHRIST's *sake,*" let us contend earnestly for imputed righteousness; because it is the brightest jewel in his mediatorial crown. " *For the sake of immortal souls,*" let us hold fast and hold forth this precious truth; because it yields the strongest consolation to the guilty conscience, and furnishes the most endearing, as well as the most prevailing inducement to universal obedience.

" To ascribe pardon to *CHRIST's passive,* eternal
" life to his *active* obedience, is fanciful rather than
" judicious." The remark is just; not so the quotation; *Aspasio* is somewhat disfigured by your distortion of his features; he limps a little, by your dislocation of a limb There is, in his language, guard enough to check every attempt, either to dissolve the union, or sever the coagency, of the different parts of our LORD's righteousness.

But let us give *Aspasio* a fair hearing. Thus he expresses himself, " To divide them (the *active* and *passive*
" righteousness) into detached portions, independent
" on each other, seems to be fanciful rather than judi-
" cious. To divide into detached portions, is more than to distinguish between the one and the other. The latter *Aspasio* practises, the former he disavows. " Independent of each other,"—do these words stand for nothing? Have they no meaning, that here you shew them no regard, and never recollect them throughout your whole epistle? Had you honoured them with any degree of notice, several of your objections must have been precluded; and if the more candid reader pleases to bear them in memory, several of your
objections

objections will, at the very first view, fall to the ground. Besides, the person who tells us, the case *seems* to be so, is not so peremptory, as he who roundly affirms it to *be* so; the former is all that *Aspasio* has advanced. Though I am willing that you should correct his style, yet I must beg of you, Sir, not to make him quite so positive; let him have the satisfaction of being modest, even where he has the misfortune, in your opinion at least, to be erroneous.

" *CHRIST's* universal obedience from his birth " to his death, is the one foundation of my hope," says *Aspasio*. To which you assent, and with a laudable vehemence, reply, " This is unquestionably " right." I wish, Sir, you would ponder your words before you speak, at least before you print, that there may be something fixed and certain, on which *we* may depend, and by which *you* will abide. One would think, after this acknowledgment, pronounced with such an air of solemnity, you could never so far forget yourself, as to open your mouth against the obedience, the universal obedience of *CHRIST*, which surely must include both what he *wrought*, and what he *suffered*. You confess it to be your *foundation*,—the foundation of your *hope*, the *only* foundation of your hope; can you then, without the most amazing inconsistency, either wish to secrete the doctrine, or offer to discountenance the expression?

" There is no manner of need to make the impu-" tation of *CHRIST*'s active righteousness a separate " head of discourse."—No manner of need, even tho' you declare, that this active righteousness, together with the expiatory death, is the only foundation of your hope! Can you think it possible to treat of *such* a topic too particularly, too distinctly, too minutely?—*Aspasio* has shewn the need, or assigned the reason for this method of handling the subject; because it sets the fulness of our LORD's merits in the clearest light, and gives the completest honour to GOD's holy law.

law. Have you alledged any thing to disprove, or so much as to invalidate his plea? Ought not this to have been done before your assertion can be valid, or even decent?

Besides, are there not persons in the world, who fondly imagine, that if they can but have pardon thro' *CHRIST*, they shall by their own doings secure eternal life? When such persons are in danger of overlooking the active obedience of the REDEEMER, why should you not for their sakes allow us to make the imputation of his righteousness " a separate head " of discourse?" That, seeing the transcendent perfection of *CHRIST*'s work, they may cease from confiding in their own *; lest it be said to them another day, *I will declare thy righteousness, and thy works, that* for the grand purpose of justification *they shall not profit thee* †.

We must therefore take leave to dwell upon the active righteousness of our LORD; we must display its perfection, in opposition to all the vain pretensions of human qualifications, endeavours, or attainments; we must demonstrate, that as the heavens are higher than the earth, so is this divine obedience higher than all the works of the children of men; yea, so transcendent in itself, and absolutely perfect, as to be incapable of any augmentation. All the good deeds of all the saints, could they be added to it, would not increase in any degree its justifying efficacy; it is like all the other works of GOD, concerning which we are told, *nothing can be added to them.* This brings to my remembrance a most beautiful and sublime representation, which you must have read in the evangelical prophet; *Every valley shall be exalted, and every mountain and hill shall be made low, and the crooked shall be made straight, and the rough places plain, and the glory of the LORD shall be revealed, and all flesh shall see it together.* Here mountains are de-

---

* Heb. iv. 10.   † Is. lvii. 12.

demolished, valleys are elevated, and the earth is levelled into a spacious plain, on purpose to accomplish what Mr *Wesley* supposes unnecessary; on purpose to give the most clear, full, striking view of the great REDEEMER, of his wonderful person, and glorious work, that he alone may be distinguished and exalted; may walk majestic and conspicuous thro' the midst of mankind, as being singly and completely sufficient for the recovery of sinners. That all flesh, not Jews only, but Gentiles also; not men of reputation only, but the meanest of mortals, the most infamous of wretches, may together see his glory, may on equal ground, without any pre-eminence of one above another contemplate and partake of his precious death and perfect righteousness, which are the one object of divine complacency, and the sovereign glory of the LORD REDEEMER. According to the import of this magnificent piece of imagery, all the differences that subsist between one man and another are abolished; nothing but *CHRIST* and his complete work are proposed, as the cause of justification and the ground of hope. Faith beholds nothing but the divine *JESUS*; it never inquires, What have I done? what have I suffered? but what has that most illustrious personage done, and what suffered? What has JEHOVAH manifested in our nature, *wrought* for the benefit and redemption of sinners?—Faith is never weary of viewing or reviewing either the active or passive obedience of *IMMANUEL*. Faith will declare, that neither of these points can be set forth in too strong or too recommending a light. Faith is ever desiring to see more and more of the SAVIOUR's worthiness, that the soul may rejoice in his excellency, and be filled with all his fulness.

May you, dear Sir, abound in this faith, and live under such views of GOD our SAVIOUR; then I flatter myself you will be dissatisfied with your present

sent opinion, and not be disgusted at the freedom of speech, used by

Your's, &c.

LETTER II.

Rev. Sir,

I AM particularly pleased at my entrance on this epistle, because it presents me with a view of Mr *Wesley* in very good humour. Instead of rebuking, he commends. He puts off the frown of censure, for the smile of approbation. I hope to follow the amiable example; to approve and applaud, wherever opportunity offers, and truth permits. And though I shall be sometimes obliged to oppose or refute; yet I shall do both with all the tenderness and lenity, which may consist with a proper vindication of the truth.

"The third and fourth dialogues contain an admi-
"rable illustration and confirmation of the great doc-
"trine of *CHRIST's* satisfaction.—This is generously acknowledged. Yet even here it so unhappily falls out, that complaisance gets the start of judgment. Did you advert, Sir, to the state of the controversy, or see the consequence of *Aspasio's* arguing, you must either give up a favourite tenet, or else dissent from his doctrine.

Aspasio maintains, that *CHRIST's* sufferings were punishment; real, proper punishment. Now could *CHRIST*, an innocent person, be punished, without bearing sin; the very sin of others? Could *CHRIST*, a divine person, bear the sin of others, and not do it perfectly away! Or can they, whose guilt was punished in *CHRIST*, and whose sin is perfectly done away by *CHRIST*, can they perish eternally? But I forbear. Yourself, and the judicious reader will easily apprehend

apprehend my meaning, and discern the point, to which these questions lead. All the benefit I propose by this remark, is, to convince Mr *Wesley*, that he is not incapable of a mistake;—that he has tripped a little, in what he *commends*, and therefore may possibly make a false step, in what he *condemns*.

Unless I may be allowed to propose this additional advantage, the rectifying an impropriety in some people's apprehensions, concerning our LORD's vicarious sufferings. It is usual to say, "He bore the punish- "ment, not the guilt; the penalty, not the fault." Which seems to be a distinction more scrupulous than judicious; answers no other end, but that of derogating from our REDEEMER's grace, and weakening the foundation of our hopes.

The guilt of sin, I take to be what the apostle calls, αμαρτια, the transgression of the law. From hence arises the obligation to punishment. This guilt our LORD *so truly* bore, that he was no less liable to the arrest of justice, and the infliction of vengeance, than if he himself had committed the most enormous crimes.—*He bare*, says the HOLY GHOST, *the sin of many*. But punishment cannot be reckoned the same as sin, any more than wages can be accounted the same as work. If then our LORD bore sin itself, he must bear every thing criminal, that is included in it; no circumstance of demerit or aggravation excepted.

He bore the *fault*, therefore he makes us without fault in the sight of GOD; and will present us faultless before the throne, with exceeding joy.—He bore the *guilt;*—therefore our LORD's sufferings were real punishment, justly inflicted by the supreme JUDGE, and, on principles of justice, discharge us from all punishment whatever. He bore the *filth;*—therefore he felt, what those wretched souls endure, who die in their iniquities; his eternal FATHER forsook him, and hid his face from him as from an abominable object.

This

This renders our SAVIOUR's propitiation great, wonderful, glorious. Seeing this, believing this, we have nothing to fear. Conscience is satisfied, and the accuser of the brethren is silenced. Nothing can be laid to our charge by the righteous law, and nothing remains to awaken the indignation of the righteous JUDGE.—Whereas, if this was not done, we have reason to be terribly apprehensive. If *CHRIST* bore not the guilt, then sinners must bear it in their own persons; if he took not away the filth, then it must lye on transgressors, and render them loathsome for ever. If the fault was not transferred to him, then it must abide upon us, and be our everlasting ruin.

Neither does this doctrine in any degree detract from our SAVIOUR's dignity. It rather gives him the honour due unto his name, *JESUS*. As in the scales of a balance, the lower the one descends, the higher the other mounts; so the deeper our MEDIATOR's humiliation sinks, to the more exalted height does his glory rise. The more horrible the condition to which he submitted, the more illustriously his goodness shines, and the more clearly the perfection of his work appears.

Satisfaction was made to the divine law, says *Aspasio*. " I do not remember any such expression in " scripture," replies Mr *Wesley*.—But do you not remember this expression in the epistle to the *Galatians*, *CHRIST was made under the law* * ? Why was he made under the law, but to fulfil its precepts, and undergo its penalty? and is not this a satisfaction to its demands?

The

---

* *Gal.* iv. 4. There is, I think, something uncouth in this expression, *made under the law*. γινομενος 'tis true very well comports with both the clauses, ιχ γυναικος & υπο νομον. But in the *English* translation, the participle might, not ungracefully, be varied, perhaps in some such manner; The *Son of GOD was made of a woman*, and *became subject to the law*.

The truth is, the divine law was violated by our sins. It was absolutely impossible for us to make any reparation; therefore *CHRIST* in our nature and in our stead submitted to its obligations, that he might magnify its injured authority, and render it in the highest degree venerable; might make even its tremendous sanctions and rigorous requirements, the very basis of grace, mercy, and peace.—Divinely-noble contrivance! unspeakably-precious expedient! By this means, vengeance and forbearance have met together; wrath and love have kissed each other, in the redemption of sinners. The law says, I am fulfilled. Justice says, I am satisfied. While both concur to expedite and ascertain the salvation of a believer.

"This way of speaking of the law, as a person "injured, and to be satisfied, seems hardly defen-"sible." Does not the apostle speak of the law as a person? a person that *liveth**, to whom some are *married*, and to whom others are *dead*? *Aspasio* will always think himself, and his manner of speaking, sufficiently defensible, so long as he has the apostolical practice for his precedent.

Having such a precedent, he wants no other; otherwise he might plead the authority of Mr *John Wesley*; who, in his explanatory notes on the *New Testament*, says, " The law is here spoken of (by a " common figure) as a *person*, to which as to an " husband, life and death are ascribed †." And if the law be an husband, may not an husband be *injured?* may not an injured husband insist upon being satisfied?

" All the benefits of the new covenant are the pur-" chase of *CHRIST*'s blood;" this is *Aspasio*'s belief. To this you assent, " *Surely they are.*"—With pleasure

---

* *Rom.* vii. 1, 4. The word ῷ at the end of the first verse is spoken of the *law*, not of the *man*, as Mr *Wesley* and others have very justly observed. It should therefore be translated not *he*, but *it*.

† See Explan. Notes, *Rom.* vii. 1.

pleasure I should receive your suffrage, was I not afraid that this is your meaning; they are *so* the purchase of his blood, as not to have any dependence on, or any connection with, his most perfect obedience.

I was alarmed by the close of your last paragraph, and my suspicions are increased by the following negative interrogation; " After this has been fully pro-
" ved, where is the need, where is the use of con-
" tending so strenuously, for the imputation of his
" righteousness?"

Aspasio has informed you, Sir, in the second dialogue. He has there shewn the advantage of unfolding, circumstantially and copiously, this momentous truth.—To give you farther satisfaction, he has quoted the words of an eminent divine, of which the following are a part,—Whoever rejects the doctrine of the im-
" putation of our SAVIOUR's righteousness to man,
" does, by so doing, reject the imputation of man's
" sin to our SAVIOUR, and all the consequences of
" it."—If you are not satisfied with Mr *Stynoe*'s reasons, you are remitted to St *Paul*. In *Rom.* v. (a chapter of distinguished dignity and importance) he teaches mankind, that *CHRIST died* for the ungodly; that we are justified thro' his *blood*, are saved from wrath by his *death*. After all this had been fully proved, where was the need, where was the use of insisting largely upon that obedience of ONE, by which many are made * righteous? or upon that righteousness of ONE, which is imputed to many for justification of life? Yet this the inspired writer evidently does.

Answer the foregoing question, in behalf of the apostle, and you will answer it in behalf of *Aspasio*; or if you decline the office, give me leave, Sir, to answer it on behalf of them both. The blood of CHRIST is never considered as independent on, or detached from, the righteousness of CHRIST. They united their blessed efficacy in accomplishing the work of our redemption;

* Rom. v. 19.

redemption; we always look upon them as a grand and glorious aggregate, in their agency inseparable, though in meditation distinguishable. Being thus distinguishable, at proper times, we meditate upon each distinctly. We display each with all the particularity possible, and cannot but contend for the imputation of one, as well as of the other. The farther we dig into either of these spiritual mines, the greater fund of treasures we discover. The more we glorify the SAVIOUR, the more we strengthen faith, and the greater addition we make to our comfort, our peace, our joy.

Aspasio inquires, If CHRIST was our substitute as to penal suffering, why not as to justifying obedience? You reply,—" The former is expressly asserted " in scripture, the latter is not expressly *asserted* there." A small inaccuracy here, Sir! the former is no more a scripture-expression, than the latter; while the latter is no less the doctrine and sense of scripture than the former.—A little piece of forgetfulness likewise! since you just now acknowledged, that " CHRIST's " universal obedience was the *one* foundation of your " hope." But how can his obedience be any foundation of your hope, if in this capacity he was not your substitute? Take away the circumstance of substitution, and there is no more ground for your reliance on the obedience of CHRIST, than for your reliance on the obedience of *Gabriel*. *We are made the righteousness of GOD*, because we are *IN him*, as our proxy and our head; because he wrought the justifying righteousness, not only in our nature, but in our name, not only as our benefactor, but as our representative.

" As sin and misery have abounded through the " first *Adam*, mercy and grace have much more a- " bounded through the second. So that now none " have reason to complain." Here indeed we have *Aspasio*'s words, but in a patched and disfigured condition. One part taken from page 181, and another wrenched from page 177. Let any one read the
whole

whole of those passages, and judge whether they can be fairly applied to the doctrines of election or predestination. Yet Mr *Wesley* is resolved, at all adventures, with or without occasion, to introduce these subjects of deep and perplexed disputation. Therefore he replies, " No, not if the second *Adam* died for all, " otherwise all for whom he did not die, have great " reason to complain."

Here, Sir, do you not force an inference from *Aspasio*'s words, foreign to his design ? He is speaking of those who betake themselves to *CHRIST*, and are recovered through his righteousness. Such persons he particularly mentions. Of such alone he discourses; without considering the case of others, who, despising or neglecting the REDEEMER, reject the counsel of GOD against themselves.—Would it not be as edifying to the reader, and as agreeable to your office, if you should join with *Aspasio* in displaying the free, superabundant, infinitely-rich grace of our GOD; altogether as becoming this, as to divert his aim, and retard his steps, when he is pressing forwards to this prize of our high calling in *CHRIST JESUS ?*

Aspasio's words are, " When we betake ourselves " to *CHRIST JESUS*, we shall find, that, as sin " and misery have abounded, *&c.*" Please to observe, Sir, how he limits his discourse, consequently is obliged to defend nothing, but what corresponds with such limitation.

Had the *Israelites* any cause to be dissatisfied with the provision made for their sustenance and their cure, when the serpent of brass was lifted up on the pole, and when the bread from heaven lay round about their tents ? No more have sinners any cause to think themselves aggrieved, when the salvation of GOD is evidently set before them in the gospel ; is brought to their very door, in the preaching of the word, and they are allowed, importuned, commanded to receive it by faith. This is enough for me.

Enough

Enough this for any transgressors, who want, not to gratify curiosity, but to inherit life.—If they, or you, Sir, chuse to pry further, and to intrude into the divine secrets, I must leave you to yourselves; saying, as I depart, *The secret things belong unto the LORD our GOD; but those things which are revealed, belong unto us and our children* *.

" The whole world of believers."—" This is an " expression which never occurs in scripture."—It affords me a kind of presumptive proof, that solid objections are not at hand, when such shadows are lifted into the service.—I should be under no pain if you could prove your charge, beyond all contradiction. To what would it amount? Why, that *Aspasio*, having occasion to mention a certain topic, happened not to make use of the very syllables and letters made use of in scripture. And do you or I, Sir, in all our sermons, journals, preservatives, and Christian libraries, undertake to use none but scriptural expressions? Had we done this, one benefit might indeed have accrued to the public. It would considerably have reduced our volumes.—But I trifle as well as Mr *Wesley*. You proceed to enforce your remonstrance, by adding,—" Neither has the expression any countenance from scripture." I am really ashamed to detain our readers any longer upon so trivial a point. Therefore what I am going to reply, is only a word to yourself. You, Sir, can tell who it is that affirms in a certain hymn;

> For ev'ry man
> 'Tis finish'd, 'tis past—
> The world is forgiv'n
> For *JESUS's sake*.

The world forgiven! What, all the world? every child of *Adam*; they who believe not on *CHRIST* and die in their sins? This you cannot mean; this you dare not assert; this, I think, no mortal can suppose. You yourself

* Deut. xxix. 29.

yourself therefore, by " the world," must intend " the believing world;" and are you offended at *Aspasio* for commenting on your text? for expressing plainly what is implied in your own words?

In the LORD shall all the house of Israel be justified. This text *Aspasio* quotes, and acquiesces in the common version, upon which you animadvert. " It " ought unquestionably to be rendered *by* or *thro'* the " LORD." How hard is *Aspasio's* lot! If he does not use the exact language of scripture, he is criminal at your bar, witness the preceding objection; if he does use the exact language of scripture, as in the present instance, you indite him for an erroneous translation. So that it is next to impossible to escape your censure.

In the LORD, you affirm, is not the pure language of scripture, it is a wrong translation, " and ought " *unquestionably* to be rendered *by* or *through* the " LORD." Yet *quisquis adhuc uno partam colit asse Minervam*—Whoever has learned *Hebrew* no more than a month, will assure our *English* reader, that the prefix ב is the very first word in the Bible. Must it there be translated *by* or *thro'* the beginning?—If our young scholar have only his psalter, he can shew the same particle occurring three times within the first verse. In *the counsel*—in *the way*—in *the seat.*—Twice in the second verse; *His delight is* in *the law*—in *his law will he exercise himself.* Three times more in the remainder of the psalm, *shall bring forth fruit* in *his season*—*shall not stand* in *judgment.* Neither in *the congregation of the righteous.*—Now let the *English* reader judge for himself, whether the *Hebrew* prefix must " *unquestionably* be rendered" in all these places " *by* or *through.*" By or through his season! by or through the congregation! But I stop, there is no need to apply all the passages. Neither is there any need of critical skill in languages, to determine concerning any *one* of them. Common sense in this case is sufficiently

sufficiently qualified to be our critic and our arbitrator. —I only wish, Sir, you had produced the evidence for the corrected version. Then the public might have seen on which side the ballance were likely to turn; and which were the most cogent logic, "*Aspasio*'s doc-"trine is false, therefore the translation is wrong; "or the translation is fair, therefore his doctrine is "true."

By this time, I believe, the *unlearned reader* will begin to discern, what degree of credit is due to your criticisms upon the original, and to your alteration of the common version, when they are supported by nothing more, than your bare assertion.—I also begin to be apprehensive, that our canvassing the sense of words, and sifting the dead languages, will be no very agreeable entertainment to *any* reader. I will therefore for the future be more concise in the execution of this business; especially as I have here given a specimen of what might be done. I will try, if it is not possible, to animate what would otherwise be dull, and to blend godly edifying with critical disquisition.

Ye are complete in him. With this translation also Mr *Wesley* finds fault. "The words literally rendered are, "Ye are filled with him."—I am ready to grant, that places may be found, where the preposition ἐν must be understood according to your sense. But then every one knows that this is not the native, obvious, literal meaning; rather a meaning swayed, influenced, moulded by the preceding or following word. The literal signification of ἐν αὐτῷ is as we have rendered it. —Nor is there the least occasion to depart from the received interpretation; it is suitable to the context, and to the scope of the whole epistle.

However, we will suppose your criticism to be just. Does this destroy or enervate *Aspasio*'s argument? Would you have one meaning contradict or supplant the other? "Ye are filled *with* him, therefore ye are "not complete *in* him?" Does the former sense include or imply the latter? Can you, or I, or any one be filled with every requisite for our recovery and happiness, yet not be complete? It seems, therefore, you get nothing by this criticism, but the satisfaction of doing violence to the phrase, without any improvement of the sense, or any advantage to your cause.

" The whole passage (you affirm) relates to sanctifi-
" cation, not to justification." Where is your proof, Sir? This we always expect. This Mr *Wesley* seldom, if ever, condescends to give. " Yes," he says, " any " unprejudiced reader may observe it." A strange kind of proof! reducible to no figure in logic, unless there be a figure styled *presumption*. Was I to answer for the unprejudiced reader, I think he would observe the very reverse. The words of the apostle are not a little forcible against your sense of the passage, as will appear from the transitive adverb *also*. The next and the subsequent verses, we allow, relate to sanctification: if this verse does the same, such is the manner of the apostle's reasoning, " In whom ye are " sanctified, in whom also ye are sanctified." Whereas, if the first clause denotes the justification of the *Colossian* converts thro' the righteousness of CHRIST, if the following periods describe their sanctification, as a consequence of this most happily operating privilege, then the reasoning is just, and the transition graceful. " In him ye are completely justified, in him " also ye are truly sanctified."

The whole passage is calculated to teach us, that CHRIST is the *fulness of our sufficiency*. In him, and in him alone, there is enough to answer all the purposes of wisdom, righteousness, sanctification, and redemption.—It is intended likewise to admonish us, that we should rest satisfied with him alone, in opposition to all the fond inventions of men; who would introduce something else for the ground of our confidence, and the cause of our consolation, as though it was said;—

If indeed our *LORD JESUS CHRIST* had been an ordinary person, or merely a created being, ye might well be offended at my doctrine. Ye might then with some colour of reason seek to the maxims of philosophy for wisdom, or to the works of the law for righteousness. But *CHRIST* is an immensely-glorious person, for *in him are hid all the treasures of wisdom and knowledge.*—*CHRIST* is an incomparably-exalted sovereign,—for *he is the head of all principalities and powers.*—Yea, *CHRIST* is the supreme incomprehensible JEHOVAH; for *in him dwelleth all the fulness of the GODHEAD bodily.* Being therefore transplanted into him by faith, ye are complete. Partakers of him; ye have every blessing and all good. Thought cannot imagine, nor desire crave, any thing farther, greater, higher.

Matchless privilege! exalted felicity! O may the knowledge, the experimental knowledge of it, fill our hearts, as *the waters cover* the abyss of the *sea!* Then will we sing the hymn which once expressed your sentiments, and still expresses mine.

> * " Join earth and heav'n to bless
> " The LORD our righteousness.
> " The mystery of redemption this,
> " This the SAVIOUR's strange design;

Man's

---

* See p. 56. of *Hymns and spiritual songs*. Anonymous indeed, but universally ascribed to Mr *Wesley*. In these excellent lines, how strongly marked are the sentiments of the gospel! Our offences so fully imputed to *CHRIST*, as to be accounted his. His righteousness so fully imputed to us, as to be accounted ours. In him we are *complete*, because his most obedient life, and his all-atoning death are ours. We are guiltless, not thro' our repentance, or reformation, but because he has died for us. We are righteous, not on account of any graces or attainments of our own, but because he has lived for us. To these truths I most cordially subscribe. This is that good old wine that once made Mr *Wesley's* heart glad. He has since tasted new; but I hope he will be brought to say, " *The old is better.*"

" Man's offence was counted his,
" Ours his righteousness divine.
" In him complete we shine,
" His death, his life is mine:
" Fully am I justified,
" Free from sin, and more than free,
" Guiltless, since for me he died,
" Righteous, since he liv'd for me."

The text lately quoted from *Isaiah*, is part of a paragraph eminent for its dignity and usefulness. We then considered a fragment of it in a critical view; let us now examine the whole of it with a devotional spirit. Thus examined, I trust it will be no longer a dry bone, but *a feast of fat things full of marrow.* Permit me to propose a correct translation of the original; to add a short illustration of the meaning, and then take my leave for the present.

" Look unto me and be saved all the ends of the
" earth, for I am GOD, and there is nought else *.
" By myself have I sworn, the word of † righ-
" teousness goeth out of my mouth, the word
" shall not return. To me every knee shall bow,
" and every tongue shall swear ‡, saying, Sure-
ly

* *None else*— אין עוד exactly rendered, signifies *there is not besides.* Not any person, nor any thing. *No person* able to lend an helping hand. *No thing* capable of yielding the least assistance.

† *The word of righteousness*, צדקה דבר I apprehend is equivalent to St *Paul*'s λόγος δικαιοσύνης, and signifies, if not the whole gospel, that precious doctrine, which is the gospel in epitome. For the vindication of this version, see *Vitringa in loc.*

‡ *Shall swear.* Our translation seems to discontinue the divine speech here; which weakens the force, and diminishes the dignity of the passage. I apprehend JEHOVAH is still speaking, and in the following words, prescribes the form of the confession, or dictates the words of the oath, in which sinners shall testify their allegiance,—even the allegiance of faith. Agreeably to this supposition, I would translate the word אמר *saying,*

"ly * in the LORD have I righteousness † and strength.
"To him shall men come, and all that are offended
"in him, shall be ashamed. In the LORD shall all
"the seed of Israel be justified, and in him shall they
"glory."

Here the SON of GOD presents himself in all the glories of his person, and all the riches of his grace; presents himself as the object of faith, and the author of salvation; to be received by sinners, without any recommending qualities, or any pre-eminence of one above another.—But hear his gracious words:

Look unto me, wretched ruined transgressors, as the wounded *Israelites* looked unto the brazen serpent. Look unto me dying on the cross as your victim, and obeying the law as your surety.—Not by doing, but by looking and believing; not by your own deeds, but by my works, *and* my sufferings, *be ye saved*. This is the mysterious but certain way of salvation. Thus shall ye be delivered from guilt, rescued from hell, and reconciled to GOD. Who are invited to partake of this inestimable benefit? *All the ends of the earth.*

saying. It will then denote not *one*, or a few, but every tongue mentioned in the foregoing verse. פן I am aware is of the feminine gender, but every reader knows how often the *Hebrews* neglect the nicety of grammatical construction, and every reader sees that the idea of אש or of a *person*, is comprehended in the word *tongue*.

* The prophet's אן *surely*, is something like the apostle's ἀλλὰ μενοῦνγε, *yea, doubtless, Phil.* iii. 8. The HOLY GHOST teaches believers to speak with vehemence upon this point, to signify their stedfast and resolute affiance in the glorious RE-DEEMER, together with the mighty and matchless importance of this faith. I have taken in this idea, because it is suggested by the *English* translation, though I prefer the *exclusive* sense *only;* as implying an absolute and total renunciation of every other confidence.

† *Righteousness*. This is the precise signification of נפחר which being in the plural number, seems to denote *completeness*. A righteousness, perfect, entire, and lacking nothing; having every thing necessary for our pardon, our acceptance, our everlasting justification.

earth. People of every nation under heaven; of every station in life; of every condition, and every character, not excepting the chiefest of sinners.

Is it possible that the obedience of *one* should save innumerable millions? It is not only possible, but indubitable. *For I am GOD* infinite in dignity and power; therefore all-sufficient, yea, omnipotent to save; to save all that come unto me; be the multitudes ever so great, or their cases ever so desperate.—(Is nothing to be done by transgressors themselves? Are no conditions to be fulfilled on their part?) None, —*there is nought beside me*. No person can take any share in this great transaction. Nothing can in the least degree co-operate with my merits. Should you add to my obedience and death, all that saints have performed, and martyrs have endured, it would be like adding a grain to the sands of the ocean, or a moment to the days of eternity.

Such is my compassionate invitation, and this my inviolable decree. *I have* not only spoken, but *sworn;* sworn by myself, and all my incomprehensible excellencies. *The word of righteousness*, that which relates to the grandest of all subjects, and most important of all interests, is planned, adjusted, and unalterably determined. Now, even now, *it goes out of my mouth*, is declared with the utmost solemnity, and established by veracity itself. The word shall not return, either to be repealed by me, or frustrated by any other.— What is the decree confirmed by this most awful oath? We are all attention to hear it. *To me every knee shall bow*. Every soul of man, who desires to inherit eternal life, shall submit to my righteousness, and as an unworthy creature, as an obnoxious criminal, obtain the blessing wholly thro' my atonement.—*To me every tongue shall swear*. Be man's supposed virtues ever so various, or ever so splendid, all shall be disclaimed, and my worthiness alone shall stand. Renouncing every other trust, they shall repose the confi-

dence

dence of their fouls on me alone, and make public confeſſion of this their faith before the whole world. —But we, O LORD, are ignorant, we cannot order our ſpeech by reaſon of darkneſs.—This then ſhall be the form of your oath, ſuch the tenor of your confeſſion.

Surely—It is a moſt wonderful, yet a moſt faithful ſaying, extremely comfortable, and equally certain. *Only*—not in myſelf, not in a poor frail creature, but *in* the incarnate JEHOVAH alone, in his divinely-excellent deeds, and unutterably-meritorious ſufferings, *I have righteouſneſs*, a righteouſneſs without ſpot, without defect, and in all reſpects conſummate; ſuch as ſatisfies every requirement of the law, and moſt thoroughly expiates all my iniquities; ſuch as renders me completely accepted before my judge, and entitles me to everlaſting life. From the joyful knowledge, the perſonal appropriation, and the perpetual improvement of this ineſtimable privilege, I have *ſtrength* for my ſanctification. Now do I indeed delight myſelf in the LORD, who, perfectly reconciled, and infinitely gracious, has done ſo great things for me. Now do I cordially love my neighbour; and being ſo happy myſelf, unfeignedly long for his eternal happineſs, that he may be a partaker with me of this great ſalvation.

To this ſovereign decree, the prophet ſets, as it were, his ſeal, or elſe, in a tranſport of joy, he foretells the accompliſhment of it. Yes, my brethren, *to him*, even to this gracious *REDEEMER, ſhall men come.* I ſee them flying as clouds for multitude, as doves for ſpeed. They believe the report of his goſpel, and receive of his fulneſs—Whereas, *all they that are offended in him*, that cannot away with his doctrine, which pours contempt upon all human excellency, and will allow no righteouſneſs to avail but that which is divine; who refuſe to come unto him, poor, and miſerable, and ſtript of every recommendation; all they *ſhall be aſhamed*. The fig-leaves of their own duties, or their own endowments, ſhall neither adorn them for glory, nor
ſcreen

screen them from wrath,—but shall abandon them to vengeance, and cover them with double confusion. While, on the other hand, *all the seed of Israel*, every true believer, shall be justified in the LORD. Against these persons no accusation shall be valid; no condemnation shall take place: so magnificent is the majesty, so surpassingly-efficacious are the merits of their SAVIOUR, that in him they shall not only confide, *but glory;* not only be safe, but triumphant; clothed with his incomparable righteousness, they shall challenge every adversary, and defy every danger.

To this portion of scripture I have led back your thoughts, that I might not close with any disgusting sentiments, but might leave a sweet savour on your mind, on the reader's mind, and on the mind of

Rev. Sir,
Yours, &c.

LETTER III.

Rev. Sir,

LET me, now, resume my observations on your epistle. Which I do, not for the sake of disputing, but for the cause of truth.

The gospel contains many sublime and glorious truths. But there is *one*, which, beyond all others, characterizes its nature, its import, and design; which makes it most eminently to differ from every other form of religion, professed or known in the world. I mean the doctrine of *free justification*, thro' the righteousness of *CHRIST*. This is to the religion of *JESUS*, what the particular features and turns of countenance are to each individual person.

I have sometimes amused myself, with standing by a painter, and observing him at his work. Here I have been surprised to see, how much a very little stroke would alter the aspect of his draught; would turn the gay into a melancholy, or the composed into a frantic countenance. Several of Mr *Wesley*'s touches are to appearance small; but, I fear, they will be found to disfigure more than a little the heavenly portrait; and give a new, not the native, air, to *the truth as it is in JESUS*.—But I proceed; my business being to prove, not to blame.

Sinners who betake themselves to the all-sufficient SAVIOUR for redemption, are fully accepted by GOD, for his beloved SON's sake. This is justification through imputed righteousness, says *Aspasio*.—" That remains to be proved," answers Mr *Wesley*. —I think, it is pretty largely, and, I would hope, it is satisfactorily proved, through the whole book.— Nay, I find Mr *Wesley* himself ere long acknowledging, that " as to the doctrine we are agreed." Either therefore you have received the proof, which you demand; or else you can submit without conviction, and agree without cause of agreement.—Not to take advantage of such slips, I would rather enlarge upon what may be useful.

I would ask Mr *Wesley*; In what other way sinners can be justified or accepted, save only through imputed righteousness?—Through their own good *deeds*, and holy *tempers*? This supposes the fruits to be good, while the tree is corrupt; and would make salvation to be of works, not of grace.—Thro' their *own faith*, standing in the law? Then they are justified before a perfect GOD, by an imperfect endowment; and life eternal is obtained, by the exercises of their own mind, not by the merits of *JESUS CHRIST*. —Are they justified *without any* righteousness, either wrought by themselves, or received * from another? This

---

* Οι λαμβανοντες, *They who receive the gift of righteousness.* Rom. v. 17.

This is an unworthy thought; this were an unsufferable practice; JEHOVAH himself being judge, *He that justifieth the wicked is an abomination* *.

Say not, GOD is a free agent, and not bound to observe his own law. Say rather, the rule of righteousness revealed in the law, is his most stedfast will; unchangeable as his nature.—Consider also, what this law requires.. A satisfaction for sin, not defective, but completely sufficient; a performance of the command, not sincere only, but absolutely perfect.—Will GOD, in justifying a sinner, disregard, contradict, overthrow his own law? In no wise. Since then it insists upon what no mortal can yield, must not at all flesh perish for ever?

This would be the unavoidable consequence, if matters rested on human abilities. But here the blessed gospel comes to our relief; shewing us, that GOD, in his immense mercy, and unsearchable wisdom, has found out a way, at once, to satisfy the unalterable law, and save insolvent man; to justify even the chief of sinners; yet without the least violation of justice, truth, or holiness.—What is this way? His own SON accomplishes the great work.—How? By relaxing the precepts of the law, that we may perform them? by disannulling the sentence of the law, that we may escape it? Heaven and earth shall pass away, before any such dishonourable expedient takes place. On the contrary, he gives satisfaction to the sentence, by suffering the tremendous punish-
ment

---

* *Prov.* xvii. 15. This is an invariable maxim. It is that word of GOD, which endureth for ever. Yet it is no objection to *his* method of justifying the ungodly. Because he first imputes his SON's righteousness unto them; thereby renders them truly and perfectly righteous: then pronounces them such; and, as such, receives them to pardon, to favour, and eternal life.—Does not the text, thus considered, afford an incontestible argument for the necessity of an imputed righteousness?

ment denounced: and he fulfils the precept, by yielding the finless obedience required.—Because this was to be finished in the nature which had transgressed, therefore he was made man. Because this was to be truly, or rather infinitely meritorious, therefore the man was one person with the GODHEAD.

Still it may be inquired, How the obedience of another can relieve my distress? How indeed! But by GOD's transferring my guilt to him, and imputing his obedience to me. By this method, the thing is clearly and completely effected. In this method, I see a propriety and an efficacy, that silence my doubts, and comfort my heart. Accordingly, it is written, in the scriptures, *GOD was in* CHRIST *reconciling the world unto himself, not imputing their trespasses unto them*. GOD; the work was too arduous to be performed by a created agent. Therefore GOD himself was in *CHRIST*. None less than the almighty LORD could execute the business. But if HE undertake it, how successfully must it be carried on, and how gloriously finished!—*Reconciling the world;* not setting poor transgressors to reconcile themselves, but himself contriving all, providing all, doing and suffering all that was needful for this great purpose; being himself the creditor, the sponsor, and payer of the debt.—How was all this brought to pass? By *not imputing our trespasses unto us;* but taking them all upon himself; bearing them all, in his own body, upon the tree; and sustaining the vengeance due to all our crimes.—Thus was the holy ONE and the just *made sin for us; that we,* sinful dust and ashes, *might,* in the very same manner, *be made the righteousness of GOD in him.* The former could be only by imputation; and so only can be the latter.

If men talk of being accepted for *CHRIST*'s sake, yet reject the imputation of righteousness, they must have very inadequate notions concerning the relation which *CHRIST* bears to his people, and the nature of his mediatorial undertaking.—Does this seem obscure? I explain myself.—A person may conduct himself so honourably and excellently, as, on account of his worthy deeds, to obtain favour in behalf of another; and this, without being his surety, or any thing like his proper righteousness. Witness the famous instance of the two brothers, *Amyntas* and *Eschylus*.

The former was a gallant hero; who exposed his life, and lost his arm, in the defence of his country. The latter was an abandoned and infamous profligate; whose crimes had brought him to the bar of public justice. The hero, on the day of trial, appeared as an advocate for his brother. He spoke nothing, but only lifted up to view the maimed and dismembered arm. This silent oratory struck the assembly; and pleaded so powerfully, that the criminal was unanimously acquitted.—Here was an acquittal of one, in consideration of the merits of another. But then the obnoxious party had no special interest in those merits. They were not acquired or exercised, with a particular reference to his good. He could not say, they are mine. Neither did they make him, in any degree, or in any sense, righteous.—Whereas, the reverse of all this is true, with regard to *JESUS CHRIST*, and justified sinners. This you and I, Sir, have asserted. Let us never retract the good confession. But, as it is the truth of the gospel, let us still and for ever say,

In HIM complete we shine,
  Because
Ours is righteousness divine.

Theron, speaking of the terms *inherent* and *imputed*, calls them nice distinctions and metaphysical subtilties. Mr *Wesley* makes *Aspasio* apply the depretiating remark to the active and passive righteousness of *CHRIST*. Whereas he says no such thing. He means no such thing. He is treating of a subject totally

tally different. And was he to maintain such a sentiment, every one must observe, it would entirely overthrow his whole scheme.

"You oblige us to make use of metaphysical subtilties, by confounding these very different ideas, that is, *CHRIST*'s active and passive righteousness,"—I could hardly believe my eyes, for some time; though both of them attested, that this was produced as a quotation from pag. 187. In which page, and for a considerable space, before and after, the subject of debate is the difference between inherent and imputed righteousness.—I was, I own, quite vexed, to see *Aspasio* so maltreated; his discourse so misrepresented; and so little regard paid to literary justice. And glad I am, that I did not give vent to my thoughts, just at that instant. I might have been too warm, and not have spared the rod. But, upon cooler consideration, I began to recover, and the prescription of *Horace* was of service,

Amara lento temperat risu.

I began to call your conduct, not artifice or sleight of hand, but incogitancy or thought misapplied. As you had been thinking so long upon the other topic, it dwelt upon your imagination; kept this from your attention; and led you both to mistake and to miscall things. Like a certain preacher, who, having lost his fortune in the bubbles of the year 1719, and having occasion to mention the deliverance of the *Israelites* from *Egypt*, told his audience, that *Pharaoh* and his host were all drowned in the *South* sea—Poor man! he meant the *Red* sea.

Mr *Wesley* proceeds: "We do not confound the active and passive righteousness."—Does *Aspasio*, Sir? he that considers them particularly and distinctly? he that examines each with a critical and minute exactness? If this be to confound, order and confusion have changed their nature.

"Neither

" Neither do we separate them." It is somewhat difficult to understand, what you mean by separating the active and passive righteousness of our LORD. —Separating them, as to their influence? Then you must be sensible, this is never done by *Aspasio*. You cannot but know, that he disclaims such a refinement. He protests against such a practice.—Do you mean, treating them as things really distinct, tho' always uniting their agency? Then I am at a loss to reconcile Mr *Wesley* with himself. For, in the very next paragraph, he thus expresses himself. " Thro' " the merits of his life and death, every believer is " justified." Are not the merits of his life here *distinguished* from the merits of his death? Does not the former expression denote his active, the latter his passive obedience? Or would you be understood to mean, " thro' the merits of his life, which are nothing " else but the merits of his death?" If you would not speak in this manner, so unworthy of your better judgment, you do the very thing which you blame.—This is done still more apparently, in one of your hymns. Where we see, not only a separation, but a distinct use and application of the separated subjects.

> Grant this, O LORD; for thou hast dy'd,
> That I might be forgiven:
> Thou hast the righteousness supply'd,
> For which I merit heaven.

I could easily excuse Mr *Wesley*, for being a little inconsistent with himself; did he not also venture to confront the apostle, by the following assertion. " Nei- " ther have we any authority from scripture, for either " thinking or speaking of one separate from the other." —Does not St *Paul*, in one passage, speak of the obedience? in another, of the death of CHRIST? Does he not, in one place, enlarge upon the righteousness? in another upon the blood of CHRIST? If so, we have an authority from scripture, we have

the

the example of the chiefest apostle, for this way of thinking and speaking.

We have also a concurrent testimony from the genius and import of the original language. Do not ὑπακοη and δικαιουν signify somewhat different from αιμα and θανατος? Are there any approved writers, who use these words promiscuously? as so many synonimous and convertible terms? If not, the voice of grammar will vindicate the propriety of our conduct, while we assign a separate discourse to each subject, and exhibit them severally in the most distinct view.

Are not light and heat always united in the sun? Is the naturalist to blame, who considers them distinctly; and examines each property, in a separate treatise? You would commend this practice in the philosopher, as the way to enter thoroughly into the knowledge of his subject. And why should you explode or censure it, in the Christian divine? Are not theological truths as worthy of a circumstantial and accurate investigation, as philosophical? Will they not as amply reward our diligence, and yield as rich advantage to the serious inquirer?

The righteousness which justifies sinners, is already *wrought out*, says *Aspasio*.—" A crude unscriptural expression," replies Mr *Wesley*.—It may be so. But if the expression is plain and true, I will sit down content. This, however, you will allow me to observe, that it is no new one, and is not far from scriptural. *Worketh righteousness*, you know, is a scriptural phrase. Does the word *out* spoil it, or the word *already?* I suppose, the latter may be most offensive. Yet you speak, in this very paragraph, of being " jus-
" tified by the merits of *CHRIST*'s life and death." Are not these matters already transacted? is not the merit of them already perfect? or can any language express these things more clearly, and affirm them more strongly, than those emphatical words in one of your own hymns?

Let

Let us for this faith contend,
Sure salvation is its end:
Heav'n already is begun,
Everlasting life is won.

Pardon me then, Sir, if I still suspect, that the doctrine and its consequences, rather than the expression and its crudity, awaken your jealousy. If this doctrine be admitted, if the justifying righteousness be already wrought, it must absolutely overturn all your pre-requisites, qualifications, and conditions; conditions of repentance, obedience, and I know not what besides. We must say to every one of them, as *Jehu* said to the messengers of *Joram: What hast thou to do with* the grand article of justification? *Get thee behind me.* Could they be fulfilled, they would come a day too late; like the sickle when the harvest is reaped. Could they be fulfilled in *all* their imaginary dignity, they would, in this relation, be needless; like a proposal for augmenting the splendour of the sun.

" The righteousness which justifies sinful man, was
" *set on foot*, when GOD sent forth his SON, from
" the habitation of his holiness and glory, to be born
" of a woman and made subject to the law.—It was
" *carried on*, through the whole course of our SA-
" VIOUR's life; in which he always did such things,
" as were pleasing to his heavenly FATHER.—It
" was *completed*, at that ever-memorable, that grand
" period, when the blessed IMMANUEL bowed his
" dying head; and cried, with a strong triumphant
" voice, IT IS FINISHED."—Upon this extract from *Aspasio*'s discourse, Mr *Wesley* exclaims, " O vain phi-
" losophy!"—Philosophy! *this* philosophy, Sir! Never did I hear, till this moment, such doctrines ascribed to philosophy. But this I have heard, and this I believe, that *the world*, even the learned and philosophic world, *by their boasted wisdom knew not GOD;* nor GOD's method of salvation, by the sufferings of an innocent,

innocent, and the obedience of a divine perſon. Their philoſophy prejudiſed them againſt it; puffed them up with a vain conceit of their own ſufficiency; and ſet them at the greateſt diſtance from ſubmitting to the righteouſneſs of GOD.

I wiſh, Sir, you would ſhew me, in which of the philoſophers I might find theſe ſacred ſentiments; or a grain, or a ſpice, or a ſavour of them. I have, for a conſiderable time, laid aſide my *Plato*, and have no more inclination to turn over my *Seneca;* becauſe I can ſee nothing like this divinely-precious truth, adorning and enriching their pages. But if you will diſcover this golden vein in their works, I will immediately renew my acquaintance with them; and will do the philoſophers a piece of juſtice, which Mr *Weſley* denies them. I will not call their philoſophy vain, but *the wiſdom of* GOD, *and the power of* GOD.—A righteouſneſs wrought out, and a redemption obtained for us! the former divine! the latter eternal! theſe, rightly underſtood, make us, beyond all the treaſures of literature, *wiſe.* Theſe, habitually enjoyed, will, more effectually than all the delineations of morality or exhortations to virtue, render us *holy.*

A divine righteouſneſs (pardon me for dwelling on my favourite topic) already wrought! A great redemption perfectly finiſhed! And this by the abaſement, the ignominy, the indignities; by the cries, the agonies, the blood of our SAVIOUR. Yea, of our GOD, *in faſhion as a man;* in the form of a ſervant, a ſlave, an execrable malefactor.—What, like this, did a thouſand philoſophers teach? What, like this, do a thouſand of their volumes contain? to ſtab our pride; to tame our fury; and to quench our luſt? to kindle our benevolence; to inflame our devotion; to make us, in a word, *wiſe unto ſalvation?*

"The plain truth is, *CHRIST* lived and taſted "death for every man."—To be ſure then, ſince every man is not ſaved by him, he lived and died only to
make

make their salvation possible.—From this and other hints, I guess your opinion to be, that *CHRIST*, by his life and death, obtained only a possibility of salvation.—[Which salvation is to become our own, upon performing terms and conditions, bringing with us pre-requisites and qualifications.]—If I mistake you, Sir, in this case, you have nothing more to do, than simply to deny my supposition. This exculpates you at once. I shall rejoice to hear you say, " As *CHRIST* " made us, and not we ourselves; in like manner he " saves us, and not we ourselves. No human endow- " ments, no human performances, but *CHRIST* alone " is *the author of eternal salvation.*"

Should you reply, True—*CHRIST* is the author of eternal salvation, but *to those* only *who obey him;*— I must then ask, what obedience *CHRIST* requires ? The law says, " Do and live." *CHRIST*, the end of the law, says, " Believe in M E, and live. Be " verily persuaded, that I am sufficient for thy salva- " tion, without any working of thine at all. Is not " the SON, the SON of the most high GOD, given " unto thee in the divine record ? Be satisfied with " *his* doing and suffering, without wishing for, or " thinking of, any thing more, to procure thy final " acceptance."—Let no one account lightly of this obedience. It is the obedience of faith. The obedience suited to the name *JESUS*. Obedience to the first and great command of the gospel. Beyond all other expedients, it excludes boasting; and, at the same time, produces that genuine love, that filial fear, which the law of works requires in vain.

Only to make a thing possible, and to effect it, are widely different. When our king fits out a fleet, and gives his admiral a commission, to harass the *French* coasts, and destroy the *French* shipping, he makes the thing possible. But to carry this design into execution; to accomplish the enterprize, now become practicable; is a far more arduous task, and a far more honourable

nourable achievement. How strangely do those writers derogate from the dignity and glory of the REDEEMER, who would ascribe to him, what corresponds with the former; and attribute to man, what bears a resemblance to the latter!

If *CHRIST* only made our salvation possible, then *we* are to execute the plan. We are to face the enemy, to sustain the charge, and silence the battery: we are to climb the steep, to enter the breach, and bring off the standards. And so, in all reason, the honour and praise must be our own.—Whereas, the gospel gives all the honour to the Captain of our salvation. He bore the heat and burden of the dreadful day. He made reconciliation for iniquity, and brought in everlasting righteousness. So that all our officious attempts, like a pinnace arriving after the victory, should be told, *It is finished;* the great salvation is already wrought. And instead of being dissatisfied or disappointed, methinks, we should rejoice, unfeignedly rejoice, in the accomplishment of the glorious work.

If it should occur to the reader's mind, that the Christian life is represented as a warfare; and that we ourselves are commanded to fight, tho' under the banner of our divine leader; to this doubt I would answer,—*The Canaanite is still in the land;* and we fight, not to gain the country, but only to subdue the rebels.

" Whoever perverts so glorious a doctrine, shews " he never believed."—This may be the substance of what *Aspasio* maintains; tho' not represented so fully or so clearly, as he has expressed himself. However, such a small wrong we will readily excuse. It was done with no sinister intention, but for the sake of brevity.

To this position Mr *Wesley* replies; " Not so."— That is; they did really and truly believe. But, after their belief, they apostatized, and fell from the faith. They were, some time, the members of *CHRIST*, and temples of the HOLY GHOST; but, quickly

severed

severed from their divine head, they became the slaves of the devil, and brands for the everlasting burning. Their names were, indeed, written in heaven. But, it seems, the heavenly records were less faithful than the parish-register. They were quickly erased, and their place in the book of life knew them no more.

Or thus—They did as really and truly believe, as those who are now in the mansions of glory. But, after their true *knowledge of the name of the* LORD JESUS; after their full conviction of his sufficiency and faithfulness for their salvation; even such as inclined and enabled them, to *put their trust in him alone,* for their acceptance with GOD; they were disappointed. Though *CHRIST* called them *his sheep,* as thus *hearing his voice;* yet he did not *give unto them eternal life,* according to his promise; but suffered Satan to *pluck them out of his hand.*

These sentiments have no very probable, much less have they a pleasing or recommending aspect. Let us inquire, whether they comport with St *John's* determination of the case. Speaking of such backsliders, he says, *They went out from us, but they were not of us.* Mr *Wesley,* to be consistent with himself, should say on this occasion; " Not so; they were of you, but they " fell away from you."—The apostle proceeds; *For, if they had been of us, no doubt, they would have continued with us.* Had they been really converted, they would most undoubtedly have continued in our doctrine and fellowship. Their revolt from our *doctrine,* is a manifest proof, that they never truly received it, nor with their heart believed it. Their departure from our *fellowship,* is an evident indication, that they were, notwithstanding all their professions, still carnal, and never renewed by grace.

Mr *Wesley* produces a text from St *Peter,* with a view to support his objection. They who *turn back as a dog to his vomit, had once escaped the pollutions of the world, through the knowledge of* CHRIST. Here and elsewhere I perceive the cannon roar, but without feeling the ball. Before this piece of sacred artillery can be brought to bear upon us, it will be necessary to prove, that the knowledge of *CHRIST*, or even believing in *CHRIST*, always signifies true faith. In some places, it certainly does. In other places, it signifies no such thing. *Though I have all knowledge*, says the apostle; yet even with this specious endowment I may *be nothing*. There is a knowledge, says the same author, which, instead of *edifying*, or establishing the soul in godliness, *puffeth up* with pride. We are likewise assured, that *Simon* the sorcerer, though in the gall of bitterness, and in the bond of iniquity, yet had *knowledge of the things which concerned the kingdom of GOD, and the name of* JESUS CHRIST; nay, that *he also believed*, yet had neither lot nor portion in the inestimable blessing.

Let us attend to the apostle's manner, and we shall be led to put the same interpretation upon the phrase, as it is used in the passage before us.—These people are not described like the true believers, to whom he addresses the epistle. Here is no mention of their being *partakers of a divine nature;* of being *born again by the incorruptible seed;* or of having their *souls purified by the SPIRIT*. They are only said to have escaped the pollutions of the world.—Again; the word expressive of these pollutions is μιασματα, which denotes the grossest excesses, and most scandalous iniquities. Consequently, their abstaining from such abominations, implies no more than what is called a negative goodness, or a mere external reformation. Their lusts had been restrained only, not subdued. Therefore the unhappy wretches were easily overcome by their old corruptions.—It is farther observable, that St *Peter* never considers these persons as new creatures. He calls them by no other name, than the *dog* and the *sow*. Such they were at first; no better, under all their profession of Christianity; and no other, even in their

foulest

fouleſt relapſes. When they returned again to their vomit, or their filthy practices, they returned to their own.

There is, then, a knowledge of *CHRIST*, which is only ſuperficial and notional; floats idly on the underſtanding, but neither penetrates, nor ſanctifies the heart. There is alſo a knowledge of *CHRIST*, which is wrought by the SPIRIT, and ingrafted into the ſoul; which receives the gift of righteouſneſs, and brings juſtification into the conſcience. The comfort and joy of which mortify the love of ſin, and produce the life of holineſs. This knowledge, Sir, may you and I teach; in this knowledge may our hearers and readers abound; and may the *divine* power give us, by means of this knowledge, all things pertaining to life and godlineſs!

The goodneſs of GOD leadeth to repentance.—" This " is unqueſtionably true," ſays Mr *Weſley*. " But " the nice metaphyſical doctrine of imputed righte- " ouſneſs."—Should you not rather have ſaid, the nice metaphyſical *phraſe?* ſince, as to the *doctrine*, we are, according to your own confeſſion, agreed; bound therefore, each of us, equally bound to clear it of the conſequences, with which it may be charged, by the author of the Preſervative, or by any other objector.—And as to the phraſe, I cannot underſtand, by what authority Mr *Weſley* calls it *metaphyſical*. *Theron*, it is true, uſes the word, and applies it to the preſent ſubject. But does not Mr *Weſley* know, that *Theron* often perſonates an enemy, and ſpeaks the language of unbelief?—Be pleaſed, Sir, to explain your term; and ſhew, in what ſenſe it is compatible with this article of my faith? " I am acquitted and " counted righteous before GOD, only through the " imputation of my SAVIOUR's obedience and death?" Which is, both in ſtyle and ſentiment, truly evangelical; but, in no degree, that I can diſcern, metaphyſical.

When

When Mr *Wesley* adds, " This leads not to repen-
" tance, but to licentiousness ;" he speaks what we
understand, not what we allow.—Will any one say,
that speculative reasoning upon the goodness of GOD,
or contemplating it barely in our ideas, leadeth to re-
pentance ? But, when we taste and enjoy, when we
apply and appropriate, his profusely-rich liberality in
CHRIST; we are thereby prompted to neglect,
abuse, and dishonour our great benefactor ? Or shall
it be said, the divine goodness, manifested in common
providence and inferior instances, tends to awaken
love and work godliness ? But the same divine good-
ness, shining forth in the most illustrious manifesta-
tion, that men or angels ever knew ; shining forth
with a glory, a richness, a perfection, sufficient to
transport heaven and earth with joy unspeakable :
this goodness tends to excite contempt of G O D,
and to cherish carnal indulgence ? Such an insinua-
tion, so depretiatory to the righteousness of the bles-
sed *JESUS*, I had much rather have heard in a
Jewish synagogue, than have seen in Mr *Wesley's*
writings.

No, Sir; this and this alone leadeth *a sinner* to re-
pentance. Not all the munificence of the DEITY ;
neither the rain from heaven, nor fruitful seasons ;
neither the fatness of the earth, nor the abundance of
the seas ; can take away the enmity of our nature,
and reconcile our affections to G O D. Nothing, no-
thing but a sense of pardon and acceptance, thro' the
work finished on IMMANUEL's cross.—If you please
to review the text, you will not affirm, that the a-
postle is asserting the efficacious influence of provi-
dential goodness on the hearts of men. He is evi-
dently inveighing against the gross and almost gene-
ral abuse of such bounty. Though it ought, it does
not produce gratitude and duty. It would indeed
upon upright, but it does not thus operate upon
depraved minds. No cause is adequate to this effect,

but

but free justification through *JESUS CHRIST*.

"The believer cannot but add to his faith, works "of righteousness."—During his first love," says Mr *Wesley*, "this is often true. But it is not true "afterwards, as we know and feel by melancholy "experience."—How, Sir! do you yourself feel this? Where then is your sinless perfection? Can they be perfect, whose love ceases to glow, and whose zeal loses its activity? Does Mr *Wesley* himself make this confession? Let him then say with us;—and let us say, with invariable stedfastness, and with increasing gratitude,—Blessed be GOD for perfection in *JESUS CHRIST!*

Do you learn, Sir, what is here acknowledged, by observations made upon others? Then those others, I apprehend, if they do not exercise themselves in good works, either have no faith, and deceive both you and themselves,—or else they intermit and discontinue the exertion of their faith. Which neither detracts from the efficacy of the principle, nor disproves *Aspasio*'s opinion. It is not said, the believer never trips, nor falters in the course of his obedience; but he always adds to his faith, the duties and works of obedience. Whenever the former acts, the latter constantly ensue. So long as we live by the faith of the SON of GOD, we shall not fail to bring forth those fruits of righteousness, which are through *JESUS CHRIST*.

This is strongly maintained, by *Aspasio*, in another place. "It is as impossible for the sun to be in his "meridian height, and not dissipate darkness, or dif- "fuse light; as for faith to exist in the soul, and not "exalt the temper, and meliorate the conduct."— This is very forcibly implied, in our LORD's interrogation to his disciples; *Where is your faith?* It must be dormant and inactive, like the sap of the trees in winter, or like the faculty of reasoning in sleep. Otherwise it would banish your fears, even amidft the raging ftorm; and produce an undaunted confidence in GOD your SAVIOUR.—The defign of all this is, to evince the wifdom of the gofpel, which lays fuch a ftrefs upon faith: fo frequently urges the neceffity of faith, above and before all things; reprefenting it, as the principle work of the divine SPIRIT, and the great inftrument of receiving falvation. Hence it appears, that the facred plan is not formed in vain; much lefs is it calculated to fupprefs or difcourage real holinefs.

"We no longer obey, in order to lay the foun-
"dation for our final acceptance." Thefe words I read with pleafure.—" That foundation is already
"laid in the merits of *CHRIST:*" Thefe I contemplate with ftill greater fatisfaction.—But when I come to the following claufe, " Yet we obey, in or-
"der to our final acceptance thro' his merits;" with difappointment and regret I cry, How is the gold become dim! how is the moft fine gold changed!

A foundation, *for what? Afpafio* would reply, For pardon, for reconciliation, and for everlafting falvation; for peace of confcience, for accefs to GOD, for every fpiritual and eternal bleffing.—A foundation, of *what kind?* In all refpects perfect; incapable of any augmentation; not to be ftrengthened, enlarged, or improved by all the duties and all the deeds of prophets, apoftles, martyrs; becaufe it has omnipotence for its eftablifhment.—A foundation, *for whom?* For finners; for the vileft and moft miferable of finners: that all guilty and undone wretches may come; and though ever fo weary, ever fo heavy laden, may caft their burthen upon this Rock of ages; in full affurance of finding reft, and obtaining fafety.

This is chearing; this is charming. What pity it is, that fuch an illuftrious truth fhould be clouded, fuch a precious privilege fpoiled, by that ungracious fentence! "We obey, in order to our final accept-
"ance."—But is this, Sir, your conftant profeffion?

I muft

I must do you the justice to own, that you have happier moments, and more becoming apprehensions.—When you join in public worship, this is your humble and just acknowledgment; " Although we be un-
" worthy, through our manifold sins, to offer unto
" thee any sacrifice; yet we beseech thee to accept
" this our bounden duty and service."—When you criticise upon *Aspasio*, the note is changed, and this is the purport of your strain; " We beseech thee to
" accept us, on account of these our services; for we
" do them, O LORD, with a professed view to this
" end,"—To implore acceptance for our duties, confesses them to be mean and contemptible. Whereas, to expect acceptance on their account, strongly intimates their excellency; that they are worthy in a very high degree; so as to obtain favour, not for themselves only, but for a miserable creature also, who confesses himself subject to manifold sins.

I said, " on account of"—For, if you obey, *in order* to your final acceptance; surely, you must expect final acceptance and eternal life, 'on account of your own obedience. A poor object displays his sores, and relates his distress, in order to obtain your alms. Does he not then expect your alms on account of his sores, his distress, and his piteous tale?—What a coalition is here between Mr *Wesley* and the subjects of the triple crown! I find the whole council of *Trent* establishing his sentiments by their anathematizing decree. These are their words; " If any one shall say, that the righ-
" teous ought not, for their own good works, to ex-
" pect the eternal reward, through the merit of *JE-*
" *SUS CHRIST*, let him be accursed *."—Do you speak of the merit of *CHRIST?* So do they. Do you, in some sense, allow *CHRIST* to be the foundation?

---

* *Si quis dixerit, justos non debere, pro bonis operibus, expectare æternum retributionem, per Jesu Christi meritum, anathema sit.* De bon. oper. can. xxvi.

dation? So do they. Are your works to rear the edifice, and perform the moſt reſpectable part of the buſineſs? So are theirs.

By this time, I believe, the thoughtful reader will gueſs the reaſon, why you oppoſe and decry imputed righteouſneſs. You are ſolicitous, it ſeems, not barely for works of obedience, but for their value and credit in the affair of ſalvation; for their ſignificancy and influence, in winning the good-will of JEHOVAH. Since this is your notion, you may well be offended at *CHRIST*'s imputed righteouſneſs. This will admit of no partner or coadjutor. This, Sir, in the caſe of juſtification, pours contempt upon all your moſt laborious exerciſes, and admired attainments. Yea, this being divine and inconceivably excellent, pours all around a blaze of glory, in which all our puny doings are loſt, as the ſtars in the meridian ſunſhine.

" We obey in order to final acceptance."—Methinks, this diſcovers no more gratitude, than wiſdom. Is it not an officious indignity to that noble goodneſs, which has ſet forth *JESUS CHRIST* for a propitiation? Is it not a contemptuous diſregard of that heavenly voice, which ſaid, with ſo much ſolemnity, *In him I am well pleaſed* with the children of men? —Does this exalt, does it not degrade the SAVIOUR? Does it mortify, does it not cheriſh the pride of man? —According to this ſcheme, the merits of our LORD are the foundation, not immediately of our acceptance, but of that ſituation only, in which we are ſuppoſed capable of acquiring it ourſelves. They are, in ſhort, no more than a mere pedeſtal; on which human worth, or rather human vanity may ſtand exalted, and challenge the favour of heaven.

Ah, Sir! acceptance with GOD, is an immenſely-rich and glorious bleſſing; a high and tranſcendently-precious privilege; incomparably too high and glorious, to be obtained, in any degree, by ſuch mean obedience

ence as yours and mine.—The pardon of rebels against the King of kings! the reception of leprous sinners into the bosom of heaven! shall such effects, than which nothing can be greater; shall such benefits, than which nothing can be richer; be ascribed to human obedience? What, but the very distraction of our disease, can have occasioned or can account for a thought so extreme in absurdity?—[Shall we, sordid wretches, with our ulcerous sores, our withered limbs, and a stupor over all our faculties; shall *we* think ourselves able to do *something* for HIM, who needeth not the services of angels? nay, to do something considerable enough, to found a claim to that transcendent honour and happiness, the light of his countenance?] —Our adorations! our thanksgivings! our praises! our prayers! our preaching! our sacramental duties! what are they all but filthy rags *, compared with his inconceivable holiness and glory? What part of his work do we attempt, but we debase it with our deplorable imperfections, or pollute it with our very touch?—Shame then belongs to us, shame and confusion of face, whenever we look to ourselves or our own performances. While all our comfort, all our hope, is to be derived from the only righteous one *CHRIST JESUS*.

If we know not enough of our own meanness and impotency,

---

* *Is*. lxiv. 6. In such a light, I cannot but look upon the services and works of frail man. In such a light they are represented, in various parts of our public devotions. And if we are but humble enough to confess ourselves *sinners*, in such a light they *must* appear to every discerning and impartial eye. Since nothing, even in hell itself, is more loathsome, or imparts a more horrid defilement, than sin.—If such services are a sweet-smelling savour to GOD, it is owing to that copious incense, (θυμιαματα πολλα, *Rev.* viii. 3.) which arises from the golden censer and the golden altar, (*Rev.* viii. 3.) It is wholly owing to the infinite dignity and all-recommending efficacy of *CHRIST*'s blood, intercession, and righteousness.

impotency, let us liften to the prophet *Ifaiah* *. In order to our acceptance with GOD, he informs us, *Lebanon* with all her ftately cedars *is not fufficient to burn; nor all the beafts*, that range thro' her extenfive fhades, *fufficient for a burnt-offering*. Nations, whole nations, avail no more than fingle perfons. Should they unite their abilities, and exert all their efforts, to do fomething which may recommend them to JEHOVAH †; all would be mean, ineffectual, defpicable. Mean, *as the drop of a bucket*, which falls to the ground, and none regards it. Ineffectual, *as the duft upon the balance*, which wants even that fmall degree of impetus, neceffary to turn the moft nicely poifed fcales. Defpicable *as the atom that floats* in the air, and has not weight enough to fettle itfelf on any object.—Should you reply, In all thefe things there is fome, though very little fubftance; the prophet farther declares, that *all nations* in the world, with all their virtues, accomplifhments, and works, would, before the infinitely-majeftic GOD, be as nothing, lefs than nothing, yea, vanity itfelf; incapable, abfolutely incapable of winning his favour, or doing any thing worthy of his notice ‡.—Bleffed
therefore,

* If. xl. 15, 16, 17.

† Do we want to learn the prophet's aim and defign in this magnificent paragraph? we may, to our great fatisfaction, confult his fagacious and devout commentator *Vitringa*. *Hic altius furgens oratio, non tantum omne me: itum abjudicat carni, fed docet etiam et inculcat, effe hæc omnia quæ gentes ad placandum numen finxerunt, merum nihil et inane. Nullum plane pondus afferre in commendatione caufæ fuæ apud Deum: imo effe nihilo ipfo et inani inferiora, fi quid nihilo minus fingi et cogitari poffit. Non poteft in natura: fed fingi poteft et obtinet in œconomia fpirituali. Eft enim ibi quod ita non prodeft ad obtinendam juftitiam apud Deum, ut fimul noceat. Cujus generis funt omnia* ινρчμαλα *et commenta fapientiæ carnis. Non tantum Deo non commendant, fed potius iram et indignationem divinam provocant*

‡ May I be allowed to elucidate the noble paffage quoted above?

therefore, for ever bleſſed be divine grace, that we have a great High Prieſt, in whom GOD is pleaſed; is

above? Sure I am, the reader will not be diſpleaſed with the digreſſion, unleſs the annotator fails in the execution, and has the misfortune

> ——— *Egregium opus*
> *Culpa deterere ingeni.*

The prophet, ſtruck with the contemplation of a moſt glorious perſonage, cries out, like one tranſported and amazed, *Who?* Never was any thing comparable to him, either exiſting in nature, or imaged by fancy. *Who hath meaſured the waters,* the unfathomable deep, and the boundleſs wave; meaſured them, not in his capacious ciſtern, but *in the hollow of his hand? Who hath meted out heaven,* an expanſe in which worlds revolve, and extended to immenſity; meted it, not with an outſtretched line, but *with the ſpan* of his fingers? *Who hath comprehended the duſt of the earth,* all the ſolid contents of this prodigiouſly-large globe, as a little pittance *in the ſmalleſt meaſure? Who hath weighed the mountains,* with all their ponderous ridges, and the hills, with all their maſſy rocks, as a man weigheth an ounce or a dram *in* his *ſcales?*—Here I would only obſerve the judicious choice of objects. By far the moſt diſtinguiſhed and magnificent, that the univerſe affords. The abyſs of waters, and the circuit of the ſkies! the dimenſions of the earth, and the elevation of the mountains! Compared with which, the loftieſt groves are leſs than the hyſſop on the wall; and the moſt ample cities are ſmaller than a grain of muſtard ſeed.

Then follows a compariſon, more admirable, if it be poſſible, than this fine deſcription. *Behold!* The nations, whether on the neighbouring continent or in the remoteſt iſles, are, before this exalted Being, as the ſmall drop of a bucket, which is almoſt too ſcanty to deſerve our notice. They are as the ſmaller duſt upon the balance, which is not ſufficient even to turn the hovering ſcale. They are as the ſmalleſt atom, which has not weight enough to reach the ground, nor force enough to reſiſt the ſlighteſt undulations of the air. Yea, all the nations of the earth, amidſt all their pomp and grandeur, with all their boaſted accompliſhments and admired works, are, before this incomprehenſible GOD, as a mere nothing.—Can

language

is well pleased; and his very soul delighteth: whose sacrifice, and whose work, have merited all the good, that sinners can want, or the ALMIGHTY can bestow.

If we are not yet duly humbled, nor willing to profess ourselves beholden to divine grace alone; if we still resolve to be principals or partners with the one MEDIATOR, in the purchase of the inestimable jewel, let us fear, lest *the LORD our righteousness* resent such a dishonour done to himself; and swear in his wrath, that we shall have neither lot nor portion in this matter. Of this he has expresly warned us by his apostle; *If ye be circumcised* CHRIST *shall prophet you nothing*. What would St *Paul* teach us by this solemn protestation?—That no *Jew* can be saved? Himself was an *Hebrew* of the *Hebrews*; circumcised the eighth day.—That a Christian would, by receiving circumcision after his conversion to *CHRIST*, forfeit all his privileges? No; for he himself circumcised *Timothy*, to gain him a fair hearing from the judaizing bigots.—Or is circumcision here used, by way of synecdoche, for the ceremonial law? teaching

language go farther? Can imagination take a bolder flight? Yes; the astonishingly-rich ideas of the prophet add a heightening, a redoubled heightening even to this inimitable picture. The kingdoms of the world, with all their inhabitants, and all their honours, are less than nothing; are less than vanity itself, in the estimate of the almighty JEHOVAH.

This, if I am not greatly mistaken, is one of the most highly finished sketches of the *beautiful* and *sublime*, extant in the whole compass of letters.—Let us always remember, that the majestic person, whom it describes, is our atonement and righteousness (ver. 2.), is our shepherd and guide (ver. 11.); it will then be one of the most consolatory and delightful truths, in all the book of GOD.—And O! may we never forget, that the small drop of the bucket, the smaller dust in the balance, the volatile atom, and that which is less than nothing, are intended to shew us, what figure our own endeavours, works, and duties make in the sight of almighty GOD. We shall then have a doctrine, most powerful to humble us, to abase us, and to teach us to renounce our own righteousness.

ing us, that, as the *Mosaic* rites were now abolished, an attempt to continue the observance of them, would be an unpardonable opposition to the designs of Providence? The charitable compromise, recorded in the xivth to the *Romans*, leads to a different conclusion. —Or did those seducing teachers, who required this conformity from the Gentile converts, require them to renounce *CHRIST*, and relapse into mere Judaism? Neither is this at all supposable. They only required such a conformity, " in order to their accept-" ance thro' his merits;" which they never rejected, but only placed as a foundation for their own.

What then can be meant by, *CHRIST shall profit you nothing, if ye be circumcised?* If ye make circumcision, or any thing whatever, besides the righteousness of *CHRIST*, necessary to your acceptance with GOD, ye shall receive no advantage from all that the REDEEMER has done and suffered. This is to halt between works and grace, between *CHRIST* and self. And such divided regards, he will interpret as an affront, rather than an acceptable homage. Indeed, this is, in Christians, the grand apostasy. By this they deny the sufficiency of their SAVIOUR's most consummate righteousness. They cast themselves entirely out of the covenant of grace, and must expect no salvation but by doing the whole law.

This is the awful apostolic caution. To which let me subjoin the plain apostolic instruction—*Ye are accepted,* says St *Paul,* not partially, but entirely; not occasionally, but finally, *in the BELOVED.* All acceptance, of whatever kind, or whatever date, is wholly in him, not in any thing of our own.—The author to the *Hebrews* affirms, that *CHRIST hath obtained redemption,* not left it to be accomplished, either in greater or smaller measure, by our diligence and duties. No; he himself hath obtained, both present and final, yea, complete and *eternal redemption for us.* And will you, Sir, ascribe to your own obedi-ence,

ence, what the apoſtle ſo expreſsly aſcribes, and ſo entirely appropriates, to the bleſſed JESUS?—The ſame writer aſſures us, that *CHRIST, by one offering, hath perfected for ever them that are ſanctified.* Them that are cleanſed with the blood of ſprinkling, he hath not only diſcharged from the guilt of ſin, but rendered them unblameable and unreprovable; before the Majeſty of heaven. He hath done all that is neceſſary for their full, perfect, and everlaſting acceptation. Yes; whether it be in life or death; whether it be at the throne of grace, or the tribunal of judgment; during the ſpan of time, or thro' the ages of eternity; all that is neceſſary for our perfect acceptation is done: done by an infinitely-better hand, than our own; by an infinitely-better expedient, than any human obedience.

Do I, by theſe remonſtrances, ſet at nought true holineſs? or ſuppoſe a ſalvation ſeparate from holy obedience? You, Sir, cannot entertain ſuch a ſuppoſition; ſince, in your very laſt remark, you was diſſatisfied with my inſiſting on the *inſeparable* connection of a living faith, and works of righteouſneſs.—I honour and prize works of righteouſneſs. I would inceſſantly inculcate, both the indiſpenſable neceſſity, and the manifold utility, of holy obedience. We are redeemed, that we may be zealous of good works. We are created in *CHRIST JESUS,* that we may be able to do good works. And by good works we are to glorify our FATHER which is in heaven.

Only I would have good works know their proper ſtation, and their proper office. I am far from ſetting at nought the ſervices of the hand or the foot. But I ſhould very much diſapprove their deſign, I ſhould utterly deſpiſe their pretenſions, if they ſhould offer to intrude themſelves on the province of the eye, or act as the organs of ſight. Apply this ſimile to the obedience of man, and juſtification before GOD, or acceptance with GOD, you will then ſee, in what

rank

rank I place, in what esteem I hold, both the one and the other.

As I would have obedience know its proper place, so I would have it take a right form. The obedience, which you propose, is the obedience of the bond-man, not of the free. A slave, bought with our money, obeys in order to be accepted. A servant, hired to dispatch our business, obeys in order to receive his wages. But the child obeys, because he is beloved; because he is the heir; and all things, which the father hath, are his.

" Obey in order to acceptance!"—Indeed, Sir, you quite mistake the principle and source of Christian obedience. Nor shall I undertake to rectify your mistaken apprehensions, lest you should scorn to learn from an inferior. I will refer you to a set of teachers, from whom you need not blush to receive instruction. But as this may demand a very particular consideration, I shall postpone it to some future opportunity, and assign it to a distinct epistle.

In the mean time, if you should ask, why I have been so copious upon this point? I answer, because it is a matter of the utmost importance. An error on this subject, is as detrimental to our spiritual welfare, as a fault in the first concoction is to the animal constitution. A mistake concerning acceptance with GOD, must set in a false light every religious truth, and shed a malignant influence on every religious sentiment.

If you ask, why I have repeated the obnoxious proposition, almost as frequently as the rams horns sounded the fatal blast, on the day when *Jericho* was overthrown? I answer, For the very same purpose. To overthrow, if possible, so pernicious a notion; to lay it as low, as the fortifications of that devoted city. And I hope, neither Mr *Wesley*, nor any other, will attempt to rebuild it, lest they *lay the foundation thereof*, in the dishonour of the blessed REDEEMER, *and set up the gates of it*, in the distress of precious souls. Both which effects, I am perſuaded, are very remote from your intention. That they may be equally remote from your preaching, your writing, and all your doctrine, is the ſincere wiſh of, &c.

LETTER IV.

Rev. Sir,

I HAD, in the warmth of my concern, almoſt forgot to take notice of a text, which you produce from 1 *Tim.* vi. 17, 18, 19.; and, which is ſomewhat ſtrange, produce as a proof, that the apoſtle requires Chriſtians " to obey, in order to their final " acceptance."

Is *Paul* then become the apoſtate? and do the curſes which he has denounced againſt the ſeducers of the *Galatian* converts, fall at length on his own head? He placed *Timothy* at *Epheſus*, as a bulwark againſt the encroachments of other doctrines. Was it with a reſerve for liberties of this kind, which he himſelf ſhould take? Can we think his mind ſo much altered, ſince he told thoſe very *Epheſians*, that, without ſeeking acceptance through their obedience, *they were already accepted in the BELOVED!* Does he now retract the bleſſed truth? adviſing the rich, to raiſe a cloud of golden duſt, that it may cover their ſins, and waft them to the ſkies? at the ſame time, excluding the poor from the fellowſhip of this new goſpel, and the hope of glory. Is he grown aſhamed of that righteouſneſs of GOD, which, he aſſured the *Romans*, was the power of GOD unto ſalvation, only through believing? And are we, Sir, grown weary of that pure doctrine, which was reſtored to us, by our glorious reformers? Are we willing to give up the depoſitum, and return to the more than *Egyptian* darkneſs of friars and monks? with whom

— *Cælum*

— — Cœlum est venale DEUSque!

But to the point.—I shall transcribe the text, and add a short paraphrase; which may, perhaps, explain the meaning, and best refute the objection. *Charge them that are rich in this world, that they do good, that they be rich in good works, ready to distribute, willing to communicate; laying up in store for themselves a good foundation, that they may lay hold on eternal life.* Charge them, those believers * among you, *who are rich in this world; that they do good,* that, as members of CHRIST, they shew kindness, and exercise beneficence to others. *That they be rich in good works,* abounding in those works and labours of love, which flow from faith, or a comfortable persuasion of their interest in CHRIST. *Ready to distribute,* on all proper occasions, with chearfulness and delight; as counting it more blessed to give, than to receive. *Willing,* even without solicitation, *to communicate;* and not only embracing, but seeking every opportunity of relieving the necessitous. Lightly esteeming all that is called wealth here below; and *laying up in store for themselves* another kind of treasure, [even CHRIST, who is the pearl of price, and the true riches.] This will be *a good foundation* of hope, of comfort, and joy: *against the time to come,* whether it be the trying season of sickness, the awful hour of death, or the more tremendous day of judgment: That, placing their affections on him,

[* The exhortation is addressed, not to the ungodly, but to true believers; who had received CHRIST, and were saved through grace; consequently, had no need to *win* or *attain* eternal life, but only to make it, in their own apprehension, or to their own consciences, more and more *sure.* Had they been unconverted people, the apostle would, like his divine MASTER discoursing with the rich, but unregenerate *Nicodemus,* have struck at the root of their misery; and spoke of more important things, than distributing a little shining dust among the poor.]

him, and having their treasure in him, they may be found wise merchants : not grasping uncertainties and shadows, but *laying fast hold on* * sure and substantial possessions ; even *on eternal life.*

"*We establish the law:* we provide for its honour by the perfect obedience of *CHRIST;* says *Aspasio.*—Can you possibly think," replies Mr *Wesley,* "that St *Paul* meant this ?"—Before I answer this question, give me leave to ask another. Have you, Sir, done justice to *Aspasio ?* Is what you quote, the whole of his interpretation ? Have you not secreted a sentence, which speaks the very thing you blame for omitting ?

A member of the house of Commons, haranguing the honourable assembly, took the liberty to assert, " The gentlemen in the ministerial interest, never " propose any thing for the good of their country."—This was no sooner uttered, than a warm partizan of the other side starting up, complained loudly of calumny and scandal. Hold, Sir, for a moment, said the interrupted orator. Let me just finish my sentence, and

---

* *Take fast hold on*—thus I would translate that emphatical compound word ιπιλαϐωνται. Which agrees with the experience of the Christian, and is not without the authority of the critic.—With *the experience of the Christian.* Since believers, by the exercise of faith, producing all good works, are continually maintaining and increasing their hold of *CHRIST;* and of that eternal life, which is given them in him.—With *the authority of the critic.* For the word signifies, " to seize " with great vehemency; to lay hold on with both hands, as " upon a thing we are glad to have got, and will be loath to " let go again." Leigh's *Crit. Sacr.*—That it does not, in this connection, denote an apprehending of somewhat not taken hold of before, is evident from verse the twelfth, where this very exhortation is directed to *Timothy* himself : who was an eminent man of GOD, and the subject of particular prophecies; was a believer of the first class, and an undoubted heir of life and immortality : who needed not therefore *to attain,* but to live in the stedfast hope and unintermitted expectation of the glorious inheritance.

and then give vent to your vehement invectives. My intention was to have added; " but we in the oppo-
" sition readily agree to their measures."—Upon hearing this explanation, the house smiled, and the hasty zealot sat down ashamed.

Let me produce the whole period now under consideration. Then I believe, the reader will allow, that Mr *Wesley* has imitated this hasty gentleman, in one instance; and whether he has not some reason to imitate him in another, I shall leave to his own determination.—Immediately after the display of free justification, or of *righteousness imputed without works* *, *Aspasio*, aware of the possibility of abusing his doctrine, asserts the indispensable necessity of holiness. This done, as quite cleared from the accusation, he triumphs with the apostle; " *Do we then make void* " *the law, through faith*, in the imputed righteous-
" ness of our LORD? *GOD forbid! yea, we esta-*
" *blish the law.* Considered as the original *covenant*
" of life, we provide for its honour, by the perfect
" obedience of CHRIST. Considered as the inva-
" riable *standard* of duty; we enforce its observance,
" by the most rational, manly, and endearing mo-
" tives †."—Here, Sir, was hardly any room for the precipitancy of interruption, because the whole passage lay before you. And it is a little surprising, that you should see and animadvert upon the former clause; yet neither see, nor regard the clause immediately following.

" Did such a thought (of establishing the law, by
" the atonement and righteousness of CHRIST) ever
" enter into St *Paul's* mind?"—Let the preceding context determine. Has the apostle been opening the true sense of the precepts, that they might be rightly understood? Has he been inculcating the inviolable obligation of the precepts, that they might be duly practised; Has he not been asserting a justification ab-
solutely

* Rom. iv. 6.   † *Theron* and *Aspasio*, vol. I. p. 192.

solutely free, effected by the righteousness of GOD, without any co-agency from the righteousness of man? Does he not, in the last words, professedly encounter the objection, which, in every age, has been raised against this sacred doctrine? " Hereby you neglect and " dishonour the divine law." No; says the inspired apologist, the law is hereby *established*, and shewn to be more stable than earth or heaven. The grand legislator himself shall be humbled to its obedience; the GOD who gave the law, shall bleed for its penalties; rather than a tittle fail of its due accomplishment.— Magnified thus, the law indeed is, and made for ever honourable. And though *Aspasio* does not exclude our practical regards, I do verily, for my own part, believe; that the former sentiment, against which you exclaim, was uppermost with the apostle, and is the chief design of the text.

Yes, Sir,; it was the apostle's chief design, to shew the perfect consistency of free justification with the most awful glories of the DEITY; and thereby lay a firm foundation for the hope of a sinner. Had justice, which is the essential glory of GOD's nature, or the law, which is the revealed glory of his will—had either of these been violated, by the evangelical scheme; benign and desirable as it is, it must have been utterly rejected; it could never have taken place; the whole world must have perished, rather than such an injury be offered to any of the divine perfections. Therefore St *Paul* most sweetly teaches, and most satisfactorily proves, that, instead of being injured, they are most illustriously displayed by the obedience and death of *CHRIST*. By this means, JEHOVAH is inflexibly just, even in justifying the ungodly; and his law is highly exalted, even in absolving the transgressor, that believeth in *JESUS*.

Here is firm footing; here is solid rock.

Solid r *e*, on which the sinner may rest, who is well nigh sunk in despair; while the waves and billows of
divine

divine indignation go over his alarmed soul.—*Firm footing*, on which he may proceed, who sees the importance of his eternal interests, and does not risk them on the vague notion of mere mercy; dares not give into the modish religion, which leaves such venerable things, as the juſtice of the Moſt High and the law of the Moſt Holy, deſtitute of their due honour; and leaves such impotent creatures as men, to shift for themselves, by doing the beſt they can.

" The plain meaning is, we eſtabliſh both the true
" ſenſe, and the effectual practice of the law: we
" provide for its being both underſtood and practiſed
" in its full extent."—How can you make this proviſion, if you ſet aſide the conſummate obedience of *CHRIST; who is the end of the law for righteouſneſs;* for accompliſhing that righteouſneſs, which its precepts deſcribe, and its conſtitution demands.

O! Sir, did you conſider, what that meaneth, which the apoſtle ſtyles το ἀδυνατον τυ νομυ you would not uſe this language. Can *we*—can ſuch miserable ſinners as *we*, ever dream of effectually practiſing, in its full extent, that law, which condemns every failure; which requires truth in the inward parts, which inſiſts upon perfection, abſolute perfection, in every inſtance, and on all occaſions; charging us,

With all intenſe, and unremitted nerve,
To hold a courſe unfaltering;

to the very end of our lives, and from the beginning of them too?—Attend, I intreat you, Sir, to this moſt ſublime ſanctity of the divine law. Then, inſtead of ſaying, we provide for its performance in the *full extent* of its demands; you will probably ſay, with a more becoming modeſty, we provide for its performance, in a way of willing, chearful, ſincere obedience, ſtill looking unto HIM for juſtification, who has, in our name, and as our ſurety, fulfilled it to the very uttermoſt.

It is, I apprehend, one of your leading errors, that you form low, scanty, inadequate apprehensions of GOD's law; that law, which is a bright representation of his most pure nature; a beautiful draught of his most holy will, and never, since the fall, has been perfectly exemplified in any living character, but only in the man *CHRIST JESUS*.—From this error, many others must unavoidably follow; a disesteem of imputed righteousness, and a conceit of personal perfection; a spirit of legal bondage, and, I fear, a tincture of Pharisaical pride.

Should Mr *Wesley* ask, why I harbour such a suspicion concerning his sentiments in this particular? I answer, Because, here, he speaks of practising this law, which is so exceeding broad, in its full extent. Because, elsewhere, he represents the violations of this law, whose least tittle is of greater dignity than heaven and earth, as small matters; as petty offences; or, to use his own words, as " things not exactly right."—But more of this hereafter.

Aspasio, to vindicate the equity of the future judgment, declares, " I see nothing arbitrary in this pro-
" cedure; but an admirable mixture of just severity,
" and free goodness. On those, who reject the a-
" tonement, just severity. To those, who rely on
" their SAVIOUR, free goodness."—Mr *Wesley*, as though he would exculpate the ungodly, asks, " Was
" it ever possible for them not to reject it?"--What says our infallible Counsellor; the TEACHER sent from GOD? *They will not come to M E, that they may have life.* They rejected his counsel. They would not cease from their own works, and betake themselves wholly to the righteousness of *CHRIST*. This method of salvation they disliked. It was foolishness unto them. Therefore they were disobedient to the heavenly call.—Does this take away their guilt? Must GOD be reckoned unjust in punishing, because men are obstinate in their unbelief?

GOD

GOD does not require me, as you too injuriously hint, to "touch heaven with my hand," in order to escape damnation. But he invites and requires me, to accept of *CHRIST* and his salvation. If, intent upon any imaginary accomplishments of my own, I overlook the gift; or if, eager in the pursuit of worldly gratifications, I trample upon it; is not the fault entirely my own? Does it not proceed from the folly of my mind, or the bad disposition of my heart; and leave my conduct without excuse?

Justification is complete, the first moment we believe; and is incapable of augmentation. Thus *Aspasio* speaks. Thus Mr *Wesley* replies, "Not so "—And has he, for his authority, a single text of scripture? No; but the whole council of *Trent;* one of whose canons dogmatizes in this manner: " If any shall affirm, that righ-
" teousness received is not preserved, and increased
" likewise, by good works; but that good works are
" only the fruits and signs of justification obtained,
" not the means of increasing it also, let him be ac-
" cursed *."—I am sorry, Sir, to see you again in such company. And I would hope, if it were not an unhandsome reflection, you did not know your associates. Yet it is strange, that a *Protestant* divine should have been so inattentive to the main part of his character; or should be able to forget, that complete justification, through the righteousness of our LORD alone, is the very essence, soul, and glory of the *reformation*.

But let us examine the point.—Justification, I apprehend, is one single act of divine grace. It must, therefore, be either done, or undone. If done, in my very idea of the act, it includes completeness. So that to speak of incomplete justification, is a contradiction

---

* *Si quis dixerit, justitiam acceptam non conservari, atque etiam non augeri coram Deo per opera bona, sed opera ipsa fructus solummodo et signa esse justificationis adeptæ, non etiam ipsius augendæ causam, anathema esto.* Sess. vi. can. 24.

diction in terms; like speaking of dark sunshine, or a round square.

An incomplete justification seems, in the very nature of things, to be an absolute impossibility. Even an earthly judge cannot justify, where there is the least departure from integrity. He may overlook; he may shew clemency; he may forgive. But he cannot, in such a case, pronounce righteous. Much less can we suppose, that justification should take place before an infinitely-pure and jealous GOD, unless all guilt be done away, and the person be rendered *completely righteous*.

Besides, can *that* justification be other than complete, which is brought to pass by the most majestic SON of GOD? by his perfectly-holy nature; by his infinitely-precious sufferings; and by his inconceivably-meritorious obedience? This, if any thing in the world, must be absolutely complete; beyond compare, and beyond imagination complete; to speak all in a word, complete in proportion to the dignity, perfection, and glory of the accomplisher.

Is any such notion, as an incomplete justification, to be found in the Bible? St *Paul* says, *Whosoever believeth is justified;* to all intents and purposes justified. No, says Mr *Wesley;* he may be justified only in part or by halves.—He that believeth, adds the apostle, *is justified from all things*. No, replies Mr *Wesley;* many that believe, especially in the infancy of their faith, are justified only from *some* things. There is no necessity, that justification should be complete, when or where-ever it exists.

Is there no necessity? Why then does the voice of inspiration assert, that *the righteousness of GOD* is upon them that believe? Can a man have that incomparably-magnificent righteousness, and yet be incompletely justified? Does not the same inspired writer declare,—that this perfect and divine righteousness is upon *all;* not upon *some* only, but upon *all* believers? whether they be weak or strong; whether in the first

moments

moments of their conversion, or in the last stage of their warfare.—Yes; and he farther assures us, that *there is no difference*. No difference, with regard to the righteousness itself; for it is the *one everlasting* righteousness of the incarnate GOD. No difference, as to the reality of its imputation; for it is *unto all, and upon all*. No difference, in the way of receiving it; which is *by faith in JESUS CHRIST*. Consequently, no difference in the fruits or effects; which are pardon and acceptance, free and full justification.

Is Mr *Wesley*, like the *Popish* party, an advocate for a first, for a second, for I know not how many justifications? According to this scheme indeed, justification may be an incomplete thing. But the misfortune attending this scheme, is, that it has no foundation in scripture. The scripture knows nothing of it; the scripture declares against it; and aknowledges, as but one faith, but one baptism, so but one justification.

This is the grand scriptural maxim; *HE hath, by one oblation, perfected for ever them that are sanctified.* The oblation is one, needing no repetition, and no appendage. It does not partially accomplish, but perfects the business of justification; perfects it, not at the last only, but from first to last; yea, for ever and ever; in behalf of all those who are sanctified; or made partakers of this great sacrifice, and this divine atonement.

This is the fine scriptural illustration; *The heir, even while he is a child, is lord of all.* You have, perhaps, a son born. Upon this child you multiply your favours and caresses. He grows in wisdom and stature. Yet neither your favours, nor his growth, add any thing to his sonship, nor augment his right to your inheritance. With both these he was invested, the first moment he drew breath. So, we are no sooner justified, than we are heirs; *heirs of GOD, and joint-heirs with CHRIST.* The perception and enjoyment of this privilege may increase. But the
privilege

privilege itself, like the birth-right of the first-born, is incapable of augmentation.

Would Mr *Wesley*, with the followers of *Arminius*, exclude the righteousness of CHRIST; and introduce something of man's as the efficient, or as a concurrent, cause of justification? Then likewise his notion of a gradual, a variable, an incomplete justification, must ensue. Whether it be faith, which he would introduce for this purpose, or repentance, or sincere obedience, or whatever else he pleases; according to the measure of these works or graces, must be the degree of justification; and not only as to different persons, but as to the same person, at different times.

Farther, since all these endowments are, so long as we continue in the present state, imperfect; our justification must, according to this plan, unavoidably partake of their imperfections. It cannot be entire and laking nothing, till mortality is swallowed up of life.—But how contrary is this to a cloud of witnesses from the scriptures! *Ye are*, even now, *justified*. *He hath*, even in this present time, *reconciled you to GOD*. Through the birth and death of IMMANUEL, there is not only *peace on earth*, but *good-will towards men;* ιυδοκια, favour, complacency, and love, from the holy GOD, to the fallen soul. And is not this complete justification?

" There may be as many degrees in the favour, as " in the image of GOD."—This objection turns upon a supposition, that the favour of GOD towards us is occasioned by the image of GOD in us: which is the doctrine of the law; the very language of Heathenism; and has not a savour of that gospel, in which *CHRIST is all*. And I think myself more concerned, to remove such very prejudicial mistakes, than to sift and adjust any nice speculations, relating to degrees of the divine favour. *Aspasio* has touched this point. Referring you to his observation, I shall confine myself to a more interesting subject.

It

It is *CHRIST*, who *has redeemed us to* G O D, to the favour and fruition of GOD, *by his blood;* by his blood alone, without any aid from our goodnefs, or any co-operation from any creature.—His work pleafes G O D. His work magnifies the law. His work is incomparably the nobleft of all things in heaven or earth. This therefore is our recommendation to the divine Majefty. Interefted in this, we ftand perfectly righteous before the KING immortal, and fhall be eternally acceptable in his fight.—It was only on account of *Abraham*'s fupplication, that G O D fhewed compaffion to *Abimelech*. It was only on account of *Job*'s interceffion, that the LORD was pacified towards his three friends. And it is only on account of *CHRIST*'s righteoufnefs, that the HIGH and HOLY ONE beholds any child of *Adam* with complacency and delight. To *JESUS* alone belongs the honour of reconciling, juftifying, faving the innumerable millions of redeemed finners. And is not the LAMB that was flain, worthy to be thus honoured, and thus exalted ?

Is then our own internal and external goodnefs of no avail in this matter ?—Let us hear the eloquent *Ifaiah*, the evangelift of the *Jewifh* church : *The lofty looks of man fhall be humbled, and the haughtinefs of men fhall be bowed down; and the LORD*, the LORD JESUS CHRIST, *alone, fhall be exalted in that day.* —Does this text, it may be faid, relate to the gofpel, and the cafe of acceptance with GOD ? Or is it poffible to make what follows, confiftent with fuch an interpretation ?—Let us fee, whether it be not, by the HOLY GHOST himfelf, made perfectly confiftent with fuch a fenfe.

The day of the LORD of hofts, in the prophetical fcriptures, generally and principally fignifies the time of the gofpel-difpenfation ; when the L O R D puts the finifhing hand to his revelation ; gives the brighteft difplay of his grace ; and gathers together all things in *CHRIST*. This

This day, and its influence, shall cause a wonderful revolution in, what is called, the religious, virtuous, moral world. It shall fall like a thunderbolt upon every idol, set up in the hearts of men; shall prove their wisdom to be folly; their ability to be impotence; all their works to be worthless.

This prophecy, being so repugnant to our notions, and so disgustful to our inclinations, is asserted and enforced with the greatest particularity, both as to persons and to things.

As to *persons*.—*For the day of the LORD of hosts shall be upon* whom? upon the sordid wretch, or the scandalous sinner? Rather upon *every one that is proud and lofty* in his own conceit; pluming himself with the notion of some imaginary pre-eminence above his neighbour. It shall be likewise *upon every one, that is lifted up* in the esteem of others; either on account of *Roman* virtue, or *Athenian* philosophy, or *Pharisaical* zeal. And, notwithstanding his aspiring pretensions, or glittering accomplishments, *he shall be brought low;* shall be degraded to the rank of a lost, undone, helpless sinner.

So that none shall have it in his power to say, " I " am better than thou. I stand upon more honour-" able terms with my MAKER, and am a fitter ob-" ject for his favour." They shall all be like prisoners, confined in the same dungeon, and liable to the same condemnation. Every one of them equally destitute of any plea for justification; and all of them, as to acceptance with their CREATOR, without any difference. No difference, in this respect, between the accomplished gentleman, and the infamous scoundrel; no difference between the virtuous lady, and the vile prostitute. No difference at all, as to the way and manner of their obtaining salvation. So that the whole may appear to be of grace.

As to *things*.—This part of the subject is illustrated by a grand assemblage of images; comprehending all
that

that is most distinguishable in the visible creation, and denoting whatever is most admired or celebrated among the sons of men.—Oaks and cedars are the most stately productions of vegetable nature. Therefore *the day shall be upon all the cedars of Lebanon, and upon all the oaks of Bashan.*—Hills and mountains are the most conspicuous and majestic elevations of the earth. Therefore the day shall be *upon all the high mountains, and upon all the hills that are lifted up.*—Towers and cities are the most magnificent works of human art. Therefore the day shall be *upon every high tower, and upon every fenced wall.*—*The ships of Tarshish* are put for the wealth, the advantages, and the various improvements, procured by navigation and commerce. *Pleasant pictures* may represent every elegant and refined embellishment of civil life.—The whole collection of metaphors, seems to express all those attainments, possessions, and excellencies, which are supposed to add dignity to our nature, or stability to our hopes; to constitute a portion, in which we ourselves may rest satisfied, or a recommendation, which may entitle us to the favour of heaven.

Yet all these things, before the requirements of GOD's law, and before the revelation of his righteousness, shall be eclipsed and disgraced. *Thrown to the bats,* and consigned over to obscurity; *thrown to the moles,* and trampled into the dust. So that, in the pursuit of eternal life, none shall regard them; or else regard them, only to despise them.

Thus, says the prophet a second time.—To render the work of humiliation effectual, he redoubles his blow. May our whole souls feel the energy of his vigorous expressions! Thus *shall the loftiness of man be bowed down, and the haughtiness of men shall be laid low.* All notion of personal excellency set aside, they shall be base and vile in their own eyes; acknowledge the impossibility of being reconciled by any duties of their own, and place all their confidence on the propitiating death and meritorious obedience of *JE-SUS CHRIST*. *They* lefs than nothing; *H E* all in all.

With this important fentiment I clofe my letter; not without an ardent wifh, that it may fink into our thoughts, and dwell upon both our hearts.

Yours, &c.

LETTER V.

Rev. Sir,

YOUR laft, and feveral of your other objections, appear more like notes and memorandums, than a juft plea to the public, or a fatisfactory explanation of your opinion. They have rather the air of a caveat, than a confutation; and we are often at a lofs to difcern, how far your remonftrance is either forcible or appofite.

Brief negatives, laconic affertions, and quick interrogatories, opened by no pertinent illuftrations, fupported by no fcriptural authority, are more likely to ftagger, ftun, and puzzle, than to *fettle our notions in religion*. You feem, Sir, to have forgotten, that propofitions are not to be eftablifhed, with the fame eafe, as doubts are ftarted; and therefore have contented yourfelf with a brevity, which produces but little conviction, and more than a little obfcurity.

This brevity of yours is the caufe, and, I hope, will be the excufe, of my prolixity; which, I perceive, is growing upon my hands, much more than I intended. If you had been pleafed to fhew your arguments at full length, and to accompany with proof your gloffes upon fcripture, the reader would then have been able to determine the preponderating evidence between yourfelf and *Afpafio*; and my trouble

ble had been confiderably leffened, perhaps quite fpared.

An inftance of the foregoing remark, is the objection which follows.—St *Paul* often mentions *a righteoufnefs imputed*, fays *Afpafio*. " Not *a* righteoufnefs," fays Mr *Wefley*; " never once; but fimply righteouf-" nefs."—St *Paul* mentions δικαιοσυνην, the righteoufnefs which is imputed, both with and without the *Greek* article. And do neither of thefe fignify *a* righteoufnefs? This is a piece of criticifm, as new to me, as it is nice in itfelf.—Befides, where is the difference between *a* righteoufnefs, and righteoufnefs? Is not every righteoufnefs, *a* righteoufnefs? Is not every perfon, *a* perfon? and every prodigious refinement, *a* prodigious refinement?—I thought, Mr *Wefley* had known how to employ his time better than in fplitting, or thus attempting to fplit hairs.

To what purpofe, Sir, is this exceffive refinement? Many of your readers, I apprehend, will find it difficult to conjecture. For my own part, I freely confefs, that I could not, for a confiderable time, difcern your aim. Nor can I, even now, difcover any other defign, than a forced endeavour, to exclude the righteoufnefs of *CHRIST;* and introduce a miftaken fomething of your own, to officiate in its ftead. —As the thread of your criticifm is fpun extremely fine, we muft examine it with the clofeft attention. But firft let me juft take notice,—

That *Afpafio*, in confequence of his obfervation, deduced from the apoftle's language, afks, What or whofe righteoufnefs can this be? To which Mr *Wefley* anfwers: " He tells you himfelf: faith is imputed for " righteoufnefs."—But have you never read *Afpafio*'s interpretation of this text? If not, be fo impartial, as to caft your eye upon the *tenth* dialogue. There he confiders this paffage at large, and lays before you his expofition of the words; not impofing it, without affigning a reafon; but, together with his expofition,

prefenting

presenting you with the grounds of his opinion. If you can overthrow them, try your strength and your skill. They stand ready to receive your attack; being, at present, in full possession of the field.

However, if you will not advert to *his* thoughts, allow me, if I can, to penetrate *yours*. "St *Paul* "never mentions *a* righteousness, but simply righte- "ousness." Thus, I presume, you argue—"Not *a* "righteousness; that might seem to denote some *real* "righteousness; some actual conformity to the di- "vine law, imputed to sinners for their justification. "—Whereas, if faith be substituted instead of this "real righteousness; if faith be all that to us, which "our own obedience to the law should have been, "and which *Aspasio* supposes the righteousness of "*CHRIST* is appointed to be; if faith itself be all "this to us, then we are made righteous without *a* "righteousness. Something is accounted to us for "righteousness, which is really no such thing.—Then "we shall be under no necessity of submitting to the "righteousness of our GOD and SAVIOUR, but may "easily be furnished out of our own stock."

Is not this, or something like this, your way of reasoning? Do you not, in this manner, understand faith imputed for righteousness? not as deriving all its efficacy, all its significancy, from its most magnificent object; but as being itself the efficient of justification; the very thing for which we are accepted; in opposition to " the wicked and vain commentaries " of the *Calvinists*, which say, that all this is resident " in *CHRIST*, and apprehended by faith."

This led me to use that singular expression, " a " mistaken something." Since this is an egregious mistake of faith; of its nature, its end, its import.— Of its *nature*. For it is a going out of self, and a flying to *CHRIST*, for pardon, for peace, and for every spiritual blessing.—Of its *end*. For it is ordained, to preclude all boasting; that itself may be nothing;

nothing; that its owner may be nothing; that the grace of GOD, and the righteoufnefs of *CHRIST*, may be all in all.—Of its *import*. For it fays, according to the prophet, *In the LORD*, not in myfelf, *have I righteoufnefs*. It would expoftulate, in the words of the apoftle, with its overweaning and doating admirers; Ye men of *Ifrael*, why look ye fo earneftly on me; as tho', by my own power or dignity, I had procured your reconciliation, and rendered you accepted? The GOD of *Abraham*, *Ifaac*, and *Jacob*, has glorified his SON *JESUS*, and appropriated this honour to *his* obedience and death. In the matter of juftification, it is my bufinefs, not to furnifh a contingent, not to fupply any part, but to receive the whole from his fulnefs.

On *CHRIST's* death finners are to rely, as the caufe of their forgivenefs; on *CHRIST's* obedience, as the ground of their acceptance. " How does this " agree with pag. 68. ?"—Be pleafed to turn back, Sir; and, with a very little attention, you will perceive the agreement. Then let me defire you to turn inward; and you will, probably, difcern more than a little difingenuity in your own procedure; fince you refolve to ftop your ears againft the author's explanation, his very particular explanation and reftriction of his own meaning *.—If you was examining a mathematical fyftem, you would always carry in your memory, the leading problems or introductory axioms. If you did not, your own judgment would blame you.

And

---

* In pag. 68. *Afpafio*, fpeaking of the obedience and death of *CHRIST*, profeffedly declares: " However, therefore, I " may happen to exprefs myfelf, I never confider them, as " acting in the *exclufive* fenfe; but would always have them " underftood, as a grand and glorious aggregate. Looking " upon our SAVIOUR's univerfal obedience, which commen- " ced at his incarnation; was carried on through his life; and " terminated in his death;—looking upon all this, in its *col-* " *lective* form, as the object of my faith, and the foundation " of my hopes."

when you neglect to do the same, in canvassing a theological treatise, does not your own conscience reprove you?

Our LORD commends such kinds of beneficence *only*, as were exercised to a disciple, in the name of a disciple. Here Mr *Wesley* asks; "Is not this a slip "of the pen?"—Read the passage, Sir; and answer yourself. What are our LORD's words; *Inasmuch as ye have done it to these my brethren.* Have you not then as much reason, to charge our divine MASTER with a slip of the tongue, as to charge *Aspasio* with a slip of the pen? It is undeniably plain, that he does in fact commend only such kinds of beneficence, as were exercised towards *his brethren.* And I presume, you will readily grant, that *his brethren*, the nobler relation, cannot be more extensive than *his disciples*, the inferior.

"Will not our LORD then commend all kinds of "beneficence, provided, &c."—Excuse my cutting short your speech. You are rambling from the point. What *CHRIST will* do, is quite another question. *Aspasio* neither denies, nor affirms any thing, on this subject. All that he considers, is, what appears to be really done, in that particular description of the last day, and its awful process. Nor will he scruple to affirm, a second time, that our LORD applauds such acts of beneficence *only*, as were exercised to a disciple; to believers; to his brethren.

The righteous Judge specifies this sort of munificence, because it is a sure indication of one begotten by the word of truth. It is a test, which none but the saints and faithful in *CHRIST JESUS* will come up to. And a Christian is most properly distinguished, not by what he does in common with others, but by the different principle from which he acts.—Of this particularity *Aspasio* takes notice, on purpose to warn, as well as to exhort his readers. *Exhort* them, that they may abound in works of generosity. *Warn* them, that

that their works may spring from the right source, faith in the divine REDEEMER.

"You are not willing to call works of beneficence, "tho' exercised to a Samaritan or a Heathen," transient bubbles.—No more is *Aspasio*, in the sense and manner, which you would insinuate. He calls them such, not absolutely, but relatively. Not in themselves, but with respect to an affair, infinitely too great for them to transact, either in whole or in part. In this view (as relative to justification) St *Paul* calls them *dung*, which is despicable and sordid. Surely then *Aspasio* may call them *bubbles*, which are shewy but insignificant.—I don't call the desk, on which I write, a mere egg-shell. Yet I should not hesitate to say, it is scanty as an egg-shell, if appointed to transport an army to the *Indies*; feeble as an egg-shell, if set up as a wall of munition, against a battery of cannon.

How must Christians exceed the Scribes and Pharisees? To this *Aspasio* replies, Not only in being sincere; in having respect unto all GOD's commandments; but also in possessing a complete righteousness. Nor can this be any thing less, than the perfect obedience of our great MEDIATOR.—" Did our LORD "mean this? Nothing less."—Peremptorily affirmed; but not so easily proved.—Yes, you add; " he spe- " cifies, in the following parts of his sermon, the very " instances, wherein the righteousness of a Christian " exceeds that of the Scribes and Pharisees."—He does so. But is it not an absolutely-complete righteousness? A meekness, without the least emotion of resentment. A purity, without the least stain of evil concupiscence. A love, a long-suffering, a perfection, such as our FATHER which is in heaven excercises. Now if this does not exceed the righteousness of all the Christians in the world, or if this is to be found in any character, save only in the character of our

great

great MEDIATOR, I retract, most freely retract my opinion.

The discourse relates to that righteousness, by which we are saved; or by virtue of which we enter into the kingdom of heaven *. And why, Sir, why will you not resign the honour of obtaining salvation, to the most blessed IMMANUEL's blood and obedience? Why will you hedge up your people's way to the immortal mansions, by teaching them to depend upon duties and attainments of their own?—Should any one, hearing this doctrine, that the law of the ten commandments requires a perfect, sinless obedience; that none can be delivered from the wrath to come, or enjoy eternal life, without this unsinning, perfect obedience: should such a one, struck with surprise and anxiety, inquire, " Who then can be saved?" What answer would Mr *Wesley* give?—The answer we would make, is obvious and full of consolation. " No " man, by his own performances. But salvation is " to be sought, salvation is to be obtained, by the righ-
" teousness

---

* *Christus magna asseveratione pronunciat, Pharisaicam illam justitiam, quæ non perfectissime habet integram legis impletionem, non posse ingredi regnum cœlorum. Suorum igitur justitiam vult esse abundantiorem, hoc est, suos vult ad judicium Dei afferre abundantissimam, plenissimam, et perfectissimam justitiam, ut per ac propter eam possent ingredi regnum cœlorum. Eam vero, quia in se non inveniunt, fide quærunt et apprehendunt in impletione legis, a Christo pro nobis præstita.* Vid. CHEMNITII *Harm. Evang.* p. 722.

A truly valuable work, in which the learned reader will find many traces of lively devotion; many pieces of solid criticism, and many fine views opened, to see more clearly the wisdom, beauty, and transcendent excellency of our blessed REDEEMER's life. This book is particularly estimable, for displaying with great perspicuity, and enforcing with proportionable zeal, that distinguished article of Christianity, *justification thro' the righteousness of* JESUS CHRIST; which is, as our author very emphatically speaks, *ipsissimum evangelii fundamentum.*

"teousness of another; even by the consummate o-
"bedience of our LORD JESUS CHRIST."

He brings this specious hypocrite to the test.—
"How does it appear," you ask, "that this young
"ruler was a hypocrite?"—It appears from his conduct. For he came kneeling to our SAVIOUR, as one sincerely desirous of learning his duty; yet, when instructed in it, he would not perform it.—It appears from your own character of him. You say, "He lo-
"ved the world." Then the love of the FATHER was not in him. That he pretended to the love of GOD, is evident from his own words. That he had no real love, is certain from your own acknowledgment. If pretence without reality be not hypocrisy, please to inform us, what is.—It is farther apparent from your descant on the case. "Therefore he could
"not keep any of the commandments in their spiritual
"sense." And it is a sure, as well as important truth, that whoever pretends to keep the commandments, yet does not keep them in their spiritual meaning, is a deceiver of himself; a deceiver of others; a hypocrite.

"The keeping of the commandments," says Mr *Wesley*, "is undoubtedly the way to, though not the
"*cause* of eternal life."—How then came it to pass, that our LORD JESUS CHRIST should declare, *I am the way?* The way, to what? To the favour of GOD; to the fruition of GOD; to every spiritual blessing; or, in other words, to eternal life.—After such a claim, from such a person, may I not, without the imputation of undue confidence, deny your assertion in your own form of speech? "The keeping
"of the commandments *undoubtedly* cannot be the way
"to eternal life;" since this is an honour, this is a prerogative, which the all-glorious REDEEMER has challenged to himself.

Hence your distinction between the *way* to, and the *cause* of, appears to have no countenance from scripture. And will it not, upon a review, appear to have as little support from reason? Cast your eye upon yonder bridge. It is thrown over a deep and wide river. It is the way, the only way, whereby I cross the water, and arrive at the opposite bank. If so, is it not likewise the cause of my safe arrival on the other side? There may be, in this case, other causes, concomitant or subordinate. But the bridge is the grand one; that which every body chiefly regards; and to which my passage is always ascribed.

CHRIST therefore is the way, the only way, to life and immortality. By his precious blood, and by his divine righteousness, we pass the gulf of wrath and destruction. By the things which he has done, by the pains which he has endured, we enter the realms of peace and joy. Accordingly, we are exhorted *to walk in him;* and are assured, that as many as walk in this way, *shall renew their strength.* This is, what the apostle calls, *the new and living way.* This is, what the Psalmist styles, *the way everlasting.* And tho' other ways may *seem right unto a man, yet the end thereof are the ways of death.*

A doubt, perhaps, may arise in the reader's mind, suggested by the words of the prophet; *An high way shall be there, and a way, and it shall be called the way of holiness.* True. The way is *CHRIST*, the incarnate GOD, with all his gifts, privileges, and blessings. *It shall be called the way of holiness.* *. None can

---

* *If.* xxxv. 8. Upon this subject, Dr *Owen* speaks excellently. " *CHRIST* is the medium of communication between
" GOD and us. In him we meet, in him we walk. All in-
" fluences of love, kindness, mercy from GOD to us, are
" through him; all our returns of love, delight, faith, o-
" bedience unto GOD, are all through him. He being that
" *one way*, GOD so often promiseth his people: and it is a
" glorious way, *If.* xxxv. 8. *An high way, a way of holiness,*
" a way that none can err in, that once enter it. Which is
" further set forth, *If.* xlii. 16. All other ways, all other paths,
" but this, go down to the chambers of death: they all lead
" to walk contrary to GOD."

See

can enter and advance therein, yet continue carnal and unclean. All that travel this road, renounce the hidden things of darkness, and do the works of righteousness. It does not indeed find, but it assuredly makes, the passengers righteous. And though holiness is not their way, yet it is a principal part of their business, while they walk in *CHRIST*.

Aspasio, having occasion to speak of *Abraham*'s faith, quotes the words of the apostle ; *By works his faith was made perfect*. Which he thus explains ; " His " faith hereby answered its proper end, and appeared " to be of the true, the triumphant, the scriptural " kind ; since it overcame the world, overcame self, " and regarded GOD as all in all."—To this Mr *Wesley* replies, with the solemnity of a censor, and the authority of a dictator ; " No. The natural sense of " the words is, By the grace superadded, while he " wrought those works, his faith was literally made " perfect."—Your proof, Sir. What have you to make good this interpretation ? There is not a word in the text about grace superadded. This is not assigned as the cause of a perfected faith. Nay, the sacred writer expressly assigns another. *By works*, says St *James*, his faith was made perfect. No, says Mr *Wesley;* but by *grace superadded*. St *James* affirms one thing ; Mr *Wesley* affirms the contrary ; and who am I, that I should decide between two such disputants ? But I believe, the reader will, without my interposal, easily chuse his side.

Perhaps, you will reply, If this is not the true sense,

See a treatise, entitled *Communion with GOD*. By JOHN OWEN, D. D. Which presents us with the spirit and quintessence of the gospel ; with the noblest privileges and strongest consolations of Christianity ; animating us thereby to all the duties of holy obedience.—Here are pinks and roses in the path. Milk and honey in the cup. Marrow and fatness on the table. In many treatises, the author has done worthily ; but in this, I think, he excelleth them all.

sense, produce a better.—One less opposite to the natural import of the words, and the apparent meaning of the apostle, is already produced. Do you insist upon another? I will then refer you to abler judges.—Shall I send you to an expositor, whom you yourself admire? Dr *Doddridge* thus comments upon the text. "*His faith was perfected by works;* the inte-"grity of it was made fully apparent, to himself, to "angels, to GOD."—Shall I remit you to an expositor, who can neither deceive, nor be deceived? The GOD of glory says, *My strength is made perfect in weakness. Made perfect!* How? Is there any such thing as a superaddition to GOD Almighty's power, while he exerts it in behalf of his people? This none can imagine. But it is hereby manifested, to their comfort, and his glory. The same word is used concerning *Abraham*'s faith, and concerning the GOD of *Abraham*'s strength. Why then should it not be understood in the same sense? Here it is τελειόω; there it is ἐτελειώθη. And, in both places, it signifies, not lite-"rally made perfect," but illustriously displayed.

Shall I send you to a familiar illustration? I view, from my window, a young tree. The gardener, when he planted it, told me, it was a fruit-tree, a pear-tree, a right *beaute du roy*. It may be such a tree, and have its respective seed in itself. But this did not then appear. If, when autumn arrives, its branches are laden with fruit, with pears, with that delicious kind of pears; this will be a demonstration of all those properties. This will not make it such a particular tree; no, nor make it a good and fruitful tree; but only shew it to be of that fine sort, or make its nature and perfections evident.

St *James* speaks of the justification of our faith; thus proceeds *Aspasio*. And thus replies Mr *Wesley;* " Not unless you mean by that odd expression, our " faith being made perfect."—I mean such a perfection of faith as is mentioned above. Other perfection

I find

I find not, either in books or men. Was faith perfect, in *your* sense of the word, love, joy, and all holiness would be perfect likewise. Correspondent to the principle, would be the state of the production. There would be no longer any cause for that petition, which the disciples put up; *LORD, increase our faith.* Nor for that supplication, which you and I, so long as we continue members of the church of *England,* must use; " Give unto us the increase of " faith, hope, and charity!"

You call the justification of our faith an " odd ex- " pression."—Is it not founded on the tenor of the apostle's discourse? Is it not the native result of the apostle's inquiry? *Shew me* thy faith. Prove it to be real and unfeigned. Prove it by such acts, as demonstrate you trust in *JESUS* alone for everlasting life. If it stands this test, we shall acknowledge it to be that precious faith, whose author is *GOD,* and whose end is salvation.—Is not *that* a justification of faith, which displays its sincerity, and renders it without rebuke? Somewhat like this would be reckoned a justification of any person, or of any other thing, and why not of faith?

Something, you see, Sir, may be said in vindication of this expression. However, if it be thought improper; if it tend to create any confusion in our sentiments; or to draw off our attention from that grand idea, which is peculiar to the word justification; the idea, I mean, of being made righteous before GOD; I freely give it up; I will alter it in my book, and use it no more.

He that doth righteousness, is righteous: he manifests the truth of his conversion, and justifies his profession from all suspicion of insincerity.—". Nay;" says Mr *Wesley,* " the plain meaning is, He alone is truly righ- " teous, whose faith worketh by love."—*Your* exposition may be true, and *Aspasio*'s no less true. I leave the reader to determine, which is most exactly suitable

able to the apostle's arguing.—He is speaking of the *Christian* righteousness; that which renders us righteous before GOD; that which flesh and blood could never have discovered; which therefore was graciously revealed in the gospel, and is the principal subject of gospel-preaching. As then there were, and always would be, many pretenders to the noble privilege, St *John* lays down a maxim or a touchstone, to distinguish the sincere from the hypocrite. *He that* uniformly *doth righteousness*, in a way of sanctification; he, and he only, *is* to be acknowledged by us, as truly *righteous* by way of justification.

Far be it from me, Sir, to be fond of wrangling. Where you hit upon the truth, or come pretty near it, I shall never be eager to oppose. On the contrary, I shall be very desirous to agree; and preserve, as much as possible, both the unity of opinion, and the harmony of affection.—Your own interpretation shall take place. Only let your *working* be the sign and fruit of a righteous state, not that which makes or constitutes us righteous. The righteousness of fallen creatures, *is* not of themselves, but *of me, saith the LORD*. It is brought in and accomplished by HIM, whom GOD hath set forth to be their MEDIATOR and SURETY. So that we are made righteous, not by doing any thing whatsoever, but solely by believing in *JESUS*. Our character as the redeemed of the LORD, is, οἱ ἐκ πίστεως; *Men*, having their existence, their subsistence, their all, *by faith*. Hence it comes to pass, that we really are, what the apostle affirms, in the following words, *righteous, even as he is righteous*. Not barely righteous, as the moral Heathens, by dint of human resolution; not barely righteous, as the reputable *Jews*, by the influence of their legal sanctions; but righteous with that *very righteousness*, which adorns and exalts, and will eternally distinguish the only begotten SON of GOD.

It remains to be inquired, *what* faith is most likely
to

to operate, in this excellent and happy manner? I mean, to *work by* love.—Let me illustrate the point by a short apologue; then release the reader from his attention, and the writer from his task.

A certain king had two favourites, whom he honoured with his peculiar regard, and enriched with a ceaseless liberality. They both, insensible of their vast obligations, became traitors and rebels. Being convicted of treason against their sovereign, he was determined to overcome their evil with good. Accordingly, when they had nothing to plead in their own behalf, he generously forgave them both. The one he dismissed from prison, and suffered to live unmolested on his private inheritance. The other he restored to all his high preferments, and public employs. He adorned him again with the robe of honour, and admitted him again into the bosom of favour.—Which of them, now, will feel the warmest affection for their sovereign? Which of them will be most ready to serve him on all occasions? and, if need be, to hazard even life in his defence?—He, doubtless, on whom most was bestowed.

And is not *that* person most likely to work and obey, from a principle of love, who believes, that his divine LORD has not only bore the curse, but fulfilled the law for him? has given him, not barely an exemption from punishment, but a title to eternal life? yea, has clothed him with his own most perfect and glorious righteousness. By virtue of which, he will, ere long, be presented faultless before the throne of judgment, and have an abundant entrance into the everlasting kingdom.—Will not the faith of such unspeakably-rich grace, pacify the conscience, and purify the heart? awaken gratitude to our heavenly Benefactor, and enkindle zeal for his glory? cause us to discharge all the duties of our station chearfully, and withstand every allurement to evil resolutely?

Surely, we may say of this faith, what *David* said
of

of *Goliath*'s fword; *There is none*, there is nothing like it. For all thefe bleffed purpofes, it is beyond compare, and I fhould think, beyond difpute, efficacious —That you, Sir, may know more of this faith, and difpute lefs againft it, is the fincere and fervent wifh of, &c.

LETTER VI.

Rev. Sir,

AS this letter may probably be pretty long, I fhall not increafe the prolixity by a preface; but enter upon it, without any farther introduction.

Whofo doth thefe things, faith *David, fhall never fall.* Which *Afpafio* thus interprets, " fhall never " fall into final apoftafy."—You are pleafed to reply; " *David* fays no fuch thing. His meaning is, Whofo " doth thefe things to the end, fhall never fall into " hell."—It would be a great wonder, I muft own, if he fhould. But if he happens to fail, at fome times, and in fome inftances, what becomes of him then?— However, let you and I, Sir, be at as little variance as poffible. Where is the extraordinary difference between yourfelf and *Afpafio?* If a profeffor of religion falls into hell, muft he not previoufly fall into final apoftafy; and if he falls into final apoftafy, muft he not inevitably fall into hell?

When you infert the claufe, *to the end*, do you interpret? do you not rather interpolate the facred text? The words of the Pfalmift relate to the prefent time, נעש *doth*, not יעשה *fhall do*. They contain an encouragement to thofe, who, at this inftant, bring forth the fruits of evangelical righteoufnefs. The encouragement is deduced from the comfortable doctrine of final perfeverance. It carries this chearing import; " Whofoever believes in JEHOVAH, as
" laying

"laying all his sins upon *CHRIST*, and giving him eternal life freely; whosoever, from this principle of faith, sincerely loves and willingly obeys GOD; he shall never fall."—The words are אל ימי לעולם, *He shall never be moved*. A phrase common among the *Hebrews*, to denote the stability of a man's happiness. An immoveable thing never falls, either one way or another. So, this righteous person shall never fall; either into final apostasy, which is the greatest misery here; or into hell, which is the consummation of misery hereafter.

But I begin to apprehend what you mean, and of what you are jealous. Your exclamation unravels all; "How pleasing is this to flesh and blood!"—Under favour, Sir, I cannot conceive how this doctrine should be pleasing to flesh and blood. Flesh and blood, or corrupt nature, is proud. Any scheme of perseverance, to be accomplished by our own strength, would indeed be agreeable to the vanity of our mind. But a perseverance, founded on the fidelity and the power of GOD; a perseverance, which acknowledges itself owing, not to any human sufficiency, but to an union with *CHRIST*, and the intercession of *CHRIST;* this is a disgusting method. This is what the natural man cannot away with. You will find the generality of people utterly averse to it.—Flesh and blood will not submit, either to be made righteous before GOD, by the imputed righteousness of *CHRIST;* or to be made faithful unto death, by the never-failing faithfulness of *CHRIST*. Try your friends; try your followers; try your own heart on this point.

To the humble believer, I acknowledge, this is a most pleasing and consolatory doctrine. He who feels his own impotence; who knows the power of his inbred corruptions; and is no stranger to the wiles of his spiritual enemy; he will rejoice in the thought, that *nothing shall pluck him out of his* almighty REDEEMER's *hand*. That his advocate with the FATHER,

FATHER, will suffer *neither principalities, nor powers, nor life, nor death, nor things present, nor things to come, nor any other creature, to separate him from the love of G O D.*—Without such a persuasion, we might too truly say of the Christian's joy, what *Solomon* said of worldly merriment ; *I said of laughter, It is mad; and of mirth, What does it?* If he, who is to-day basking in the divine favour, may before the morrow be weltering in a lake of fire ; then joy, even joy in the HOLY GHOST is unreasonable ; and peace, even that peace which passeth all understanding, is chimerical. A building without a basis ; at least, *a bowing wall and a tottering fence.*

Let us examine the doctrine, which Mr *Wesley* says is so pleasing to flesh and blood; or, in other words, to carnal people.—What is the thing which the Psalmist teaches, and *Aspasio* professes ? That the persons who are described in the psalm †, shall never apostatize from the true faith, or from true obedience. Is this so agreeable to carnal people? Is it not rather unwarrantable in Mr *Wesley* to suppose, that carnal people either possess true faith, or perform true obedience, or can be pleased with either ? Especially, since the apostle assures us, that *the carnal mind is not subject to the law of GOD, neither indeed can be.*

Besides, are not the duties mentioned by the Psalmist, offensive to flesh and blood ? Do they not require, or imply, the mortification of our carnal appetites,

---

‡ The xvth *psalm*, I apprehend, describes the perfect character. That perfection, which *CHRIST* really fulfilled ; and is the righteousness, in which G O D is well pleased. The children of the truth are, by the same SPIRIT, led to imitate this character, according to the measure of their faith. Yet so imperfectly, that when compared with it in their own persons, they have reason to pray, *Forgive us our trespasses.* Though, when considered as clothed with the fulfilment of all in *CHRIST*, they may assure themselves of acceptance with GOD, and an everlasting title to the divine favour.

tites, and the discipline of our unruly affections? Can it be a welcome piece of news to flesh and blood, that this mortification shall take place? instead of being remitted shall increase? and never, never be discontinued, till mortality is swallowed up of life?—If so, *the old man which is corrupt*, must be pleased with the curb, and the dagger must delight in its own restraint, and its own destruction.—Such a paradox we must believe, before we can espouse Mr *Wesley*'s notion, that flesh and blood are pleased with the doctrine of a final perseverance in self-denial, in righteousness and true holiness.

" Should your repentance be without a failure, and
" without a flaw; I must still say to my friend, as our
" LORD replied to the young ruler, *One thing thou*
" *lackest*. In all these acts of humiliation, you have
" only taken shame to yourself. Whereas, a righ-
" teousness is wanting, which may magnify the law,
" and make it honourable."—These are *Aspasio*'s words; upon which Mr *Wesley* animadverts. " One
" thing thou lackest, the imputed righteousness of
" CHRIST. You cannot think this is the meaning
" of the text."—Neither does *Aspasio* affirm this to be the meaning. He only uses the words by way of accommodation. Could you demonstrate, that our LORD intended no such thing, yet the sentence may not improperly express *Aspasio*'s opinion; and if so, be not unfit for his use.

However, let us inquire into the exact meaning of the text. A very little search will yield the desired satisfaction. *Sell all thou hast, and give to the poor, and thou shalt have treasure in heaven.* *Treasure in heaven* was what the young gentleman lacked. Could this be any other than *CHRIST* himself? Is not *CHRIST* the treasure, hid in the field of the gospel? Is not *CHRIST* the inheritance, reserved in heaven for us? Is not a communion with *CHRIST*, and an enjoyment of *CHRIST*, the supreme felicity of our nature?

nature?—*David* was of this mind, when he publicly declared, *Whom have I in heaven but thee?*—St *John* was of this mind, when he solemnly averred; *He that hath the SON, hath life.*—Whoever is of another mind, has very inadequate, very unworthy notions of heaven and its happiness.—Now if *CHRIST* himself was the *one thing* needed, surely his righteousness could not be secluded. His blood and obedience inseparably accompany his person. He that hath the bridegroom, hath his riches also.

In opposition to this sense, it is affirmed, " Certain-"ly the one thing our LORD meant, was the love "of GOD."—The love of GOD is *certainly* an eminent blessing. Possessed, I should imagine, only by those, who have first obtained eternal life, by *knowing the true GOD and JESUS CHRIST*. But does our love of GOD magnify the law; satisfy justice; or obtain heaven? Are we pardoned, are we reconciled, are we justified, on account of our love of GOD?—The young ruler wants *that*, which may open to him the kingdom of heaven; and *that*, whereby he may inherit eternal life. Mr *Wesley*, setting aside pardon, reconciliation, justification, together with the one perfect righteousness, which procures them, ascribes all to our love of GOD. And, by this means, not to the true love, arising from the knowledge of him, as manifested in the gospel; as having first loved us, in granting us remission of sins, freely through *JESUS CHRIST.*—This notion may pass current at *Rome* *, not among the *Protestant* churches. Our own church has most expressly disclaimed

---

* The council of *Trent*, by her interpreter *Andradius*, thus expresses herself; *Christus obedientia sua non meruit credentibus in ipsum salutem et vitam æternam ; sed hoc tantummodo meruit, quod propter ipsum infunditur nobis charitas inhærens; ut illa demum sit, quæ hominem Deo non tantum gratum, sed pergratum ; non tantum acceptum, sed peracceptum reddat ad vitam æternam.* Vid. Chemnit. Exam. Conc. Trident. p. 146.

claimed it. Speaking of CHRIST and his precious blood-shedding, she adds ; " Whereby *alone* we are " made partakers of the kingdom of heaven."

" Is the obedience of CHRIST insufficient to ac- " complish our justification ?"—Here you would correct both the language, and the doctrine. The language : for you say, " Rather I would ask, Is the " death of CHRIST insufficient to purchase it ?"— To purchase justification, you suppose, is more proper and expressive, than to accomplish. As this may seem a strife of words, I shall dismiss it without much solicitude. Only I would transiently observe, that to accomplish, denotes more than to purchase. It denotes the constituent cause ; what the schoolmen call, the matter of justification, or the very thing which effects it. If your favourite phrase implies all this, let it have the pre-eminence.

Next, you correct the doctrine, by saying, " *I* " *would rather ask, Is the* death *of CHRIST* insuffi- " cient *to purchase justification?*"—I answer, If you consider the death of CHRIST, as exclusive of his obedience, it is insufficient. If you do not, there is no great reason for your starting a doubt, where we both are agreed. And indeed it is scarce worth my while to take notice of it. I will therefore return to the distinction, which you think proper to make, between accomplishing and purchasing justification.— Why, Sir, would you set aside the former phrase ? Does it not imply, that which justifies ? that very thing, which commends us to GOD ? that *very righteousness*, in which we stand accepted before him ? Does not this way of expressing, guard most effectually against the errors of Popery, and exclude all co-efficiency of faith, of works, or any thing else whatever ?—I said, the errors of Popery. For a *Popish* synod will allow, that we are not justified without the righteousness of CHRIST, by which he hath merited justification for us ; but declares, at the same time,

If any man shall say, we are formally righteous, by that very righteousness, let him be accursed.—According to this, which is no very good confession, the righteousness of CHRIST purchases, but does not accomplish; it merits our justification, but does not constitute our justifying righteousness. See, Sir, whither your refinements are leading you.

The saints in glory, says *Aspasio*, ascribe the whole of their salvation to the blood of the LAMB. " So " do I," replies Mr *Wesley;* " and yet I believe, he " obtained for all a possibility of salvation."—Is this objection pertinent? Does *Aspasio*'s assertion contradict your belief? Does it not comprize, all that you avouch, and much more? Is it possible, that Mr *Wesley*, who is such a master of logic, should argue in this manner? " The saints in glory ascribe all their sal- " vation to CHRIST's blood; therefore he did not " obtain a possibility of salvation for all men."—What a forced conclusion is this! What wild reasoning is here! Such premises, and such an inference, will probably incline the reader to think of a sun-beam and a clod, connected with bands of smoke.

If you was determined to make this passage faulty, you should have opposed it with the following declaration of your faith, " Yet I believe, that CHRIST " obtained *no more than* a possibility of salvation for " any." Then you would have something suited to your purpose; but not agreeable, either to sound sense, or sound doctrine.—Not to *sound sense.* Your possibility of salvation is, if people perform the conditions. How then can they ascribe *the whole* glory to CHRIST? At this rate, they do a piece of injustice to their own resolution and diligence; as these, by fulfilling the conditions, had a hand in obtaining the reward, these ought to have a share in receiving the honour.—Not to *sound doctrine.*—*Aspasio* believes much more than a possibility of salvation by *JESUS CHRIST*. He believes a full and complete salvation; according to

that

Let 6. ASPASIO VINDICATED.

that noble text, *It is finished.* A salvation, not to be acquired, but absolutely given; according to that precious scripture, *GOD hath given to us eternal life.* Not upon some terms or pre-requisites, but without any condition at all; according to that most gracious invitation, *Whoever will, let him take of the water of life freely.*—This I look upon as sound doctrine. But will your notion of a conditional salvation, proposed by way of bargain, and granted upon terms, comport with this *gift of grace?*

No more than a *possibility* of salvation!—Yes, Sir, *CHRIST* obtained a great and a free salvation. Great; for it comprizes the pardon of all sin, original and actual; a restoration to entire and unalterable favour; together with a title to everlasting life and glory.—This is such a provision for our happiness, as becomes the immense goodness, and inconceivable majesty of an incarnate GOD; such as not only supplies our wants, and satisfies our desires, but surpasses our very wishes; transporting us with wonder, and filling us with joy.—To accomplish all this, we may reasonably suppose, nothing less could be sufficient, than the active and passive righteousness of HIM, who is gone into heaven, angels, and authorities, and powers being made subject unto him.—Since this matchless ransom has been paid; since these grand conditions are performed; there is no obstruction from the divine justice, or the divine truth. All that ineffable and eternal blessedness is now become *free;* is granted to sinners, to rebels, to the most unworthy; they are allowed, yea, invited to receive it, to possess it, to rejoice in it as their own portion; and without the proviso of any good thing in themselves, purely on account of their SAVIOUR's all-sufficient work.

I read in sacred history of *Eleazer the son of Dodo the Ahohite, one of the three mighty men with David; how he arose, and smote the Philistines, until his hand was weary, and his hand clave unto his sword; and the*

LORD

LORD wrought a great victory that day; and the people returned after him only to spoil. And were not these mighty men typical, faintly typical of our almighty REDEEMER? Did not *JESUS* also arise, and work a great victory? Has he not triumphed gloriously over sin, and all our enemies? And what have we to do, but only to return, and divide the spoil, and share the benefits of his conquest?—May we not boldly say? " My sin is done away, because *CHRIST*
" has bore it on the cursed tree. I stand accepted be-
" fore GOD, because *CHRIST* has finished the righ-
" teousness, which renders me unblameable and un-
" reprovable. I shall receive the HOLY GHOST,
" because *CHRIST* is my advocate; and prays the
" FATHER, that he will give me another comfort-
" er. This sacred comforter, by shewing me the
" riches of *CHRIST*, will more and more sanctify
" my nature." To think and live in this manner, is to take the spoil after our victorious leader.

Let me close and confirm this sentiment, with a passage from that inimitable penman, the prophet *Isaiah;* who, for his remarkably-clear views of CHRIST, may almost be admitted into the number of evangelists; and, for his exquisitely-fine descriptions of CHRIST, greatly exceeds all orators and all poets. *Who is this that cometh from* Edom, *with dyed garments from* Bozrah? *This that is glorious in his apparel, travelling in the greatness of his strength?—I that speak in righteousness, mighty to save.—Wherefore art thou red in thine apparel, and thy garments like him that treadeth in the wine-fat?—I have trodden the wine-press alone, and of the people there was none with me.*

The prophet, like one thrown into a sudden surprise, with a beautiful abruptness, cries out, *Who is this?* What extraordinary appearance discovers itself to my sight? Is it a human, or a divine form, *that* I behold? He *cometh from Edom* the country, *from Bozrah* the
capital,

capital, of our profeſſed national enemies. Is he for us, or for our adverſaries?—The firſt queſtion ſeems to proceed from a diſtant and indiſtinct view. He then takes a nearer ſurvey, and deſcribes the wonderful perſonage with greater particularity. This that cometh with *dyed garments*, like ſome terrible and victorious warrior, that has ſcarcely ſheathed the ſword of ſlaughter; who is all encrimſoned, and ſtill reeking with the blood of the ſlain.

The viſion becomes clearer and clearer. I ſee him (adds the rapturous prophet) *glorious in his apparel*. Highly graceful, as well as extremely awful. Bearing in his aſpect, in his whole perſon, in his very dreſs, the marks of tranſcendent dignity. *Travelling in the greatneſs of his ſtrength*. Not faint with toil, nor wearied with the fatigue of the dreadful action; but like one, that is indefatigable in the zeal, and irreſiſtible in his power; and therefore ſtill preſſing forwards, to new victories; ſtill going on, from conquering to conquer.

The majeſtic object is, all this while, advancing. At length, he approaches near enough, to hold a conference with this devout inquirer. One would naturally expect, that his ſpeech ſhould be like his aſpect, alarming and tremendous. But grace is on his tongue, and his lips drop balm. *I that ſpeak in righteouſneſs:* all whoſe words are faithfulneſs and truth; an immoveable foundation for the faith of my people. *That ſpeak of righteouſneſs* *: of that myſterious righteouſneſs, which is the delight of my FATHER, and the life of the world. To bring in which, is the deſign of my appearance on earth, and to reveal it is the office of my SPIRIT. By means of this righteouſneſs, I am *mighty to ſave:* to ſave thee; to ſave any loſt ſinner; to ſave them, as with the arm of omnipotence, beyond all that they can think, even to the very uttermoſt.

* *Vox* רבד *loqui conſtructa cum præfixa* ב, *notat paſſim, phraſi ſacra, loqui de re.*

Here the prophet seems to be somewhat at a loss, and takes leave to renew his inquiry. If thou art come, not to destroy mens lives, but to save; *wherefore art thou red in thine apparel, and thy garments like him that treadeth in the wine-fat?* These indicate, not deliverance, but destruction. These are tokens, not of forbearing mercy, but of inexorable vengeance.—'Tis true, replies the illustrious hero, *I have trodden the wine-press* *;* I have crushed my foes; I have trampled them under my feet; and repentance was hid from

---

* *Trodden the wine-press.*—I can hardly forbear taking notice of the great impropriety, with which this text and this metaphor are frequently used by our theological writers. They apply both to *CHRIST*, as bruised by his almighty FATHER; and bearing the weight of that indignation, which was due to the sins of mankind. Nothing is more common, than to make this text descriptive of his agony in the garden.—If indeed it had been said, *I am trodden in the wine-press*, the image might not be improper. But when it is said, *I have trodden*, nothing can be more unsuitable to a state of humiliation and suffering. This phrase evidently denotes conquest and triumph; enemies vanquished and totally destroyed. It should never therefore be applied to the agonizing, but to the triumphant SAVIOUR; not to *JESUS* prostrate on the ground, but to *JESUS* making his foes his footstool.

As I have taken leave to animadvert upon a common mistake, I would also take liberty to pay merit its due honour; by recommending to my reader a poetical version of this passage, given us by Dr *Lowth*, in his very elegant work, entitled *De sacra poesi Hebræorum.* Where he understands the text, in the sense suggested above; and translates it, in the very spirit of *Virgil.* As the lines are few, and the book may not be in the hands of all my readers, I will present them with a transcript.

> —— —— *Ille patris vires indutus et iram,*
> *Dira rubens graditur, per stragem et fracta potentum*
> *Agmina, prona solo; prostratisque hostibus ultor*
> *Insultat; ceu præla nova spumantia musto*
> *Exercens, salit attritas calcator in uvas,*
> *Congestamque struem subigit: cæde atra recenti*
> *Crura madent, rorantque insperse sanguine vestes.*
>   Page 62.

from my eyes. But thy enemies were the object of mine indignation. Sin, and death, and hell, are the vanquished adversaries. It is their blood, that is sprinkled upon my garments, and that stains all my raiment.—This victory I have gained, by myself *alone*. Being infinitely too great in my power, to want an associate; and infinitely too jealous of my honour, to accept of any assistance. *Of the people*, whether in heaven or on earth, *there was none with me;* to afford the least succour, or to take the least share in the glorious work. The salvation of sinners; their deliverance from wrath, and their redemption to GOD, is, in all its parts, my act, even mine, and mine only. Yours be all the benefit; mine all the glory.

The terms of acceptance for *fallen* man, were, a full satisfaction to the *divine justice*, and a *complete conformity* to the divine law. "This," says Mr *Wesley* to *Aspasio*, "you take for granted, but I cannot allow."—That *Aspasio* does not take these points for granted, I thought, even his enemies would confess. That he has attempted, at least, to make good his opinion, all the world, besides yourself, Sir, will acknowledge. What else is the design of dialogue the *third* and *fourth?* what else is aimed at, in dialogue the *seventh*, *eighth*, and *ninth?* The former treat largely of the full satisfaction given to divine justice. The latter treat still more largely of the conformity demanded by the divine law, and yielded by the divine *JESUS*.

These things, however, "you cannot allow."— Not allow a full satisfaction of divine justice to be necessary? Are you not then acceding to the *Socinian?* Not allow a complete conformity to the divine law to be necessary! Are you not then warping to the *Antinomian?* See, Sir, how you approach the rocks, both on the right hand, and on the left. May the KEEPER of *Israel* preserve yourself and your followers, from suffering shipwreck!—Every one, I think, must allow

low what you deny, who believes the divine juſtice to be infinite, and the divine law to be unalterable. A juſtice, that will admit of any ſatisfaction, leſs than complete, can never be deemed infinite. And if the divine law can reſt ſatisfied with an obedience that is defective, it is not ſo venerable as the law of the *Medes* and *Perſians*.

"*The* terms *of acceptance for fallen man*," you ſay, "*are* repentance *and* faith."—I muſt own, I don't much like the expreſſion *terms*, unleſs it be referred to the mediation of *CHRIST*. And you yourſelf, if you would act conſiſtently, ſhould not be over-fond of it, becauſe it is not ſcriptural. Tho' for my own part, I have no quarrel againſt the word, becauſe it is not the exact phraſeology of ſcripture; but becauſe I diſ-like the idea it conveys. Shall *we* treat with the DEITY, as free ſtates or ſovereign princes treat with each other? the one obtaining from the other, peace or ſome advantageous conceſſion, by complying with his terms?

To confirm your opinion, that " the terms of ac-
" ceptance for fallen man, are repentance and faith," you produce the following text; *Repent ye, and believe the goſpel*.—Here you write, like a man of ſenſe; who knows what juſt diſputation means. You lay aſide your *certainlies*, your *undoubtedlies*, your *unqueſtionablies*; and urge a proof from ſcripture.—Whether you rightly underſtand, and duly apply this proof, muſt now be inquired.

Repent ye, and believe the goſpel. This may be the meaning of the exhortation. *Repent;* relinquiſh all your wrong notions, relating to the way and manner of finding acceptance with the DEITY. *Believe the goſpel;* which opens a moſt unexpected avenue, for the communication of this bleſſing; which brings you tidings of a ſalvation, fully procured by the incarnate GOD, and freely offered to the unworthy ſinner.—The word you know, is μετανοειτε. Which, in its

primary

primary signification, denotes not so much a reformation of conduct, as a change of sentiment.

ρ. Suppose it to signify a reformation of conduct. The meaning then may be as follows. *Repent;* forsake all your vices, and all your follies; mortify every evil temper, and renounce every evil way. In order to render this practicable, *believe the gospel;* wherein a SAVIOUR is preached and displayed; who makes peace for such offenders; reconciles them to GOD; and obtains eternal redemption for them. This will sweetly withdraw your affections from iniquity, and sweetly attach them to the blessed GOD. Whereas, without this powerful expedient, you will never be delivered from the pleasing witchcraft of your lusts. Sin will always have dominion over you, so long as you are under the law, and not under grace.—Repentance, thus understood, is not the condition of obtaining salvation, but the fruit of salvation obtained.

Besides, if repentance be a gift, it cannot be a term or condition. He must be a stranger to the import of language, and the common ideas of mankind, who will take upon him to affirm the latter; and he must be yet a greater stranger to the holy word of GOD, who will offer to deny the former.—*CHRIST is exalted,* faith the apostle, *to give repentance.* Not to require it, as a condition of blessedness; but to give it, as a most eminent blessing. Not require repentance of fallen man, who is not able to think a good thought; but give it, from his unsearchable riches; and work it, by his almighty power.

You say, " the terms of acceptance for fallen man, " are, *&c.*"—Methinks, I should be glad to know, what you mean by *fallen* man. Do you mean (as you tell us, in your collection of sermons) " one dead to GOD, " and all the things of GOD? having no more power " to perform the actions of a living Christian, than " a dead body to perform the functions of a living " man?" What terms, I beseech you, can such a one fulfil?

fulfil ? Be they ever fo difficult, or ever fo eafy, it maketh no difference. The hand ftiff in death, is no more able to move a feather, than to remove a mountain.—Whatever, therefore, others may affirm, you, Sir, cannot talk of repentance, to be exercifed by *fallen* man, until he is quickened and enabled by fellowfhip with *CHRIST*, the living and life-giving head. Unlefs you chufe, either to contradict your own affertion, that fallen man is abfolutely dead to all good; or elfe think proper to maintain, that the dead may not only act, but perform fome of the moft excellent acts, and important offices.

You fhould likewife, Sir, if you would write correctly and argue forcibly, have told us, what you mean by faith. Otherwife, you may intend one thing, and I another, even while we both ufe the fame word. In this cafe, our difpute might be as endlefs, as it muft be fruitlefs.

By faith I mean, what St *John* calls, *a receiving of* CHRIST ; a receiving of him and his benefits, as they are freely given, in the word of grace and truth. If this, which is the apoftolical, be a proper definition, then it feems not to come under the denomination of a condition. They muft be exceffive refiners indeed, who would call my receiving a rich prefent, the terms or conditions of poffeffing it ; or would efteem my eating at a plenteous feaft, the terms and conditions of enjoying it. Is not this to fubtilize, till found fenfe is loft ?

Faith, according to St *Paul*, is a perfuafion, that *CHRIST loved me, and gave himfelf for me*. Where is any trace or any hint of conditionality, in this defcription ? I don't hear the apoftle faying, He loved me, provided I repent ; he gave himfelf for me, in cafe I think this, or do that : but he gave himfelf for me, when I was ungodly, and *had* performed no conditions ; when I was without ftrength, and *could* perform no conditions.—Thus he gave himfelf for me,

that

that I might have remission of sins thro' his blood; and eternal life, thro' his righteousness.—Believing these delightful truths, and receiving these heavenly privileges, I love my most adorable Benefactor; and abhor those iniquities, for which he wept, and groaned, and died. That love of *CHRIST*, is vital holiness; and this abhorrence of sin, is practical repentance. And both are the fruits, therefore cannot be the conditions, of salvation by *JESUS*.

Some holy men and excellent writers, I confess, have not scrupled to call faith and repentance the conditions of our salvation. Yet I cannot prevail on myself to admire or approve the language. I fear, it tends to embarrass the sincere soul; to darken the lustre of grace; and to afford too much occasion for boasting.

To embarrass the sincere soul.—For, if I am saved on conditions, this will naturally divert my attention from the grand, and all-sufficient cause of justification, the righteousness of *CHRIST;* which alone gives solid comfort. Instead of delighting myself in the LORD REDEEMER, I shall be engaged in an anxious concern about the supposed conditions. Whether I have performed them? Whether I have performed them aright? Whether there may not be some latent defect, that spoils all, and renders my labour fruitless? The more serious our minds are, and the more tender our consciences, the more shall we be liable to perplexity and disquietude on this head.

It eclipses the lustre of grace.—*Ye are saved by grace*, says the oracle of heaven. But if salvation be upon conditions, it cannot be of grace. It must, in some measure at least, be of works. Since it depends upon working the conditions, it is obtained by working the conditions; and the candidate has reason to look principally unto his performance of the conditions. They are to him, by incomparable degrees, the most important point. Because, without their all-significant
interposition,

interpofition, every thing elfe is as nothing. Even GOD's everlafting love, and CHRIST's everlafting righteoufnefs, are, till the conditions are fulfilled, but cyphers without the initial figure.

It affords too much occafion for boafting.—May I not, in this cafe, thank my own application and induftry? They, they exerted themfelves fuccefsfully; and behold! the promifed reward is mine. What then fhould hinder me from facrificing unto my own net, and burning incenfe unto my own drag?—At this door the notion of merit will unavoidably creep in. Becaufe my performance of the condition is meritorious of the *covenanted* reward. So far meritorious, that the reward is my due. I may demand it, as a debt. And it will be an act of apparent injuftice to with-hold it.—But fhall thefe things be faid unto the ALMIGHTY? Will thefe things redound to *the praife of the glory of his grace?* Do thefe things hide vanity from man; or confift with a falvation, that is *without money, or without price?* Not quite fo well, I believe, yourfelf will acknowledge, as the following lines.

" Let the world their virtue boaft,
" Their works of righteoufnefs;
" I, a wretch undone and loft,
" Am freely fav'd by grace:
" Other title I difclaim,
" This, *only this* is all my plea;
" I the chief of finners am,
" But *JESUS* died for me.

" Fallen man," you fay, " is juftified, not by perfect " obedience, but by faith."—" Not by perfect obe- " dience." Ah, Sir! if you had remembered the immutability of GOD, and the fpirituality of his law, you would not have challenged this expreffion. — " But by faith." Here, 'tis true, you ufe the language of fcripture. Neverthelefs it behoves a watchman

man in *Israel*, to shew how the language of scripture may be abused. Faith, you allow, is imputed to us for righteousness; therefore (you infer) not the righteousness or perfect obedience of *CHRIST*. This, if you mean any thing, or would speak any thing to the purpose, must be your way of arguing. So you would set faith and *CHRIST*'s righteousness at variance. The former shall exclude the latter from its office. Whereas, the former is only the pitcher at the fountain, while the latter is the very water of life; is that blessed, glorious, heavenly expedient, which, received by faith, justifies, sanctifies, saves.

According to your gospel, faith will say to the righteousness of the REDEEMER, ". Depart hence. I " have no need of thee. I myself act as the justifying " righteousness. *I stand in the stead of perfect obedi-* " *ence, in order to acceptance with GOD* *."—To this may we not reply? Was faith then crucified for you? has faith magnified the divine law? or is it by means of faith, that not one jot or tittle of its precepts pass unfulfilled?

If faith, in this sense, is imputed for righteousness, how can you subscribe that emphatical article, which declares, " We are accounted righteous before GOD, " *only* for the merit of our *LORD* and *SAVIOUR* " *JESUS CHRIST*." Surely, Sir, you are account-" ed righteous, for the sake of *that*, whatever it be, which stands in the stead of perfect obedience. That, whatever it be, may claim the honour; and to that justice itself cannot but award the prize.

If your notion be true, the believer ought to have his own faith principally in view. Whatever presents me perfectly obedient before GOD, is my greatest good; is my choicest portion; the best foundation for my hope, my peace, my joy. To this, therefore, so
long

* These are Mr *Wesley*'s own words, in his explication of this very doctrine. See his sermon on *the righteousness of faith*. Vol. I. p. 111.

long as I know my own interest, I must chiefly look. Whereas, *look unto* JESUS, is the direction of the HOLY GHOST. Look unto his perfect atonement, and complete righteousness, *and be saved*, is the grand unchangeable edict, issued from the throne of grace.

Perhaps, you will say, Are not the words of scripture expresly on my side? *Faith is imputed for righteousness.* True. But is the sense of scripture on your side? Suppose, I should undertake to prove, that *David* was purged from guilt, by the hyssop which groweth on the wall; this you would think a wild and an impracticable attempt. But should I not have the words of scripture, expresly on my side? *Purge me with hyssop, and I shall be clean.* Yet should I not have the least countenance imaginable from the spirit and sense of those sacred writings. Has the hyssop, a mean worthless shrub, any kind of fitness, to stand in the stead of the sacrificial blood, and make the atonement for sin? No more fitness has faith, to stand in the stead of perfect obedience; to act as our justifying righteousness; or procure our acceptance with GOD.

"What CHRIST has done."—Here Mr *Wesley* himself speaks of what CHRIST has *done*. He represents it by a very magnificent image. He lays it as the foundation of that first and most comprehensive blessing, justification. In this I most cordially agree with him. Hoping, that we shall unanimously join, to defend this important sentiment, against all opposition; and endeavour to display the REDEEMER's work, as well as his passion, in all its glorious excellency.

"What CHRIST has done is the foundation of "our justification, not the term or condition."—The prophet *Isaiah* had other notions of this matter; *If thou shalt make his soul an offering for sin, he shall see his seed.* If * is the hypothetic language; denotes a

term;

* *If.* liii. 10. אִם תָּשִׂים, Si posueris. *Vecula* אִם *valet* conditionem,

term; expresses a condition; on the performance of which, the MESSIAH *should see his seed;* should have a numberless multitude of sinners, pardoned and renewed; born again of the SPIRIT, and made heirs of salvation. The grand term, on which all these blessings depend, and by which they are made sure to believers, is, the pouring out of the MESSIAH's soul, as a sacrifice for their sins, and a ransom for their persons.

"The foundation, not the condition."—Methinks you should offer some reason for this distinction. Especially, since St *Paul* assures us, that CHRIST is, in the work of salvation, not this or that only, but he is ALL. Especially, since CHRIST himself declares, *I am*, in that grandest of all affairs, the redemption of sinners, *the beginning and the ending*. And well he may be so, since he is, as it follows in the text, *the ALMIGHTY*.

Your meaning, I presume, is, What CHRIST has done, is a foundation for the influence and significancy of our own doings. That they, under the notion of terms and conditions, may come for a share, and be his co-adjutors in the great work. This was the doctrine, established by the council of *Trent;* this is the doctrine, still maintained in the conclave of *Rome;* and is, perhaps, of all their abominations the most refined, yet not the least dishonourable to our SAVIOUR. It bears the greatest opposition to the truth of his gospel, and the freeness of his redemption.

I have heard it insinuated, that Mr *Wesley* is a Jesuit in disguise. This insinuation I rejected, as the grossest calumny; I abhorred, as falsehood itself. I acquit you, Sir, from the charge of being a Jesuit or a Papist. But no body, I apprehend, can acquit

---

conditionem, *et recte vertitur per* si. *Patet enim clarissime,* conditionem *hic conjungi cum* privilegio, *præstita couditione obtinendo.* VITRIN.

your principles from halting between Proteſtantiſm and Popery. They have ſtolen the unhallowed fire, and are infected with the leaven of Antichriſt. You have unhappily adopted ſome ſpecious Papiſtical tenets, and are liſtening to the mother of abominations, more than you are aware.

Amidſt all your miſtakes (and from miſtakes who is exempt?) I verily believe, your principal aim is, the honour of *C H R I S T*, and the edification of ſouls. Therefore I ſpeak the more freely. Was you a bigot to ſelfiſhneſs, or a devotee to vain-glory, ſuch liberty might be diſpleaſing. But I am perſuaded better things of Mr *Weſley*. He has publicly declared, that " wherein foever he is miſtaken, his mind is open to " conviction; and he ſincerely deſires to be better in- " formed." This is written in the true ſpirit of a Chriſtian. To this ſpirit I addreſs myſelf. Begging of you, Sir, with the ſincerity and tenderneſs of a brother, to conſider theſe hints impartially; leſt, being miſled yourſelf, you miſlead your thouſands and ten thouſands.

In the mean time, I hope, you will not take it amiſs, if, to my affectionate intreaties, I add my earneſt prayers: That you, Sir, and your people, may be in the number of thoſe *bleſſed men*, *unto whom GOD imputeth righteouſneſs without works*. Which I take to be the firſt and great evangelical privilege; as, I am very ſure, it is the richeſt benefit, I know how to crave, either for you, or for your moſt, *&c.*

LETTER VII.

REV. SIR,

PERSONS ſkilled in the diſſection of animal bodies, frequently mention *comparative anatomy*. May I borrow the term, and apply it to theology? I do then freely declare, that in caſe you cenſured *Aſpaſio*,

spasio, for points of divinity, *comparatively small*, you should have no opposition nor any check from this pen.

Some people, for instance, are of opinion, that the belief of a parent is considerably beneficial to his children. That, when St *Paul* says to the anxious jailor, *Believe on the* LORD JESUS, *and thou shalt be saved, and thy house;* he promises some special good, that should redound to the man's household, from his own receival of *CHRIST*. It seems, indeed, that the apostle must intend something of this nature; more than barely to say, thy family also, provided they follow thy example, shall obtain salvation with eternal glory. If this were the whole of his meaning, he need not have confined it to the jailor's domestics, but might have extended it to all the inhabitants of *Philippi*.

Such tenets, whether admitted or rejected, affect not the *main* point. Men may embrace which side of the question they think proper, and yet be found in the faith of our LORD JESUS CHRIST. But errors, relating to *that righteousness*, which is the one efficient cause of justification; in which alone GOD is well pleased, and all his perfections glorified; which is the only spring of solid peace, and true godliness; such errors are extremely pernicious. These we must withstand with resolution and zeal. We may not give place to their encroachment, no, not for an hour. The former may be compared to a fly, settled on the dish; the latter are more like poison, mixed with our food. To dislodge *that*, may not be amiss. But to prevent, or expel, or antidote *this*, is absolutely necessary. In the former number, perhaps, the reader will rank your observation, which follows. But as I have undertaken to follow you step by step, I must not disregard it.

Aspasio, speaking of *David*, expresses a high esteem for that hero, king, and saint. Allowing, that his esteem

esteem were carried a little too far; where would have been the great hurt, or the grievous offence? How, Sir, could this have led to " unsettled notions in re- " ligion *?"—I was inclined to answer your reflections, as the hero himself answered his censorious brother, *Is there not a cause?* Then passing on to another subject, as he, perfectly master of himself, and nobly superior to the affront, turned to another person. But as you seem to have injured *David*, and not done justice to the truth, I shall hardly be excused, if I dismiss the matter, without some more particular notice.

GOD himself dignifies *David* with the most exalted of all characters, says *Aspasio*.—" Far, very far " from *it*," says Mr *Wesley*. " We have more exalted " characters than *David's*."—Where, Sir? Shew me, in any of the saints, or in any of the sacred writers, a more devout, or a more divine spirit, than that which breathes in the penman of the *Psalms*. For my own part, I know nothing superior to it, in any author, or in any language. Neither can I conceive a more exalted character, than the character given of *David*, *a man after GOD's own heart*. If GOD be an unerring judge, if *his* approbation be the infallible standard, this description must express the most consummate human worth. Say whatever you will of a person, it does not, it cannot, exceed this most illustrious testimony.

" But this is said of *David* in a particular respect."
—Ay? notwithstanding the HOLY SPIRIT has declared concerning him ; *a man after mine own heart, who shall perform all my will*. If you was expounding this text, would you think it right to say ? He shall perform *all my will*, that is, he shall serve me in *some particular respect*.—" It was not said, with regard to
" his

* The reader will please to remember, that the pamphlet, which contains the remarks under consideration, is entitled *A Preservative against unsettled notions in religion.*

" his whole character." No! not when the SPIRIT of infpiration has borne this witnefs to *David; His heart was perfect with the LORD his GOD.* Could his heart be perfect, yet not influence his *whole* conduct?—" But it was faid in the fecond or third year " of *Saul*'s reign." Therefore it was not applicable to him, during the future years of his life. This is the inference you would draw. But can you really think it a juft one? or would you call *that* perfon, a man after GOD's own heart, who is fingularly pious in the days of his youth, but fwerves and declines in his advanced age?

Notwithftanding all thefe remonftrances, you pufh matters to the utmoft; as tho' it was a point of the laft importance, to prove *David* an errant back-flider. With this view, you add; " But was he a man af-" ter GOD's own heart, all his life, or in all parti-" culars? So far from it, that"—Stop, Sir, I befeech you. And, before you fpeak unadvifedly with your lips, hear what the LORD himfelf replies, to both your interrogatories; *David did that which was right, in the eyes of the LORD, and turned not afide from any thing that he commanded him,* all the days *of his life, fave only in the matter of Uriah the Hittite.* Surely, you was not aware, that fuch things are written in the book of GOD. Otherwife, you would not have contradicted them, with fo much boldnefs. I will, therefore, put the moft charitable conftruction upon your procedure, and fay with the apoftle; *I wot, that through inadvertence you did it.*

There is not a juft man upon earth, that finneth not, is a text quoted by *Afpafio*. Upon which Mr *Wefley* obferves; " Solomon might truly fay fo, before *CHRIST* " came."—According to this infinuation, what *Solomon* faid in his *Proverbs* and other books, was faid only by a fhort-fighted mortal: who might adapt his inftructions to the prefent œconomy; but was not able to plan a fyftem of morals for futurity. Whereas, as, I always supposed, that his writings were dictated by that infinitely-wise SPIRIT, before whom all times are present, and to whom all events are known. Agreeably to this suppoſition, *Paul* informs us, that *whatſoever things were written aforetime*, whether by *Solomon* or any other prophet, *were written for our learning.*—No; ſuggests Mr *Weſley*. Here is ſomething written, which appertains not to us Chriſtians. We are above it.—Are you ſo? Your reaſon for theſe lofty apprehenſions? Why, " St *John* af-" firms, *Whoſoever is born of GOD, ſinneth not.*"

True; he ſinneth not habitually; it is not his cuſtomary practice. Thus the paſſage is explained by another apoſtle; *Sin*, tho' it may make inſurrection, does *not reign in his mortal body*. Tho' it may aſſault him, yet it *has not dominion over him*.—

Again, he *ſinneth not*, is the ſame way of ſpeaking, and to be underſtood with the ſame limitation, as that text in *Job, HE giveth not account of any of his matters*. How Sir, would you interpret theſe words? It is undeniably certain, that ſometimes GOD giveth account of his matters. He gave it to *Abraham*, when *Sodom*, and *Gomorrah*, and the cities about them, were to be deſtroyed with brimſtone and fire from heaven. You would therefore, I preſume, in ſome ſuch qualified ſenſe expound the paſſage; " *He giveth not account;* " it is not his uſual way. Not a cuſtomary procedure " with the ſupreme Diſpoſer of things. He generally " requireth his creatures to tranſact with him upon " truſt; to give themſelves up with an implicit re-" ſignation to the veracity of his word, and the " good-pleaſure of his will."—The harmony of ſcripture, and the neceſſity of the caſe, call upon you to give the ſame expoſition of the text before us.

I ſaid, the neceſſity of the caſe. For you will pleaſe to obſerve, the thing affirmed, is affirmed in ſuch a manner, that it muſt be applied to every individual Chriſtian, and at the very inſtant of his commencing a true Chriſtian. The apoſtle ſays not, a ſaint of
the

the first rank, but *whosoever*. He says not, After such a one has been, for a considerable time, born of GOD; but whosoever *is born*, is but just entered upon the desirable state, *sinneth not*. The character belongs to the very weakest believer. The description is suited even to babes in CHRIST. To suppose, therefore, that it implies an entire freedom from sin, infirmity, and defect, is to suppose, that all the children of the regeneration are born in a state of manhood; or rather, are more than men, even while they are infants of a day.

Our sense of the passage is free from this impropriety, yet gives no countenance to immorality. *Whosoever is born of GOD sinneth not.* He does not, he cannot sin, like the devil, or one actuated by the diabolical nature. This interpretation is rendered probable, by the apostle's antithesis; *He that committeth sin is of the devil.* It is rendered necessary, by the preceding remark, and by the experience of Christians.—The text, thus interpreted, is applicable to the babe in CHRIST, as well as to the adult. Though either of them may fall, through the violence or surprise of temptation; yet neither of them can live and die in allowed iniquity, whether of omission or commission. They cannot have a settled love to any known sin, nor can they commit it with the full consent of their will.

Solomon, when he uttered those humbling words *, had his eye upon what you somewhere call, " the inconceivable purity and spirituality of the sacred " precepts;" upon that universal obedience which they require, in every the minutest instance.—That we do nothing, great or small, which they forbid; leave nothing undone, in heart or life, which they enjoin.—That we do all this, in the most perfect degree. Not only serving the LORD, but serving him with all our strength. Not only loving our neighbour, but loving him as our own soul. Ever exercising the utmost

---

* Eccl. vii. 20.

utmost regularity of affection and desire; even maintaining the utmost rectitude of temper and thought.—If you also, Sir, had your eye fixed upon the same law, as it delineates and demands this " inconceivable " purity and spirituality; you would not scruple to acquiesce in the wise man's confession, nor think much to adopt it as your own. You would acknowledge it calculated, not only for the *Mosaic* æra, and the meridian of *Judea*, but for all times and all places; till those new heavens, and that new earth appear, wherein dwelleth consummate righteousness.

In many things we offend all. " That St *James* does " not speak this of himself, or real Christians, will " clearly appear to all, who impartially consider the " context."—I wish, Sir, you had made this appear to *one;* even to him, whom you honour with this address. Then I should not have been obliged to ask, Of whom speaketh the apostle?—He says, *My brethren.* Does not this imply true believers, and real Christians?—He says, *We teachers* *. Does not this comprehend himself, and describe his office?—He adds, *We all.* If he himself, and real Christians, are not included in this most comprehensive clause; I would desire to know, in what terms they could possibly be comprised.

According to this interpretation, the arguing is just, and the conclusion forcible. As though he had said, —" My dear brethren, though you are truly convert-" ed to Christianity, yet do not unadvisedly engage " in the arduous and awful work of the ministry. " Remembering that we ministers of the gospel shall " be subject to a stricter judgment † than Christians " in ordinary life; and if, upon trial, we are found " faithless, shall receive a heavier condemnation †.— " The danger, let me add, is very considerable; be-
" cause

---

* The original is not κυριοι, *masters*, but διδασκαλοι, *teachers*.

† † *Judgment, condemnation—* the word κριμα may be taken in both these significations.

"cause such is the frailty of our mortal state, that the very best among us, and those conversant in sacred things, cannot always walk uprightly; but, in many instances, we trip, we stumble, we offend."

Whereas, if neither the apostle himself nor real Christians be meant, I can see no propriety nor force in the reasoning. Nay, I can see no reasoning at all, though the illative particle *for* evidently requires it. Nothing but a most insipid and frivolous assertion; "For, in many things, we that are not real Christians offend." Is this a discovery worthy of apostolical wisdom? Is this all that the inspired St *James* meant to declare? You and I could have told him and his people a great deal more. Whosoever is not a real Christian offends, not in *many* things only, but in *every* thing. To such a one nothing is pure. His mind and conscience are defiled: his whole life is sin.

We have examined this objection, as it stands in itself. Let us now take a view of it, as it may appear in its consequences.—*In many things we offend all.* "The apostle speaks not of himself, nor of real Christians." What fine work would our adversaries make with the scriptures, if we should allow them Mr *Wesley's* liberty of interpretation! Tell a *Pelagian*, that all mankind is deprived. Prove the universal depravity, by that abasing text, *All we, like sheep, have gone astray.* How easily may he reply, *All we* does not mean all mankind? The prophet speaks not of himself, nor of virtuous persons, but only of profane people, and men of the baser sort.—Tell an *Arian*, that our LORD JESUS CHRIST is very GOD. Confirm the glorious truth, by that most cogent text; *In HIM dwells all the fulness of the GODHEAD.* The heretic has nothing more to do, than, in Mr *Wesley's* manner, to answer, *All fulness* does not mean all the divine perfections, but only some pittance or portion of them.—Dear Sir, whenever you are difposed to criticife again, let me befeech you to confider a little the import of language, and the confequences of things.

Had the words been, *In many things we offend*, you might, by difregarding the context, have borrowed fome flight feeming countenance for your criticifm, from verfe the ninth ; where the apoftle is fuppofed to perfonate the wicked, *Therewith curfe we man*. But in the place under confideration, he enlarges the fentiment, and ftrengthens the language ; though free from that particular crime, he was not free from this general charge. Here therefore he fpares not himfelf; he takes fhame to himfelf, and teaches the moft upright of the human race, to plead guilty before their Judge. We the fervants of GOD; we the ambaffadors of CHRIST; we *all**—not one excepted—in many things offend.—Where then could *they*, and O.! where can *you* and *I*, look for our perfection, but only in our divinely-gracious SURETY, BRIDEGROOM, HEAD ? There let us feek it, where fome excellent lines (whofe author you may probably know) have taught us to find it.

> *Now let me climb perfection's height,*
> *And into nothing fall ;*
> *Be lefs than nothing in thy fight,*
> *While* CHRIST *is all in all.*

In the paragraph which begins, " O·children of " *Adam*," you don't diftinguifh what the law is *mac;* to fpeak, according to a new fcheme of divinity ; and what it really *does* fpeak to true believers, on the principles of the gofpel. Give me leave to rectify your miftakes, and to point out the manner in which you fhould have expreffed yourfelf.

To rectify your miftakes—You fuppofe the law, upon *Afpafio's* plan, fpeaking to this effect : " O children " of *Adam*, you are no longer obliged to love the " LORD

* *Ne feipfos quidem excipiunt apoftoli.* BENGEL. in loc.

"LORD your GOD with all your heart." Indeed you are. The obligation remains, and is unalterable. But it has been fully fatisfied, as the condition of life and immortality, by the believer's glorious SURETY.—" Once I infifted on abfolute purity of heart. Now " I can difpenfe with fome degrees of evil defire." No fuch thing. Every degree of evil defire I condemn with inexorable rigour. But every fuch offence has been thus condemned, and thus punifhed, in the flefh of your crucified LORD.—" Since *CHRIST* " has fulfilled the law for you, you need not fulfil it." Rather, you need not fulfil it, in order to the juftification of your perfons, or to obtain eternal life and glory. This, to you the greateft of impoffibilities, has been performed in your behalf, by a MEDIATOR and a REDEEMER, to whom nothing is impoffible.—" I will connive at, yea accommodate " my demands to your weaknefs." Not this, but what is much better, I fee no finful weakneffes in you, becaufe they are all covered † with the refplendent robe of your SAVIOUR's righteoufnefs; therefore I no longer curfe, but blefs you, and fign your title to everlafting happinefs.—Thus the enmity of our nature is flain: thus the precepts, even the ftricteft precepts, become amiable and defirable. We love the law, which, thro' our dear REDEEMER, is no longer againft us, but on our fide; is a meffenger of peace, and bears witnefs to our completenefs in *CHRIST*.

The manner in which you fhould have expreffed yourfelf—This is what the law fpeaks, according to *Afpafio*'s doctrine: " O believers in *CHRIST*, I am, like " my divine Author, confummate and unchangeable.
" I did

---

† Pfal. xxxii. 1. *Bleffed is he, whofe iniquities are covered.* Upon this text St Jerom very ingenioufly, and very comfortably defcants; *Quod tegitur, non videtur; quod non videtur, non imputatur; quod non imputatur, non punietur.* That which is covered, is not feen; that which is not feen, is not imputed; that which is not imputed, fhall not be punifhed.

"did require, I do require, and ever shall require, perfect love to GOD; perfect charity to your neighbour; and perfect holiness, both in heart and life. Never abating one tittle of these my requirements, I shall denounce the curse upon every disobedience; upon the least departure from absolute perfection. —But this is your comfort, believers, that the curse is executed upon your most holy SURETY. This is your comfort, believers, that my precepts have been fully obeyed by JESUS your SAVIOUR. As this was done, in your nature, and in your stead, I am satisfied, and you are justified. Now, though I can never dispense with any fault, nor connive at any infirmity; yet I behold all your faults laid upon IMMANUEL: I behold all his righteousness put upon you; and on *his* account I acquit you, I accept you, and pronounce you righteous *."

This is the language of the law to the faithful, as they are in *CHRIST JESUS*. This is the spirit of *Aspasio*'s conversation with his friend *Theron*. The native tendency of this doctrine, and its powerful agency in producing true holiness, are professedly displayed in the tenth letter; and not obscurely hinted in various other places. If you can prove, that it has a contrary tendency, you will prove, that *the grace of GOD does no longer teach us to deny*, but prompt us to

---

* I think, it is no misrepresentation, to suppose the law speaking, in this manner, to the believers.—Because to them *all things* are *become new*. Consequently, the voice of the law is new.—Because *all things are theirs*. If so, the sentence of the law is theirs. Not to overwhelm them with confusion, but to make them joyful through hope.—Because this is the language of the almighty LAWGIVER, to the redeemed of the *LORD JESUS;* and surely the law will not jar, but harmonize with its author, saying, *How shall I curse whom GOD hath not cursed?* or *how shall I defy, whom the LORD hath not defied?*

to commit *ungodliness*. An attempt, in which, with all my efteem for your perfon, and deference to your abilities, I cannot wifh you *GOD fpeed*.

"Does the righteoufnefs of GOD ever mean (as "you affirm) the merits of *CHRIST?*"—Where do I affirm this, Sir? Be pleafed to produce the paffage. At leaft refer us to the page.—*Afpafio*, in the place which offends you, fpeaks of what *CHRIST* has done and fuffered; of his active and paffive obedience. Thefe expreffions you change into "the merits of "*CHRIST;*" which being an ambiguous phrafe, may ferve to perplex the caufe, rather than clear up the difficulty. Give me leave, therefore, to reftore *Afpafio's* words, and to ftate the queftion fairly.

"Does the righteoufnefs of GOD ever fignify the "active and paffive obedience of *CHRIST?*" To this Mr *Wefley* replies, "I believe not once in all the "fcripture."—Why then, Sir, do you not difprove what *Afpafio* has advanced in fupport of this interpretation? *You* believe one thing; *he* believes another. And there is this *little* difference in the ground you refpectively go upon. He appeals to argument and fcripture. You reft the whole matter upon this fingle bottom, "I believe fo."

You proceed—"It" (that is, the righteoufnefs of GOD) "often means, and particularly in the epiftle "to the *Romans*, GOD's method of juftifying finners." —Suppofe I fhould fay, in my turn, This phrafe never means, no, not in the epiftle to the *Romans*, GOD's method of juftifying finners; I fhould then argue in your own way; bring a fhield fuited to your fword; juft as good an argument to defend, as you have brought to deftroy my opinion. What would the judicious reader fay, on fuch an occafion? Would he not fmile, and cry, "A goodly pair of difputants "truly!"

But let me afk, Does the holinefs of GOD fignify his method of fanctifying finners? Does the wifdom of GOD signify his method of making sinners wise? This no mortal has suspected; this you yourself will hardly venture to assert. Why then should we take your word, when, without assigning the least reason, you dictate and declare, "The righteousness of GOD "means his method of justifying sinners?"—You must pardon us, Sir, if we prefer St *Peter*'s judgment; his judgment in that memorable passage, *Who have obtained like precious faith in the righteousness of our GOD, even of our SAVIOUR JESUS CHRIST.* This sentence is a key to all those texts in the New Testament, and many of those in the Old, which mention the righteousness of GOD. Here it necessarily signifies the righteousness of *CHRIST*; because none else is our GOD and SAVIOUR. Here it confessedly signifies the object of justifying faith. Which cannot be the essential righteousness of an absolute GOD, but must be the vicarious righteousness of an incarnate GOD. And why should you scruple to call the righteousness of *CHRIST*, the righteousness of GOD? since his blood is called the blood of GOD. His life, which he laid down for us, is called the life of GOD. And he himself, as the author of our salvation, is called *JEHOVAH* (or GOD self-existent and everlasting) *our righteousness.*

It is possible, you may produce some commentators of eminence, who co-incide or have led the way, in this your interpretation. But may we not ask them, as well as yourself, on what authority they proceed?—Is this the plain and natural signification of the words? No; but an apparent force upon their natural import.—Does this tend to fix and ascertain the sense of the passage? No; but it gives the passage such a rambling turn, as will accommodate itself to the sentiments of Arians or Socinians, Arminians or Papists.—Is this reconcileable with the tenor of scripture? *He hath made HIM to be sin for us, who knew no sin, that we might be made the righteousness of GOD*

in

in him. Make a trial of your interpretation upon this distinguished text; see how it will accord with common sense, or the analogy of faith. That we might be made the righteousness of GOD; that is, "that we might be made GOD's method of justifying sinners." Can you yourself, Sir, upon an impartial review, be pleased with *such* interpretations of sacred writ?

How much more noble, and how much more comfortable is the easy and obvious sense, which the words, in a most beautiful climax, afford! He made *CHRIST*, who was perfectly free from sin, both in heart and life; GOD made him to be sin, justly chargeable with it, and justly punishable for it. That we, who are full of sin, both original and actual, might be made *righteous*—and not barely righteous, but (which is a much stronger expression) *righteousness itself*; yea, that we might be made, what exceeds all parallel, and passes all understanding, *the righteousness of GOD* *; might have that very righteousness for our justification, which the GOD of all perfection, uniting himself to our nature, wrought, finished, and infinitely ennobled.

Mr *Samuel Clarke*, in his annotations on this verse, on

---

* St *Chrysostom* expounds the important passage, in much the same manner. His words are worthy, not only to be copied in a note, but to be written on our hearts. Ποιος ταυτα λογος, ποιος τουτα παραστησαι δυνησεται νυν; Τον γαρ δικαιον, φησιν, εποιησεν αμαρτωλον, ινα τους αμαρτωλους ποιηση δικαιους. Μαλλον δε ουδε ουτως ειπεν, αλλ' ο πολλῳ μειζον ην. Ου γαρ εξιν ιδεαιν. αλλ' αυτην την ποιοτητα. Ου γαρ ειπεν, εποιησεν αμαρτωλον, αλλ' αμαρτιαν. Ινα ημεις γενωμεθα, ουκ ειπε, δικαιοι, αλλα δικαιοσυνη, και Θεου δικαιοσυνη.

What words can express, or what thoughts can conceive, the greatness of these things? He made the RIGHTEOUS ONE a sinner, that he might make wretched sinners righteous. This, though marvellously great, is not all. The word is not in the concrete, but in the abstract. He made the JUST ONE, not a sinner, but sin; that we might be made, not righteous only, —but righteousness itself,—yea, the righteousness of GOD.

on *Rom.* i. 17. on *Rom* x. 3. writes in the same vague and unsatisfactory manner as yourself. I could mention another celebrated commentator, who leans to this timid and trimming scheme.—I speak thus freely, because I look upon the article of justification through the righteousness of our GOD and SAVIOUR, to be the supreme distinguishing glory of Christianity. Because I consider it as the richest, incomparably the richest privilege of the Christian. To have a righteousness,—a consummate righteousness,—the very righteousness of the incarnate GOD,—dignified with all the perfections of the divine nature,—to have this righteousness imputed for our justification! matchless inconceivable blessing! This fills the believer's heart with inexpressible comfort and joy. This displays the grace of GOD, in the most charming and transporting light. This constitutes the most engaging motive to love, to holiness, and to all willing obedience.

Let us not then treat of it, in such *diluting* terms, or in such a *compromising* strain, as shall defeat the efficacy of the heavenly *cordial*, or deliver up the precious *depositum* to the enemies of the gospel. Let us rather, by a clear and full *manifestation of the truth*, of this capital and leading truth especially, *commend ourselves to every man's conscience*. Their humour may dislike it, their prejudice may reject it; but their conscience, whenever it awakes, and gains the ascendant, will embrace it; will cleave to it; and rejoice in it.

But stay. Let me proceed cautiously; not triumph immaturely. You rally your forces, and prepare for a *fresh* attack. *Aspasio* tells his friend, that the righteousness of GOD, signifies a righteousness of the most supereminent dignity; such as is worthy to be called by his name, and may justly challenge his acceptance. To this you reply, " I cannot allow it " at all."—*Aspasio* supports his opinion by scripture, by reason, and by a very respectable authority. All which

which Mr *Wesley* would confront and overthrow, by that one irrefragable proof, " I cannot allow it at all."—Surely, said I, upon reading such controversial triflings, delivered with the air of oracular responses; surely this letter must have stoln its way into the world. It was designed as a preservative for Mr. *Wesley's* private societies only. It could never be intended for public view, and general examination. Since every reader is treated, not as his judge, no, nor as his equal, but as his pupil; not as one, that is to be addressed with argument, and convinced by reasoning, but as a tame disciple, that is to acquiesce in the great preceptor's solemn " SAY SO."

To your next paragraph I have no material objection. I might indeed complain of an unfair quotation; but I shall only observe, that you would discard the expression, *imputation of righteousness*, and insert in its stead, *interest in CHRIST*. You had not always, Sir, such an aversion to the phrase imputed: witness that stanza in one of your hymns;

> Let faith and love combine
> To guard your valiant breast;
> The plate be righteousness divine,
> Imputed and imprest.

However, in this place I am willing to gratify you: because it will be difficult to show, how a sinner can have a real interest in *CHRIST*, in what he has done and what he has suffered, any other way than by imputation. I am willing to gratify you, provided you do not entertain that strange conceit, of an *incomplete* interest, or an interest in half the REDEEMER; but look upon the holiness of his nature, the obedience of his life, and the atonement of his death, as the one undivided ineffable treasure, in which every believing sinner is interested; as that which is the all-sufficient cause of his justification; rendering acceptable, first his person, then his performances;

ances; and, at the last, introducing him, with dignity and triumph, into everlasting habitations.

Here I lay down my pen; unless you will permit me to relate a little piece of history, not foreign to your last sentiment.—A certain general happened to observe a common soldier distinguishing himself, on the day of battle, with uncommon activity and courage; determined to reward merit where-ever it was found, he advanced the brave plebeian to a captain's post; who had not long enjoyed the honour, before he came to his benefactor, and, with a dejected countenance, begged leave to resign his commission. The general, surprised at such an unexpected request, asked him the reason. Your officers, said the petitioner, being gentlemen of family and education, think it beneath them to associate or converse with a rustic. So that, now, I am abandoned on every side; and am less happy, since my preferment, than I was before this instance of your Highness's favour.—Is this the cause of your uneasiness? replied the general; then it shall be redressed, and very speedily: to-morrow I review the army, and to-morrow your business shall be done.—Accordingly, when the troops were drawn up, and expected every moment to begin their exercise; the general calls the young hero from the ranks; leans his hand upon his shoulder; and, in this familiar endearing posture, walks with him through all the lines.—The stratagem had its desired effect. After such a signal and public token of his prince's regard, the officers were desirous of his acquaintance; and courted, rather than shunned, his company.

And will not the favour of the blessed *JESUS*, give us as great a distinction, and as high a recommendation, in the heavenly world? Will not the angelic hosts respect and honour those persons, who appear washed in his blood; clothed with his righteousness; and wearing the most illustrious tokens of his love, that he himself could possibly give?—In these tokens of his love may we and our readers be found! Then shall we meet one another with courage and comfort, at the great tribunal; with honour and joy, amidst the angels of light; with everlasting exultation and rapture, around the throne of the LAMB.

Under such pleasing hopes I take my leave at present, and remain your, &c.

LETTER VIII.

Rev. Sir,

YOU introduce the paragraph that comes next under our consideration, by a very just distinction. *Aspasio* had observed, that a rebel may be forgiven, without being restored to the dignity of a son. To which you reply; " A rebel against an earthly king " may; but not a rebel against GOD: in the very " same moment that GOD forgives, we are the sons " of GOD."—This is perfectly right. But hence to infer, that the conversation of our two friends is no better than " an idle dispute," is not very polite, and not at all conclusive. Because remission of the offence, and restoration to favour, may come in the same moment, and yet be different blessings. That afflicted patient, mentioned in the gospel, had at the same instant his ears opened, and the string of his tongue loosed. Were these effects, therefore, one and the same kind of healing?—Besides, why are forgiveness and sonship united in the divine donation? Because the sufferings of a sinner, and the obedience of a son, were united in the divine REDEEMER. So that we must still have our eye, our believing and adoring eye, upon the meritorious righteousness of our LORD.

" Pardon and acceptance, though," &c. Here I see nothing but the *crambe repetita*.—The words of " *Job*,"

"*Job*," &c. Here I see nothing but the usual argument, our master's *ipse dixit*. Therefore we will pass on to the next period.

Two texts of scripture are produced. You set aside *Aspasio*'s interpretation, to make way for one of your own. Which might have passed without suspicion, if it had appeared in your sermons, or been delivered from your pulpit; where a person may be content with the general sense, without entering upon a critical nicety. But, by rejecting *Aspasio*'s exposition, you seem to intend a peculiar degree of accuracy. Let us then examine the passages with such a view.—*Grace reigneth thro' righteousness unto eternal life;* " that " is, the free love of GOD brings us, thro' justifi- " cation and sanctification, to glory."

In this, I question, Sir, whether you are exactly orthodox. You lead the reader to suppose, that sanctification is as much the cause of glory as justification; that *CHRIST*'s work, and our graces, have just the same weight; act in the very same capacity; have, at least, a joint influence, in procuring eternal life.— You should rather have expressed yourself in some such manner; " The free grace of GOD brings us, " through the joyful privilege of justification, first to " sanctification, or the love of his blessed self; then to " glory, or the enjoyment of his blessed self."

Besides, you neglect the significancy of that beautiful and emphatical word, *reigneth*. On this much stress ought to be laid in reading the sentence; therefore it ought not to be totally overlooked in explaining the sentence. Grace is *discovered* in other instances; grace is *exercised* in other blessings: but by giving us eternal life; by giving it freely, even when we are undeserving guilty creatures; this ever-amiable attribute *reigneth*. It is manifested with every grand and charming recommendation. It appears, like the illustrious *Solomon*, when seated on his inimitably-splendid throne of ivory and gold; or like the magnificent

magnificent *Ahasuerus*, when he *shewed the riches of his glorious kingdom, and the honour of his excellent majesty*.

Another particular I cannot persuade myself to admire. You change the word *righteousness* into *justification;* instead of saying, " Brings us through righ-" teousness ;" you say, " Brings us through justifica-" tion." By this language, you scarce distinguish yourself from any heretic. You may rank with the Arian, or with the Sectarist of any denomination. They will, every one, allow the necessity of justification, in order to final felicity ; but not the necessity of a righteousness adequate to the demands of the law, as a foundation for this blessed hope.—You do just the same injury to *CHRIST* and his righteousness, which obtain this inconceivable recompense of reward; as you would receive from a messenger, who carries a rich present to your friend, but will not acknowledge from whom it comes. It comes, he confesses, from some man ; but obstinately refuses to say from Mr *John Wesley*. Whereas, *Aspasio* scruples not to own, nay, rejoices to declare, from whence the invaluable benefit of justification proceeds : Not from works of the law ; no, nor from works of the SPIRIT ; from nothing done by us, from nothing wrought in us ; but wholly from the blood and obedience of *JESUS CHRIST*.

The next passage, on which you descant, is, *That they may receive forgiveness, and a lot among the sanctified.* Thus you translate the original. *Aspasio*, not affecting needless novelty, is content with the common version. *That they may receive forgiveness of sins, and inheritance among all them that are sanctified, by faith that is in ME.*—Why do you omit the word *sins ?* Forgiveness, I own, implies it. But the apostle chuses to express it. By which means, the sentence becomes more full and emphatical. Grace is more highly honoured, and man more deeply abased.—I wonder also, why you should prefer *lot* to inheritance, which is
the

the usual translation. The latter word conveys a much more noble and pleasing idea to the *English* reader, than the former.—*Receive forgiveness of sins;* not earn it (let us mark this) by performing conditions, but receive it, as an absolute gift. Just as *Joseph*'s brethren received the portions sent them from the viceroy of *Egypt*'s table.—*Receive an inheritance;* consisting of all spiritual blessings here, and a title to everlasting blessedness hereafter. All which are bestowed as freely, as the several portions of land in *Canaan* were, by *Moses* and *Joshua*, consigned over to the tribes of *Israel* for a possession.—*Among those that are sanctified.* If you should inquire, how sinners are sanctified? The answer is added; *by faith which is in ME.* Not *for* faith, as your conditional scheme supposes; but *by* faith: by accepting the blessings mentioned; by looking upon them as our own; through the divine gift; and by living in the delightful enjoyment of them. Thus our hearts are won to GOD, and filled with his love. Thus they are weaned from vanity, and renewed in true holiness.

Is the satisfaction made by *CHRIST*'s death, sufficient to obtain both our full pardon, and our final happiness? *Aspasio* has answered this question in the negative. He has confirmed his opinion, by the authority of scripture, and the testimony of reason. Mr *Wesley* thinks it enough to reply; " Unquestionably it " is sufficient, and neither of the texts you cite prove " the contrary."—How easy, by this way of arguing, to overthrow any system, and silence demonstration itself!—But pray, Sir, be pleased to recollect yourself. Did you not, a little while ago, extol *Aspasio* as " un- " questionably right," because he made the *universal* obedience of *CHRIST*, from his birth to his death, the one foundation of his hope? Yet here you condemn him, as " unquestionably wrong," because he does not attribute all to *CHRIST*'s death *exclusively*. Will Mr *Wesley* never have done with self-contradiction?

tion? why will he give me such repeated cause to complain,—*Quo teneam vultus, &c.*

If it was requisite for Christ to be baptized, argues *Aspasio*, much more to fulfil the moral law.—" I can" not prove," replies Mr *Wesley*, " that either the one " or the other was requisite, in order to his purcha" sing redemption for us." Why then do you admit his obedience to the moral law, as an essential part of the foundation of your hope? A tottering foundation methinks, which is laid in a doctrine you cannot prove.

But if you cannot prove it, may not others prove it for you? You are not called to prove this point, Sir, but only to disprove what *Aspasio* has advanced in confirmation of it.—That it was requisite for our LORD to be baptized, he himself acknowledges. Speaking of that sacred rite, he says, *Thus it becometh us to fulfil all righteousness*. It becometh; was it not requisite for *CHRIST*, always to act the becoming part? in every circumstance to demean himself, according to the utmost decorum and highest dignity of character?—" This was not requisite to purchase re" demption for us." For what then was it requisite? Not to wash away any stain from the holy JESUS. Not to obtain any blessedness for the SON of the HIGHEST. Since, as the SON of the eternal GOD, he had an undoubted right to all the blessings of heaven and earth, of time and eternity.

" But it was not requisite, that he should fulfil the " moral law."—No! Do *you* then establish the law? Are not you the *Antinomian*, who would have sinful men saved, yet the divine law not fulfilled, either by them or their SURETY? This is a strange way of magnifying the great standard of all righteousness. Rather, it is the sure way of dishonouring and debasing it.—What says our LORD? *I came, not to destroy the law, but to fulfil* *. Did this signify, as some expository

* *Matth.* v. 17. Some expositors would persuade us that

expository refiners suggest, only to vindicate and illustrate the law; to explain its highest meaning, and rescue it from the false glosses of the scribes; the business might have been done by the prophets and apostles. No occasion for the KING of heaven to appear in person. His ambassadors might have transacted the whole affair of vindication and explanation. But to fulfil every jot and tittle prescribed in its commands; to suffer all the vengeance and the whole curse denounced in its penalty; this was a work worthy of the SON of GOD,—practicable by none, but the SON of GOD;—and, being executed by HIM, is truly meritorious of pardon and life for poor sinners; of the restoration to the divine favour, and of their admission into the heavenly kingdom.

The moral law is inviolable in its nature, and of eternal obligation. This is a truth of great importance: with this is connected, and on this depends, the absolute necessity of vicarious righteousness. I am no longer surprised, that you dispute against the latter, since you question or deny the former.—But consider, what our LORD says farther upon this subject, in the fifth of St *Matthew*, and the eighteenth verse. Perhaps, you will reply, "I have
"both

---

the word πληρῶσαι signifies *fully to explain*. This sense I am far from discarding; but in this sense I can by no means acquiesce. It neither gives us the whole, nor the principal part of our LORD's meaning. Let us place the matter in a different light; then I believe the scantiness of the interpretation, and the impropriety of the notion, will appear unto all men.—We will suppose an ungodly person who has learned from books, the spiritual and extensive import of the divine law. Having a ready utterance, he explains it clearly, properly, fully. Does any mortal say of this lip-practitioner, that he *fulfils the law?* No such thing. A system of precepts can never be fulfilled, without a due and punctual obedience. To open, to adjust, to enforce a set of injunctions, is as far from fulfilling them; as to give a description of a battle and a conquest, are different from fighting the enemy, and gaining the victory.

Let 8. ASPASIO VINDICATED.

" both confidered it, and expounded it, in my fer-
" mons." You have; but in fuch a manner, as, I
hope, you will live to retract. Thus you expound
the awful text, and turn it into a piece of unmeaning
tautology. " *One jot or one tittle fhall in no wife pafs,*
" *till heaven and earth pafs;* or, as it is expreffed im-
" mediately after, *till all* (or rather *all things*) *be ful-*
" *filled,* till the confummation of all things *." You
would make ἕως ἂν παρέλθῃ ὁ οὐρανὸς ὃ ἡ γῆ, and ἕως ἂν τᾶυτα γένηται, fy-
nonymous phrafes, expreffive of the fame thing.
Thus ftands the paffage, interpreted according to your
criticifm. " Till the confummation of all things, one
" jot or one tittle fhall in no wife pafs from the law,
" till the confummation of all things." See! to what
miferable fubterfuges a man of learning is driven, in
order to evade the force of a text, which militates
ftrongly for the meritorious obedience of *CHRIST.*

How much more juft, more noble, more ufeful, is
the common expofition, and the obvious meaning?
Which we may thus introduce—Thefe are the terms
of life and happinefs to man.—Whofoever falls fhort,
GOD himfelf pronounces accurfed. And will the
UNCHANGEABLE go back from his purpofe;
make abatement in his demands; or come to a com-
pofition with his creatures? No verily. *He is of one
mind, and who can turn him* †? *It were eafier for hea-
ven and earth to pafs* ‡, for all nature to be unhinged,
and the univerfe to drop into diffolution, *than for one
jot*

---

* Sermons by JOHN WESLEY, vol. II. p. 173.
† Job xxiii. 13.
‡ Ἕως ἂν παρέλθῃ ὁ οὐρανὸς ὃ ἡ γῆ, a proverbial expreffion, to denote
the utmoft impoffibility. See it explained *Luke* xvi. 17. In
this connection, it fignifies the abfolute certainty of our
LORD's declaration, both as to its truth and as to its accom-
plifhment.—If I may borrow the language and the imagery of
Horace, they will not unfitly exprefs, what is affirmed con-
cerning the law.
  Si fractus illabatur orbis,
  Immobilem ferient ruinæ.

jot or tittle of this unalterable law to pass without a perfect accomplishment * in every the minutest instance. By CHRIST's sufferings alone the law was not satisfied, says *Aspasio*. "Yes, it was," replies Mr *Wesley*.—Then all the indefatigable and important labours of his life, all his exemplary and shining graces, must be mere superfluities. At least, they could have no merit, but were necessary only by way of setting an example.

The prophet was of another mind; *The LORD is well pleased for his righteousness sake.* By this righteousness, not barely by his sufferings, *he will magnify the law and make it honourable.*†—The apostle was of another mind. *GOD sent forth his SON, made of a woman, made under the law.* What? only to bear its curse? only to undergo its penalty? not to fulfil its preceptive part? which is confessedly the principal part in every law; and to enforce which, all penalties are added.—You yourself *ought* to be of another mind. For you have already and truly observed, that pardon and

* Εως αν παντα γενηται "The word *all*," says Mr *Wesley*, "does "not mean all the law, but all things in the universe." How forced a construction! How contrary to grammar? Since the law, and the things which it comprehends, are the immediate antecedent.—How much more properly and consistently has Dr *Doddridge* explained the passage! "*Till all things,* which "the law requires, or foretells shall be *effected*. The trans- "lation here given, is most literal, and most comprehensive, "The law *has its effect*, when its sanctions are executed, as "well as when its precepts are obeyed."—Let me add; in case of a violated law, *then only* it is fulfilled, or has its effect, when both the former and the latter respectively obtain their end.

† *If* xlii. 21. I am sensible, there are expositors, who give a different turn to these noble words. But I had rather take the voice from heaven for my guide, than all the expositors in the world; even that voice, which declared concerning *CHRIST*, and his work, *CHRIST* and his righteousness, In these *I am well pleased*. Which is one of the most capital sayings in the Bible, and a clue to lead us into its whole meaning.

and acceptance always go together. "In the same moment that GOD forgives, we are the sons of GOD." And wherefore? The reason is, because the sufferings of a sinner, and the obedience of a Son, went together in the REDEEMER. And without this union, the redemption of man had not been complete.

"The law required only the alternative, Obey or die."—Some of your errors are less considerable; this I take to be a first-rate mistake. According to this supposition, *Cain* and *Judas*, and all the damned, are righteous. Because they *die;* they bear the curse; they suffer everlastingly; and thereby conform to one of the law's alternatives.—One of the *law's* alternatives? No, here I am wrong. It is one of *your* alternatives. The divine law knows no such thing: no law on earth knows any such thing. Sanctions and penalties annexed to a law, are never looked upon as equivalent to obedience, but only as preservatives from disobedience.—In all the compass of your reading, have you ever met with a law, that makes such proposals to its subjects? "Conform to the regulations established, and "you shall enjoy my privileges, you shall share my "honours. Or, if you chuse to violate all my whole- "some institutions, only submit to the penalty, and "you shall have an equal right to the immunities and "preferments."

"The law required no man to obey and die too." —But did it not require a transgressor to obey and die? If not, then transgression robs the law of its right, and vacates all obligation to obedience.—Did it not require the SURETY for sinful man, to obey and die? If the SURETY dies only, he only delivers from punishment; but this affords no claim to life, no title to a reward, unless you can produce some such edict from the court of heaven, Suffer this, and thou shalt live. I find it written, *In keeping thy commandment there is great reward.* No where do I read,

In undergoing thy curfe, there is the fame reward.—Whereas, when we join the active and paffive obedience of our LORD, the peace-fpeaking blood, with the life-giving righteoufnefs, both made infinitely meritorious, and infinitely efficacious, by the divine glory of his perfon; how full does our juftification appear! How firm does it ftand! It has all that the law can demand, both for our exemption from the curfe, and for our title to blifs.

Before I take my leave of this topic, let me make one fuppofition, for which your way of thinking affords the jufter ground. Suppofe our *LORD JESUS CHRIST* had yielded a perfect conformity to the precept, without ever fubmitting to the penalty; would this have been fufficient for the juftification of a finner? Here is one of your alternatives performed. Upon the foot of your principles, therefore it would, it muft have been fufficient.—But this is fo wild an opinion, fo contrary to the whole current of fcripture, that to produce it, is to refute it.

Where fcripture afcribes the whole of our falvation to the death of *CHRIST*, a part of his humiliation is put for the whole. To this Mr *Wefley* objects; "I cannot allow it without proof."—I wifh you would remember the golden rule, (of doing as you would be done by,) and, fince you infift upon proof from others, not be fo fparing of it in your own caufe: I wifh likewife you would impartially confider what *Afpafio* has advanced, upon the fubject.—Has he not given you the proof you demand?—" No; he was obe-
" dient unto death, is no proof at all."—But is that the only thing urged? If one argument is inadequate, muft all be inconclufive? Becaufe you have routed one detachment, have you therefore conquered the whole army? However let us fee, whether this detachment, weak as you fuppofe it, may not be able to fuftain your attack.

Does not the fcripture afcribe the whole of your falvation to the death of *CHRIST?* To this queftion
Afpafio

Aspasio replies, This part of our LORD's meritorious humiliation is by a very usual figure put for the whole.—The death of *CHRIST* includes not only his sufferings, but his obedience.—The shedding of his blood was at once the grand instance of his sufferings, and the finishing act of his obedience; in this view it is considered, and thus it is represented by his own ambassador, who, speaking of his divine Master, says, " He was obedient unto death, even the death of the " cross."—" This," you reply, " is no proof at all, " as it does not necessarily imply any more, than that " he died in obedience to the FATHER."

How do some people love to cramp the enlarged, and debase the magnificent sense of scripture! Surely this text implies; and not implies only, but forcibly expresses both the active and passive obedience of *CHRIST*. It is not ἀπέθανε, *he died;* but γινομενος υπηκοος, *he became obedient.*—Can you see nothing of his active righteousness in these words? For my part, I can see very little besides.—This is what the following clause confirms—Let common sense be judge—Obedient, not barely *in* death, but *unto* death, like that expression of JEHOVAH, by the prophet, *Unto hoary hairs I will carry you.*—Does not this give us a retrospect view of youth and manhood, as well as lead our attention forward to old age? In like manner, *obedient unto death;* does not this refer us to all the previous duties and virtues of a righteous walk; while it leads us to the closing scene of all, a resigned exit? Does it not most naturally mean, obedient through the whole course of life, even to the last all-completing instance, a voluntary submission to death?—How easy and obvious is this interpretation! how grand and graceful is this meaning!

I can no more admire your taste (considered) as a critic, than I can admire your doctrine (considered) as a divine. Give me the expositions of scripture, which act, not like the nocturnal damp, but like the morn-
ing

ing fun; not fhrivelling and contracting, but opening and expanding thofe flowers of paradife, the truths of the gofpel, that they may difplay all their charming beauties, and breathe out all their reviving odours. I think, upon the whole, we have very fufficient cauſe to affert, and to abide by our affertion; that when the fcripture afcribes the whole of our falvation to the death of *C H R I S T*, a part of his humiliation is put for the whole; and in thus fpeaking, the HOLY SPIRIT copies after himſelf. For if the death inflicted on the firſt *Adam* included every evil confequent upon the fall; the depravity, as well as the miſery of the creature; it was meet that the death to which the fecond *Adam* fubmitted, ſhould include every good needful for our recovery; the obedience as well as the fufferings of the REDEEMER. It was meet that the price expreffed by the fame word, ſhould be as extenfive as the punifhment.

"But how does it appear that he undertook this "before the foundation of the world?" At what time does Mr *Wefley* fuppofe, that *CHRIST* undertook the work? Not till fin entered and man apoftatized? Was it then an incidental (upftart) expedient, fetched in to remedy fome unforefeen difafter? Was it a device, which owed its birth to fome unexpected contingency, occafioned by the perverfenefs of the creature? Far, far from it.—It was the grand, original, all-comprehending plan, the way in which GOD, long before time commenced, decreed to manifeft the glory of his grace, and the luftre of all his perfections. The world was made as a proper theatre, on which to difplay and execute this moſt magnificent ſcheme; and all the revolutions of human affairs, like ſo many under plots in the drama, are fubfervient to the accomplifhment of this capital defign.—" Known unto " GOD are all his works," determined by GOD are all his counfels, from the beginning of the world, more efpecially this grandeſt of all the divine difpenfations;

fations ; this mafter-piece of his unfearchable wifdom.

"But was this by a pofitive covenant between "CHRIST and the FATHER?" *Afpafio* proceeds to illuftrate and confirm the doctrine of an everlafting covenant between the almighty FATHER and his co-equal SON. He produces feveral texts of fcripture, to each of which you object as infufficient for his purpofe: each of your objections I fhall anfwer, only by adding a fhort comment, explanatory of their fpirit and force—" This proves no previous contract;" that is, I deny it, and therefore it cannot prove your point. " Neither does this prove any fuch thing." That is, I cannot or will not fee the proof. And therefore there is none.—" That expreffion does not necef- "farily imply any more" than I pleafe to allow.—" In " the way or method he had chofen;" of which I am the fole complete judge, and my judgment ought to be decifive in the cafe.—Thus would Mr *Wefley* have, not *Afpafio* only, but the public alfo, receive his dictates (*tanquam a tripode*) as abfolute oracles.—For here is only bare affertion, or bare denial, without any vouchers, but his own word; without any authority, but his own declaration.

In *pfalm* the xlth, the conditions of the covenant are circumftantially recorded, which were the incarnation and obedience of the eternal SON. " A body " haft thou prepared me—lo! I come to do thy will." " Nay, here is no mention of any covenant, nor any " thing from which it can be inferred." *How many times fhall I adjure thee*, faid *Ahab* to *Micaiah, that thou tell me nothing but that which is true?* And how many times fhall I intreat Mr *Wefley* to object nothing, without affigning fome reafon for his objection? at leaft not to think of convincing my judgment, and converting me to his opinion by a bare *fay fo*.—But I have done—Perhaps I have trefpaffed upon the patience of the reader, in expreffing my difappointment fo frequently; perhaps I may alfo bear too hard upon Mr *Wefley*,

Wesley in asking for proofs, when it may be no small difficulty to produce them. To return—" Nay here " is no mention of any covenant, nor any thing from " which it can be inferred."—That the word *covenant* is not mentioned, is very true ; that there is no reference to any such thing, is not so certain : let us consider the whole passage.—" Sacrifice and burnt-of-" fering thou didst not require." If sacrifice and slain beasts are not the object of the divine complacency, in what will the LORD delight ? The next words declare, " A body hast thou prepared me :" Since the law cannot be fulfilled without *doing*, nor justice satisfied without *dying*, " lo ! I come," says the second person in the TRINITY, " to undertake both : since " this undertaking must be accomplished by ONE " who is finite, that he may die ; and infinite, that " he may conquer death ; I will accomplish it in the " divine and human nature. For this purpose a body " hast thou prepared me ; in this body lo ! I come, " willingly and chearfully I come, to perform, to su-" stain, to fulfil all ; and so to do thy great, thy gra-" cious will."—May we not rationally suppose this spoken by way of (restipulation, or) compliance with the FATHER's demands ? that the matter is thereby brought to a solemn contract ?

Dr *Hammond* thought this no irrational supposition; therefore gives us, upon the following words, a perfectly-corresponding comment. In the volume of the book it is written of me. " Which is no other than " a bill, or roll of contract between the FATHER " and *CHRIST;* wherein is supposed to be written " the agreement, preparatory to that great work of " *CHRIST*'s incarnation, wherein he, undertaking " to fulfil the will of GOD, to perform all active, " and also all passive obedience, even unto death, had " the promise from GOD, that he should become the " author of eternal salvation to all that obey him."

Thus says our learned countryman. And what says the

the blessed apostle? whose exposition and application of the passage you seem to have forgotten, at least, not to have thoroughly weighed. Having quoted the passage, argued from it, and displayed the benefits obtained by this all-sufficient propitiation, he adduces a text from *Jeremiah* relating to this very subject, and explaining its nature: whereof the HOLY GHOST also is a witness; of what? of the justification and sanctification of sinners, both founded on, both effected by, the sacrifice of the dying *JESUS*. Transactions, which both the prophet and the apostle consider under the notion of a covenant, as is plain from the following quotation: " For after that he had said " before, This is the covenant which I will make " with them in those days." Hence it appears, that the author to the *Hebrews* saw something in the words of the Psalmist, from which the doctrine of a covenant might be inferred.

Another copy of this grand treaty is recorded, *If.* xlix. from the first to the sixth verse. " I have read " them, but cannot find a word about it in all those " verses; they contain neither more nor less than a " prediction of the salvation of the Gentiles." They contain a prediction, and somewhat more; they describe the way whereby this most desirable event shall be brought to pass. This the LORD himself declares shall be by way of covenant; " I will give thee for a " covenant to the people."—This verse we may look upon as a key to the preceding. It teaches us to consider them as descriptive of the august covenant; of its establishment, its parties, and its terms. Indeed the verses themselves lead us to the same view; for what is a covenant? A contract, wherein a condition is prescribed, a promise is made, and both are ratified by a mutual agreement.—The condition is prescribed in those words, *Thou art my servant, O Israel* *, in

whom

* *Israel* is the name of the church, often given to her in

X 2   this

whom I will be glorified. The promise is made in those words, *Thou shalt raise up the tribes of Jacob, restore the preserved of Israel, and be my salvation unto the ends of the earth.* The agreement is specified or implied in those words: (*I have spent my strength for nought, yet) surely my judgment is with the LORD, and my work with my GOD.*

The great *Vitringa*, after having expounded the whole clause, concludes in this manner: " Antequam
" ab his verbis, sensu fœcundissimus, summam do-
" ctrinæ evangelicæ complexis, discedam, monere ve-
" lim, eadem clarissime deformare totum mysterium
" conventionis pacis, inter Deum patrem et Messiam
" filium ejus, in humana carne appariturum, initæ,
" perinde ac in locis quæ ex aliis excerpo, *Psal.* xl. 7.
" *Zech.* vi. 13. Pater ut Dominus, filio ut Messiæ,
" offert gloriam longe amplissimam, mediationis et
" salvationis Judæorum et Gentium, quæ gloria, om-
" nium quæ mente concipi possunt, est maxima, sub
" lege sive sub conditione profundissimi obsequii ser-
" vilis ; eaque stipulatio utrinque ratihabetur *."

If, upon a stricter review, this prophecy be found to express no such thing as a covenant, I am very willing

this prophecy. *CHRIST* and his church, by virtue of the union between them, have the same names. As she is sometimes called by his name, " The LORD our righteousness;" —so he is here called by her name *Israel.* See *Jer.* xxxiii. 16.

" * Vitring in loc. Before I leave this paragraph, which is
" so rich in sense, and contains the very substance of evangeli-
" cal doctrine, I would observe, that it most clearly and ex-
" actly delineates the mysterious council of peace, planned be-
" tween GOD the FATHER, and his divine SON. The FA-
" THER as supreme LORD, offers to his SON the MES-
" SIAH the highest glory, that which shall result from justify-
" ing, sanctifying, and saving, with an everlasting salvation,
" both Jews and Gentiles. This glory, the greatest which
" thought can conceive, is proposed on the terms, or under
" the condition of his deep humiliation, even to the state and
" obedience of a servant. The whole passes into a solemn
" contract, and is ratified on either side."

Here

willing to give up the proof; so much the rather as it makes no part of *Aspasio*'s discourse, is only just mentioned in a note, and stands not in the main body, but only as a corps de reserve.

By the covenant of works, man was bound to obey in his own person.—Here you take *Aspasio* up very short, and reply, " So he is under the covenant of " grace, tho' not in order to justification." This is the very thing he means. Nor could you easily have mistaken his meaning, if you had only done him so small a piece of justice as to read the whole paragraph; of which, since you seem either willingly, or through inadvertence, to be ignorant, I will beg leave to transcribe it :—" Between the covenant of works, and " the covenant of grace, this I apprehend is the diffe- " rence. By the former man was indispensably bound " to obey in his own person ; by the latter, the obe-
" dience

Here our author subjoins an extract from כרשית רבה a rabbinical treatise. Which is very remarkable; for such a writer, singularly just; one of the most curious, as well as valuable pieces of *Jewish* antiquities that ever fell in my way. I believe it will afford no unpleasing entertainment, perhaps some spiritual benefit to the reader. For which cause I take leave to transcribe it.—" GOD began to enter into a covenant with the " MESSIAH, and said, MESSIAH, my righteous one, the " sins of thy chosen people are likely to bring thee into a state " of great toil and extreme affliction ; thy lips shall taste gall, " thy tongue shall cleave to the roof of thy mouth, thy body " shall be wasted with sorrow and sighing. Is thy love to thy " people inviolable? Art thou willing to rescue them on these " conditions? If thou undertakest their recovery, well; if " not, they are rejected from this moment, and perish for e- " ver.—To this MESSIAH replied, LORD of eternity, I am " pleased with the office, I accept these conditions ; and am " willing to undergo all tribulation, that my people may en- " joy a resurrection (to the life of grace and the life of glo- " ry.)—Then said the holy, blessed GOD, Be it so. Imme- " diately the MESSIAH took upon him our miseries, as it is " written in the book of the prophet *Isaiah*, He was op- " pressed and he was afflicted."

"dience of his SURETY is accepted, instead of
"his own.—The righteousness required by both, is
"not sincere, but complete; not proportioned to the
"abilities of fallen man, but to the purity of the law,
"and the majesty of the LAWGIVER." You see
the whole argument turns upon a *complete* righteousness, such as satisfies the law, and is an adequate ground for justification. This, I imagine, fallen man is not obliged, by the covenant of grace, to perform; if so, we shall be at a loss to find any such thing as grace; if so, we can have no hope of obtaining salvation with eternal glory. There will be too much reason for applying, to all mankind, those awful words of the prophet; *In the day thou mayst make thy plant to grow, and in the morning thou mayst make thy seed to flourish; but the harvest shall be a heap, in the day of grief and desperate sorrow.*

Blessed be GOD the melancholy strain is superseded.—Though the terms in the first covenant were a perfect obedience; though the terms once fixed continue unalterable; yet, in the new covenant, there is a change and substitution as to the performer, without any relaxation as to the performance. Instead of personal obedience, we are justified through the obedience of our MEDIATOR, *We are made the righteousness of GOD in him.* That is, we are furnished with a plea, as prevalent for our justification and admission into the divine favour, as if we had retained our innocence untainted; and, in every respect, conformed ourselves to the righteousness which the law of GOD requires*.—Thus the salvation of sinners

neither

---

* 2 Cor. v. 21. This is Dr *Doddridge*'s interpretation of the passage; and it speaks a noble, a joyful truth, only it does not express the whole truth. The righteousness of GOD is more than equivalent to untainted innocency; is more than tantamount to the most perfect human obedience. It is a righteousness of infinite worth, far surpassing the integrity of *Adam* in paradise, or the sanctity of angels in heaven. It is a gift, incomparably, yea, incomprehensibly great, efficacious, glorious.

neither clashes with the truth, nor interferes with the justice of the supreme LEGISLATOR —On the contrary, it becomes a *faithful* and *just* procedure of the most high GOD, to justify *him that believeth on JESUS*.

"The obedience of our Surety is accepted instead of our own." "This is neither a safe, nor a scriptural way" "of speaking."—That the obedience of CHRIST is accepted for our justification, is a doctrine warranted by scripture; it may therefore very justly be reckoned a scriptural way of speaking. And if *his* obedience is accepted for this purpose, *our own*, was it ever so considerable, could come in for no share of the work. Our own, though ever so gorgeously arrayed, must stand aside, or be cast into shades, just as the stars hide their diminished, or rather extinguished heads, when the sun appears in his meridian splendour, because the obedience of CHRIST is of infinite dignity and value. And infinite value is such, as not only transcends all other services, but renders them mere nothings in the comparison. For this reason, the apostle counted all endowments, but *loss* for CHRIST, and the prophet represents all nations as nothing before GOD.

"I would simply say, We are accepted through the Beloved."—If you rightly understood what is meant, when the apostle speaks of being accepted in the BELOVED, you would have no fault to find with *Aspasio*'s comment. St *Paul* means we are accepted, not by any obedience performed in our own persons, but solely by the obedience of that infinitely excellent, and infinitely beloved ONE CHRIST JESUS, whose righteousness being imputed to us, and put upon us, causes us not only to be pardoned, but to be highly esteemed, dearly beloved, and blessed with all spiritual blessings.

Here I cannot but observe, that you have changed the

the apostle's expression. He says, "Accepted * *in* "the Beloved;" you say, "Accepted *through* the Be- "loved." I am willing to believe this was an oversight, you had no sinister design; but still I think you should take more heed to your pen, and not alter the inspired word, lest you blemish the language, or injure the sense. Perhaps you will ask, What difference is there between accepted *through,* and accepted *in,* the beloved? I will illustrate the difference by a similitude. A creditable housekeeper gives a good character to a servant that leaves him, by virtue of which he is accepted, and admitted to some other valuable employ. This character is his introduction, yet this makes no addition to his real value. Acceptance through the Beloved, may import no more, than such an admission through such a recommendation. Whereas, accepted *in* the Beloved, implies not only a recommendatory passport from *CHRIST*, but a real union with *CHRIST*, whereby we are incorporated into his sacred body, and partake as truly of his righteousness, as the members partake of the life which animates the head. By this our persons are really ennobled; this imparts the highest dignity to our nature. We are not only recommended to, but rendered meet for, the favour, the complacency, the beatific presence of GOD, being one with *JESUS*, and therefore loved even as *JESUS* himself is loved †.

The second covenant was not made with *Adam* or any of his posterity, but with *CHRIST* in those words. "For any authority you have from these "words, you might as well have said, it was made "with the HOLY GHOST."—No;" *CHRIST*, not the HOLY GHOST, was the seed of the woman.—This is an answer much in your own strain.— But let us consider farther.

You

---

* Εχαριτωσεν ημας εν τω Ηγαπημενω.

† *John* xvii. 23. They *in* me, says our LORD. Therefore, on this account, or viewed in this relation, *thou hast loved them, as thou hast loved me.*

You allow, I presume, that the first covenant was made with *Adam*, as our public fœderal head:—That all his posterity were included in it, being to stand or fall together with him: Herein, says the apostle, "*Adam* was a figure of him that was to come." If so, the second covenant must be made with CHRIST, as our public fœderal head. He and all his seed are included in it; and as it was impossible for him to miscarry, they must be joint partakers of the benefits. Accordingly, he is styled the MEDIATOR of the new covenant, by whose most acceptable and prevailing interposition, all its blessings are obtained: he is styled the Surety of the covenant, engaging to pay the whole debt for poor insolvent creatures; the debt of penal suffering, and the debt of perfect obedience.— The Testator of the covenant, whose are its riches, and whose are its privileges, who has also of his unbounded goodness bequeathed them as so many inestimable legacies to indigent men. Methinks those are such charming truths, such divinely-comfortable doctrines, that you should consider them thoroughly before you oppose them, least you do a greater act of unkindness to your readers, than that which is charged, though very injuriously, upon *Job*: *Thou has stripped the naked of their cloathing, and sent widows away empty.* And when you are disposed to consider these points thoroughly, ask yourself this question: Is it possible to conceive that CHRIST should be the MEDIATOR, the Surety, the Testator of the covenant, if it was not made with him, and the execution of it undertaken by him?—Or, is it possible to suppose, that the all-glorious SON of GOD should be the MEDIATOR, the Surety, the Testator of the covenant, yet leave others to perform the conditions; which are incomparably the most important, interesting, and difficult parts of the transaction?

"These words were not spoken to CHRIST, but
"of him." True, *of* him as given for a covenant of

the people. " There is not the least intimation of any " such covenant." You will not deny that CHRIST is signified by *the feed of the woman.*—It is said, *He shall;* a language expressing authority, and requiring conformity. As CHRIST is the supreme uncontrollable GOD, this could not be required; and would never have been said, without his actual consent: here then is implied his approbation of the office. It is farther said, The serpent shall bruise his heel.—He shall become incarnate, and after a life of much sorrow, and many tribulations, shall be put to a most tormenting death. Here is the condition of the covenant. It is added, He shall bruise the serpent's head; shall destroy the works of the devil, and repair the ruins of the fall; shall deliver from the wrath deserved, and recover the inheritance forfeited.—Here is the recompence or reward of the covenant.

Should you ask, Is it supposable that *Adam* understood the words in this compass of meaning? Perhaps not. But if we do not understand them in a more exalted and extensive sense than our first father, what advantage do we reap from the full revelation of the gospel?—The full revelation of the gospel pours as much light upon this, and other of the ancient oracles, as the experiments of our modern anatomists have poured upon the structure and œconomy of the human body.—This grand original text, read with the comment of the New Testament, speaks all that *Aspasio* has suggested; all that our fallen state could want, or our very hearts can wish.

You have mustered up several objections, yet there is room for more; I will therefore for once act as your auxiliary, and turn against *Aspasio*. " He supposes " the covenant to be made with CHRIST. Where- " as the scripture represents the covenant as made " with various men, particularly and personally, in " various ages."—True, it is recorded, that GOD made a covenant with *Abraham,* with *Isaac,* with *Jacob,*

cob, and with *David* the father of *Solomon:* but were they in a capacity to enter into covenant with their Maker; to stand for themselves, or be surety for others? I think not.—The passages mean no more, than the LORD's manifesting in an especial manner, the grand covenant to them; ratifying and confirming their personal interest in it; and farther assuring them, that *CHRIST*, the great covenant-head, should be of themselves, and spring from their seed.

This accounts for that remarkable and singular mode of expression, which often occurs in scripture; *I will make a covenant with them;* or, *This is my covenant with them.*—Yet there follows no mention of any conditions, only a promise of unconditional blessings; because the former have already been performed, and nothing remains but to confer the latter; so that the meaning of the divine Speaker is, I will admit them to an interest in this covenant, and make them partakers of its privileges.

I should now conclude, but Mr *Wesley* will not suffer me to quit the subject. He farther insists, " The " words manifestly contain, if not a covenant made " with, a promise made to *Adam* and all his posterity." —*If not*—He begins to hesitate in his assertion; to fluctuate in his opinion; and I could hope, to see his mistake.—" The words contain a promise."—And have you never read, that the covenant of GOD, or the various renewals and ratifications of the covenant of grace, are styled *covenants of promise?* which consist of pure promises, and dispense free gifts?

Observe the tenor of the new covenant, as it stands ingrossed by the pen of inspiration. *This is the covenant, which I will make with the house of Israel after those days, saith the LORD; I will put my laws into their mind, and on their hearts will I write them: and I will be to them a GOD, and they shall be to me a people. And they shall not teach every man his neighbour, and every man his brother, saying, Know the LORD:*

LORD :—for all shall know me, from the least of them, even unto the greatest of them.—For I will be merciful unto their unrighteousnesses, and their sins and their iniquities will I remember no more.—Where are your conditions in this draught? Where are any terms required of impotent man? Is it not all promise, from the beginning to the end? That repentance, and that faith, for whose conditionality you plead, are they not both comprehended in this heavenly deed; and comprehended under the form of blessings vouchsafed, not of tasks enjoined?—Does the contract run in this manner? I require and command; or in this strain? I grant and bestow. The LORD says, *I will put my laws; I will write them.*—The work shall not be laid on my creatures, but done by myself. *They shall be my people, and I will remember their sins no more.* What? provided they perform such and such duties. I read no such clause. I see no such proviso.—All is absolutely free; dependent on no performance of ours; but flowing from sovereign, supreme, self-influenced goodness.

Just such is that delightful declaration, *I will make an everlasting covenant with them, that I will not turn away from them to do them good; but I will put my fear in their heart, that they shall not depart from me.*—What you call conditions must be comprised in *my fear*. This is represented as a singular benefit, which GOD imparts; as a gracious temper, which GOD implants; and both as dependent, not on the fidelity of man, but on the power and veracity of GOD.—Another of your conditions, I presume, is perseverance unto the end.—This, in the covenant of grace, is not enjoined, but secured; secured, not by a strict prohibition of apostasy, but by the omnipotent interposition of JEHOVAH. *I will put my fear;* so put my fear into their hearts, *that they shall not depart from me;* shall never draw back unto perdition.—Thus the covenant becomes not transient, but everlasting. Thus the promise is not precarious, but sure to all the seed.

There

There seems to be as great a difference between this evangelical, and your legal method of stating the covenant; between suspending the benefits on human endeavours, and grounding them on divine agency, as between hanging the anchor on the top of the mast, and fixing it at the bottom of the sea.

Let me add one more text, which now occurs to my thoughts, *Ye are the children of the prophets, and of the covenant which GOD made with our fathers, saying unto Abraham, And in thy seed shall all the kindreds of the earth be blessed* *. Here the covenant is first mentioned in general; then particularly specified.—*In thy seed shall all the kindreds of the earth*— be laid under conditions? be obliged to execute terms? No; but *shall be blessed;* blessed with all blessings, temporal, spiritual, eternal.—*In thy seed;*— that is, in *CHRIST*,—without any regard to qualifications or deeds of their own; entirely by virtue of an interest in his consummately-excellent actions, and consummately-precious sufferings.—Then the apostle singles out one special and distinguished blessing of the covenant; a conversion from *darkness to light, and from the power of Satan to the service of GOD;* or, as it is expressed In the following verse, *a turning from all iniquity.*—This is still exhibited to our contemplation, as the fruit of the covenant of grace; as the thing for which it makes provision, not introductory to, but consequent upon, our participation of it.

If therefore, in speaking of holiness and obedience, we represent them as the promises, rather than the demands of the covenant, we evidently follow the apostle's example. Were we to take the contrary course, we should act as prudently as the sportsman, who, entering his horse for a plate, chuses to have him walk backwards, rather than run forwards: Would this increase his speed? Would this help him to outstrip

* Acts iii. 25.

strip his rivals? or enable him to win the prize?—Shall we, in order to avoid the charge of *Antinomianism*, rush into this absurdity? I am persuaded you could not wish to see so egregious a piece of folly, even in your enemy; much less in   Your, &c.

LETTER IX.

Rev. Sir,

I Wish you would consider with some attention, that emphatical memento of the apostle, *Since ye knew the grace of GOD in truth.* Here he intimates, that we may have a knowledge of grace, which is not genuine; not free from corrupt mixture, not true.—It may be so discoloured with error, or blended with so much of the law, as no longer to appear like itself.—The language of such persons, is somewhat like the language of the *Israelites*, after their return from captivity, who spoke neither the *Hebrew*, nor the Heathenish dialect; but expressed themselves half in the speech of *Ashdod*, and half in the speech of *Zion.*

It is true, says *Aspasio*, I cannot perform the conditions.—" It is not true," says Mr *Wesley*. This is pretty blunt, and pretty bold too; for it is, in effect, affirming, that a man dead in trespasses and sins is able to perform conditions. Mr *Wesley* is not aware, that " *CHRIST* strengthening us," is one of the benefits of the covenant, comprehended in these words, *I will put my laws into their minds.*

" The conditions of the new covenant are, Repent " and believe." It has been already shewn, that they are represented by the HOLY GHOST, not as conditions, but as blessings; not as conditions required, but as blessings bestowed; not as conditions on which depends the accomplishment of the covenant; but as happy fruits, or precious effects, of the
                                                                                                covenant;

covenant; made, and making good to sinners, who are wholly without strength.

'Tis equally true, says *Aspasio*, this is not required at my hands. " 'Tis equally true," says Mr *Wesley*, " that is absolutely false."—This is, doubtless, a *home*-thrust.—It behoves us to provide some ardour of proof for our defence; and this the scripture furnishes abundantly. It furnishes us with more than *robur et æs triplex*. The scripture sets forth justification, salvation, and all blessedness, as things perfectly free; detached from all works; dependent on no conditions, but the gifts of sovereign goodness, and infinitely-rich grace.

Though you, Sir, treat *Aspasio* in so unceremonious a manner, we will be more complaisant; you shall receive such entertainment from us as the king of *Babylon*'s ambassadors received from *Hezekiah*. We will, on this occasion, shew you *the house of our precious things, the silver and the gold, the spices and the precious ointment, and if* not *all*, yet some of *the house of our armour* *.

We are saved, that is, we have all the benefits of the new covenant—By grace—*By grace ye are saved.* —*It is of grace, and no more of works.*—*Who hath saved us, not according to our works, but according to his purpose and grace* †.

Freely—*Being justified freely.*—*The things that are freely given to us of GOD.*—*Whosoever will, let him take the water of life freely* ‡.

By way of gift—*If thou knowest the gift of GOD.*— *The gift of GOD is eternal life.*—*The free gift came upon all men, to justification of life* ‖.

Without the law—*The righteousness of GOD without the law.*—*That we might be justified, not by the works of the law.*— *If the inheritance were of the law* §.

Not

---

* 2 Kings xx. 13. † Eph. ii. 5. Rom. x. 6. 2 Tim. 1. 9.
‡ Rom. iii. 34. 1 Cor. 2. 12. Rev. xxii. 19. ‖ John iv. 10. Rom. vi. 23. v. 18. § Rom. iii. 21. Gal. 16. iii. 18.

Not by works—*Not of works, but of him that calleth us.—Not by works of righteousness which we have done, but according to his mercy he saved us.—Not having mine own righteousness, which is of the law* *.

By righteousness, not performed, but imputed—*Faith* (in *CHRIST*, as our all) *is imputed for righteousness.—GOD imputeth righteousness without works.—To whom it* (that is, the merits of a dying and rising SAVIOUR) *shall be imputed* †.

Not by guiltless behaviour, but by remission of sins—*Blessed are they whose iniquities are forgiven, and whose sins are covered.—GOD was in CHRIST, reconciling the world unto himself, not imputing their trespasses unto them.—To give knowledge of salvation by the remission of their sins* ‡.

Not each by himself, but all by one—*They shall reign in life, by one CHRIST JESUS.—By the obedience of one, shall many be made righteous.—By one offering, he hath perfected for ever those that are sanctified* ‖.

By faith alone—*Being justified by faith.—A man is justified by faith, without the deeds of the law.—Thro' him, all that believe are justified from all things* §.

Not on account of faith, as a condition performed; but on account of CHRIST, the pearl of inestimable price; which faith receives, applies, and uses.—*Who has* by himself *purged away our sins, by himself finished our transgressions, made reconciliation for our iniquities, and brought in an everlasting righteousness* ++.

This is the doctrine of scripture. Because it is of the greatest importance, you see, with what care it is stated, and with what copiousness displayed, with what zeal it is urged, and with what vigilance guarded.—How solicitously the sacred writers use every form of speech that may exclude all human works; may

set

---

* Rom. ix. 11. Tit. iii. 5. Phil. iii. 9. † Rom. iv. 5, 6, 23, 24, 25. ‡ Psal. xxxii. 1. 2 Cor. v. 19. Luke i. 77. ‖ Rom. v. 17, 18, 19. Heb. x. 14. § Rom. v. 1. iii. 28. Acts xiii. 39. ++ Heb. i. 3. Dan. ix. 24.

set aside all conditions and pre-requisites, in order to supersede all glorying, and ascribe the whole of our justification to the free grace of GOD, and the sole merits of CHRIST.

After all these testimonies of scripture, shall we still maintain that the covenant of grace consists of conditions; depends upon conditions; is such as we cannot expect to have made good till certain conditions are, by us, duly and truly fulfilled? *Dagon* may as well stand in the presence of the ark, as such a notion in the face of these evangelical texts.

All, all is free to us sinners, though it was not free to CHRIST our SAVIOUR.—He paid the price; he performed the conditions. If you would know what *price* was paid; what *conditions* were performed, and on what *terms* we inherit the blessing; you, Sir, may receive information from Mr *John Wesley*, who says in his comment, " All the blessings of the new " covenant are secured to us by the one offering of " CHRIST." According to this commentator, they are not only procured for us, but *secured* to us. How could either of these be true,—much more, how could the latter be fact,—if the blessings were suspended on any performance or any acquisition of ours? If I am not to enjoy them *until* I discharge this or that duty, they are not procured for me; if I am not to enjoy them *unless* I become possessed of this or that quality, they are not secured to me; not secured to me, as the estate is to an heir, even whilst he is a minor, but only as the prize is to a racer, in case, by exerting his speed and his strength, he arrives first at the goal; which was never yet called security, but allowed to be mere uncertainty.

As to this point, *others* may receive information from the prophet *Zechariah*: *By the blood of thy covenant, I have sent forth thy prisoners out of the pit, wherein was no water* *. *Thy prisoners,* those wretched

* Zech. ix. 11.

ed creatures, who were in a state of guilt, and under the sentence of death; subject to the tyranny of the devil, and liable to the damnation of hell. In this dismal state they were, as in a *pit* unfathomably deep; from which there seemed no possibility of escape, nor any method of deliverance: *A pit, in which there is no water*, nothing but absolute misery, without a gleam of hope, or a drop of comfort. *I have sent them forth* into a place of liberty; where they obtain pardon, and enjoy peace, are satisfied with the plenteousness of my house, and drink of my pleasures as out of a river. All this, by the *blood of thy covenant*.—Blood was the righteous term, blood was the dreadful requirement, even that infinitely precious blood of *CHRIST*, on which the covenant of our freedom was established, and by which its rich blessings are procured. Which is called *thy covenant* *, *O daughter of Zion*, thou church of the first-born, because it was made in thy name; made with thy divine Surety, and for thy unspeakable good.

This is not only false, but " most dangerously false. " —If we allow this, Antinomianism comes in with a " full tide." Pray, Sir, what do you mean by *Antinomianism?* such a contrariety to the law, as debases its dignity; deprives it of its proper honour and proper end †?

Surely then, not *Aspasio*'s, but Mr *Wesley*'s tenets, are chargeable with this kind of heterodoxy; since they would cause the law to be put off with a mite, when millions of talents are its due;—oblige it to be
content

---

* *Thy covenant.* The words are not addressed to *CHRIST*, but to his church. As the *Hebrew* את being in the feminine gender intimates.

† The end of the commanding law is righteousness, *Rom.* x. 4. The end of the violated law is punishment, *Gal.* iii. 10. Both these ends are answered by the interposition of an obedient and crucified REDEEMER, but on no other scheme, and in no other manner whatever.

content with errant deficiency, when the most sinless obedience, and the most exalted perfection are what it demands.

Do you mean by *Antinomianism*, such a contrariety to the law, as disregards its duties, and violates its precepts? Then the apostle *Paul* shall reply, *The grace of GOD, which bringeth salvation, hath appeared unto all men; teaching us, that, denying ungodliness and worldly lusts, we should live soberly, righteously, and godly.*—*The grace of GOD*, his infinitely-free favour, of which we have a specimen in the preceding texts, which scorns to be shackled with conditions, or meanly dependent on human endeavours.—This grace, requiring nothing of the creature, but *bringing salvation*, spiritual and eternal salvation, finished by the incarnate CREATOR, and free for the chiefest of sinners. This grace being revealed in the gospel, being discerned by faith, and thus appearing in lustre, and with power, to *all men*—to men of every rank, every age, every character; making no difference between the servant and his master, between the ruddy stripling and the hoary sire; between the vile prostitute and the chaste vestal, but opening its inexhaustible treasures, to be received by one as well as the other —This grace does what? " Cause Antinomianism," or practical ungodliness, " to come in with a full tide?" Quite the reverse.—It represses it like an immovable barrier. It *teaches us to deny* [*], to renounce ungodliness, *all ungodliness;* not only external gross abominations, but *wordly lusts* also, every vitious inclination, and every irregular desire. Farther, it teaches us to live *soberly*, with regard to ourselves, *righteously* towards

---

[*] The word is ἀρνησάμενοι, which does not signify, to abolish totally, or to destroy utterly; but to disavow and renounce, to refuse admittance, or not to yield compliance. There may be, even in the regenerate, some remainders of ungodliness: but, influenced by grace, they will constantly turn a deaf ear to its solicitations, or resolutely say nay to its demands.

wards our neighbours, and *godly* to our great CREATOR.

The original word is particularly beautiful and significant; it is not ῥιζοῦν, *prescribeth*, by way of rule, nor ἐπιτάσσων, *enjoineth*, by way of authority; but παιδεύων, *teacheth*, by way of instruction, pointeth out the effectual method of obeying the precepts, and conforming to the rule. A tyrant may command his slave to write, or make a proficiency in writing. A kind tutor forms him to it, shews him how to do it, and renders, what otherwise would be an irksome, perhaps an impracticable task, both easy and pleasant.— So this grace, clearly manifested in the understanding, and cordially apprehended by the will, renders every duty of holiness both practicable and pleasant; it gives us a heart and a hand, and ability to exercise ourselves unto universal godliness.

CHRIST has performed all that was conditionary for me, says *Aspasio*. " Has he repented and believed " for you?" says Mr *Wesley*; a question already answered in the dialogues.—" No;" replies Mr *Wesley*, " not answered, but evaded. He performed all that " was conditionary in the covenant of works, is no- " thing to the purpose; for we are not talking of that, " but of the covenant of grace." Give me leave to tell you, Sir, that you are greatly mistaken here; we are talking, at least we ought to be talking, of the covenant of works, when we talk of the covenant which *CHRIST* came under. It was a covenant of works to him, which, by his execution of it, became a covenant of grace for us. He became answerable for our debt; the debt was exacted, without the least abatement. In this respect, GOD *spared not his own Son*: And is not this the tenor, are not such the effects of a covenant of works?

CHRIST is called the *Surety of a better covenant;* that is, a surety provided and admitted by a better covenant: in this peculiarity, infinitely momentous and

and comfortable, the new covenant is better; because it brings in a substitute, to discharge what was contracted under the old, which neither provided, nor allowed, nor knew any such thing.—It is written, *CHRIST was made under the law*, therefore not under a covenant of grace. If you can shew me, in the construction of the law, any hint of faith in the merits of another, or any mention of repentance unto life, I will retract my opinion, that *CHRIST* performed whatever was conditionary; I will do honour to those genteel expressions, and submit to those cogent arguments, " 'Tis not true—'Tis nothing to the " purpose—'Tis absolutely false."

" If *CHRIST*'s perfect obedience be ours, we " have no more need of pardon than *CHRIST* him- " self. The consequence is good, you have started " an objection which you cannot answer."—It is answered in the dialogues; whether in a satisfactory, or insufficient manner, the reader must determine.—But suppose we admit the consequence; it implies no more than the apostle affirms—*By one offering he hath perfected for ever them that are sanctified.* Let me transcribe your own * explication of this passage.—" He " hath done" (observe, you yourself speak of *CHRIST*'s doing; in this place *only* of *CHRIST*'s doing; yet I would not be so injurious to your good sense, as to imagine that you exclude his *suffering*) " all that was needful, in order to their full reconci- " liation with GOD." This exposition I approve, as far as it goes; only you have omitted one very weighty circumstance, comprehended in the word " ever;" by this doing and suffering, believers are fully and perfectly reconciled, not for a day only, or for any particular time, but *for ever*. The pardon is irrevocable; the blessing unalienable. Not like the *moon*, which now waxes, and anon wanes; but like the *sun*, which

---

* Explanatory notes *in loc.*

which is always the fame; ever fhines with the fame plenitude of rays; and needs only to appear, in order to appear unchangeably bright.

This reminds me of a more direct anfwer to your difficulty. The repeated pardon, which believers implore, is only a witnefs bearing to the truth, or a repeated manifeftation of it to our confciences.—Will you find fault with this doctrine? Might you not, for the very fame reafon, fay, if the atonement of *CHRIST*'s death was abfolutely perfect, there could be no need of his interceffion at GOD's right hand? Yes, for the actual application of the great atonement, and the continual communication of its happy fruits, this interceffion is neceffary. So, though our juftification is complete, though our fins have all been laid upon the LORD, and are not to be done away by fome duties of our own, but already done away by the *facrifice of* HIMSELF; yet the application of this bleffing, the revelation of it to our hearts, is daily, hourly, inceffantly needful. Therefore he faith, fpeaking of his vineyard the church, *I will water it every moment.*—Whereby? in what manner? what fpiritual bleffings correfpond with watering the thirfty foil?—The difcovery of complete pardon, of complete acceptance, of complete falvation in *CHRIST*. This will make the foul like a watered garden;—this will caufe joy and holinefs to bloffom as a rofe.

Both the branches of the law, the preceptive and the penal, in the cafe of guilt contracted, muft be fatisfied. " Not fo."—If not, one of them muft pafs unfatisfied and unfulfilled. Whereas, our LORD declares, that *heaven and earth fhall pafs away, fooner than one jot or one tittle of the law fhall fail* of its accomplifhment. Will you undertake to prove, either that the preceptive, or elfe that the penal part of the law, does not conftitute fo much as one jot or one tittle of its contents? Then, and then only, your af-
fertion

fertion may confift with our LORD's declaration. This will be an undertaking as adventurous as your next is difingenuous.

"Not fo; CHRIST, by his death alone" (fo our church teaches), " fully fatisfied for the fins of the " whole world."—*By his death alone*, that is, in contradiftinction to all human works, as efficient or adjutant caufes: *fully fatisfied*, that is, without having, and without needing the concurrence of any human fatisfaction. It is fpoken in oppofition to our endeavours, not to his own moft glorious obedience. But do you really want to be informed that our church means no fuch thing, as you would infinuate? Have you never heard her profefs, and require to believe, what *Afpafio* maintains? If not, be pleafed to read the quotations from her homilies, which he has produced, vol. III. pag. 48, 49.*. Read thefe, and I cannot but think, you have modefty enough to blufh at an attempt, to palm upon the public, fuch an apparent mifreprefentation of our venerable mother.

"The

---

* As this book may poffibly fall into the hands of fome perfons, who have not the book, entitled *Theron* and *Afpafio;* I will, for their fakes, tranfcribe one of the teftimonies, to which we are referred.

In the homily concerning the falvation of mankind, we read the following words :—" The apoftle toucheth three things, " which muft go together in juftification. On GOD's part, " his great mercy and grace. On *CHRIST*'s part, the " fatisfaction of GOD's juftice, or the price of our redemp- " tion, by the offering of his body, and fhedding of his pre- " cious blood, with fulfilling of the law perfectly. On our " part, true and lively faith in the merits of *JESUS* " *CHRIST*, which yet is not ours, but by GOD's working " in us." You fee, according to the judgment of our reformers, not only the offering of *CHRIST*'s body, and the fhedding of *CHRIST*'s blood, but alfo his perfect fulfilling of the law, are the adequate price of our redemption. Yet Mr *Wefley* is pleafed to exclude the latter; and ventures to affirm that he has the authority of our church for fuch an opinion, and for fuch a practice.

"The same great truth, is manifestly taught in the xxxift article."—What? That *CHRIST*, by his *death alone*, or by *shedding his blood alone, without fulfilling the law perfectly*, satisfied for the sins of the world? Then the articles and the homilies most flatly contradict one another.—Upon this you ask, "Is it therefore fair, is it honest, for any one to plead the articles of our church in defence of absolute predestination?" Indeed, Sir, I know not what you mean by this interrogatory, or at what you aim. Does *Aspasio* plead the articles for any such purpose? Not that he should be afraid, in case there was an evident occasion, to advance such a plea, and perhaps might put Mr *Wesley* to greater difficulty than he is aware of, in order to elude the force of it.—But he does not in this place come within view of the point; nor so much as remotely hint at it. No, nor in any part of the two volumes, does he once touch upon *absolute predestination*, much less does he plead the articles of our church in its defence. So that your inferential word "therefore" is a conclusion without premises.

Absolute predestination is a phrase not to be found in all the dialogues, or in any of the letters. But it is a phrase which Mr *Wesley* thinks to be alarming and disgusting, on which Mr *Wesley* has learned to say many horrible and shocking things; therefore be it right or wrong, be it true or false, *Aspasio* shall be charged with the obnoxious expression.—When he mentions predestination, it is in the very words of scripture; without dwelling upon the subject; without resting his cause upon it; without attempting either to explain or to establish it. This he leaves, and ever will leave, to clearer hands and abler pens.—As to your "absolute," this is not what *Aspasio* speaks, but what Mr *Wesley* would make him speak; a word, which in this connection he never used, nor so much as dreamed of using; for which reason, I call it, not *his*, but

but *yours*:—May I not then retort your own queſtion? and aſk, Is it fair, is it honeſt, to put into your friend's mouth words which he never uſed, and then exclaim againſt them?

What follows in this paragraph is prodigious indeed. " Seeing the xviith article barley defines the " term;" that is, the church does not believe the doctrine, nor require any ſuch belief from her members? Why then does ſhe ſelect it for one of the articles? why pronounce it agreeable to GOD's word? why forbid diſputation againſt it? Pity, but we had been acquainted with this fine diſtinction when we were ſtudents at *Oxford.*—We then declared our approbation of the academical ſtatutes; we engaged to obſerve them all, and confirmed our engagement with an oath.—But how eaſily might we have eluded the obligation, if, when called upon for conformity and obedience, this ſalvo had come into our heads; " The " univerſity does not, in theſe ſtatutes, ſet forth our " duty, but barely defines the terms; ſhe does not " inſiſt upon a conformity, but only flouriſhes a little " upon terms, and leaves us to obey or diſobey, as " we ſhall feel ourſelves inclined."

" Barely defines the term, without either affirming " or denying the thing."—How! does ſhe not affirm the *thing*, when ſhe ſtyles it an *excellent benefit of GOD?* declares it to be *full of ſweet, pleaſant*, and *unſpeakable comfort* to the godly? that it *greatly eſtabliſhes and confirms their faith of eternal ſalvation*, and *fervently kindles their love towards* GOD? " Not affirm the " thing!"—when ſhe expreſsly aſcribes ſuch fruits and conſequents to it! This is not only affirming, but affirming with the higheſt approbation, like proclaiming the king, and placing the crown upon his head.

In one part of your *Preſervative*, you enumerate, and very properly diſplay, what you call " the five " benefits of baptiſm."—Suppoſe a *Quaker*, upon read-

ing this passage, should say, " Friend *Wesley,* thou
" barely defineth the term, thou neither affirmeft nor
" denieft the thing.—This is no proof that thou thyfelf
" believeft a tittle of water-baptifm, or wouldft have
" thy readers believe the reality of any fuch ordi-
" nance." Should the *Quaker* argue thus, he would
argue juft like yourfelf. But I apprehend he would
not be fo boldly difingenuous, he would rather con-
fefs; " Friend *John* doth certainly maintain and be-
" lieve thefe things; but his opinion is miftaken, and
" his arguments are inconclufive."—" The xxxift
" article totally overthrows predeftination, and razes
" it from the foundation." If fo, it makes one ar-
ticle contradict another; confequently, weakens the
authority, and undermines the credibility of them all.
In this article are two points more particularly proper
for our inquiry: The *great falvation,* and the *number
of the faved.*—I cannot but query, whether you be-
lieve the former, or rightly underftand the latter?

The *great falvation,* expreffed in the following
words; " The offering of CHRIST once made, is
" that perfect redemption, propitiation and fatisfac-
" tion for all the fins of the whole world, both ori-
" ginal and actual." If I take thefe words as I am
enjoined, in the literal and grammatical fenfe, I muft
believe, that CHRIST engaged to fatisfy offended
juftice, for every fin which I have committed, or fhall
commit, throughout my whole life. My paft fins at
that time had no more exiftence, than my future fins
have at this hour; but both were equally laid upon
my LORD.

Having undertaken this greateft of all works, I
muft believe that he fully accomplifhed it; and actu-
ally fatisfied for all my tranfgreffions, of every kind
and every date.—A poffibility, or mere *chance* of being
redeemed, can never be reckoned a perfect redemp-
tion; neither would our SAVIOUR have paid down
a pofitive price for a precarious conditional good;
much

much less would he have paid an immense, an infinite price, upon a bare uncertainty, whether it should take an effect, or ever obtain its defired end.—I believe therefore, that the fatisfaction is made for *me;* that GOD has received the all-fufficient atonement in behalf of all my provocations; and that there is no more ground of condemnation for me a vile finner, than there is room for the profecution of an infolvent, all whofe debts are defrayed, even to the very laft mite.

The number of the faved, expreffed in thofe words —*the fins of the whole world.* This I acknowledge to be the language of fcripture; and I promife myfelf you will bear with me, while I offer my thoughts concerning the occafion and the import of fuch language.

In the *antediluvian* and *patriarchal* ages, the LORD JEHOVAH confined his favour to a few particular families.—When he formed his *Ifrael* into a commonwealth, he chofe them to himfelf, and feparated them from all other nations. To them he gave his oracles, his ordinances, and his covenants; yea, he honoured and indulged them with his divine prefence: In this the *Ifraelites* gloried; they appropriated this privilege to themfelves, and held other people at a diftance, looking upon them as ftrangers, and without GOD in the world; hence that chofen feed fpares not to fay, " We are thine; thou never bareft rule over them; " they were not called by thy name."—At the commencement of the MESSIAH's kingdom, the LORD purpofed to change the fcene, and vary the difpenfation, by admitting both *Jews* and *Gentiles* to an intereft in the great falvation; as they were equally chargeable with fin, and equally liable to the curfe, they fhould now ftand upon a level, be equally fharers in that divine SAVIOUR, who fubmits to be made fin, and to be made a curfe for both alike. This the HOLY GHOST exprefsly and repeatedly promifed, *He* (that is, the REDEEMER which is to come) *fhall fpeak peace unto the Heathen; his do-*

minion shall be from sea even unto sea, and from the river even to the end of the earth.

Notwithstanding such prophecies, and such promises, our LORD himself, when he entered upon his ministry, acted a discriminating part, and kept up the *partition-wall;* in pursuance of that declaration, *I am not sent, but unto the lost sheep of the house of Israel.* When he sent forth his disciples to preach and to teach, he gave them also a command to shew the same partial regard; *Go ye not into the way of the Gentiles.* This conduct of our LORD, both under the Old Testament and the New, confirmed the *Jews* in their self-flattering notion, that they were, and ever should be, a favourite nation, and a peculiar people. The *Gentiles,* on the other hand, were no less discouraged: apprehending, that as they were, so they ever should be, *aliens from the commonwealth of Israel.* But in order to convince the *Jews* of their mistake, in claiming the blessing of *Abraham* to themselves, and in order to assure the poor discarded *Gentiles* that they should be *fellow-heirs and of the same body;* our LORD, in his last charge to his apostles, alters the style of his commission, and enlarges the sphere of their several departments. It is now no longer, *Go not into the way of the Gentiles;* but quite the reverse, *Go teach all nations, all the world,* yea, and *every creature; Whosoever believeth,* whether *Jew* or *Gentile, shall be saved.*

Still the *Jews* were hardly induced to give the right hand of fellowship to their brethren the *Gentiles.*—For St *Peter* cries, with some indignation; *Not so, LORD.* Still the *Gentiles,* hardly persuaded that they should be partakers of the grace, reasoned against themselves; *The LORD hath utterly separated me from his people.* Therefore the LORD, to intercept all the desponding objections of the *latter,* and to bring down the high disdainful imaginations of the *former,* declares in a variety of places, that the difference no longer subsists, that *CHRIST* has thrown down the partition-wall,

and

and laid all plain, and common, and free.—Though the giving of the law pertained to *Israel only*, the *LORD JESUS* gave himself a ransom for ALL PEOPLE. Though the paschal lamb extended its influence only to the circumcision, the LAMB of GOD is a *propitiation for the sins of the whole world*, even though it be not circumcised. And now GOD would have all men, whether bond or free, *Jews* or *Gentiles*, *Greeks*, or *Barbarians*, to be saved, by coming unto the knowledge of the faith.

This account gives us the true cause, and points out the intended use, of such universal phrases. They are calculated to abate the pride of the *Jews*, to encourage the despised *Gentiles*; and by excluding *none*, they give encouragement for *all* to come, because, though every *individual* person will not be saved, yet *whosoever cometh shall in no wise be cast out*. By this interpretation, the phrase is neither inconsistent with other texts, neither does our church contradict herself.

Upon the whole, you will please to observe, that I should never have touched upon this subject, had not your objections, far fetched and forced as they are, given me a kind of challenge. And now I have touched upon the subject, it is not as a champion for the cause, but only to shew the weakness and the inconsistency of your arguing, how little you avail yourself even on a point, where you think opposition vain, and your arm irresistible.

"Believers, who are notorious transgressors in "themselves, have a sinless obedience in *CHRIST;*" this passage you select as faulty, I presume, because it is opposite to your favourite tenet, "*perfection* in per- "sonal holiness.—By *notorious*, I mean *acknowledged, confessed, indisputably such*. If you are not such a transgressor, why do you daily confess yourself, "a "miserable sinner?" Why do you acknowledge, that you are "tied and bound with the chain of your sins;" and declare before all men, that "there is no health
"in

"in you?" All this Mr *Wesley* speaks with his lips, and, I would hope, believes in his heart. Yet all this does not amount " to a *notorious* transgressor." Pray then, good Sir, inform us, what sort of transgressor is described by all these expressions.

You cry out, "O syren song!" The Psalmist would have taught you a better exclamation. If this is the case, *let us rejoice with trembling.*—Are we notorious transgressors in ourselves? The consciousness of this is the strongest motive to humility.—Have we a sinless obedience in *CHRIST?* The belief of this is an abundant source of joy. When you add, " Pleasing " found to *James Wheatly! Thomas Williams! James " Rily!"* I am quite ashamed of your meanness, and grieved at your uncharitable rashness. How unworthy is such a procedure, either of the gentleman, the Christian, or the man of sense! Unworthy the *gentleman*, to stigmatize by name, and expose to the most public infamy. Unworthy the *Christian*, whose charity concealeth, rather than divulgeth and proclaimeth upon the house-tops. Unworthy the *man of sense*, who knows that the miscarriages of a professor are no argument against the soundness of a doctrine. If they were, would not your own principles totter? Nay, how could Christianity itself stand?

Elijah failed in his resignation, and even *Moses* himself spake unadvisedly with his lips. " It is true," says Mr *Wesley*, " But if you could likewise fix some " blot upon venerable *Samuel*, and beloved *Daniel*, it " would prove nothing." I have no desire to fix a blot; but if I find it in the most accomplished character, this proves the proposition, which *Aspasio* maintains; " That the very best of men fall short; that " the very best of men will be found *guilty*, if *tried* " *by the righteous law :*—That the very best of men " have nothing more to plead *for acceptance* with the " HIGH and HOLY one, than the criminal, who " yesterday murdered his benefactor, to-morrow is

" to

" to be executed for his crime, and is now flying to
" the redemption that is in CHRIST JESUS for
" the chief of sinners."

" No scripture teaches that the holiness of Christians
" is to be measured by that of any *Jew*." I should
be afraid to advance such a position, after having read
that general exhortation, *Be ye followers of them, who
through faith and patience inherit the promises;* and
those more particular references to the ancient saints,
comprised in the *eleventh chapter to the Hebrews.*
Were not they *Jews?* Does not the apostle propose
them as *patterns* for our imitation? Is not this his
language, *Let us* act in conformity to their practice?
—*The spirit of CHRIST was in them;* and " they ob-
" tained, (even from the supreme JUDGE) a good
" report." Agreeably to this divine testimonial, we
are directed to learn from *Abel,* a fiduciary depend-
ence on the great atonement ; and from *Enoch,* a life
of communion with a reconciled GOD. The pro-
phets are recommended to our contemplation, as " ex-
" amples of suffering affliction, and of patience."
Elijah is set before us as an instance of persevering
and successful prayer : and we are directed to walk in
the steps of our father *Abraham*'s faith. This was the
counsel of an apostle to others ; this was the aim of an
apostle with regard to himself; therefore I think, it
can never be unworthy of you, or unfit for the most
advanced among your disciples. For my part, I shall
reckon myself truly happy ; I shall bless the day,
whereon I was born ; if I may but be enabled to fol-
low the footsteps of these illustrious leaders, though

— — *non passibus æquis.*

That Christians ought to rise above the level of the
common *Jews,* I freely own. Mr *Wesley*'s mistake
seems to lie in confounding the *common* with the *un-
common,* in not discerning the difference between *any*
and *every;* between *some* and *all.* Some *Jews* were
blessed with extraordinary endowments ; they had dis-
tinguished communications of the spirit of wisdom and
holiness.

holinefs. They were as the " ftones of a crown, lifted up as an enfign upon his land." Their great atchievements and eminent attainments are defcribed in the aforementioned chapter, which may truly be ftyled the *golden legend;* great things impoffible to flefh and blood, they both performed and fuffered; fuch as characterife a faint of the higheft rank.—To imitate thefe, is the duty of *all* Chriftians; to equal them, is the privilege of *few*.

Let me *illuftrate* this fentiment; the reader, I apprehend, will hardly think it needs *confirmation*.—Every graduate in the univerfity, much more every minifter of the gofpel, ought to exceed the fchoolboy in learning and knowledge.—Yet there have been fchoolboys with whom few minifters, and fewer graduates, will venture to compare themfelves. A recent inftance of this kind, we have in the famous *Baratier*. This wonderful youth, when he was but four years old, fpoke *French* to his mother, *Latin* to his father, *High Dutch* to his maid. At the age of fix, he explained the *Hebrew* text, as ready as if it had been his native *German*. When other lads are fcarce able to read with fluency and propriety their mothertongue, he was not only acquainted with, but mafter of five feveral languages. In his eleventh year he publifhed a learned *Latin* differtation, and tranflated a book of travels out of *Hebrew* into *French*. While a mere boy he was qualified to difpute with profeffors of the fciences, was honoured with a feat at an ecclefiaftical fynod, and admitted to the degree of doctor in philofophy. Upon this narrative I fhall only obferve, that many of the *Jews*, whofe names are immortalized in fcripture, were, in faith, in godlinefs, and all that is exemplary, fo many *Baratiers*.

" Do not the beft of men frequently feel diforder in " their affections? Do they not often complain, When " I would do good, evil is prefent with me?" " I " believe not." What a proof is here! How well
suited

suited to its office! which is to control the current and over-rule the evidence of ancient and modern consent. But why don't you believe what *Aspasio* supposes? Is your disbelief grounded on fact? Are you acquainted with any people, who feel no disorder in their affections? who always do good in the completest manner? and never have evil present with them? If so, what are their names? where do they live? We would go many miles to see them. You have no aversion to the mention of names, when censure is the motive, and public disgrace the effect; why should you be so reluctant, when honour and distinguished respect would be the consequence?

Do they not say, *We groan, being burdened* with the workings of inbred corruption? " This is not the " meaning of the text. The whole context shews " the cause of that groaning was their longing to be " with CHRIST." You need not on this occasion rummage the context, or take a journey to find what is at your door. The sentence itself shews, as plainly as words can shew, the cause of their groaning. We groan, it is not said because we long to be with CHRIST. This might be a truth; but this is not the cause assigned, " We groan because we are burdened." Burdened with what? *Aspasio* answers, with a body of sin and death, or with what the apostle himself styles τὸ θνητόν. This, whatever it means, was the load that encumbered them, oppressed them, and made them sigh ardently for deliverance. Does not this signify all the infirmities and disorders of the present mortal state? Among which the sad effects of inbred *corruption*, are none of the least. These gave those magnanimous, but pious souls, more uneasiness than all other kinds of affliction whatever *.

The

* " We groan, being burdened, with a sense of our spirit-
" ual infirmities, and with the workings of inbred corruption."
This is *Aspasio*'s interpretation. " We groan, being burdened
" with numberless infirmities, temptations, and sins." This is

The cure of sin will be perfected in heaven. "Nay, " surely in paradise.—*Aspasio* knows no difference between paradise and heaven. Paradise is the kingdom where *CHRIST* reigns; and is not this heaven? Paradise is the region where the tree of life grows; and is not this heaven? Heaven denotes the place; paradise describes its nature, a place of consummate bliss and absolute perfection, where is the fulness of joy and pleasure for evermore.—However, if it can be proved, that they are different abodes, and imply different states * ; then *Aspasio* would be understood to say, the cure of sin is completed in paradise; or as soon as the believer drops his flesh, and enters the invisible world.

This (a perfect conformity to GOD) is a noble prerogative of the beatific vision. "No;" says Mr *Wesley*. Though St *John*, one would think, had settled and ascertained this point beyond all contradiction—*We shall be like him, for we shall see him, as he is.*— " We shall," which intimates, that at present we are not perfectly like him—" For," which denotes the efficient cause of this advancement and felicity; this complete

---

Mr *Wesley*'s interpretation, in his Expository notes on the New Testament. Yet here he denies what there he affirms.— It is said, I think of *Ishmael*; *His hand will be against every man*. Mr *Wesley* goes a step farther. His hand is against *himself*, as well as against every body else.

* St *Paul*, I am aware, speaks of heaven and speaks of paradise, 2 *Cor.* xii. 2, 4. So does *David* speak of *rising up into the hill of the LORD*, and of *standing in his holy place.*—But as the same thing, though variously expressed, is meant by the *Psalmist*, I think we may not unreasonably understand the *Apostle* in the same manner. If they had been different habitations, methinks he would have mentioned *paradise* first, and then the third *heavens*. Otherwise he tells the story but awkwardly; for he first mentions his arrival at the third heavens, and then at paradise; that is, according to Mr *Wesley* ; first he was led into the *presence*, and then introduced to the *antechamber.*

complete transformation into the divine image.—
" We shall see him," no longer through a glass, but
face to face. We shall receive the clearest manifestation of his ineffable holiness and glory, which will
have just the same effect upon our souls as the imprinted seal has upon the melting wax.

" It would then come too late. If sin remains in
" us till the day of judgment, it will remain in us
" for ever." You suppose, that the beatific vision is
not enjoyed, till the day of judgment. But in this
you seem to err, not knowing the scripture. I have
a *desire*, says the apostle, *to be dissolved*.—And what
is the consequence, the immediate consequence of
dissolution ? *To be with CHRIST;* in his presence ;
before his throne ; and is not this the beatific vision ;
Willing (says the inspired writer) *to be absent from
the body, and present with the L O R D.* Here is no
hint of any intermediate state, but the very moment
in which the saints depart from their bodies, they are
present with the L O R D ; and if with the L O R D,
then in the highest heavens ; then at the fountain-
head of felicity ; then amidst the *beatific vision.*—To
heaven *Elijah* was conveyed in his fiery chariot ; and
into heaven the first *martyr* was received by his compassionate S A V I O U R. Neither of them waited in
some intervening mansion, as a kind of *lobby* to the
heaven of heavens. This is the *Popish* notion, and
very closely connected with the chimera of purgatory ;
so closely connected, that if you take away the former,
the latter drops into nothing.—I am sorry, your opinions, Sir, are so much like the errors of the man of
sin.

Our present blessedness does not consist in being free
from sin. " I really think it does." Spoke like Mr
Wesley. " I think," is still the *argumentum palmarium*.
" I think," is the heavy artillery, which is to demolish brigades at a blow ; only here it is strengthened
and enforced by that emphatical word " really."—

But if our present blessedness does *really* consist in being free from sin, where are your blessed persons? We may truly say,

Apparent rari nantes in gurgite vasto. VIRG.

No; this can hardly be said. *Virgil*'s description is too full; instead of seeing a very *few*, here and there one, popping up their heads, in the great and wide ocean of the world, we are not able to find so much as an *individual.* Shew us *one*, only *one* of these angels in flesh and blood, and it sufficeth us. Whereas, if you persist in maintaining your *sinless perfection*, yet cannot produce a single instance, to exemplify your notion, will you not give too just a handle for that sarcastic reflection, used on another occasion?

*With witnesses many this cause did abound, (drown'd,
With some that were hang'd, and some that were
And some that were lost, and some never found.*

These are *Aspasio*'s words—" It (our present im-
" perfection) perpetually reminds us of a most im-
" portant truth, that our present blessedness consists,
" not in being free from all sin, but in having no sin
" imputed to us." He took particular care to guard his meaning from misconstruction, by adding the word *all:* lest this word, because it is little of stature, should be overlooked, he printed it in *Italics.* But all this precaution is thrown away upon Mr *Wesley.* He takes no notice of this same little word; nay, he shuts it entirely out of his quotation; as though he should say, " Where is the harm of clapping under the
" hatches such a puny insignificant monosyllable? I
" would have it to know, I shall ere long turn adrift
" more plump and portly words than that."

Aspasio also took care to confirm his sentiments by a reference to scripture; he supported himself by the authority of King *David.*—Mr *Wesley* having a little while ago laboured to depretiate, now ventures to contradict

tradict the royal *Pfalmift. Bleffed* (fays the Pfalmift) *is the man*—who is free from fin ? who is perfectly fanctified? This is not the doctrine which the fweet finger of *Ifrael* teaches; but bleffed is he *whofe tranfgreffion is forgiven, whofe fin is covered.* Deeply impreffed, and quite charmed with the contemplation of this moft fubftantial happinefs, the facred writer proclaims it; repeats it; yes, a third time he celebrates it; crying out with ardour of joy, *Bleffed is the man, unto whom the LORD imputeth no iniquity* *. Neither that iniquity which was formerly committed, nor that which ftill defiles †.) Bleffed indeed! May I live under a firm perfuafion of my own particular intereft in this unfpeakable privilege! May I find it made good to my foul, at the univerfal judgment! Then let others take the kingdoms of this world, and all the glory of them.—And as for *Afpafio*, he may reckon his credit fafe, and his opinion fully authorifed, while he efpoufes the doctrine, and ufes the very words of the unerring SPIRIT.

" If we are not free from fin, we are not Chriftian " believers."—What an affertion is here! *Affertion*, for I dare not call it a *truth*.—If it was, who then could be faved? Not one of a thoufand; not two of a million; no, nor Mr *John Wefley* himfelf, fince out of his own mouth he ftands condemned. He makes this acknowledgment concerning himfelf and his followers, " We know by melancholy experience what " it is to neglect works of righteoufnefs." To corroborate his confeffion, he adds, " We know and feel " by melancholy experience, what it is to fwerve from " our firft love. We feel by experience."—He is willing to run the hazard of tautology, rather than any fhould fufpect the fincerity and truth of his proteftation.

* *Pfal.* xxxii. 1, 2. Should any objection arife from the next fentence, the reader may fee it anticipated, and fuperfeded, in *Theron* and *Afpafio*, vol. II. p. 258, 259. of this edition.
† Pfal. xv. 3.

testation.—And can you after such a confession, after such a protestation, pretend to be free from sin? Is all this which you know of yourself, and *feel by experience*, consistent with a *sinless* state? Just as much as a' *lethargy* is consistent with the vigour of *health*, or a shameful *flight* with a glorious *victory*. See, Sir, how you are entangled in your own net; how, without being chafed by an enemy, you run yourself aground. Nor will all your dexterity, so long as you avow such palpable inconsistencies, be able to set you clear.

You attempt to confirm your opinion by the apostle's declaration; *Being made free from sin.*—But he and you mean different things by the same words.—He means being freed from the *dominion of sin.*—This is agreeable to his own explanation; sin (ου κυριευσει) shall not lord it over you;—it may *assault* you; it may *harass* you; it may gain some *advantage* over you; but it shall not obtain a *final victory*, not play the *tyrant* over you. To the expedience and necessity of this freedom, if ever we would approve ourselves disciples of *CHRIST*, or Christians indeed, I readily subscribe:—whereas, you mean being free from the very *remainders* of sin. " Having a purity" ('tis your own explanation) " free from all mixture of " its contrary, and a resignation excluding every de- " gree of self-will." Against the existence, or the possibility of this freedom, so long as we sojourn in a body of flesh, I enter my protest.

If we were perfect in piety, *C H R I S T*'s priestly office would be superseded. " No, we should still " need his Spirit, and consequently his intercession." But were we perfect, we should receive the Spirit without an intercessor.—An intercessor implies an alienation between the two parties; or something which, without the intervention of a third person, would create alienation.—The priestly office, whether of atoning, or of interceding, is founded on a state of guilt; to this it bears an essential and invariable relation.

tion.—Does *CHRIST* exercise his priestly office in behalf of angels? No, because they excel in strength, and are perfect in holiness.—Will *CHRIST* exercise his priestly office, when all his saints are received into glory? No, because then there will be an absolute consummation both in body and soul, both in righteousness and happiness, and the mediatorial kingdom be delivered up to the FATHER.—Did *CHRIST* exercise his priestly office before *Adam* fell? No, because sin had no existence then, and then the language was, *Let man be blessed;* not, *Deliver him from going down into the pit*.

The objections laid to my charge in this paragraph, and the whole side of the leaf, proceed upon your favourite notion; *perfection* of holiness, even while we continue in houses of clay. As I look upon your foundation to be a mere delusion, I must of course conclude, all that you build upon it to be chimerical and delusory; therefore, till you prove your supposition, I have no reason to concern myself with any of your consequences deduced from it, or with any of your allegations relating to it. On one clause, however, let me bestow a slight animadversion.

Aspasio says, a sense of remaining inbred corruption will reconcile us to death; Mr *Wesley* replies, "Indeed it will not: nor will any thing do this like perfect love."—Here I think you have missed the mark. Nothing can reconcile us to death but that which takes away its sting; and this is done only by the atonement of *CHRIST*. Nothing can reconcile us to death, but that which delivers us from its terror; and this is effected only by the sacrifice of our great HIGH PRIEST, which has converted the king of terrors into a messenger of peace: nothing can reconcile us unto death, but that which makes it desirable to depart, and gain to die; and this is owing, wholly owing to him who died for us, that whether we wake or sleep, we should live together with him.

Old

Old *Simon* found, that nothing could reconcile him to death, so much as a believing view of the LORD's CHRIST. Seeing GOD made flesh; seeing him as his own SAVIOUR, he was enabled not only to acquiesce in the summons, but to welcome it as a deliverance.—He was enabled to say with composure, and complacency, LORD, *now lettest thou thy servant depart in peace.*—Not because I am weary of this imperfect state; not because I am perfect in divine love; but because *mine eyes have seen thy salvation.* Though you may not like to imitate a *Jew*, I most heartily wish for myself, Let me die the death of this most venerable *Hebrew*, and let my latter end be like his!

If you still persist in your opinion, that nothing can reconcile you to dissolution like the imagined *perfection* of your love, not the *blood*, by which the saints overcame; not the *righteousness*, by which they reign in life; not the grace and power, which have swallowed up death in victory: I must then caution you to take heed least you cross, or attempt to cross the *river*, in the boat of *vain confidence.* You have abridged, if I mistake not, the *Pilgrim's Progress*, therefore can be at no loss to understand my meaning.

One clause, I said,—but I correct myself.—There is another, so very extraordinary, that you might justly charge me with inattention little short of stupidity, if I should pass it over without notice. These are the words,—" If we were perfect in piety, (St *John's* " word is perfect in love,) we should still be encom- " passed with infirmities, and liable to mistakes, from " which words or actions might follow, even tho' the " heart was all love, which were not exactly right."

This is strange! wondrous strange indeed! Perfect, yet " encompassed with infirmities!" Perfect, " yet " doing actions, and speaking words not exactly " right!" You are as singular in your *idea*, as you are strenuous for the *doctrine of perfection.*—I know not any *Protestant* writer that pretends to maintain the latter,

latter, yourself only excepted; and as to the former, I think it could never enter into the head of any thing living, but Mr *Wesley's* only. Perfect, "yet encom-"passed with infirmities," is just as found divinity, as true, yet addicted to lying, is found morality.

This is not the worst property of your notion of perfection, that it is absurd and self-contradictory. A sentiment may be *absurd*, yet not very *pernicious*. But this is an error of the most malignant kind. This was at the bottom of the Pharisees pride, and spirited them on to seek justification by the works of the law. They knew full well, that their obedience was not complete, it did not come up to their sacred and exalted standard; but they had learned to soften and extenuate their disobedience, into matters " not exactly right." —This is the cause, why people professing Christianity, see no form or comeliness in *CHRIST*, so as to desire him, with desires that cannot be uttered. 'Tis true they are not perfect, they often offend;—but then the offences are only human *infirmities;* words and actions " not exactly right." With this, which is indeed " the syren song," they lull their souls into an insensibility of their ruined state, and a disregard of the all-sufficient REDEEMER.

Cursed (says the law) *is every one that continueth not in all things*, whether they be great or small.— And will you regard that as a mere infirmity, and consistent with perfection, on which the divine law denounces a curse; which the divine law threatens with all misery here, and with everlasting vengeance hereafter? The apostle would probably chastise the author or abettor of such a conceit, in the following manner: " Wilt thou know, O vain man, that what " thou callest a matter " not exactly right," is most " horribly odious in the eye of GOD's infinite puri-" ty; deserves eternal death in the estimate of his " infinite justice; and could never have been pardon-
" ed

"ed but by the atoning death of his infinitely-majes-
"tic Son!"

"Encompassed with infirmities, yet the heart all
"love! Words and actions not exactly right, yet the
"man all perfection!" These are all paradoxes which
I never saw equalled, only in the writings of some
high-flown Papists. Mr *Wesley*'s words are not far
from a translation; they are, to a nicety, the sense
of those very offensive passages which I meet with in
a couple of Popish zealots. *Andradius*, interpreter of
the council of *Trent*, writes thus; " * Venialia pec-
"cata tam sunt minuta et levia, ut non advertentur
"perfectioni charitatis, nec impedire possunt per-
"fectam aut absolutam obedientiam."— *Lindenus*,
another champion for the same bad cause, expresses
himself in a more elegant, but in no less shocking a
manner. " † Levicula vitiola lapsuum quotidianorum,
"aspergines et nævulæ sunt: quæ per se non maculant
"et contaminant, sed quasi pulvisculo leviter asper-
"gunt vitam Christianam: ut nihilominus tamen per
"se sint perfecta, et undique immaculata renatorum
"opera in hac vita."—If Mr *Wesley* pleases to con-
sider these passages, I hope, he will be induced to alter
his phrase, and rectify his notions.—If he pleases to
translate these passages, his followers may have an op-
portunity of seeing, how nearly he approaches to
some of the worst errors of Popery; and may hence
be admonished not to imbibe, without due examina-
tion,

* Venial sins are so minute and trivial, that they do not
oppose the perfection of our love, nor can they hinder our
obedience from being absolutely perfect.

† The little trifling faults which are owing to our daily
slips or mistakes, are like specks, or almost imperceptible moles
upon the body, which of themselves do not stain or defile:
but as it were, with small particles of fine dust, lightly sprin-
kle the Christian life; so that, nevertheless, the works of the
regenerate may be of themselves perfect, and in all respects
immaculate, even in this life.

tion, his doctrines; nor submit, with an implicit credulity, to his dictates.

" The charges of the law are all answered."—At this sentence Mr *Wesley* is highly offended. As the lion is said to lash himself into rage, so my objector stirs himself up into a graceful indignation; stirs *himself*, for there is nothing in the passage, or in the context, to awaken such a flame of zeal. If Mr *Wesley* had understood *Aspasio*, according to the whole tenor of his discourse, there would have been no room for bringing Count *Zinzendorf* upon the carpet, nor for making that injurious conclusion, *Then neither GOD nor man can claim any obedience to the law.*—This is what *Aspasio* means: The claims of the law, as a covenant of works;—the claims of the law, as being the condition of life and glory;—the claims of the law, as requiring perfect obedience on pain of eternal death; these claims are all satisfied by our most blessed and gracious SURETY.—If not, they are still incumbent upon us, and upon every child of man. A burden this, which neither *we nor our fathers were able to bear*, which, heavier than the sands of the sea, would have sunk us all into the nethermost hell.—This doctrine, therefore, is not " *Antinomianism* without a mask;" but it is the doctrine of *righteousness without works* [*], and of justification *without the deeds of the law* [†].

" Then neither GOD nor man can claim any obe-
" dience to the law." Yes, GOD Almighty may, and GOD Almighty does claim our obedience to the law; as a rule of life, he requires a conformity to its precepts, as to the image of himself; he demands a performance of its duties, as the means of bringing glory to his name, and paying submission to his authority. And none will be so readily disposed, none will be so effectually enabled, to obey the *whole* law as those who see themselves made righteous by the obedience

---

[*] Rom. iv. 6.   [†] Rom. iii. 28.

obedience of *CHRIST*, who are thereby delivered from that tremendous curse, denounced on all ungodliness and unrighteousness of men.

Aspasio thus exhorts his friend,—Let me defire you to imagine, rather may the blessed SPIRIT enable you to believe, that your sins are expiated, through the death of *JESUS CHRIST;* that a righteousness is given you, by virtue of which you may have free and welcome access to GOD.—" This is not " scriptural language," says Mr *Wesley*. Therefore it cannot be sound doctrine, is his way of arguing. Harmless enough I must own. But what follows is not quite so modest. " I would simply say ;" and surely what *I* would say, must be *unexceptionably right:* This is the conclusion we are to make ; otherwise what you alledge, is of no weight at all.—" I would simply " say, By him we have access to the FATHER." This is beyond all objection proper.—It is taken from the apostle, and it includes what *Aspasio* expresses.— The apostle's language is the ingot of gold ; *Aspasio's* sentiment is a thread drawn, or a leaf beaten from it. Methinks, before I dismiss this topic, I would desire you to turn back a moment, and reconsider what you have affirmed.—Your sins are *expiated,* is not this scriptural language ?—What else meaneth that expression of the apostle ? Εις το ιλασκεσθαι τας αμαρτιας τν λαυ. " To " make expiation for the sins of the people *."—A righteousness is given you, is not this the scriptural way of speaking ? " They who receive *the gift of* " *righteousness*, shall *reign in life*."—" By which you " have *free access to GOD ;*" is not this both the dialect, and the doctrine of the HOLY GHOST ? " We " have access with confidence (not through our punc- " tual performance of any conditions, but) through " the faith of him ;" by a fiducial reliance on our

LORD's

---

* *Heb.* ii. 17, Εις το ιλασκεσθαι,—*Ad expiare,* i. e. *ut expiaret peccata populi, quibus expiatis, Deus nobis redderetur propitius.*

LORD's most precious obedience, blood, and merit.

"I have seen such terrible effects of this unscriptural way of speaking."—Here I fancy you slip into a little mistake; you forgot the distinction between the *use*, and the *abuse* of a doctrine, a distinction which you can easily make on other occasions. You have doubtless seen people, who use the most scriptural way of speaking, yet act unsuitably to their language; what reflections arose in your mind, and what inference did you draw upon observing such an inconsistency? You said perhaps, "Their voice is *Jacob*'s voice; but "their hands are the hands of *Esau*.—Hence it appears, that they are hypocrites.—They pretend one "thing, and are really another."—Make the same reflection, and draw the same inference, when you hear people talking of *imputed righteousness*, yet see them loosing the reins to ungodliness; then you will be consistent with yourself, and with truth; ascribing the terrible effects, not to the wholesome doctrine, but to the vitiated mind.

Where sin abounded, &c. Mr *Wesley* rejects *Aspasio*'s interpretation of this text, and offers one of his own; one, which he had given us a little while ago; and now serves a second time, without any considerable variation, at our table.—I shall only refer the reader to page 150. where he will find this text considered, and Mr *Wesley*'s exposition canvassed.

In this and the two following paragraphs you find fault with the phrase *imputed;* yet you say, "Concerning the thing there is no question." You would discard that particular form of expression; yet you add, "As to the doctrine we are agreed." Then, according to your own confession, all these your objections are a mere strife of words.—Surely such a man as Mr *Wesley* should know how to make a better use of pen, ink, and paper, than to litigate about letters and syllables.—If I thought myself contending only
about

about the most precisely proper form of expressing the same thing, I should be ashamed of my employ, and would this instant lay down my pen; whereas I apprehend, that we are not agreed as to *doctrine*, that there is a material and very wide difference between us.—My opinion, or rather, my *faith* is, that our LORD's obedience to the moral law in professed submission to its authority, and in exact conformity to its precepts; his performance of all holy duties, and his exercise of all heavenly graces, that all this is a most essential and distinguished part of his merit, that this is of higher dignity and greater value than the whole world, and all the righteousness in it.—That the divine law is hereby more signally honoured, than it could have been honoured by the uninterrupted obedience of *Adam* and all his posterity.—That GOD's justice, holiness, truth, receive greater glory from these unparalleled acts of duty, than from all the services of angels and men in their several wonderful orders; that this *active* righteousness, together with his most meritorious *sufferings*, are the ground and cause of my acceptance with GOD, are the very thing which procures and effects my justification, making me not barely acquitted from guilt, but truly righteous, yea, perfectly righteous, and that before the GOD of infinite penetration and purity.—This is a view of the doctrine, incomparably magnificent and inexpressibly comfortable. If you agree with your friend in all these particulars, speak and write conformably to such agreement; then you will never again hear from him in this manner, neither will he receive any more such favours from you as the letter now under consideration; then we shall be perfectly joined together " in the same mind, and in the same " judgment."

Alas! this union, I fear, is not so easily to be effected.—Mr *Wesley* still insists, and still urges, " The au- " thority of our church (which *Aspasio* pleads) and of " those

" those eminent divines (whose testimony *Aspasio* al-
" ledges), does not touch those particular forms of
" expression."—Justification through imputed righ-
teousness, or being made righteous through the obe-
dience of *CHRIST*, I suppose are the forms of ex-
pression intended. These, it seems, none of the quo-
tations *confirm*, *establish*, no, nor *touch*, in Mr *Wesley's*
opinion at least; but I am inclined to hope, that the
generality of readers will be of a different persuasion,
and allow that the quotations and the expressions
touch and resemble one another, as much as the wings
of the cherubim in the ancient sanctuary *.

" Does not touch." No! not yet? Then we must
have recourse to some other authority; and such a one
I have at hand as you would hardly venture, or even
wish to gainsay; I mean the authority of *John Wesley*,
M. A. who declares, in his exposition of the New
Testament—" This is fully consistent with our being
" justified by the imputation of the righteousness of
" *CHRIST*." Now I shall only remonstrate, in imi-
tation of the apostle; " If thou thyself usest this
" phrase, why wouldst thou compel others to lay it
" aside? Or, why art thou displeased with others,
" for a practice which thou allowest in thyself?"

Surely you will not say, *imputation* of righteousness
is quite a different thing from *imputed* righteousness.
—Does not the former evidently include the latter?
Can there be a proclamation of pardon, without a
pardon proclaimed? Can there be the purchase of
an estate, without an estate purchased; or the impu-
tation of righteousness, without a righteousness im-
puted? If others should affect such subtile and self-
deluding evasions, Mr *Wesley* cannot, Mr *Wesley must
not*, he has precluded himself; nay, he has, with his
own mouth, given a verdict against himself. Is it
not

---

* Both the cherubims were of one measure, and one size:
and their wings touched one another in the midst of the house,
1 *Kings* vi. 25, 27.

not recorded in thofe lines, fubjoined to your character of a methodift?

> *Let faith and love combine*
> *To guard your valiant breaſt;*
> *The plate be righteouſneſs divine,*
> *Imputed and impreſt.*

This *imputed righteouſneſs* was once a delightful theme; your fong in the houſe of your pilgrimage. Why is it now a burthenfome ftone, which you would fain fhake off from yourſelf and others? Are you become *rich* in yourſelf, and *increaſed with goods* of your own acquiring? We know full well for what reafon the *phraſe* and the *doctrine* are rejected, exploded, and reproached by the *Romiſh* fuperftition, becauſe they diſplay, in the brighteft light, the beauty of FREE GRACE. They hold the door againſt all kind of human merit; they cut off every, the moſt diftant pretenfion for glorying in man, and refer all the honour of falvation to *JESUS CHRIST* alone. Admit juftification through the imputed righteoufnefs of *CHRIST*, and the grand bulwark, or the main pillar of *Popery*, falls to the ground? while a ſolid foundation is laid for that triumph and gratitude, expreſſed in the inſpired hymn, *Let us be glad and rejoice* exceedingly, but *give the honour* (all the honour) *to HIM* [*].

The righteoufnefs of GOD, fignifies the righteoufnefs which GOD-man wrought out. " No;" fays Mr *Weſley*. Your reaſon, Sir, for this negative? A child may deny; a man of judgment will difprove.—Does not Mr *Weſley* difprove, when he adds? " It " fignifies GOD's method of juftifying finners."— Juft as forcibly as the " *Jews* difproved the Meffiah- " ſhip of *JESUS* of *Nazareth*, when they cried, " Thou the MESSIAH! No: thou art a *Samaritan*, " and haft a devil." What they alledged wanted a proof, altogether as much as what they denied.—
What

[*] Rev. xix. 7.

What Mr *Wesley* here alledges is a thread-bare objection, already confidered, and already confuted. Yet, since it relates to a point of the utmost moment, and that which is the main hinge of our controverfy, I fhall not be deemed officious, if, as the fhot has been once again difcharged, I once again lift up my fhield againft it.

"The righteoufnefs of GOD fignifies GOD's method of juftifying finners." We have already fhewn how low an interpretation this is; how infipid in itfelf, and incompatible with the current language of fcripture: on the other hand, how fublime and confolatory is the fenfe which *Afpafio* gives! A righteoufnefs which GOD HIMSELF has provided without any co-operation from his creatures:—The righteoufnefs of that moft exalted, yet moft condefcending SAVIOUR, who is GOD and man in one CHRIST; a righteoufnefs, dignified with all the perfections of the GODHEAD, therefore worthy to be the comfort, the joy, the never-ceafing boaft of his people; and fufficient, infinitely fufficient, to fave even the moft vile, the moft bafe, the moft defperately ruined finners.

This is a righteoufnefs, as much fuperior to all human attainments, to all angelic accomplifhments, as the heaven of heavens is higher than a clod of the valleys.—This is a righteoufnefs which could never have entered into the heart of man or angels to conceive, but will be the caufe of their admiration, and the fubject of their wonder to endlefs ages.—This fenfe fully accounts for thofe rapturous expreffions of the prophet, when fpeaking of the all-furpaffing gift, he thus addreffes his fellow-finners; *Rejoice greatly, O daughter of Zion; fhout, O daughter of Jerufalem; behold, thy King cometh unto thee;—he is righteous, and having falvation.* He is completely righteous in his nature, has fulfilled all righteoufnefs in his life and death, and has thereby obtained for thee, a full pardon,

don, a finished salvation, a sure title to eternal glory.
—This accounts for those more rapturous expressions of the sacred writers, when, in the fervour of their gratitude, they call upon the whole creation to celebrate the goodness of the incarnate JEHOVAH. *Sing, O ye heavens, for the LORD hath done it; shout, ye lower parts of the earth: break forth into singing, ye mountains; O forest, and every tree therein; for the LORD hath* (in his own person, by his own obedience and suffering) *redeemed Jacob, and glorified* (not human abilities, not human works but) *himself,* and his own righteousness, *in* the restoration of *Israel* *.

In short, this is a righteousness, which exalts GOD's justice; which magnifies the law, displays all his awful and amiable attributes in their fullest lustre.—To contrive it, was unsearchable wisdom; to bestow it, is invaluable treasure.—It answers, in the completest manner, all the grand and gracious purposes both of GOD's glory and of man's salvation. True gospel this! glad tidings indeed! an expedient for our recovery

very

---

* *If.* xliv. 23. Should any one say, Is this the sense of the prophet? I ask, Is not this the fullest, grandest, divinest sense? Is it not a sense perfectly true? Is it not warranted by the gospel-revelation? Is it not demanded by that declaration of our SAVIOUR; *They* (the ancient scriptures) *testify of me?* Some writers, I am aware, interpret this and other similar passages, without taking in the unspeakable blessings of CHRIST and his grace. But these interpreters seem to act a very injudicious, and no less unfaithful part. I will suppose them expounding and illustrating that great command of creating power, *Let the earth bring forth grass, and the herb yielding seed.*—Will they model their exposition, or fetch their illustration from what appears on the ground in the barren month of *December?* Surely, if they have any taste or judgment, they will form their comment, by the fertility, the plenty, the unbounded luxuriancy of *April* and *May.* There is much the same difference between the righteousness of an incarnate SAVIOUR and all other gifts of divine goodness, as there is between the vegetable productions of the vernal, and the almost total sterility of the wintry months.

very greater than our hearts could wish. We may truly say, while meditating on this gift of confummate righteousness; *Where sin has abounded, grace has much more abounded.* The bricks are fallen down, but the most glorious Repairer of our breaches has built with hewn stone. Well might the apostle, having this supremely-excellent righteousness in his view, look down with the most sovereign contempt upon every other (cause of) confidence; upon every other object of trust; and reckon them *dross* and *dung*.—Well might he declare that he would never be ashamed of the gospel, in which is this transcendently-noble righteousness, in all its magnificence, riches, and glory.

Do you think me rather too warm upon the subject? Let me once again remit you to St *Chrysostom;* read his exposition of that charming sentence, *The righteousness of GOD,* Hom. &c. This venerable father of the church speaks the thing as it is. He does not mingle our wine with water, but gives us the genuine truth, and triumphs because of the truth.

The doctrine of an imputed righteousness seems to have been typically taught, by the remarkable manner of clothing our first parents. All they could do for their own recovery, was like the patched and beggarly mantle of fig-leaves; this they relinquish, and GOD himself furnishes them with apparel; animals are slain, not for food, but sacrifice; and the naked criminals are arrayed with the skins of those slaughtered beasts.—The *victims* figured the expiation made by *CHRIST*'s death, the *cloathing* typified the imputation of his righteousness. "That does not appear," cries Mr *Wesley*. *Aspasio* has produced an authority from the famous *Milton*. I could reinforce it by another from the elegant *Witsius*. If you are not satisfied with either, or both these testimonies, I will give you a reason for the sentiment.—The victims most properly shadowed forth the expiation of guilt, by the Redeemer's blood; becaufe it is the peculiar end of facrifice, to make atonement for fins; the cloathing moſt pertinently denoted the Saviour's righteouſneſs, which is deſcribed, both by the prophet and the apoſtle under this very image—*He hath covered me with the robe of righteouſneſs*, ſays the prophet *Iſaiah*. *The fine linen*, which arrays the bride of the Lamb, *is the perfect righteouſneſs of the ſaints* *.—ſays the beloved diſciple. It is like a royal veſture, or a rich ſuit of apparel, *upon all them that believe*, adds the apoſtle *Paul*. The impartial reader, I promiſe myſelf, will allow theſe paſſages, if not to be abſolutely deciſive, yet to have ſomewhat more weight, than that atom in your ſcale. " This does not appear." As for ſanctification, this may very reaſonably rank among the effects of being cleanſed by the blood, and adorned with the righteouſneſs of *CHRIST*. Theſe bleſſings produce peace of conſcience, and love of GOD. Juſt as commodious cloathing produces warmth, and promotes health. And what is love of GOD, but holineſs of heart in the ſeed, and holineſs of life in the fruit?

As this (the nature of true holineſs) is a matter of the laſt importance; is a point, on which multitudes, I fear, are miſtaken; I will leave it uppermoſt in your thoughts, in the reader's, and in thoſe of, Rev. Sir, your, &c.

LET-

---

* *Rev.* xix. 8. Τα δικαιωματα, being in the plural number, I think may be tranſlated, *juſtitia omnibus numeris abſoluta*. A righteouſneſs of all kinds, and all degrees, or comprehending every kind, and defective in no degree.—Would you ſee the beauty of this fine linen, or the wardrobe in which it is depoſited, conſult, *Iſ.* xlv. 24. *Theron* and *Aſpaſio*, vol. II. * pag. 68. &c. where the paſſage is explained, with copiouſneſs and particularity; O! that it was alſo explained with a propriety and energy ſuitable to its eminent importance!

* i. e. vol. III. in this edition.

LETTER X.

Rev. Sir,

WE are now entering upon a new province. Our business will be chiefly of the *philological* kind. We shall treat principally of *words*. But as they are the words which the HOLY GHOST teacheth, they are like the combs erected in yonder hive. Not empty syllables, made only for sound; but rich with divine sense, and full of the honey of the gospel, replete with the manna of heaven.—May this pen be, to the reader, like *Jonathan*'s rod, when, dipt in the delicious juice, it *enlightened his eyes*, refreshed his spirits, and cheared his heart!

" Almost every text," you are pleased to affirm, " quoted in this and the following letter, in support " of that particular form of expression, (imputed righ- " teousness,) is distorted above measure from the plain, " obvious meaning, which is pointed out by the con- " text."—Let us examine these abused and distorted texts, in order to discover, from whence the misfortune happened; how the violence was done; whether by Mr *Wesley*'s pen, or by *Aspasio*'s tongue.

The first is from the book of *Job*. Which, as it is greatly venerable for its antiquity, and singularly to be regarded for its importance, I shall beg leave to consider at large.—A sinner is described, lying under a dangerous sickness; and brought, by the force of his disease, to the brink of the grave; by the multitude of his sins, to the very borders of hell. In this deplorable condition, *If there be a messenger with him, an interpreter, one of a thousand, to shew unto man his uprightness; then he is gracious unto him, and saith, Deliver him from going down into the pit; I have found a ransom* *.

If

---

* *Job* xxxiii. 23, 24. I have the rather chosen to lay this whole passage before the reader, because a new interpretation

If there be with him a messenger of the living GOD; a faithful ambassador of *CHRIST*, who may administer spiritual assistance to the poor afflicted creature.—*An interpreter*, who knows how to open the scriptures, and rightly to divide the word of truth ; who is a preacher of righteousness, and can properly apply the word of grace.—This is not every one's talent; nor within the compass of every man's abilities. He is *one of a thousand*, to whom GOD hath given the tongue of the learned ; enabling him to speak a word in season, and suit the condition of each respective patient.—*To shew unto man his uprightness;* that is, says Mr *Wesley*, " to convince *him* of GOD's ju- " stice, in so punishing him."

But is this the instruction, which such a distressed sufferer wants? Is this the word of reconciliation, which every true minister, in ancient times, did preach, and in latter times does preach? Or is there any need of a choice instructor,—one skilled in the counsel of GOD, to teach what the common dictates of reason demonstrate?—In this interpretation, I can neither discern the true critic, nor the clear reasoner, nor the sound divine.

Not the *true critic.* He would acknowledge, that the antecedent in this clause יושר אדם, is not GOD, but man. To *man* therefore, if we regard grammatical propriety, the pronoun *his* must be referred.— Not

is given to the word *messenger.* Here, it is supposed to denote a faithful and skilful minister of the gospel. In the dialogues it is supposed to describe our LORD *JESUS CHRIST* himself. I scarcely know, which sense to prefer. Perhaps, both may be included, the author, as well as the instrument, of comfort to the sick and sinful man.—However, the point in debate between Mr *Wesley* and *Aspasio*, is not affected by the different application of this word. *His uprightness*, according to either exposition, *may* signify the MESSIAH's obedience and sufferings; *must* signify these things; provided these are the only justifying righteousness of a sinner ; the only way of obtaining the divine favour, and removing every evil.

Not the *clear reasoner;* he would observe the emphasis of the word *then* *. Implying some discovery, or some conviction, in consequence of which, deliverance from death ensues, or with which it is connected. Can this be a discovery or a conviction of GOD's justice, in punishing him? No verily.—Much less therefore can I discern the *found divine.* He knows, and affirms constantly, that this is the consequence of the MESSIAH's righteousness alone; which, being imputed to the sinner, becomes, for the blessed purpose of justification unto life, *his* †.

So

* Verse 24.

† " *The uprightness,*" says Mr *Caryl,* " chiefly intended " here, is *the righteousness of CHRIST,* in and by which we " are reconciled to and made one with GOD. We never see " where our uprightness is, till we see there is nothing that " makes us stand upright in the court of heaven, but only " *CHRIST* our righteousness.—This is the great duty of the " messengers and interpreters of *CHRIST,* to declare to man " this righteousness for his uprightness. And that hence it is " (as *Elihu* speaks) that G O D is and will be gracious unto " him."

Mr *Caryl,* in expounding the book of *Job,* has acquitted himself like a master in *Israel.* His thoughts are beautiful and animated. His criticisms are correct and judicious. His language, considering the time in which he wrote, is remarkably pure and strong. His doctrines are truly edifying, because, generally speaking, they are evangelical.—What is a very necessary, but very difficult task, in explaining this part of scripture, the connection of the sentiment is discovered, the bearings and dependencies of the argument are pointed out; and the transitions from one passage to another, shewn to be, not wild and disorderly, but just, regular and graceful.

The only fault attending this work, is prolixity. I wish some skilful hand would, by rendering it less copious, render it more useful. I cannot but think, it might be a profitable employ for young students in divinity, to exercise themselves in abridging Mr *Caryl,* Dr *Owen* upon the *Hebrews,* Mr *Charnock* upon the attributes, or some such valuable, but voluminous authors. These, and many other works of the same luxuriant growth, would, if put into the alembic, afford us the very spirit of the gospel, and the richest cordials for our souls.

So that *Aspasio* seems to have the import of language, and the scope of the context, both on his side. And I may venture to add, he has the consolatory genius of the gospel, yet more strongly pleading for his interpretation. It must yield but cold comfort, to tell a poor wretch, confined to the bed of languishing, and alarmed with apprehensions of eternal vengeance; but cold comfort must it yield, to tell such a one, that he has deserved all this misery, and is justly punished. Whereas, to inform him of a righteousness, sufficient to do away all his transgressions; sufficient to reconcile him, and render him acceptable, even to the chastising GOD; sufficient to obtain his deliverance, very probably from death, most assuredly from hell; this is a reviving report indeed. This will make the bones, which sin and misery had broken, to rejoice.

Then, the sinner and the sufferer, attentive to this instruction, and applying this righteousness, is made partaker of pardon. GOD, the sovereign LORD of life and death, *is gracious unto him; and faith*, in the greatness of his strength, as well as in the multitude of his mercies, *Deliver him from going down into the pit* of corruption, as a pledge of his deliverance from the pit of perdition. For *I have found a ransom*, satisfactory to my law, and to my justice. I have received an atonement, in behalf of this once obnoxious, now reconciled transgressor.

He shall receive the blessing from the LORD, and righteousness.—This you will render *holiness*. But have you no *Hebrew* lexicon to inform you, that the word which signifies holiness, is very different from the expression used by the Psalmist? He says רדק׳, whereas holiness is expressed by קדש. Besides, have you not observed, that *your* interpretation would betray the Psalmist into apparent tautology? He had, in the preceding verses, displayed the duties of practical godliness, and the graces of inherent holiness. The

person

person he describes, possesses the latter, and practises the former. To say, therefore, he shall receive holiness, when he has it already, would not suit *David*'s correctness; however it may suit Mr *Wesley*'s fancy, or Mr *Wesley*'s design.—In this clause, the evangelical moralist touches upon another particular, which enters, as an essential part, into the character of a godly man; even *the righteousness which is of faith;* denoted by the blessing of pardon, and the gift of righteousness. Take away this, and there is no acceptance with GOD. Take away this, and the gates, mentioned in the close of the psalm, are unalterably shut. Unless we are furnished with this passport, the everlasting doors never lift up their heads.—If you exclude this peculiarity, the description is very imperfect, and the picture extremely deficient. Whereas, this adds the finishing touch, and gives *true* perfection to both.

Several passages are quoted, in which the word צדקה occurs. Sometimes you would have it signify *mercy;* sometimes *justification;* sometimes *spotless holiness.* But what proof do I find, for establishing any of these significations; which differ so much from one another, and still more from the truth? Nothing but the customary argument, " So it unquestionably " means."—Now you must unquestionably know, at least every novice in the language knows, that the genuine and native sense of צדקה is *righteousness*. The word expressive of mercy, is חמד ; neither in sense nor sound alike.—As to *justification*, the phrase never denotes that blessed effect, but the divine and meritorious cause which produces it.

Shall I, in this inquiry, appeal to the best lexicons, the most approved translations, or the ablest interpreters? No, I will refer you to the decision of an interpreter, who is superior to all lexicons and all translations; I mean, the author of the epistle to the *Hebrews*. He translates this very word, as it enters into the name of *Melchisedec*. And he translates it, not

not mercy, not juftification, no, nor fpotlefs holinefs, but righteoufnefs; even that righteoufnefs, whofe fruit is peace with GOD, and peace in our own confcience. Now, will you play the critic upon this infpired writer? and fay, Unqueftionably it means, not what the apoftle has determined; not what *Afpafio*, fupported by his authority, has adopted; but what I think fit to dictate?

An oppofer of our LORD's imputed righteoufnefs, who had more difcretion or more fubtilty than Mr *Wefley*, would have argued in this manner: " The " original word, I muft confefs, ought to be tranfla- " ted *righteoufnefs*. This is undoubtedly the princi- " pal and leading fignification of the term. But then " the circumftances and the context oblige us to un- " derftand it, in the notion of mercy, of fpotlefs ho- " linefs, or of any thing elfe that ferves our purpofe." —This would be more modeft and more plaufible, tho' not more juft and folid, than your confident affertion.

Suppofe we fhould admit this pretence, what does the critic gain thereby? Muft he not have recourfe to that noble and comfortable doctrine, for which we plead? Let the word be tranflated *mercy*. Why is mercy fhewn to finners? Is it not on account of the righteoufnefs of their SURETY? Let it be tranflated *goodnefs*. Wherefore is goodnefs exercifed to rebellious men? Is it not becaufe of the fatisfaction made by their crucified LORD? Render it whatever you pleafe, provided it conveys the idea of favour vouchfafed, or of the benefits conferred, it muft terminate, ftill terminate, in that grand central point, the incarnation, obedience, and death of IMMANUEL.

Zion fhall be redeemed with judgment—" After fevere " punifhment," you fay,—The *Hebrew* prepofition, fignifying *after*, is אחר. I find no trace of any fuch word in my edition of the Bible. You may as well render or interpret the paffage, *in the midft*. And then, if fome other critic fhould be inclined to tranflate

late it, *before* or *round about;* we should have a large compass of meaning; but where would precision and exactness be found?—But why is *Zion* to be redeemed *after* severe punishment? Has her punishment any influence or sway in the work of her redemption? Does the punishment of man pave the way for the salvation of GOD? Are sinners to wait for pardon and reconciliation, till they have been severely punished? This is very discouraging doctrine; and, blessed be GOD, it is absolutely without foundation. The gospel says, *To-day, even to-day,* sinners, *if ye will hear his voice, ye shall enter into rest.* You need not tarry till you have been severely chastised; but this instant believe in the *LORD JESUS,* and you shall be saved. The *LORD JESUS* has been wounded and bruised in your stead. He has received all the punishment which you have deserved. Yea, as a ransomer, he has paid double, as a victim, he has suffered double *, for all your sins.—Considering these things, I am still disposed to abide by *Aspasio's* plain and obvious interpretation; not to go out of my way, in quest of the pricking brier and grieving thorn, when I meet with roses and lilies in the common road.

In the LORD have I righteousness. This will not satisfy our critic. It must be *through* the LORD.— What piddling criticism is this, even in case it was true, and answered some specious end! But it is by no means true. Every body knows, that the prefix ב signifies *in;* and every body but Mr *Wesley* would blush to assert the contrary. Neither does it answer any valuable end, but the reverse. It degrades the exalted sense, and impoverishes the rich blessing. To have righteousness *in* the LORD, is abundantly more expressive of glorious grace, than barely to have righteousness *through* the LORD. *Mordecai* had riches and honours *thro' Ahasuerus,* and his royal favour; *Esther* had riches and honours *in Ahasuerus,* as her

royal

* If. xl. 2.

royal husband; *he* by being a courtier, *she* by being a consort to the most magnificent monarch in the world.

If Mr *Wesley* piddled in the foregoing, he flashes in the following passage. He assures us that עולמים פין means *spotless holiness*. This is really a bold stroke in criticism. But, like many other bold enterprises, it is likely to prove, not a birth, but an abortion.— עולמים *spotless!* You might as well have rendered it *toothless*. It has no more to do with the idea of spotless, than it has to do with the idea of an ivory tooth, or a polished tooth-pick. Literally translated, it signifies *ages;* and may denote the *perpetuity* of this righteousness, and of its beneficial effects. It *was* from the beginning, it *is* at this day, and it *will be* even unto the end, mighty to save. It is the one refuge and hope of sinners, in every age of the world, and under every dispensation of religion. Thro' all the changes of time it has been, and thro' the unchangeable eternity it will be their chief joy, and their crown of rejoicing.

What righteousness shall give us peace at the last day, inherent or imputed? To this question *Aspasio* has replied, in a very explicit manner, by presenting us with a pertinent extract from *Bishop Hall*, and by commenting upon a most important prophecy of *Isaiah*. In both which, all human righteousness is set aside, and our peace is derived entirely from the glorious SHILOH *; from him, who made peace by the blood of his cross, and whose name is THE PRINCE OF PEACE; having this heavenly blessing, and the right of conferring it, as the peculiar privilege, or unshared prerogative of his crown.

Mr *Wesley* is pleased to deny this doctrine, and to associate

---

* Gen. xlix. 10. שילה *Schilo. Nomen Messiæ peculiare, tranquillatorem designans.* That is, the maker of peace, and the author of tranquillity, for rebellious and wretched men.

associate with the Papists *, in ascribing our peace (and if our peace, then our salvation) "partly to in-"herent, partly to imputed righteousness."—But does our church so? Hear her own words. " We do "not presume to come to this thy table, O merciful "LORD, trusting in our own righteousness;" much less then will she dare to approach his judgment-seat, trusting in any such thing.—Does the apostle *Paul* do so? Hear his own protestation, *That I may be found in CHRIST, not having mine own righteousness, which is of the law;* which consists of my personal obedience, and inherent holiness; but having this, as the source of my peace, and the strength of my salvation, *the righteousness which is of GOD by faith*; even that inconceivably precious righteousness, which GOD my SAVIOUR wrought, and which a sinner by faith receives.—Did Mr *Wesley* himself always do so? Let those lines bear witness; of which neither the poet nor the divine need be ashamed.

My righteous servant, and my S O N,
 Shall each believing sinner clear;
And all who stoop t'abjure their own,
 Shall in his righteousness appear.

Will that righteousness give you peace, which you abjure? Or, is it pious, is it prudent, is it consistent, to trust in a righteousness, which you absolutely renounce? That which you abjure (a stronger word could not be used) you consider, not barely, as despicable, but as utterly abominable. Whereas, that which gives you peace at the awful tribunal, must
not

* The doctrine of the Papists, avowed by a writer of their own, is; " Our confidence and hope in the day of judgment "dependeth, not only upon our apprehension of CHRIST's "merits by faith, but also upon our conformity to CHRIST, "in charity and good works."—The reader may see this presumption rebuked, and this error refuted, in Dr FULK's *anno- tations on the Rhemish Testament*. 1 John iv. 17.

not only be excellent, but incomparably excellent and valuable.—See, my friend, how *thine own mouth condemneth thee, and not I* : yea, *thine own lips teſtify againſt thee* *. O ! that you may return to your firſt ſentiments, and to your firſt love † ! and no longer expoſe yourſelf and your doctrine to be a by-word among the people. If you perſiſt in ſuch palpable inconſiſtencies, who can forbear taking up that taunting proverb, *A double-minded man is unſtable in all his ways ?*

But

* Job xv. 6.

† That Mr *Wesley* may not be aſhamed to retract a miſtaken ſentiment, I will break the ice, and lead the way. If it be ſhameful to renounce error, and ſacrifice all to truth, I do very willingly take this ſhame to myſelf.—In a copy of verſes, which I formerly wrote, ſacred to the memory of a generous benefactor, I remember the following lines :

Our wants reliev'd by thy indulgent care,
Shall give thee courage at the dreadful bar.
And ſtud the crown thou ſhalt for ever wear.

Theſe lines, in whatever hands they are lodged, and whatever elſe, of a like kind, may have dropt from my pen, I now publicly diſclaim. They are the very reverſe of my preſent belief. In which I hope to perſevere, ſo long as I have any being.

Far be it from me to ſuppoſe, that any work of mine ſhould, in order to create my peace, or cheriſh my confidence, *be coupled with CHRIST's moſt holy act.* I ſpeak the words of our church, and I ſpeak the ſenſe of the prophet. *I will truſt, and not be afraid.* Wherefore ? Becauſe I am inherently holy ? Rather, *becauſe GOD is my ſalvation.* GOD manifeſt in the fleſh, has finiſhed my tranſgreſſion, and made an end of my ſin. And in this moſt magnificently-gracious work will I rejoice. I ſpeak agreeably to the declaration of the HOLY GHOST. *Fear not, for thou ſhalt not be aſhamed, neither ſhalt thou be confounded.* Why ? becauſe thy inherent goodneſs ſhall prevent thy confuſion ? No; but on a footing, infinitely more ſolid ; for a reaſon, infinitely more ſatisfactory. *Becauſe thy MAKER is thy huſband.* The conſequence of which is, all thy debts and deficiencies are upon him ; all his conſummate righteouſneſs is upon thee.

But stop. A passage from St *John* is introduced, to support this opinion. "*CHRIST* died for us, "and lives in us, *that we may have boldness in the* "*day of judgment.*"—That *CHRIST* died for us, and lives in us, I readily acknowledge: but where do you find any of the apostles, from these premises, drawing *your* conclusion? St *John*, whom you quote, has no such logic. His inference is deduced from a very different topic. You give us a fragment of the apostle's words; why don't you exhibit the golden bowl complete? We shall then quickly perceive, that it contains a more sweet and salutary draught, than you have provided for our refreshment.

Ἐν τουτο τετελειωται η αγαπη μεθ' ημων, ινα παρρησιαν εχωμεν εν τη ημερα κρισεως.
Which we translate, *Herein is our love made perfect, that we may have boldness in the day of judgment* *. As you are fond of criticising upon the original scriptures, here you might have done it justly and honourably. Here you might have altered and reformed our translation; while every capable judge would have owned your service to be seasonable and important. The true sense of μεθ' ημων is *with us*, or *with regard to us*. That is, GOD's love, celebrated with inimitable † energy and beauty in the preceding verse; GOD's love towards us is herein made perfect; this is its grand and crowning effect, that we should have, not a bare hope, but an unappalled boldness at the day of judgment.

As

* 1 John iv. 17.

† Ὁ Θεος αγαπη εστιν, *God is love.* This I call *inimitable*. Nothing can be more simple, yet nothing is more sublime. For my part, I know not how to attempt an illustration of the noble sentiment. It strikes the mind, as light strikes the eye. No art can make *this* more bright; and no paraphrase can make *that* more delicate, more majestic, more affecting.—How flat some of the finest things said by the ancient philosophers; how flat they read, when compared with this animated stroke of divine eloquence, the reader, if he pleases, may see, in CONTEMPLATIONS ON THE STARRY HEAVENS.

As though he had said, GOD having reconciled us to himself, by the blood of his SON;—having renewed us after his own image, by his blessed SPIRIT, testifying of CHRIST in our hearts;—having carried us through all the dangers of life, and raised our bodies from the dust of death; he crowns and consummates all these most indulgent acts of his grace, by giving us an undaunted and triumphant confidence, at the day of universal audit. According to this interpretation, your own text is against your opinion; and refers this joyful assurance, not to our love of GOD, but to his love of us; not to inherent righteousness, but to free grace *.

Aspasio thus translates St *Peter's* words; *Who have obtained like precious faith in the righteousness of our GOD and our SAVIOUR JESUS CHRIST* †. Mr *Wesley* gives us to understand, that this translation is wrong. It should be faith *through*—and not through the righteousness, but through the *mercy* of our GOD and SAVIOUR.—He will not allow the *Greek* preposition ἐν to signify *in*; though I can prove it to have been in peaceable possession of this signification, for more than two thousand years. And the substantive δικαιοσύνη must not denote *righteousness*, though it pleads, as a warrant for this weighty sense, the incontestible authority of St *Paul*. Give me leave to tell you, Sir, that I can produce a multitude of proofs, to overthrow your first puny alteration; but produce, if you can, a single passage from the whole New Testament

* Should it be said, in case you thus interpret the first part of the text, how will it connect with what follows? Perfectly well.—And none need wonder, that we shall appear with such boldness at his coming: since they cannot but observe, that *as he is, so are we in this world*. We are actuated by his SPIRIT; we resemble him in all our conversation; and hence it is evident, that we are one with him.

† 2 *Pet.* i. 1. Τοῖς ἰσότιμον ἡμῖν λαχοῦσι πίστιν ἐν δικαιοσύνῃ τοῦ Θεοῦ ἡμῶν ἐ σωτῆρος ἡμῶν Ἰησοῦ Χριστοῦ.

Testament *, to uphold your last daring innovation.

Here I cannot but observe, you abandon your favourite commentator *Bengelius;* of whose merit and excellence you speak so highly and so justly. He says, in his notes upon the place, The righteousness of GOD our SAVIOUR, is the righteousness of *CHRIST;* which faith apprehends, and which is opposed to a man's own righteousness.—What is more surprising, you depart from your own comment; nay, you expressly contradict your own comment. To edify the readers of your exposition, you inform and assure them, that this phrase signifies " both the active " and passive righteousness" of *CHRIST.* To gainsay what *Aspasio* has advanced, you more than insinuate, that it signifies no such thing, but only " the " mercy of our LORD,"—Nay, to corroborate the true sense, and determine the words invariably to the active and passive righteousness of *CHRIST,* you add, " It is this alone by which the justice of GOD is sa- " tisfied." If then Mr *Wesley* would reconcile what he writes in his expository notes, with what he writes in his animadversions on *Aspasio,* he must maintain, that by the *mercy* of GOD alone, his justice is satisfied.

I will not exclaim, on this occasion, as you have too freely and not very genteelly done, in your letter to Mr *Law,* " Exquisite nonsense †!" But this I may venture

---

* *The righteousness of GOD, the righteousness of GOD our SAVIOUR,* never denotes, in all the apostolical writings, the attribute of *mercy.* If it does, and Mr *Wesley* can make it appear, I will confess myself mistaken, and thank him for correcting my error.

† Mr *Wesley,* in the *abridgment* of his letter to Mr *Law,* inserted in the *Preservative from unsettled notions,* has expunged this and some other indecently-harsh expressions. In so doing, he has done well. Since the *contemptuous* and the *reproachful,* even when really deserved, can have no tendency to confirm our argument, but to provoke resentment. They

venture to say, Contradiction, didst thou ever know so trusty a friend, or so faithful a devotee? Many people are ready enough to contradict others. But it seems all one to this gentleman, whether it be another or himself, so he may but contradict.

Permit me, for a moment, seriously to expostulate the case. Why should you be so averse to the righteousness of our GOD and SAVIOUR? Why should you ransack all the stores of your learning and knowledge; nay, descend to unwarrantable criticisms, and quite unworthy your superior abilities, in order to exclude this most glorious truth from the Bible? in order to exterminate this most precious privilege from the church? Attempt, if you think proper, to pluck the sun from the firmament, to hide the light from our eyes, and withdraw the air from our lungs. But do not attempt to rob us of what is far more valuable than all these blessings, by depriving us of this inestimable treasure, the righteousness of *CHRIST*.—Which, being a righteousness immaculate, all-surpassing, divine, swallows up and annihilates our guilt; as the immense waves of the ocean would swallow up and annihilate the drop of ink, that now hangs on the point of my pen.—Which, being a righteousness immaculate, all-surpassing, divine, will present us before our GOD, and before his angels, without spot and blemish; in robes more beautiful than the colours of that resplendent bow, which is bended on the skirts of yonder cloud.

Therein *is revealed the righteousness of GOD;—* " GOD's method of justifying sinners." See this interpretation examined, and this objection answered before.

We establish the law, as we expect no salvation, without

are not the most promising means of joining us together, in the same mind and the same judgment; but rather the sure way, to widen the breach, and increase animosity.

without a perfect conformity to it *,—namely, by *CHRIST*. " Is not this a mere quibble?" says Mr *Wesley*.—Quite the reverse. It is no *low conceit*, but an exceeding serious and momentous truth. It is no play upon the *sound* of words, but expresses a doctrine of great solidity, and of the last importance. Tell me, ye that cavil at this method of establishing the law, by what other expedient you propose to effect it?—By your past conduct? That, you must acknowledge, has been more or less a violation of the law.—By the present obedience? That, you cannot deny, falls short of the sublime requirements of the law.—By your future behaviour? Well, I will suppose, that, in some future period, you reach the very summit of perfection. Still the law will have much to complain of, and will lay much to your charge. You have not magnified it by a holy nature. You have not presented it with the consummate righteousness of your whole heart, and your whole conversation. You have not begun, from the first moment of your existence, and persevered in this perfect conformity, to the last breath you drew. In this case, either the law must recede from its most righteous demands, and the immutable GOD must compromise matters with his creatures, or else you can never enter into life. *Unless* you renounce all such impotent attempts, and arrogant conceits; talk no more of " practising it, in " its full extent," but betake yourself to *CHRIST*, *who is the end of the law* †, *for accomplishing* that

righ-

* The reader is desired to peruse *Aspasio*'s own words, vol. III. pag. 92, 93. There his sentiments are more fully explained; but the passage is not transcribed, on purpose to avoid increasing the size of this piece; which already swells to a larger bulk than the writer proposed.

† *Rom.* x. 8. *CHRISTUS*, faith, *Bengelius, est* τελος νομο, *justitiam et vitam, quam lex ostendit, sed dare nequit, tribuens. CHRIST* is the end of the law. How? By bringing in that righteousness

righteousness, which its precepts demand, but which the frailty of man cannot perform.

Thus we establish the law, as the consummate standard of righteousness; as the original condition of life; and as that most venerable system, with which, as well as with its divine Author, there is no variableness or shadow of changing.—And does this method of securing the dignity of the law, hinder or discourage a dutiful observance of its commands? If not, your objection derived from that well-known text, *Without holiness no man shall see the* LORD, is

— — *telum imbelle sine ictu.*

If this be the most rational, and the most sure way of producing the love of GOD, which is the very essence of true holiness, then your objection recoils, and falls upon the head of your own cause.—Can there be a more powerful, a more endearing motive to love the LORD my GOD, than a persuasion of his ineffable love to me, in giving his dear SON, so to fulfil, so to satisfy the law on my behalf, that I am thereby delivered from all my offences; am vested with a perfect righteousness; and on the foot of justice, as well as mercy, stand entitled to eternal life?

"Though I believe, that *CHRIST* hath *lived* and " *died* for me, yet I would speak very tenderly and " sparingly of the former."—How widely then does your practice differ from the apostle's? *We believe, and therefore have spoken*, confidently and incessantly, in season, and out of season. No, says Mr *Wesley*, " We

righteousness, and giving that life, which the law shews, and shews the want of, but neither itself gives, nor can enable us to acquire.

CHRISTUS, saith St *Augustine*, *est legis finis, interficiens & perficiens.* The ceremonial law he has slain, and taken out of the way. The moral law he has fulfilled for us, and we in him. Inasmuch as, through faith in his name, his obedience becometh ours.

"We believe, and therefore we speak tenderly and
"sparingly."—If you believe, that *CHRIST* has
lived for you, and fulfilled all righteousness in your
stead, surely you should give him the honour of this
wonderful loving-kindness, and both preach, and talk,
and sing of his goodness. It should be as a fire shut
up in your bones; and you should speak, that your-
self may be refreshed, and your LORD may be glo-
rified.

But you "fear dreadful consequences:" What!
where the divine holiness fears none; and the divine
prescience sees none? Are you then more deep-sight-
ed, to discern these distant evils, than omniscience?
Methinks, I would not have spoken thus, unless I had
been wiser than the SPIRIT of inspiration.—Do
you not, by cherishing and avowing such apprehen-
sions, find fault with the glorious gospel, in which
this righteousness is revealed? revealed, as its most
eminent article, and most distinguishing peculiarity?
—A doctrine taught, and a blessing granted, and
both from heaven! yet not fit to be displayed, incul-
cated, and insisted on! What a contemptible idea must
this give of our holy religion, and of our holy reve-
lation, to an inquiring infidel?

"I would never speak of them (the active and pas-
"sive righteousness of *CHRIST*) separately."—This
insinuates, what *Aspasio* disavows; and what you can-
not hint, without apparent injustice to his sentiments.
—"I would speak of it (the former) as sparingly as
"do the scriptures." Here you appeal to those wri-
tings, which must either condemn your conduct, or
their own propriety. At your leisure consider the
case, and you will find the dilemma unavoidable.—In
the mean time, be so candid as to read a short note,
inserted in *Theron* and *Aspasio*, vol. III. pag. 115;
where you may see, that the scriptures are far from
speaking sparingly on this point. It is their favourite
and

and fundamental topic. It runs through them, as a golden woof through a warp of silver; or as the vital blood through the animal structure.—And whatever *you*, Sir, may be inclined to do, I hope no lover of *CHRIST* will be persuaded to secrete this invaluable truth of the gospel. Shall *such* a truth skulk in a corner, or speak only in a whisper? No; let us proclaim it upon the house-tops; and wish, that the joyful sound may reach the very ends of the earth.

The gift of righteousness must signify a righteousness not their own.—*Aspasio*'s expression is, not *originally* their own. Originally he said, with a view of hinting, that, in some other sense, it was and is their own; their own, by way of imputation, though not by way of operation. This word, in order to make the sentence appear absurd, Mr *Wesley* drops. But whether such a practice be free from guile, or what the apostle calls *cunning craftiness*, let the impartial reader judge.

Aspasio's interpretation of the phrase, authenticated by the language of scripture, Mr *Wesley* sets aside; and introduces another, whose only recommendation to the public is, " I come from *Wesley*'s pen."— Do you so? then we will allow you all proper regard. But because you come from Mr *Wesley*'s pen, must you therefore displace propriety, and supplant truth? make an inspired writer argue incorrectly, nay, jar with himself? This is rather too much for you to assume, even though you came recommended by a greater name.

" The gift of righteousness, signifies the righteous-
" ness or holiness which GOD gives to and works
" in them." Let us observe the apostle's aim, and the process of his reasoning.—His aim is to illustrate the manner of our justification. For this purpose, he forms a contrast between *Adam*'s transgression, and *CHRIST*'s obedience. *Adam*'s transgression, which he himself committed, ruins all that spring from him.

This

This is the leading propofition, Now, if the facred difputant knows how to reafon accurately, or to draw a conclufion juftly, the conclufion muft be to this effect; fo likewife *CHRIST*'s obedience which he himfelf performed, recovers all who believe in him. Through *Adam*'s difobedience, without the confideration of their own mifdoings, the former are made finners; through *CHRIST*'s obedience, without the confideration of their own good qualities; the latter are made righteous.—Though I am far, very far from difefteeming the holinefs wrought in us, yet what place has it here? In the article of juftification it is utterly excluded. It has no fhare in the accomplifhment of that great work; and every attentive reader will fee, that it enters not into the apoftle's prefent argumentation.—Befides, if the gift of righteoufnefs fignifies the holinefs wrought in us, then we fhall reign in life, by means of a perfonal, not of an imputed righteoufnefs, by means of an imperfect, not of a complete obedience.—Then all the people of GOD will be juftified, not by the obedience of ONE, but each by his own, feverally and diftinctly. Which is contrary, not only to a fingle, but to many exprefs paffages of this very chapter.

I faid, " Every attentive reader will fee."—Some perhaps may fay within themfelves, Is not this fpoken in Mr *Wefley*'s manner? the loofe prefumptive way of arguing, which you blame in him?—To which it is anfwered, I am far from refting my point upon this prefumptive proof: it is not the pillar which fupports my caufe; but only a feftoon which adorns my pillar.—However, was it accompanied with no proofs fatisfactory to others; it muft to Mr *Wefley*, whom I fuppofe one of the attentive readers, have the force of demonftration. Hear his own words, in his comment on this very portion of fcripture: " As the fin of *A-*
" *dam*, without the fins which we afterwards com-
" mitted, brought us death; fo the righteoufnefs of
" *CHRIST*,

"*CHRIST*, without the good works which we af-
"terwards perform, brings us life *."—It is a righ-
teoufnefs without the good works which we after-
wards perform; therefore it is a righteoufnefs, not o-
riginally our own, but another's. It is not that which
GOD works in us, but prior to it, and independent
on it. If *Afpafio* had fuborned an evidence, and put
words into his mouth, he could not have devifed a
more direct and full confirmation of his doctrine,
than this volunteer witnefs depofeth.—I thank you,
Sir, for giving me fo valuable an explanation of the
gift of righteoufnefs, and its bleffed effects. I thank
you likewife for furnifhing *Afpafio* with fo inconteft-
able a vindication againft the objections of the author
of *The Pefervative*.

The obedience of ONE, fo highly extolled by the
apoftle, is *CHRIST*'s actual performance of the
whole law.—This you deny. I wifh you had favour-
ed me with your reafons for this denial; but my wifh-
es of this kind are conftantly difappointed. However,
I will follow our LORD's direction, and do unto o-
thers, even as I would they fhould do unto me. I
will give you a reafon for my own or *Afpafio*'s inter-
pretation.—The apoftle is treating of *Adam*'s actual
breach of the law. If fo, the proper antithefis muft
be *CHRIST*'s actual performance of the law.—In
the following verfes he explains himfelf. Let *them* be
the comment on our text, and the gift of righteouf-
nefs means, *the righteoufnefs of ONE; the obedience
of ONE.* This righteoufnefs we have in *JESUS
CHRIST* our LORD; all other is inherent in our-
felves. Juftification by this righteoufnefs, is alone
confiftent with free grace; juftification by any other,
is (inconfiftent with it, is) fubverfive of it.

Farther, as you are a critic in the *Greek*, you need
not

---

* Here Mr *Wefley* fpeaks in perfect agreement with St
Chryfoftom; Ο Χριϛος τοις εξ αυτȣ, και᷉οιγε ȣ δικαιοπραγησασι, γιγονε πρεξε᷉ε-
ται δικαιοσυνης.

not be informed, that St *Paul* uses three several words, δικαιωμα, δικαιοσυνη, υπακοη. Now can you shew any passages, in which all these words are used to signify sufferings or death? Nay, can you shew me any single passage, in which any one of them occurs in this signification? If you cannot, what shadow of authority have you, for putting this construction upon the words, in the present case? What shadow of authority for saying, with that unlimited confidence, *CHRIST*'s "dying for man, is *certainly* the *chief* part, if not the "*whole* which is meant by that expression * ?"—If you attend to the tenor of the apostle's argument, or inquire into the import of his language, perhaps you will see cause, not only to alter, but even to reverse, this your positive assertion.

Let me subjoin an extract from St *Chrysostom*, suited to this and the preceding paragraph; and worthy of our serious consideration. From which it will appear, that *Aspasio* is by no means singular in his sentiments, but speaks the doctrine of the ancient church.

Τυτῷ ἐςιν Ιησυ Χριςυ ο Αδαμ· πως τυτῷ, φησιν; ὁτι ωσπερ ικηνῷ τοις ιξ αυτυ, καιτοιγε μη φαγυσιν απο τυ ξυλυ, γιγονεν αιτιῷ θαναtυ τυ δια την βρωσιν εισαχ- θεντῷ, υτω ξ ο Χριςῷ τοις ιξ αυτυ, καιτοιγε κ δικαιοπραγησασι, γιγονε προξενος † δικαιοσυνης, ην δια τυ ςαυρυ πασιν ημιν εχαρισατο· δια τυτο αιω ξ καtω τυ ΕΝΟΣ εχιται, ξ συνεχως τυτο τις μεσον φερει λεγων, ὡσπερ δι' ΕΝΟΣ ανθρωπυ η αμαρ- τια εις τον κοσμον εισηλθε· ξ, ιν τω τυ ΕΝΟΣ παραπτωματι οἱ πολλοι απεθανον·
                                                                                    &.

* The obedience of one, St *Chrysostom* expounds by, τοs κα- τορθωσαντος. Would Mr *Wesley* venture to affirm, that *dying well*, not *doing well*, is *certainly* the chief thing signified in κατορθωσαντος? A pretty daring criticism this! Does not the word rather signify, a course of well-doing; terminated (if you please) in, not constituted by, a correspondent death?

† Προξενος, an expressive word; it seems to denote such a procuring of righteousness for sinners, as corresponds with the provision made, by some hospitable housholder, for the strangers who are come to be his guests. In which they bear no part, either of the expence, or of the trouble. Προξενα σοι τυτο, *Hujus rei sum tibi auctor; hanc rem tibi comparo.* Steph. Thesaur. in voc.

ξ, Ουχ ως δι' ΕΝΟΣ αμαρτησαντος, το δωρημα ξ. Το κριμα εξ ΕΝΟΣ εις κατα κριμα ξ παλιν, Ει γαρ τω τη ΕΝΟΣ παραπτωματι ο θανατος εβασιλευσε δια τω ενος ξ, Αρα ως δι' ΕΝΟΣ παραπτωματος ξ παλιν, Ωσπερ δια της παρακοης τυ ΕΝΟΣ ανθρωπυ αμαρτωλοι κατεσαθησαν οι πολλοι· ξ υκ εριταται τυ ΕΝΟΣ, ιν' οταν λεγη σοι ο Ιυδαιος, πως, την καταρθωσαντος τυ Χριςυ, η οικυμενη εσωθη; δυνηθης αυτω λεγειν, πως, τνος παρακυσαντος τυ Αδαμ, η οικυμενη κατεκριθη*.

That the righteoufnefs of the law might be fulfilled in us. That is, by our reprefentative, and in our nature.—" Amazing!" cries Mr *Wefley*. But why amazing? Is not this the common import of the moft common actions? Do not you and I make laws in and by our reprefentatives in parliament? May not every

debtor,

* *Chryfoft. tom*. III. pag. 71, 72. *Edit. Savil*. " *Adam* is a
" type of *CHRIST*. How ? In this refpect; as the former
" was the caufe of death to all his defcendents, though they
" did not (like him) eat of the forbidden fruit; fo *CHRIST*
" is the caufe (προξενος) author, procurer of righteoufnefs to all
" his feed, though they have not (like him) been perfonally
" obedient; even of that righteoufnefs, which he finifhed for
" us on the crofs. For this reafon,—*to afcertain and appropri-*
" *ate the honour of this righteoufnefs to CHRIST; as a work*,
" *not wrought by us, nor wrought in us, but completed for us*
" *on the curfed tree*.—He infifts and dwells upon that very ob-
" fervable circumftance. *One*. He iterates and reiterates the
" emphatical word ONE. He introduces it again and again,
" and can hardly prevail upon himfelf to difcontinue the re-
" petition, As by *one man* fin entered into the world—Thro'
" the offence of *one* many be dead—Not as it was by *one* that
" finned, fo is the free gift—The judgment was by *one* to
" condemnation—By *one* man's offence death reigned by *one*
" —As by the offence of *one*, judgment came upon all men
" unto condemnation—As by the difobedience of *one* many
" were made finners.—Thus does the apoftle again and again
" introduce the word ONE, and can hardly prevail on him-
" felf to difcontinue the repetition. That if a *Jew* fhould afk,
" How can the world be faved by the well-doing of one, or
" by the obedience of *CHRIST?* You may be able to reply
" on his own principle, How could the world be condemned
" by the evil-doing of one; or by the difobedience of *Adam?*

debtor, when his surety has given full satisfaction to the creditor, say, I have satisfied, I have paid, in my bondsman?

To invalidate this interpretation, you alledge, that the apostle "is not speaking here of the *cause* of our "justification, but the *fruits* of it." Among all the excellent things, which, in your studies and in your travels, you have learned; have you never learned, that between saying and proving there is a wide difference? Never did I meet with a person, who seemed so totally ignorant of this very obvious truth. —Well; we must take your word, without proof; but I hope, not without examination. "The apostle "is speaking of the fruit." Is then the fulfilling of the law the fruit of justification? This is the first time, I apprehend, that any such thing was deliberately affirmed. It is the cause, the adequate, the immediate, and indeed the only proper cause of justification. But the fruits are peace of conscience, and love of GOD; the spirit of adoption, and the hope of glory.

Shew me, Sir, where *δικαιωμα*, in conjunction with *τυ νομυ*, signifies the fruits of justification; and not those demands of the law, which must necessarily be satisfied before justification can take place.—Especially; when the phrase is corroborated by that other strong expression, *πληρωθη*. An expression used by our LORD concerning himself, and the design of his coming into the world. Applicable to him alone, who is the end of the law for righteousness; and descriptive of that obedience, by which alone the law is magnified.

This sense, says *Aspasio*, agrees with the tenor of the apostle's arguing. "Not here;" replies Mr *Wesley*.—Let us then consider the aim, and trace the progress of the apostle's reasoning. He is clearing up and confirming that great privilege of the gospel, *There is no condemnation to them that are in JESUS CHRIST*. This, you will allow, is not the fruit of justification, but justification itself. As this wants no argument to confirm it, let us proceed in our attention to the sacred writer. There is no condemnation to those who are true believers in *JESUS CHRIST;* who, in consequence of this belief, walk not after the flesh, but after the SPIRIT.

Perhaps, some man will say, How can this be? since even true believers fall short. Nay, they offend, and therefore must be liable to the curse.—*For* this reason, they are delivered from condemnation; because *the law of the SPIRIT of life in CHRIST JESUS*, that new dispensation, introduced in the room of the old law, promises the privilege of pardon, and the gift of the SPIRIT; in which things the true life and real happiness of mankind consist: promises both freely, without any works, purely on account of the righteousness which is in *CHRIST JESUS*. And hereby this new, gracious, blessed dispensation, *hath made me free from the law;* which convinced me of *sin;* condemned me for sin; and bound me over unto *death*.

These are glad tidings, doubtless; but are they not attended with two inconveniencies? Does not this procedure deprive the law of its due honour, and screen the sinner from his deserved punishment?—By no means. *For that which was an absolute impossibility, on account of the* strictness *of the law, and the weakness of human nature,* GOD, to whom nothing is impossible, *has* most wonderfully *accomplished; by sending his own SON, in the likeness of sinful flesh,* to live among sinners; to come under their obligations, *and* perform the obedience demanded from them; by sending him also to be a sacrifice *for sin;* to be charged with its guilt, and undergo its punishment. By this grand expedient, he has provided for the honour and perfect accomplishment of the law. He has also *condemned* and punished *sin*, with the utmost severity.

And

And both thefe *in the flefh;* in that very nature which was guilty, difabled, ruined,

Should you farther afk, Wherefore is all this? To lay the fureft foundation, or make the moft complete provifion for our juftification. *That the righteoufnefs of the law* both its righteous fentence and its righteous precepts, whatever either of fuffering or of obedience it required from tranfgreffors, being fulfilled in *CHRIST, might be fulfilled in us;* as it was all done in our name; and as he and we are one; one in civil eftimation, for he is our Reprefentative; one in legal eftimation, for he is our Surety; one in focial eftimation, for he is our Bridegroom. For which caufe, his righteous acts are ours, and his atoning death is ours.

There was a time, when you embraced thefe fentiments; when you had fuch views of things; when fuch language came out of your mouth, which even now ftands upon record, under your own hand. See your " Principles of a Methodift." If you have forgotten them, permit me to remind you of them. " *CHRIST*," you fay, " is now the righteoufnefs " of all them that truly believe in him. He for them " paid the ranfom by his death; he for them fulfilled " the law in his life. So that now, in him and by " him, every believer may be called a fulfiller of the " law."—Since you pronounce *my* fenfe of the apoftle's words unnatural, I adopt, I efpoufe *yours* *; and fo much the more readily, as it will puzzle fagacity itfelf, to difcern a difference between them.

" I totally deny the criticifm on δικαιοσυνη and δικαιωμα." Then be fo good as to fuggeft a better. Or, if this fhould be fomewhat difficult, at leaft favour us with a

reafon

---

* Should Mr *Wefley* fay, Though I ufed thefe words, I never intended them for a comment on this paffage.—If you did not, I imagine, the compilers of our homilies, from whom they are taken, did. At leaft they regarded this text as a foundation, a warrant, a proof of their doctrine.

reason for this your total denial. Not a word of either. Strange! that a man of ordinary difcernment, fhould offer to obtrude upon the public fuch a multitude of naked, unfupported, magifterial affertions! fhould ever be ableto perfuade himfelf, that a pofitive air will pafs for demonftration, or fupply the place of argument! If this be to demonftrate, if this be to confute, the idiot is as capable of both as the philofopher.—May I not cry out, in your own ftrain? O how deep an averfion to the imputed righteoufnefs of *CHRIST* does this *Arminian* fcheme difcover! fince it will make a man gainfay, when he knows not why, or wherefore.

St *Paul* declares, that *the Gentiles who followed not after righteoufnefs, had attained unto righteoufnefs.* Upon which *Afpafio* obferves, that the righteoufnefs here mentioned, could not be any perfonal righteoufnefs. To which Mr *Wefley* replies, " It was." And to render his reply quite irrefiftible, a perfect thunderbolt in argumentation; he adds, " *Certainly*, it was." —How, Sir! did they attain perfonal righteoufnefs without feeking after it? Are *you* becoming a *Calvinift?* you that had rather be an Atheift? Could the zealot of *Geneva* go greater lengths?—*Afpafio* will not deny, that thefe Gentiles were fanctified, as well as juftified; but he will venture to affirm, that no degree of fanctification can make the perfons righteous, who are once become finners. *CHRIST*, like *Elijah*, firft cafts his mantle over them; and then, like *Elifha*, they forfake all and follow him.

The righteoufnefs which the Gentiles attained, could not be a perfonal righteoufnefs. " Certainly it was." —Then it was the righteoufnefs of the law; whereas, the righteoufnefs which they attained, is exprefsly faid to be *the righteoufnefs of faith.*—Then it was a righteoufnefs confifting of good works and godly tempers. Whereas, their righteoufnefs confifted in believing according to the apoftle's own explanation.

With

With the heart man believeth unto righteousness. Then it was the righteousness of man. Personal righteousness and implanted holiness pass, in the scriptures, under that denomination. Whereas, these Gentiles *submitted themselves to the righteousness of GOD.*—If what these Gentiles attained had been a personal righteousness, it would have been no stumbling-block to the *Jews.* Even they would have fallen in with such a system of religion, as should ascribe righteousness and salvation to their own duties and their own deeds.

You say, " It was *implanted,* as well as *imputed.*" Here, then, you acknowledge an imputed righteousness. You yourself use the phrase. You affirm it to be, if not the whole, part, at least, of the apostle's doctrine. I wish you had been of this mind when you began your letter. Then you would not have conjured me, by all that is venerable and important, to discontinue an expression, which conveys—your own—the apostle's meaning—and the meaning of the HOLY GHOST.

You join imputed and implanted righteousness. So, in case this address to yourself should pass through the printer's hand, would I join a handsome type and pertinent reasoning. Yet, I apprehend, when you sit down to examine the essay, you will regard only the latter.—What you associate, you associate properly. The first is the trunk, the last is one of the branches which spring from it; but the apostle seems, in the place before us, to be considering the first only. The last he reserves for some future occasion.—He is speaking of the righteousness, by which we are saved; and that is solely the imputed righteousness of *CHRIST.* —He is speaking of the righteousness, which was an eye-sore and an offence to the self-conceited *Jews;* and this was only the imputed righteousness of *CHRIST.*—He is speaking of a righteousness, contradistinguished to that righteousness which is described by *he that doth these things;* and this can be nothing

thing else, but the imputed righteousness of *CHRIST*.—Therefore, though love of GOD, and conformity to his image; though the pure heart, and the devout affection; are the inseparable concomitants, or rather the genuine produce of imputed righteousness; yet here they come not under consideration. To force them into this passage, is to make them appear out of due season. Such an exposition may bespeak a zealous officiousness, not a distinguishing judgment; because it confounds the order of the apostle's plan; it defeats the design of his argument, if it does not introduce self-contradiction into his arguing.

This righteousness came upon the Gentiles, *as the former and latter rain upon the earth.* To them was fulfilled the word spoken by the prophet *Isaiah; Let the skies pour down righteousness.* As the earth engendereth not the rain; has not the least influence in forming, or the least agency in procuring the refreshing showers; but only receiveth them, as the mere gift of Providence; so these Gentiles had not the least influence in effecting, nor the least agency in procuring this righteousness.—When the good news came into their territories, they were totally destitute of it; they were utterly unconcerned about it; they knew nothing at all concerning it. But seeing it revealed in the gospel; seeing it displayed as the work of GOD, and hearing it offered, as the gift of GOD, they were not disobedient to the heavenly invitation. They believed the report, they accepted the blessing, and relied upon it for life and salvation.—Then, *as the rain coming down and the snow from heaven, returneth not thither again, but watereth the earth, and maketh it bring forth and bud; that it may give seed to the sower, and bread to the eater;* so, this inestimable truth being admitted into the soul, *CHRIST*, and his righteousness, being received to dwell in the heart *; all the powers

of

---

* Eph. iii. 17.

of intellectual nature, or what St *Paul* calls *the inner man*, are exhilarated, quickened, and fructified. They bud as the rose, and blossom as the lily; they bring forth the fruits of inward love, of outward obedience, of universal godliness.

For instruction in righteousness, in the righteousness of *CHRIST*. "Was there ever such a comment before?" May I not answer, in your own words, Was there ever such a method of confutation used before?—But you add, "The plain meaning is, *for training up in holiness* of heart and of life." I wish you had thought of introducing this interpretation, by the following short preface, "I take it for granted." You would then have been sure of saying *one* truth.—But if this does not appear plain to me, as you see it did not to *Aspasio*, methinks, you should lend me your spectacles, or favour me with your reasons.

If you please to examine the passage, you will find holiness of heart and life, comprehended in one of the preceding expressions. Πρὸς ἐπανόρθωσιν signifies, For restoration of the man to a state of moral uprightness; which must include a renovation of the mind, and a reformation of the conduct. After this comes, very properly, and without any tautology, very needfully, and to the exceeding comfort of the sinner, another most valuable property of the scriptures. They instruct the reader in the *Christian righteousness;* in the justifying righteousness; in that mysterious, but incomparably-precious righteousness, which no other book in the world displays, mentions, or so much as hints. Yet, without which, we could never stand in the judgment, never find acceptance with GOD, nor be admitted into the realms of glory.—If you reject this sense, the apostle's character of the sacred volumes is very defective; it leaves out what is their supreme excellence, and most distinguishing peculiarity; what is first, and above all other things necessary for our fallen

fallen race.—A traveller undertakes to give an account of some celebrated picture-gallery. He describes the dimensions of the structure, the form of the windows, the ornaments of the roof; but he quite forgets, at least, he totally omits, the article of the paintings. Is this a masterly execution of his design? is this satisfactory to the hearer's curiosity?

He shall convince the world of righteousness—" That " I am not a sinner, but innocent and holy." How flat and jejune is this exposition! Nothing can be more so, to my taste.—" Innocent and holy!" Is this all the SPIRIT witnesses, concerning the most adorable and infinitely-deserving SON of GOD? Does this come up to the inconceivable dignity of his person, and the immensely glorious perfection of his work? Is this sufficient to comfort the conscience, smitten with a sense of most damnable guilt, and alarmed with the terrors of eternal vengeance?

The whole clause contains a platform or summary of evangelical truth; of that all-important truth, which ministers are to teach and preach; which the HOLY SPIRIT will own and accompany with his influence; and which is thereby made the power of GOD to the salvation of the hearers.—He shall convince the world *of sin;* of the guilty and miserable state, in which all mankind are plunged by nature; and in which every individual person continues, so long as he is destitute of an interest in *CHRIST,* so long as he believeth not in HIM who died upon the cross, and is gone to the FATHER.—Of *righteousness;* he shall reveal the REDEEMER's most perfect and magnificent righteousness in their hearts. That righteousness, which satisfies the justice of the MOST HIGH, and brings complete redemption to transgressors. Testifying, not barely, that he is innocent; such was *Adam* in Paradise: not barely that he is holy; such are angels in heaven. Shall the eternal CREATOR, even after his humiliation unto

death,

death, have no higher a teftimony than a fet of mere creatures? Yes, verily; the HOLY GHOST will convince the world, that CHRIST's righteoufnefs is the grand and capital bleffing, which the prophets foretold; and which not only fulfils, but magnifies the law. That it is the righteoufnefs, the very righteoufnefs of the incarnate JEHOVAH; and therefore renders every foul, to whom it is imputed, unblameable, unreprovable, complete. Glorious office this! worthy to be the object of the almighty COMFORTER's agency! in performing which, he adminifters ftrong confolation.—Then he fhall convince of *judgment;* fhall condemn and caft out the prince of this world, introducing a moft happy change into the heart and life; fhall begin and carry on the work of grace, fanctification, obedience; and all, through the joyful knowledge, together with the perfonal appropriation, of this juftifying righteoufnefs.

That we might be made the righteoufnefs of GOD in him. Which cannot be intrinfically, but muft be imputatively.—This interpretation *Afpafio* eftablifhes, attempts, at leaft, to eftablifh from the tenor of the context, from the apoftle's antithefis, and from feveral venerable names. But what are all thefe to Mr *Wefley?* No more than the arrow and the fpear to *leviathan.* Nay, not fo much. That fcaly monfter *efteemeth iron as ftraw, and brafs as rotten wood.* But Mr *Wefley,* cafed in his own felf-fufficiency, efteemeth all the aforementioned evidences as mere nothings. He totally difregards them. Reafon, grammar, precedents, are eclipfed by his bare negative, and vanifh into an infignificancy, not worthy of notice.

When *Afpafio,* fupported by fuch great authority, fays, This cannot be intrinfically, but muft be imputatively; Mr *Wefley,* fupported by his greater felf, replies, "Both the one and the other."—But does he duly advert to the apoftle's fubject, or follow the clue of the context? The *fubject* is reconciliation to GOD,

GOD, justification before GOD, or *that*, whatever it be, which is implied in not imputing trespasses. The *context* intimates, that intrinsic holiness is not yet taken into consideration, but is reserved for the next chapter. There the apostle exhorts the *Corinthians*, *not to receive this* infinitely-rich *grace* of free justification, *in vain;* but to shew its efficacy, to shew its excellency, and recommend it to the unbelieving world, by an unblameable conversation, *giving no offence in any thing.*

Justification then is the only point which the apostle, in this passage, considers; and justification is the fruit of imputed righteousness solely, not of inherent righteousness in any degree. This we must allow, unless we prefer the impositions of *Trent,* before the confession of our church. " Faith says unto us, It is not I " that take away your sins, but *CHRIST* only ; " and to him only I send you for that purpose, for- " saking therein all your good words, thoughts, and " works, and only putting your trust in *CHRIST.*" Thus speaks, and thus teaches, our reformed church. —" If any one say, that man is justified only by the " imputation of *CHRIST*'s righteousness, or only " by the remission of sins, without the co-operation " of inherent grace and holy love, let him be accur- " sed *." Thus dogmatizes, and thus anathematizes, that mother of falsehoods.—Chuse now your side. For my part, I renounce and abjure the proud and iniquitous decree. If you persist in your present opinion, there will be an apparent harmony between yourself and *Rome,* but an essential difference between yourself and *Aspasio.*

" GOD, *thro' him,* first *accounts,* and then *makes* " us righteous." How ? Does GOD account us righteous, before he makes us so ? Then his judgment is not according to truth. Then he reckons us to be righteous,

* *Si quis dixerit, hominem justificari, vel sola imputatione justitiæ, vel sola remissione peccatorum, exclusa gratia et charitate, anathema esto.* Sess. vi. can. 11.

righteous, when we are really otherwise. Is not this the language of your doctrine? this the unavoidable consequence of your notion? But how harsh, if not horrid, does it sound in every ear? Is not this absolutely irreconcileable with our ideas of the supreme BEING, and equally incompatible with the dictates of scripture? There we are taught that *GOD justifieth the ungodly.*—Mark the words. *The ungodly* are the objects of the divine justification. But can he account the ungodly righteous? Impossible!—How then does he act? He first makes them righteous *.—After what manner? By imputing to them the righteousness of his dear SON.—Then he pronounces them righteous, and most truly. He treats them as righteous, and most justly. In short, then he absolves them from guilt; adopts them for his children; and makes them heirs of his eternal kingdom.—In the grand transaction, thus regulated, mercy and truth meet together. All proceeds in the most harmonious and beautiful consistency, with the several attributes of GOD; with his whole revealed will; and with all his righteous law.

"*The righteousness which is of GOD by faith*, is "both *imputed* and *inherent*."—Then it is like interweaving linen and woollen; the motely mixture forbidden to the *Israelites*. Or rather, like weaving a thread of the finest gold, with a hempen cord or a spider's web.—The righteousness which is of GOD, is perfect, consummate, everlasting. Not so inherent righteousness, your own self being judge, and your own pen being witness.—In the righteousness which is of GOD, the apostle desires to be found, before the great and terrible tribunal of the LORD. His own righteousness, or the righteousness which is inherent, he

---

* Agreeable to this, our church speaks; *In justification, of unjust we are made just before GOD; and adds, This is the strong rock and foundation of Christian religion.* Hom. of Justif. part 2.

he abandons, as abfolutely improper for this great purpofe; being no more fitted to give him boldnefs at the day of judgment, than dung and filth are fit to introduce a perfon, with credit and dignity, to court.—The righteoufnefs which is of GOD is unknown to reafon; is revealed from heaven; and without the works of the law. Whereas, the righteoufnefs inherent, is difcoverable by reafon; was known to the Heathens; and confifts in a conformity of heart and life to the precepts of the law.—By the latter, we act, we obey, and offer our fpiritual facrifices unto GOD. By the former, we work nothing; we render nothing unto GOD, but only receive of his grace.

They are, therefore, not the fame, but totally diftinct. To blend and confound them, betrays unfkilfulnefs in the word of righteoufnefs; derogates from the honour of *CHRIST*, and tends to cherifh a legal frame, or, what the fcripture calls, *a fpirit of bondage.*—If you would approve yourfelf a workman, that need not be afhamed, rightly dividing the word of truth, thus you fhould fpeak, and thus you fhould write; the righteoufnefs of GOD is always imputed. But, being imputed, it produces the righteoufnefs inherent. Being juftified by the former, faved from hell, and rendered meet for heaven; we are fanctified alfo, and difpofed to love the LORD, who has dealt fo bountifully with us; and if to love, then to worfhip him, to ferve him, to imitate him.

My faith fixes on both the *meritorious life* and *atoning death of CHRIST.* " Here we clearly agree."—How can you clearly agree, either with *Afpafio,* or with yourfelf, or with common fenfe?—How with *Afpafio?* Since you queftion, in direct contrariety to his fentiments, whether the death of *CHRIST* be not the whole of what St *Paul* ftyles *the obedience* of ONE.—How with *yourfelf?* For did you not declare, a little

a little while ago, that fallen man " is not juſtified by
" perfect obedience ? Is not *CHRIST*'s meritori-
ous life perfect obedience ? If your faith fixes on this
perfect obedience, is it not for the purpoſe of juſtifi-
cation ?—How with *common ſenſe?* Since you ſuppoſe,
that the " ſcripture aſcribes the whole of our ſalva-
" tion to the death of *CHRIST,*" ſo entirely aſcribes
it to the death of *CHRIST*, that " there was no
" need of his fulfilling the moral law, in order to
" purchaſe redemption for us ;" what reaſon, or ſha-
dow of reaſon can you have, to fix upon what *we* call
the merit of his life? If what you ſuppoſe and affirm
be true, there was no kind of meritorious efficacy in
his life. His life and all his labours were, in this re-
ſpect, a mere ſuperfluity. Salvation might have been
obtained, and redemption purchaſed, without their
concurrence. Therefore to fix upon them, is to fix
upon a phantom, and to reſt your hopes upon *a thing
of nought*.

But ſtay. Am I not repeating the miſconduct,
which proved ſo fatal to the famous Earl of *Warwick*,
and his forces ? At the battle of *Gladmore*, while the
ſcale of victory hung in ſuſpenſe, they ſaw a conſider-
able body of troops advancing. Suppoſing them to
be enemies, the bowman made a general diſcharge,
and galled them with their arrows. But they ſoon
perceived their miſtake ; that they had been oppoſing
their friends, and annoying their allies. Perhaps, by
this time, you are become my ally. You may have
ſeen your errors ; may have corrected your notions ;
ſaying, in ratification of both, " We agree."

That is, " I would no longer exclude the merito-
" rious obedience of *CHRIST*. But this, together
" with his atoning death, I look upon as the only
" cauſe of my juſtification.—This I call his righteouſ-
" neſs ; and this, being imputed to me, becomes my
" plea, my portion, and rational foundation for my
" everlaſting felicity.—This I receive by faith ; which

"I now look upon, not as conſtituting any part of
"my recommendation, but only as receptive of the
"fulneſs laid up for me in *CHRIST*.—Though
"the law of works faith, Do and live; I am now
"made ſenſible, that the law of faith ſays, Be verily
"perſuaded, that *CHRIST* is ſufficient for thy ac-
"ceptance, without any doing of thy own at all.—
"Since *CHRIST* is given to me in the ſacred re-
"cord, given to me as a ſinner, to be received with-
"out any conditions, I joyfully accept the gift. I am
"ſatisfied with his doing and ſuffering: they are di-
"vinely excellent, and infinitely ſufficient: I neither
"wiſh for, nor think of any thing more, to obtain
"my complete ſalvation.—This way of ſalvation ef-
"fectually excludes boaſting; and at the ſame time
"produces thoſe deſirable effects,—that love of GOD;
"that delight in his perfections; that conformity to
"his will; which the law of works requires in vain."

If this is what you mean by "We agree," I would
ſeal and ratify the agreement, with the laſt wiſh, and
the laſt words of the celebrated Father *Paul*, *Eſto per-
petua*. Be this the caſe, and you ſhall have not only
the right hand of fellowſhip, but the right hand of
pre-eminence.—Only I crave one favour in return.
Diſmiſs thoſe injurious inſinuations, which cauſe your
readers to ſuſpect, that *Aſpaſio* conſiders the meritori-
ous life of *CHRIST*, ſeparate from his atoning death.
Whereas, he affirms them to be inſeparable, like the
correſpondence of motion between the two eyes. Try
if you can make one of your eyes move to the right,
while the other wheels off to the left. When you
have done this, then, and not till then, may you have
ſome reaſonable pretence for theſe your ſuggeſtions.

Alas! *quanta de ſpe decidi!* I find my hopes were
too ſanguine. We are not come to the deſired coali-
tion. In this very paragraph, you begin to fly off.
By talking of imputed righteouſneſs, you tell us,
"We are expoſed to an exceeding great hazard; even
"the

"the hazard of living and dying without holiness."
—Pray, Sir, have you seen a little piece written upon this subject by the Rev. Mr *Witherspoon?* If you have not, let me recommend it to your perusal. In case you are ignorant of that powerful influence, which justification through the righteousness of *CHRIST* has upon sanctification and true holiness, from this treatise you may learn some valuable knowledge. In case the author of this treatise is mistaken, in maintaining the indissoluble connection of justification with true godliness; and the never-failing efficacy of the REDEEMER's righteousness, to bring forth willing obedience in the believer; you may have an opportunity of rectifying his sentiments. You may give us, in your next publication, a preservative, not only against *unsettled*, but against *unsound* notions in religion.

Theron, speaking of *gems,* says, when nicely polished, and prodigal of their lustre, they stand candidates for a seat on the *virtuous* fair-one's breast.—This displeases Mr *Wesley.* Would he then have gems placed on the *vitious* or lascivious breast? Or would he have them put to no use at all, but buried in darkness? Did the ALMIGHTY pour such a brilliancy upon them, only that they might be consigned over to obscurity? Did he not rather array them with lustre and with charms, that they might display something of his own brightness; incite his rational creatures to admire his transcendent excellency, and teach his faithful people to apprehend the emphasis of that animating promise, *They shall be mine, in the day that I make up my jewels.*

"I can't reconcile this with St *Paul.* He says, *not* "*with pearls;* by a parity of reason, not with dia- "monds."—Do you rightly understand St *Paul?* Don't you dwindle his manly and noble idea, into a meanness and littleness of sense? such as befits the superstitious and contracted spirit of a hermit, rather than the generous and exalted temper of a believer;

who *stands fast in the liberty, wherewith* CHRIST *hath made him free?*—Our LORD says not, they that are *splendidly apparelled*, are apparelled unsuitably to Christianity, or in a manner inconsistent with the fear of GOD; but they *are in kings courts*, and their dress is adapted to their station. Neither does St. *Paul* forbid the *use* of pearls, or costly array, when a person's circumstances will afford them, and his situation in life may require them. He rather cautions against the *abuse*, against looking upon these glittering things, as any part of their true dignity, on which they value themselves, or by which they would be recommended to others. The word is not ενδυσασθαι, *put on* *, nor φορειν, *wear* †, but κοσμειν, *adorn*. "Let them not " place their excellency in such mean distinctions; " no, nor covet to distinguish themselves by these " superficial decorations; but rather by the substan-" tial ornaments of real godliness, and good works; " which will render both them and their religion " truly amiable."

The apostle *Peter* observes the same propriety of speech, and the same correctness of sentiment. *Whose adorning, let it not be that outward adorning of wearing of gold, or plaiting the hair, or putting on of apparel.* Was this an absolute prohibition of the several particulars mentioned, it would forbid all kind of cloathing, or the putting on of any apparel. Take the passage in your rigorous sense, and it concludes as forcibly against garments, as against ornaments; we must even go naked, and lay aside our cloaths, as well as our gems. Whereas, understood according to the natural signification of the words (ως ο κοσμος, not ως το ενδυμα) it conveys a very important, and a very seasonable exhortation; " Christians, scorn to borrow your re-" commendations from the needle, the loom, or the " toy-shop. This may be the fashion of a vain world.

But

* Mark vi. 9. † Matth. xi. 8.

"But let your embellishments, or that which beautifies and distinguishes your character, be of a superior nature. Let it be *internal;* not such as the sheep have wore, or the silk-worms spun; but such as is peculiar to the immortal mind, or *the hidden man of the heart.* Let it be *substantial;* not such as the moth corrodes, or such as perishes in using; but *that which is not corruptible;* which being planted on earth, will be transplanted into heaven, and being sown in time, will flourish to eternity.—Let it be that adorning, whose excellency is unquestionable, and *whose praise is of* GOD, even *the ornament of a meek and quiet spirit:* which will render you, not indeed like the grandees of the earth, but like the SON of the HIGHEST; shewing, that you are united to him; interested in him; and partakers of his divine nature."

"In all things, I perceive, you are too favourable, both to *the desire of the flesh, and the desire of the eye.*"
—I rather think, Mr *Wesley* is too censorious of others, and too indulgent to himself. Why may not *Theron* wear his richly-embossed gold watch, and his lady use her golden buckle set with diamonds, as well as you and I wear a silver buckle *, or make use of our silver watch? Why may not an earl or a countess † put on

I i 2 their

---

* That Mr *Wesley* may not suspect I am pleading for self-indulgence, I will give him my word, that I have never wore my silver buckles, since I was in mourning for his *Royal Highness.* Neither shall I have one uneasy thought, if I never put them on again.

† Should it be said, the persons to whom St *Peter* wrote, were in mean circumstances; therefore such grandees are out of the question. I answer, The persons *for* whom St *Peter* wrote, were all Christians to the very end of the world. Among these, though there may not be *many* grand, nor many noble, yet, blessed be GOD, there are *some.* And when these go to receive their celestial crown, we trust, it will be said,

—— *Uno ablato non deficit alter aureus.*

their robes, sumptuous with embroidery, or their coronet, glittering with jewels, as inoffensively, as you and I put on a beaver-hat, or trail after us a prunella gown? There is no necessity for this our sprucenefs. A fustian jacket would keep our backs warm, and a flannel cap our heads, as well as our more elegant array.—Methinks, therefore, we should either abstain from all needless finery in our own dress, or else forbear to censure it in others. Rather, we should all, in our respective stations, and according to our respective circumstances, use these things as not abusing them; remembering, that the fashion of this world passeth away. Looking therefore for that city of the living GOD, *whose wall is of jasper, whose buildings are of pure gold, and whose foundations are garnished with all manner of precious stones;* but whose external splendor is infinitely surpassed by the glory of GOD, which lightens it, and by the presence of the LAMB, which is the light thereof.—When we are blessed with clear apprehensions of this ineffable glory which shall be revealed; when we live under a delightful persuasion, that GOD hath given to us this eternal life; gems will have but little lustre in our eye, and less and less allurements for our heart. All the pomp of this transient world will appear to us, as the palace of *Versailles*, or the gardens of *Stowe*, would appear to some superior being; who, from an exalted stand in æther, should contemplate the terraqueous globe; and at one view take in its vast dimensions, its prodigious revolutions, and its most copious furniture.

"You are a gentle casuist as to every self-indul"gence, which a plentiful fortune can furnish."—I would consider the end for which these things were created, and point out and enforce their proper improvements. They were created, not to tantalize, but to treat us; not to ensnare, but to gratify us. *Then* they are properly improved, when we enjoy them with moderation, and render them instruments of usefulness;

fulness; when they are regarded as pregnant tokens of our CREATOR's love, and act as endearing incitements of our gratitude.—What you call my casuistry, is built upon a maxim, which will never be controverted; *Every creature of GOD is good, if received with thankſgiving.* It is nothing elſe, but an attempt to diſplay what is affirmed in the former clauſe, and to enforce what is preſcribed in the latter.

In the ſixth letter, in the ninth, and in other parts, *Theron* enumerates ſome of the fineſt productions, and moſt choice accommodations which the earth, the air, the ſeas afford.—In imitation of the apoſtle, who in one ſentence expreſſes abundantly more, than my three volumes contain; *HE giveth us all things richly to enjoy.*—In imitation of the Pſalmiſt alſo, who, in ſeveral of his hymns, eſpecially in *Pſalm* civ. celebrates the profuſe munificence of JEHOVAH; profuſe, even in temporal bleſſings, and with regard to our animal nature.—Does our nature call for ſomething to ſupport it? Here is *bread, which ſtrengthens man's heart*, and is the ſtaff of his life. Does our nature go farther, and covet ſomething to pleaſe it? Here is *wine, that maketh glad the heart of man;* regaling his palate, and exhilarating his ſpirits. Is our nature yet more craving, and deſirous of ſomething to beautify it? Here is *oil, that maketh the face to ſhine;* that the countenance may appear both chearful and amiable; that gaiety may ſparkle in the eye, while beauty glows in the cheek.—Now I cannot perſuade myſelf, nor is all Mr *Wesley*'s rhetoric powerful enough to convince me, that it is any diſcredit or any error to follow ſuch examples.

" But I mention the exquiſite reliſh of *turbot*, and " the deliciouſneſs of *ſturgeon*. And are not ſuch ob-" ſervations beneath the dignity of a miniſter of " *CHRIST?*" Mr *Wesley* does not obſerve from whom theſe remarks proceed. Not from *Aſpaſio*, but *Theron*. To make *him* ſpeak like a miniſter of
CHRIST,

CHRIST, or like a Christian of the first rank, would be entirely out of character. It would have betrayed an utter ignorance, or a total disregard of *Horace*'s rule;

Reddere personæ scit convenientia cuique.

However, I am willing to take all upon myself, and be responsible for the obnoxious sentiments. I would only ask, Is any thing spoken of, which the ALMIGHTY has not made? and shall I think it beneath my dignity, to magnify the work of his hands? Is any thing spoken of, which the ALMIGHTY has not bestowed? and shall I think it a diminution of my character, to acknowledge the various gifts of his bounty? Has GOD most high thought it worthy of his infinite majesty, to endue the creatures with such pleasing qualities, as render them a delicious entertainment to our appetites? and shall I reckon it a mean unbecoming employ, to bear witness to this condescending indulgence of the DEITY?—Particularity in recounting benefits, is seldom deemed a fault. It comes under no such denomination, in *my* system of ethics. If Mr *Wesley* has a better, in which neglect and insensibility are ranked among the virtues, I must undoubtedly, upon those principles, drop my plea. Where *they* are commendable, my conduct must be inexcusable; and if inexcusable, I fear, irreclaimable. For I shall never be ashamed to take a fish, a fowl, or a fruit in my hand, and say, "A present this from "our all-bountiful CREATOR! See its beauty, "taste its sweetness, admire its excellency, and love "and adore the great Benefactor. To us he hath "freely granted these, and other delights; though "he himself, in the days of his flesh, had gall to eat, "and vinegar to drink."

"But the mentioning these in such a manner, is a "strong encouragement of luxury and sensuality."
—If,

—If, to enumerate a *few* of these dainties*, be a strong encouragement to luxury, how much more, to create them *all*, and clothe them with such inviting properties, and recommend them by such delicate attractives?—But " the mentioning them in such a " manner." What! Is this an encouragement to sensuality? to mention them as so many instances of divine beneficence, and so many motives to human gratitude? This, methinks, is the way to prevent the abuse of our animal enjoyments, and to correct their pernicious tendency. This is the way to endear their adorable GIVER, and render them incentives to love. And the love of GOD is a better guard against luxury, a better preservative from sensuality, than all the rigid rules of the cloyster or monastery.

Upon the whole, however well-affected Mr *Wesley* may be to our civil, he seems to be a kind of malecontent with regard to our spiritual liberties; those I mean, which are consigned over to us in the *Magna Charta* of the gospel.

We have liberty, through *JESUS CHRIST*, to use not one only, but every creature of GOD; and to use them in a *sanctified* manner, so that they shall not sensualize our affections, but refine and exalt them, by knitting our hearts more inseparably to their munificent CREATOR. According to that clause in the heavenly deed, *All things are yours*. This you would curtail and diminish.

We have liberty to look upon ourselves as justified before GOD, without any works of our own; made perfectly righteous in his sight, without any personal obedience whatever; entirely through our Representative and Surety, what he has suffered in our name and in our stead. According to those gracious declarations, *In the LORD have I righteousness*; and, *By the obedience of ONE shall many be made righteous*. This you would supersede and abolish.

We

---

* The scripture calls them, *royal dainties*, Gen. xlix. 20.

We have liberty to claim and receive this unspeakable privilege, without performing any conditions, or seeking any pre-requisites; having no other qualification, than that of being lost sinners, and needing no other warrant than the divine grant, made and recorded in the word of the gospel. According to that most generous invitation, *Come, buy wine and buy milk, without money and without price.* According to that most gratuitous concession, *Whoever will, let him take of the water of life freely.* This you would clog and embarrass.

We have liberty through our LORD's atonement, to look upon ourselves as made free from all guilt; to consider our sins, as absolutely blotted out, never to appear again, either to our utter condemnation, or to our least confusion.

The three first articles of the charge, I think, are made clear, too clear and undeniable, in the course of the preceding letters. Should you challenge me to prove the last, I refer you to your assize-sermon. There you tell us, that the sins of true believers, as well as of unbelievers, will be brought to light, and exposed before the whole world, at the day of universal judgment.

Here, I must do you the justice to acknowledge, that you have not, as in your epistolary animadversions on *Aspasio*, required your audience to assent, merely because you affirm. You attempt to establish your opinion by the authority of *Solomon; GOD shall bring every work into judgment, with every secret thing, whether it be good, or whether it be evil.* But you seem to forget, that the sins of the believer are τα μη οντα, *things that are not.* CHRIST *has blotted out, as a thick cloud, our transgressions; yea, as a thin cloud our sins* *.—Consider them as moral stains, or

causes

---

* *Is.* xliv. 22. עָב *Nubes.* עָנָן *Nubecula.* Thus *Houbigant* translates the words; and, I think, very justly. The first

seems

causes of defilement; they are washed away by the blood of *JESUS*. And surely the blood of GOD must have as powerful an effect on our souls, as the waters of *Jordan* had upon *Naaman*'s body *.—Consider them as contracting guilt, or deserving punishment; they are vacated; they are disannulled; and, like the scape-goat, dismissed into the pathless inaccessible wilderness; *when sought for, they shall not be found*.—Consider them in either of these respects, or under any other character; and they are, not only covered or secreted, but abolished. Just as the darkness of the night is abolished, by the splendor of this clear, serene, delightful morning.

Bring to our sight, if you can, the millstone that is cast into the depths of the sea. Restore, to its former consistence, the cloud that is dissolved in rain; or find one dreg of filthiness in the new-fallen snow. Then may those iniquities be brought again into notice, which have been done away by the High Priest of our profession; which have been expiated by the perfect, most effectual, and glorious oblation of himself.—His people, when rising from the bed of death, will *have no more conscience of sin* in themselves. They are fully and for ever free from the accusation of others; so free, that sin shall not so much as be mentioned unto them; no, nor even remembered by the LORD their GOD any more. They are made holy, unblameable, and unreprovable in his sight. And they shall be presented, at the great day, without spot or wrinkle, or any such thing.

Thus may we, and thus may our readers, be presented! so shall we meet each other with comfort at the

---

seems to denote an immense arrangement of clouds, covering the sky. The second signifies a loose detached fragment, floating in the upper regions. The first fixed like a vault; the last sailing like a skiff. This sense diversifies the prophet's imagery; and, instead of tautology, presents us with a beautiful gradation.   * 2 Kings v. 14.

the awful tribunal, with joy amidst the angels of light, and with everlasting transport around the throne of the LAMB.—To promote this blessed event, is the sole aim of these remonstrances, and the unfeigned desire of,   Rev. Sir, Your, &c.

LETTER XI.

REV. SIR,

MY last concluded with a sketch of our Christian *liberty*, extracted from the *charter* of the gospel. We have liberty—to use all the creatures, and in a sanctified manner—to consider ourselves, as made perfectly righteous, through the obedience of CHRIST —to receive this grand prerogative, without performing any conditions,—to look upon all our sins, as totally and finally done away, through the blood of JESUS.

Perhaps you will ask, Where is your liberty from the *power* of sin? Does not this come within the extent of your charter? Most certainly. You injure our doctrine, if you deny it: we are undone irreparably, if we continue destitute of it. Every other immunity, without this crowning privilege, would be like the magnificent palace and the beautiful gardens of Pharaoh; while swarms of locusts filled them with their loathed intrusion.

But observe, Sir; freedom from the dominion of sin, is the result of all the preceding blessings. By revealing these in our hearts, and CHRIST the author of them, the HOLY SPIRIT acts as the SPIRIT of liberty. You are a philosopher; you understand the theory of light. From the association of various rays, or the mixture of many *parent-colours*, springs that first of elements, and best of material gifts, *light*. So, from the union, and united enjoyment of all those heavenly treasures, springs that most desirable

desirable liberty, the *liberty of righteousness.* 'This is that truth which makes us free. This is that knowledge, by which we are renewed after the image of HIM that created us. And these are the exceeding precious promises, by which we are partakers of the divine nature. Hence we are taught to love the LORD our GOD, and to delight in his adorable perfections. By this means, they look with a smiling aspect upon us, and are unspeakably amiable to us. Under such views, we say of sin, we say of all our evil and corrupt affections, *Do not I hate them, O LORD, that hate thee? and am I not grieved with those that rise up against thee? I hate them with a perfect hatred; I count them mine enemies.*

Our SAVIOUR's obedience. This phrase disgusts Mr *Wesley*. Therefore he cries, " O say, with the " good old Puritans, our SAVIOUR's *death* and *me-*" *rits.*"—*Aspasio* speaks with St *Paul*, *By the obedience of one.*—He speaks with St *Peter*, *Faith in the righteousness of our GOD and SAVIOUR.*—He speaks with the prophets *Isaiah* and *Jeremiah*, *In the LORD have I righteousness;* and, *JEHOVAH is our righteousness.*—Having these precedents, he need not be very solicitous, who else is for him, or who is against him.

Though not very solicitous about this matter, he is somewhat surprised at your vehement address; that you should exhort him so earnestly to " speak with " the good old Puritans." Has not your printer committed a mistake? Did not the clause stand thus in your manuscript? " With my good friends the *Armi-*" *nians.*" They indeed disapprove this expression; because it is, when rightly understood, a dagger in the heart of their cause.—But as to the Puritans, they are, one and all, on the contrary side. Their language is a perfect union with *Aspasio's*. They glory in the meritorious obedience of their great MEDIATOR. They extol his imputed righteousness in almost every page, and pour contempt upon all other works, compared

pared with their LORD's.—What will not an author affirm, who ventures to affirm or infinuate that the Puritan writers difufe this manner of fpeaking? For my part, I know not any fet of writers in the world, fo eminently remarkable for this very doctrine, and this very diction. I faid, in a former letter, we would inquire into this particular; but the inquiry is quite unneceffary. It would be like *Uriel*'s fearching for the fun, while he ftands in its orb, and is furrounded with its luftre.

"We fwarm with *Antimonians*."—And we muft fwarm with perfons, whofe hearts are enmity againft the law of GOD, fo long as *your* tenets find acceptance. Who can delight in a law, which neither has been, nor can be fulfilled by them? which bears witnefs againft them, and is the miniftration of death unto them? teftifying, like the hand-writing on Belfhazzar's wall, *Thou art weighed in the balances, and found wanting.*—Whereas, when we fee it fully fatisfied on our behalf, by our SURETY's obedience; no longer denouncing a curfe, but pronouncing us bleffed; not purfuing us, like the avenger of blood, but opening a city of refuge for the fafety of our fouls; we fhall then be reconciled to its conftitution and defign; we fhall then take pleafure in its precepts and prohibitions. We fhall fay with the Pfalmift, *LORD, what love have I unto thy law! all the day long is my ftudy in it.*

My mouth fhall fhew forth thy righteoufnefs and thy falvation—" Thy mercy which brings my falvation," fays Mr *Wefley*, in oppofition to the fenfe affigned by *Afpafio*. Which fenfe has been vindicated already. I fhall therefore not renew my arguments, but only exprefs my wonder.

As Mr *Wefley*, is a minifter of the gofpel, I wonder, that *he* fhould ftudioufly fet afide, what is the peculiarity and glory of the evangelical revelation. " Mercy " which brings falvation," is what an unenlightened *Jew* might have preached; nay, what a more ignorant

rant Heathen might have taught. But salvation thro' a divine righteousness, as the adequate and meritorious cause thereof, is the distinguishing doctrine and the sovereign excellency of the gospel.

As Mr *Wesley* is a sinner, I wonder, he should chuse to weaken the foundation of his own and our hope. Why mercy *alone*? Is it not better to put our trust in mercy, erecting its throne on a propitiation, and thence holding forth the golden sceptre? By the obedience of IMMANUEL, the law is satisfied, as to its penalty; is fulfilled, as to its precept; and is, in every respect, unspeakably magnified. This shews us the inexhaustible fountain of mercy unsealed, and every obstruction to its free and copious flow removed.

As Mr *Wesley* is zealous for the honour of GOD, I wonder, he should not prefer that method of salvation, by which every divine attribute is most abundantly glorified. This is not done, by expecting pardon and acceptance from mercy alone; but by expecting and receiving them, through our REDEEMER's righteousness and blood. Then we have a display, not only of infinite love, but of inflexible justice, and incomprehensible wisdom. Here they mingle their beams, and shine forth with united and eternal splendour.

Considering these things, I am still inclined to embrace *Aspasio*'s interpretation of this, and such like passages of scripture, wherein salvation is ascribed to divine mercy, exercised through the obedience and death of *CHRIST*, which gives as great a heightening to the blessing, as the atmosphere gives to the rays of light, or as the light itself imparts to the scenes of creation.

Those divine treasures which spring from the imputation of *CHRIST*'s righteousness. "Not a word "of his atoning blood."—I wish you would turn back to *Aspasio*'s definition of this phrase, as it is laid down at the beginning of the conference, to be the

ground-

ground-work of all the dialogues, and of all the letters. You will then perceive, that there is not a word of this kind, but *CHRIST*'s atoning blood is included in it. Without this, his righteousness had not been perfect. Without this, his righteousness could not be imputed.—Some people have a treacherous memory, and really forget things. Others have a perverse mind, and resolve not to regard them. Which of these is Mr *Wesley*'s case, I presume not to say, let his own conscience determine.

'Tis true, we " love to speak of the righteousness " of *CHRIST*." Yet not because " it affords a " fairer excuse for our own unrighteousness." For indeed it affords no excuse at all. On the contrary, it renders unrighteousness quite inexcusable, because it yields new and nobler motives to all holy obedience. —But we love to speak of the righteousness of *CHRIST*, because it is the most comprehensive expression, and the grandest theme in the world.—The *most comprehensive expression;* as it denotes all that he has done and suffered, both his meritorious life, and his atoning blood.—The *grandest theme.* Consider all those blessings, which have been vouchsafed to GOD's people, before our *SAVIOUR* appeared on earth; add all the blessings which will be vouchsafed, until the consummation of all things; consider all that good, which is comprised in a deliverance from the nethermost hell; together with all that bliss which is contained in the pleasures and glories of the heavenly state. All these to be enjoyed through a boundless eternity, and by multitudes of redeemed sinners, numberless as the sands upon the sea-shore. Then ask, What is the procuring cause of all? whence do these inestimable benefits proceed? From the righteousness, the sole righteousness of *JESUS CHRIST.*—Is it not then worthy to be uppermost in our thoughts, and foremost on our tongues? Might not the very stones cry out, and reproach our insensibility, if we
did

did not *love* to talk of this divinely-precious righteousness?

Faith is a persuasion, that *CHRIST* has shed his blood *for me*, and fulfilled all righteousness *in my stead*. "I can by no means subscribe to this definition."—You might very safely subscribe to this definition, if you would suffer St *Peter* to speak his genuine sentiments. Describing the faith of the primitive Christians, he calls it πιστις δικαιοσυνη *Faith in the righteousness*. He says nothing of the atoning blood; but does he therefore exclude it? He speaks of nothing but the justifying righteousness; and will you totally discard it? It is the central point in his faith, and shall it have no place in yours!—*Righteousness*, he assures us, was the object of the believer's faith, even the righteousness *of our GOD and SAVIOUR JESUS CHRIST.* But how could this be the object of their faith, if it was not fulfilled in their stead? Or how could they truly believe in this righteousness, if they did not regard it, as performed for them, and imputed to them?

"There are hundreds, yea thousands of true believers, who never once thought, one way or the other of *CHRIST*'s fulfilling all righteousness in their stead."—Then their faith is like the sight of the person, *who saw men as trees walking*. He saw them indeed, but very dimly, indistinctly, confusedly; and 'tis pity but they were more thoroughly instructed unto the kingdom of GOD.—Not one of those thousands, provided he fixes his hope wholly upon the merits of *CHRIST*, would reject this delightful truth, if it was offered, with scriptural evidence, to his understanding. Reject it! No surely. He would joyfully embrace it, if offered, with that single, but undeniable evidence; *CHRIST was made sin for us, though he knew no sin, that we might be made the righteousness of GOD in him.*

"You personally know many, who, to this hour, "have

" have no idea of *CHRIST*'s righteousness."—Surely then it behoves you, as a lover of souls, and as an ambassador of *CHRIST*, to teach them the way of GOD more perfectly *. So doing, you will be employed much more suitably to your function, and much more profitably to your brethren, than in your present attempt. By which, you would weaken the hands, and defeat the designs of those, who endeavour to spread abroad the favour of this knowledge, in every place; and who, notwithstanding all that you personally know, must unalterably persist in their method. Which is, to regulate their definition of faith, not by the state of your supposed believers, but by the express declaration of the unerring word. And from this, they have authority to maintain, that faith in the imputed righteousness of *CHRIST*, is a fundamental principle to every believer, who understands upon what foundation he is saved.

These your acquaintance, though they have no idea of *CHRIST*'s righteousness, yet " have each " of them a divine evidence and conviction, *CHRIST* " loved me, and gave himself for me."—In this case, don't you take rather too much upon you? Have you then the apostolical gift of discerning spirits? If not, it will be impossible for you to know the man, exclusive of yourself, who is certainly possessed of this divine evidence. You may form a charitable judgment or a prevailing hope; which seems to be the utmost you can warrantably claim with regard to others. And while you entertain this hope, we shall allow it to indicate the benevolence of your heart; but cannot admit it as a proof of your point, That people may be full of faith and love, yet have no idea of *CHRIST*'s righteousness.—We would also caution you to take heed,

* Mr *Wesley* cannot say; What! Teach a doctrine, which I disapprove! since he himself has allowed it, has approved it, has set his seal to it, again and again, in the course of these his remarks.

heed, lest, thro' an immoderate fondness for increasing the number of your converts, you are led to deceive yourself and others; registering those as real believers, whom the LORD hath not registered. By this means, you may be confirmed in your unscriptural notion, that the righteous fall away, and the faithful apostatize. Whereas, they who fall away, were righteous only in appearance; and they who apostatize, were no otherwise than professionally faithful. What you see drop from the sky, is not a star, but a meteor only.

Faith is the hand which receives all that is laid up in *CHRIST*.—*Aspasio* expresses himself thus; *CHRIST* is a store-house of all good. Whatever is necessary to remove our guilt, whatever is expedient for renewing our nature, whatever is proper to fit us for the eternal fruition of GOD, all this is laid up in *CHRIST*. And all this is received by faith, for our application, use, and enjoyment.—To this Mr *Wesley* subjoins a word of objection; but not in due season. *Aspasio* is displaying the efficacy of faith; Mr *Wesley's* argument is levelled against the indefectibility of faith. However, as it is your favourite objection, it shall not be treated as an intruder. " If we *make shipwreck of the* " *faith*, how much soever is laid up in *CHRIST*, " from that hour we receive nothing."

Have you never heard of the answer, which the *Spartan* states returned to an insolent and barbarous embassy from *Philip* of *Macedon?* You may read it in the book you are censuring; and may receive it as a reply to this, and your other surmises of this nature. It was all comprised in that single monosyllable IF.— A mere professor may make shipwreck of the doctrine of faith; a true believer does not make shipwreck of the grace of faith. No, nor ever will, unless *CHRIST's* intercession be made of none effect; *I have prayed, that* such *faith fail not.*

265. Answered already, in number 261.

Aspasio, describing the dreadful nature of the command given to *Abraham*, says, Thy hands must lift the deadly weapon ; thy hands must point it to the beloved breast ; thy own hands must urge its way, through the gushing veins and the shivering flesh, till it be plunged in the throbbing heart.—" Are not " these descriptions far too strong?" This is submitted to the judgment of the reader. I would only observe, that the more strongly the horrors of the tremendous deed are represented, the more striking will the difficulty of the duty appear ; consequently the more efficacious and triumphant the power of faith.— " May not these descriptions occasion unprofitable " reasonings in many readers ?" What unprofitable reasonings may be occasioned, I do not pretend to guess. But the just and natural reflection, arising from the consideration of such a circumstance, is ; " What " has faith wrought ! It purifies and exalts the affec- " tions. It invigorates and ennobles the soul; makes " it bold to undertake, and strong to execute, every " great and heroic work. I see, therefore, it is not " in vain, that the scripture so frequently inculcates " faith ; lays so remarkable a stress upon faith ; and " places it in the very front of all Christian duties." *This is the victory that overcometh the world*, overcometh self, overcometh all things.

How could he (*Abraham*) justify it to the world? " Not at all."—True; not to the unbelieving world. They will argue, as Mr *Wesley* on another occasion, " What! stab his son, his best-beloved, his only son to the heart? Could the GOD of goodness command such a piece of barbarity? Impossible! I could sooner be a Deist, yea, an Atheist, than I could believe this. It is less absurd to deny the very being of a GOD, than to make him an almighty tyrant."—But to the believing world, who fear the LORD, and hearken to the voice of his servants, *Abraham*'s conduct will never stand in need of a vindication. By them it will be highly extolled, and greatly admired. It will be be an undeniable demonstration of the reality and sincerity of his faith; of its very superior elevation, and invincible strength.

You take the direct and certain way to obtain substantial comfort. The righteousness of our LORD JESUS CHRIST, after which you inquire, about which you are solicitous, is a never-failing source of consolation. Thus *Aspasio* writes to *Theron.*— "What! without the atonement?" cries Mr *Wesley*. To which he adds, in a following paragraph; "So the death of CHRIST is not so much as named." This puts me in mind of an objection, no very formidable one, made against that introductory exhortation to the common prayer, Dearly beloved *brethren*. So then, said a candid examiner, *women* have no part in your worship. They are not so much as named. But I forbear. If you are not ashamed of repeating, I am ashamed of refuting, so frequently refuting such an empty cavil. And, I believe, the reader is tired with us both.

286. I have no great objection to your alteration of *Aspasio's* comment. Suppose, we compromise matters, and consider the oil poured on *Aaron*'s head, and emptying itself from *Zechariah*'s olive-tree, as typical both of the merits and the SPIRIT of CHRIST; which, like light and heat in the sun, are indissolubly connected; or, to make use of a sacred illustration, are like the living creatures and the wheels in *Ezekiel*'s vision. *When the living creatures went, the wheels went by them. When the living creatures were lift up from the earth, the wheels were lift up.* Whithersoever the former were to go, the latter went also.—For the sake of obliging Mr *Wesley*, I call this a compromise. But if he can prevail on himself to read the paraphrase on the two passages, without prepossession, he will find this association of senses anticipated by *Aspasio*.

Has the law any demand, says *Aspasio?* It must go to CHRIST for satisfaction. From which you draw this injurious consequence, "Then I am not obliged

" to love my neighbour. CHRIST has satisfied
" the demand of the law *for me.*" This objection has
already received an answer.

I shall therefore content myself with shewing, why
I call your conclusion injurious. Because, like the deaf
adder, it stoppeth the ear against my own explication
of my own phrase. A note is added, on purpose to
limit its sense, and obviate your misrepresentation.
This you totally disregard, and argue as if no such
precaution was used.—The note informs you, that
the law—the commanding law is satisfied with nothing
less than perfect obedience, and the broken law in-
sists upon condign punishment. Now, if it must not,
for satisfaction to both these demands, go to *CHRIST*
our divine husband, where will it obtain any such
thing? who is able to give it, among all the children
of *Adam?*

However, lest we offend, needlessly offend any read-
er, I promise, that, in case the providence of GOD
and the favour of the Public call for a new edition,
Aspasio shall alter his language. Thus the paragraph
shall stand; Does the law demand perfect purity of
" nature, and perfect obedience of life? It must so
" to HIM for satisfaction. Do we want grace, and
" glory, and every good gift? We may look to HIM
" for a supply; to HIM, *in whom it hath pleased the*
" *FATHER, that all fulness should dwell.*"

For all his people—With this phrase Mr *Wesley* is
chagrined. This he will not suffer to pass without
animadversion. Though he *must* know, if prejudice
has not blinded his understanding, that it is pure
scripture. Why does he not shew the same dissatis-
faction with the angel that appeared unto *Joseph,* and
with *Zechariah* the Baptist's father? The former of
whom says, He shall save *his people* from their sins.
The latter declares, He shall give knowledge of sal-
vation unto *his people,* by the remission of their sins.
Why does he not put the same question unto them,
and

and draw the same inference upon them? "But what "becomes of *all other people?*"—Sometimes Mr *Wesley* is so attached to the scriptures, that nothing will please him, but scriptural expressions. Here he is so wedded to self-opinion, that even scriptural expressions will not pass current, when they seem to thwart his own notions.

For *all his* people—From this expression, though used by a prophet, authorized by an angel, and to be found in many places of scripture, Mr *Wesley* deduces some very offensive and dreadful consequences; so dreadful, that he "would sooner be a *Turk*, a Deist, "yea an Atheist, than he could believe them."—My dear Sir, let me give you a word of friendly advice. Before you turn *Turk*, or Deist, or Atheist—see, that you first become an *honest* man. They will all disown you, if you go over to their party, destitute of common honesty.

Methinks, I hear you saying, with some emotion, What do mean by this advice? or what relation has this to the subject of our present inquiry?—A pretty near relation. Out of zeal to demolish the doctrine of election, you scruple not to overleap the bounds of integrity and truth.—Mysterious still! I know not what you aim at.—Then be pleased to review a passage, in your book on *original sin*, where you have thought proper to make a quotation from my dialogues. It relates to that great doctrine of the gospel, CHRIST becoming the representative and fœderal head of sinners. Upon this occasion *Aspasio* says, "As *Adam* was a public person, and acted in the stead "of all mankind; so CHRIST was a public person, "and acted in behalf of *all his people*. As *Adam* was "the first general representative of *this kind*, CHRIST "was the second and last." Here you substitute the word *mankind*, instead of *this kind;* and thereby lead the reader to suppose, that *Aspasio* considers our glorious Representative, as standing in this capacity to

the

the whole human race; than which nothing can be more injurious to the sense of his words.

I at first thought it might possibly be the effect of inadvertency. But could a person of Mr *Wesley*'s discernment allow himself to nod over a passage, which he knew to be of a critical and controverted import?—Perhaps, it might be the printer's fault; an error of the press. I would willingly have admitted one of these extenuating circumstances, till I came to the bottom of the page; where, to my great astonishment, I found the following words, inclosed within the marks of the same quotation, and ascribed to *Aspasio*. " All these expressions demonstrate, that *Adam*" (as well as *CHRIST*) " was a representative of *all* " *mankind*." Then I could forbear no longer crying out, *There is treachery, O Ahaziah!* A false quotation, not made only, but repeated, cannot be owing to negligence, but must proceed from design. And this, I should think, can never be defended, no, nor with a good grace excused, by Mr *Wesley*'s most devoted admirers. A studious alteration of our words, and an evident perversion of their meaning, are defensible by no arguments, are excusable on no occasion.

Quite inexcusable this practice. And is not your language equally offensive? Is not your conclusion very precipitate; when you suppose *Aspasio*, though using the words of scripture, yet representing G O D as " an almighty tyrant ?"—Surely, you had better forbear such horrid and shocking expressions. Especially, as you cannot deny, that many passages in scripture seem at least to countenance this obnoxious tenet. As you very well know, that many persons, eminent for their learning and exemplary in their lives, have written in defence of it, and bled for the confirmation of it. As we have proofs more than a few, that you are far from being infallible in your judgment; yea, far from being invariable in your opinion. Witness your former notions of matrimony: witness

the

the character you formerly gave of the *Moravian* brethren; and the esteem which you once had for the *Mystics*, and their writings.—Considering yourself, therefore, it would better become you to be diffident on such a subject, and say, " That which I know not, " LORD, teach thou me." And I imagine, it can never become you, on any subject whatever, to break out into such a language, as ought not to be named among Christians; ought to have no place but in the bottomless pit.—This is an admonition, which, while I suggest to you, Sir, I charge on myself.

The three following paragraphs relate to a doctrine, which *you* are fond to attack, and which *Aspasio* studiously declines. It constitutes no part of his plan. It forms not so much as the out-works. Be it demolished or established, the grand privilege, and the invaluable blessing, of justification, through the righteousness of *CHRIST*, remains unshaken, stands immoveable.—In applying this to ourselves, we proceed neither upon universal nor particular redemption, but, only upon the divine grant, and the divine invitation., We assure ourselves of present and eternal salvation, through this perfect righteousness, not as persons *elected*, but as persons *warranted* by the word of GOD; bound by the command of GOD, and *led* by the SPIRIT of GOD.—Therefore, while you are encountering this doctrine, I would be looking unto *JESUS;* be viewing the glory of my LORD; contemplating HIS perfection, and my own completeness in HIM.

If I divert, for a moment, from this delightful object, it is only to touch upon one of your remonstrances. You suppose, that according to the *Calvinistic* scheme, GOD denies what is necessary for present comfort and final acceptance, even to some who sincerely seek it. This is contrary to scripture, and no less contrary to the doctrine of your opponents. However, to confirm yourself in this misapprehension, you ask, " Would *you* deny it to any, if it were in *your*
" power?"

" power?"—To shew the error of such a sentiment, and the fallacy of such reasoning, I shall just mention a recent melancholy fact.

News is brought, that the *Prince George* man of war, Admiral *Broderick*'s own ship, is burnt, and sunk, and above four hundred souls that were on board, are perished. Six hours the flames prevailed; while every means was used to preserve the ship and crew, but all to no purpose. In the mean time, shrieks and groans, bitter moanings, and piercing cries, were heard from every quarter. Raving, despair, and even madness presented themselves, in a variety of forms. Some ran to and fro distracted with terror, not knowing what they did, or what they should do. Others jumped over board, from all parts; and, to avoid the pursuits of one death, leaped into the jaws of another. Those unhappy wretches who could not swim, were obliged to remain upon the wreck, though flakes of fire fell on their bodies. Soon the masts went away, and killed numbers. Those who were not killed, thought themselves happy, to get upon the floating timber. Nor yet were they safe; for the fire, having communicated itself to the guns, which were loaded and shotted, they swept multitudes from this their last refuge.—What say you, Sir, to this dismal narrative? Does not your heart bleed? Would you have stood by, and denied your succour, if it had been in your power to help? Would not you have done your utmost, to prevent the fatal catastrophe? Yet the LORD saw this extreme distress. He heard their piteous moans. He was able to save them, yet withdrew his assistance. Now, because you would gladly have succoured them if you could, and GOD ALMIGHTY could, but would not send them aid; will you therefore conclude, that *you* are above your LORD, and that *your* loving-kindness is greater than his? I will not offer to charge any such consequence upon you. I am perfuaded you abhor the thought.

"The wedding-garment here means holinefs."—Thus faying, you depart from *Bengelius*, for whom you profefs fo high a regard. *Bengelius* overlooks your expofition, and gives his vote for *Afpafio*'s. *Hæc veftis eft juftitia CHRISTI*. Awed by fo venerable an authority, you have not ventured to exclude this fenfe from your comment. You have admitted it into your expofitory notes, yet will not allow *Afpafio* to admit it into his difcourfe with *Theron*. Thefe are your words; "The wedding-garment, that is, the "righteoufnefs of *CHRIST*, firft imputed, then "implanted." Which, by the way, is not perfectly accurate, nor according to the language of the gofpel. The gofpel diftinguifhes between the righteoufnefs of *CHRIST*, and our own righteoufnefs. That which is imputed, goes under the former, that which is implanted, under the latter denomination.

However, let us confider the circumftances of the cafe, and we fhall find, that our common favourite *Bengelius* has probability and reafon on his fide. The guefts mentioned in this parable, confifted of poor outcafts, collected from the high-ways and hedges. Now we cannot fuppofe, that people in fuch a condition, and coming at a minute's warning, fhould be able to furnifh themfelves with a drefs of *their own*, fuitable to the grand occafion. Here then perfonal holinefs is put out of the queftion.—But we muft fuppofe, (which is conformable to the *Eaftern* cuftoms,) that the king had ordered his fervants, to accommodate each gueft from the royal wardrobe. That each might have this additional token of his fovereign's favour, and all might be arrayed in a manner becoming the magnificent folemnity. This exactly correfponds with the nature of imputed righteoufnefs.

Farther, the banquet, you will readily allow, is the pardon

pardon of sin, and peace with GOD, the divine SPIRIT, and eternal life. From all which, uniting their happy influence, true holiness springs. To say, that holiness is the wedding-garment, necessary for our introduction to this banquet, favours of absurdity; like saying holiness is necessary to holiness.—It is absolute legality*; for it makes the performance of all duties, the way to the REDEEMER's grace.—It implies an impossibility; the sinner, that can exercise holiness, before he receives CHRIST and his SPIRIT, is like the dead man, who arises and walks, before he is restored to life.

The grand end which GOD proposes in all his favourable dispensations to fallen man, is to demonstrate the sovereignty of his grace. " Not so."—Do you mean, *Aspasio* has not spoken so? that you have misrepresented his sense? have clipped and disfigured his coin? If this is your meaning, you speak an undoubted truth. His words are, " To demonstrate the sove-
" reignty, and advance the glory of his grace." Why did you suppress the last clause? Was you afraid it would supply the deficiency, which you charge on *Aspasio*, and express the idea of imparting happiness? If so, your fears are just enough.—Why did you not take into consideration those texts of scripture, with which *Aspasio* confirms his tenet? Ought you not to have overthrown those testimonies, before you deny his doctrine? Otherwise, you oppose your own authority, to the decision of a prophet and of an apostle.

" Not so," proceeds Mr *Wesley*. " To impart hap-
" piness to his creatures, is his grand end herein."— The devout prophet speaks otherwise; *I have created him for my glory*. The wise moralist speaks otherwise; *The LORD hath created all things for himself*. The holy apostle speaks otherwise; *To the praise of the glory of his grace*. From which, and from innumerable other places of scripture, from the reason of the thing, and from the very nature of the SUPREME BE-
ING,

ING, it appears, that the primary leading aim, in all GOD's works, and all GOD's dispensations, is his own glory. The felicity of his creatures, though not separated from it, though evidently included in it, is still subordinate to it. And surely it is very meet and right so to be. Can there be a nobler end, or more worthy of an infinitely-wise agent, than the display of those sublime perfections, for which, and through which, and to which, are all things? Could GOD make any other being the principal end of his acting, he would *undeify* himself, and give his glory to another. Does any creature imagine his own happiness to be a higher end than the divine glory? He thereby usurps the GODHEAD, making, as far as in him lies, JEHOVAH the subject, and himself the sovereign.

" Barely to demonstrate his sovereignty." The word *barely* is not used by *Aspasio*. But it gives another specimen of Mr *Wesley*'s integrity, in stating truth, and doing justice to his opponents.—It is not said, the *sole*, but the *grand* end. Therefore, would any unprejudised person conclude, there must be some other, tho' inferior purpose? No, says Mr *Wesley;* hence I infer, that it was *barely* to demonstrate his sovereignty. Do you so? Then your inference is of a piece with the quotation, *that* as valid, as *this* is faithful.

" Barely to demonstrate his sovereignty," is a principle of action fit for the great Turk, not for the most high GOD. Such a fraudulent quotation I have not often seen, no, not in the Critical Reviewers. To mark the sentence with commas, and thereby assign it to *Aspasio*, is really a master-piece, especially, after you have thrust in the word *barely*, and lopped off the word *grace*. You have treated the passage worse than *Nahash* king of *Ammon* treated the ambassadors of *David*. They were ashamed to shew their faces, under such marks of abuse and disgrace. I am no less ashamed

aſhamed of the clauſe, as you have mangled and diſguiſed it. But reſtore it to its true ſtate; let it wear its native aſpect; then ſee what is blameable, or what is offenſive in it.

The grand end which GOD propoſes in all his favourable diſpenſations to fallen man, is, to demonſtrate the ſovereignty, and advance the glory of his grace.—The *glory*, that it may appear rich, unbounded, and infinitely ſurpaſſing all we can wiſh or imagine.—The *ſovereignty*, that it may appear free, undeſerved, and abſolutely independent on any goodneſs in the creature.—That ſinners may receive it, without waiting for any amiable qualities, or performing any recommending conditions.—That, when received, it may ſtop the mouth of boaſting; may cut off all pretenſions of perſonal merit; and teach every tongue to ſay, *Not unto us, O LORD, not unto us, but unto thy name*, be the praiſe.

And ſhould we not greatly rejoice in this method of the divine procedure? That the LORD orders all things relating to our ſalvation, *to the praiſe of the glory of his grace?* Can any thing be more honourable to our nature, or more tranſporting to our ſouls? Can any thing ſo firmly eſtabliſh, or ſo highly exalt our hopes? Angels, principalities, and powers; all intellectual creatures, in all ages, and all worlds; are to look unto *us*, unto us men they are to look, for the moſt conſummate diſplay of GOD's grace. Our exaltation and felicity are to be the mirror, in which the wondering cherubim and ſeraphim will contemplate the ſuperabundant goodneſs of JEHOVAH. How *great* muſt that honour and that happineſs be, which are intended to exhibit the fulleſt, faireſt, brighteſt view of GOD's infinitely-glorious grace! How *ſure* muſt that honour and happineſs be, which are ſo intimately connected with the glory of the omnipotent King! which can no more fail of their accompliſhment,

than

than the amiable attributes of GODHEAD can be stripped of their lustre!

GOD is a boundless ocean of good. "Nay that "ocean is far from boundless, if it wholly passes by "nine-tenths of mankind."—What, if it had passed by *all* mankind, as it certainly did all the devils, would it have been the less boundless on that account? I wish, methinks, you would study the evil of sin more, and not so frequently obtrude upon us a subject, of which neither you nor I seem to be masters. Then we should neither have hard thoughts of GOD, nor high thoughts of ourselves.

You cannot suppose, GOD would enter into a fresh covenant with an *insolvent* and *attainted* creature *. These are *Aspasio*'s words. To which Mr *Wesley* replies; "I both suppose and know he did." *Satis cum imperio.* Then be pleased, Sir, to shew us *where* the Almighty entered into a covenant with fallen *Adam;* for of him we are speaking. Produce the original deed; at least favour us with a transcript. And we will take your word, when it is backed with such authority.

GOD made the new covenant with *CHRIST*, and charged him with the performance of the conditions. "I deny both these assertions." And what is your reason for this denial? Is it deduced from scripture? Nothing like it. Is it founded on the nature of things? No attempt is made towards it. But you yourself affirm, that these assertions "are the cen- "tral point, wherein *Calvinism* and *Antinomianism* "meet." Or, in other words, they tend to establish what you dislike, and to overthrow what you have taught. This is all the cause which you assign for your denial. I cannot but wish, that, whenever I engage

---

* *Insolvent* and *attainted* creature, Mr *Wesley* has changed into "a rebel."

gage in controversy, my adversary may be furnished with such arguments.

You deny the assertions now. But don't you forget what you allowed and maintained a little while ago; when you yourself, adopting a passage from *Theron* and *Aspasio*, called *CHRIST* " a fœderal " head?"—Pray, what is a fœderal head, but a person with whom a covenant is made, in behalf of himself and others?—Here your judgment was according to truth. Fit, perfectly fit for such an office is *CHRIST;* whose life is all his own, who is able to merit, and mighty to save. But absolutely unfit for it, utterly incapable of it, is fallen man; whose life is forfeited, whose moral ability is lost, and whose very nature is enmity against GOD.

I have made a covenant with my chosen.—" Namely, with *David my servant.*" True; with *David* as in *CHRIST*, or rather as a type of *CHRIST.* You cannot be ignorant, that *CHRIST* is called by this very name. The LORD, speaking by the prophet *Ezekiel,* says, *I will set up one shepherd over them, and he shall feed them, even my servant David.*— Was *David* beloved*? *CHRIST* was incomparably more so.—Was *David* GOD's chosen one? *CHRIST* was so likewise, and in a far sublimer sense, and for infinitely more momentous purposes. Was *David* GOD's servant? So was *JESUS CHRIST;* and, by his services, brought unspeakably-greater honour to the LORD his GOD, than all kings on earth, and all the princes of heaven.—Several parts of this psalm *must* be applied to *CHRIST;* and, if several of them must, the principal of them *may* and *ought*.

He will wash you in the blood which atones, and invest you with the righteousness which justifies. " Why should you thus put asunder continually what " GOD has joined?" How difficult is it to please

Mr

---

* *Beloved.* This is the meaning of דוד *David's* name.

Mr *Wesley!* When *Aspasio* spoke of CHRIST's righteousness, without particularly mentioning his blood, you said it was better to mention them both together; it behoved us never to name the former, without the latter. Yet here, when both are mentioned, and the particular use of each is specified, you complain of his putting asunder what GOD has joined; which, in truth, is no disjoining, but an illustration and amplification of the unsearchable riches of CHRIST.

GOD himself, at the last day, pronounces them righteous, because they are interested in the obedience of the REDEEMER. " Rather, because they " are washed in his blood, and renewed by his " SPIRIT." GOD will justify them in the last day, in the very same way whereby he justified them in this world; namely, because they are interested in the obedience of the REDEEMER. As for their renewal by the SPIRIT, though it will then be perfect, yet it will be no cause of their acquittal, but the privilege of those who are acquitted.—A proof of this, at least an attestation of it, the world has received from your own pen. " For neither our own in-
" ward nor outward righteousness is the ground
" of our justification. Holiness of heart, as well as
" holiness of life, is not the cause, but the effect of
" it. The *sole* cause of our acceptance with GOD,
" is the righteousness and death of CHRIST, who
" fulfilled GOD's law, and died in our stead." Excellent sentiments! In these may I ever abide! to these may you also return!

The

The practical improvement of the doctrine of a sinner's justification by the righteousness of Christ, taken from a little piece, entitled, A DISCOURSE UPON JUSTIFICATION, printed at London in 1740, which Mr HERVEY highly esteemed, and warmly recommended.

Being no improper supplement to the doctrine contained in THERON and ASPASIO, and ASPASIO VINDICATED.

1. SINCE the *justification* of a sinner is by the complete *obedience* of Jesus Christ, *imputed* to him, and received by *faith*, unto such great and glorious *effects;* we may hence learn, what reason we have to *admire* that infinity of *wisdom*, which shines forth in the *contrivance* of this wonder; and to adore that immensity of *grace*, which is displayed in this glorious *provision* made for the favourites of heaven! When the beloved *John* was favoured with a visionary sight of the *woman-bride, the Lamb's wife*, as *clothed with* Christ, *the Son* of Righteousness, and shining forth in the resplendent rays of her Bridegroom's glory; he says, he saw *a* WONDER, *Rev.* xii. 1. And a wonder it is indeed; so great, that it calls for the admiration, both of men, and of angels. This is one of those glorious *things*, that by the gospel is revealed unto us, *which the angels desire to look into,* 1 *Pet.* i. 12. And while sinful men have *the forgiveness* of their *sins through* Christ's *blood,* and the *acceptation* of their *persons* in him, *the Beloved, according to the riches of* the Father's *grace, wherein he has abounded towards* them, *in all wisdom and prudence;* it becomes them to admire and adore the same, and to cry out, with the apostle, *O the depth of the riches both of the wisdom and*

and knowledge of God! How unsearchable are his judgments, and his ways past finding out! Eph. i. 6, 7, 8. Rom. xi. 33. That the *obedience* of the Son of God should be made our *righteousness*, the righteousness of a *sinner*, to his complete *justification* before God, is such a *project* of infinite *wisdom*, such a *provision* of infinite *grace*, for the *salvation* of God's chosen, that every way becomes the great JEHOVAH! and will be the endless wonder of men and angels!

2. Since the justification of a sinner is wholly by the righteousness of another, which is a *way of life above* nature, above being discovered by nature's *light*, and seem by nature's *eye*, or discovered by the light of the *law*, and discerned by natural *reason;* we may learn hence, what an absolute necessity there is of a supernatural *revelation* thereof, in order to the soul's receiving of this *righteousness*, and so of the grace of *justification* thereby. This is one of these *things* that God has *prepared* for his people, that never *entered into the heart of* the natural *man to conceive of*, which he has neither *known*, nor *can* understand; and therefore deems it *foolishness*, or a foolish thing, for any to think they shall be justified by the obedience of Christ, exclusive of all their own works. But the people of God " receive not the Spirit which is of the world, " but the Spirit which is of God, that they may know " the things which are freely given *them* of God." And *this*, of *the free gift of righteousness, is revealed unto* them by his *Spirit,* though it is one of those *deep things of God*, which are hidden from the *natural man;* which are impossible to be known by any, but heaven-born souls, under a *special revelation* from above, 1 *Cor.* ii. 9. *&c.*

3. Since the *justification* of a sinner is by the *obedience* of Christ alone; we may hence learn, how greatly *important* the *knowledge* thereof is! The *knowledge* of this righteousness must needs be of the utmost *importance*, since *ignorance* of it, and *non-submission*

to it, (which always go together,) leave the soul in an *unrighteous* state, *Rom.* ix. 31, 32. and x. 3. All those miserable souls, who are *ignorant* of Christ's *righteousness, go about to establish their own righteousness;* and, alas! *the bed is shorter, than that a man can stretch himself upon it, and the covering narrower, than that he can wrap himself in it,* If. xxviii. 20. There is no true *rest* for a *sinner,* from the *works* of its own hands; no *covering* for a *naked* soul, from the *fig-leaves* of its own *righteousness,* though ever so artfully sewed together. Our Lord told his *disciples,* that *except* their *righteousness did exceed the righteousness of the scribes and Pharisees, they should in no case enter into the kingdom of heaven,* Matth. v. 20. These *scribes* and *Pharisees* were the *zealous,* the *religious* men of that age, the strict observers of *Moses's* law, that trusted in *themselves,* that they were *righteous,* by their own *legal* performances, and thought to get to *heaven* by means thereof. But our Lord declares, that none shall ever come *there,* but those who have a *better* righteousness, a *righteousness* that exceeds a *Pharisaical* righteousness, *i. e.* such a righteousness that every way answers to all the extensive requirements of the *law,* in heart, lip, and life; and this is no other than the *righteousness* of Christ, imputed to poor *sinners,* or made *theirs* by *imputation;* in which, being completely *justified,* according to *law* and *justice,* they shall, as *righteous* persons, be admitted into the kingdom of *heaven,* or into the glory of the heavenly *state;* while all others who trust in their own *righteousness,* and think they have done *many wonderful works,* which they dare plead for acceptance with God, shall be sent away from Christ, into eternal *misery,* with a *Depart from me, ye workers of iniquity,* Mat. vii. 22.

And as our Lord, in this his *sermon* upon the *mount,* had been expounding the law of God, in its *spirituality,* as extending to the *heart,* as well as *life;* and asserting the necessity of *keeping* the commandments, in the same extensive manner that the law *required*, in order to make a person *righteous;* so, in the conclusion thereof, he says, " Therefore whosoever heareth these sayings of mine, and doth them, I will liken him unto a wise man, who built his house upon a rock; and the rain descended, and the floods came, and the winds blew, and beat upon that house; and it fell not, for it was founded upon a rock, *ver.* 24, 25." These *sayings* of our Lord contain the *substance* of the moral *law*, and the *doing* of them unto *righteousness* before God is by *believing;* as faith lays hold on Christ, who has *obeyed* the law perfectly, as the *representative* of his people: on which account, *they* may be said to have done, or *fulfilled* the law in him; his *obedience* being *imputed* unto *them,* for their complete *justification* before God. As the *surety's payment,* among men, is accounted to the *debtor*, and is the same, in the eye of the *law*, and as effectual for his full *discharge*, as if he himself had paid the *debt*. And he that thus *doth* the law, or these *sayings* of Christ, he *likens* him *unto a wise man, who built his house upon a rock*. It is a piece of natural *wisdom*, to lay a good *foundation* for a stately *structure;* and the most *firm* that any house can be built on, is that of a *rock*. And he that is spiritually *wise, wise unto salvation*, lays the whole *stress* of it, and builds all his *hope* of life, upon *Christ*, the *Rock* of ages; in which it appears, that he is *wise* indeed. For as in nature, a *house* that is built upon a *rock*, will stand the *storm;* so the *soul* that is built upon *Christ*, shall never be removed: *The rain may descend, the floods come, and the winds beat;* afflictions, temptations, and trials of all kinds, may *beat vehemently against* that soul; but shall never *destroy* its *salvation*, nor make it *ashamed* of its *hope*. No; Christ, the *Rock* of immutability, will hold it *unshaken*, in a state of *salvation*, through *life*, thro' *death*, at *judgment*, and for *ever*. Such a soul *stands* as *immovable*, in the grace of *justification*, and *life,* as the *rock* itself, on which it is founded. *Because I live,*

live, faith our Lord, *ye shall live also*, John xiv. 19. Christ's *life* is the life of that *soul*, that depends upon him alone, for all its justification, and eternal salvation. And therefore the *wisdom* of faith is great indeed! in that it foresees the storm, and thus provides against it.

But *he*, faith our Lord, *that heareth these sayings of mine, and doth them not*, (*i. e.* that *heareth* the law's requirements, and endeavours to *obey* the same, for *righteousness* before God, and so doth them *not;* because his obedience cannot come up to that perfection which the law requires,) " shall be likened unto a " foolish man, which built his house upon the sand ; " and the rain descended, and the floods came, and " the winds blew, and beat upon that house ; and it " fell, and great was the fall of it," ver. 26, 27. Oh, the *folly* of that poor sinner, who lays the *stress* of his salvation, and builds his *hope* of life, upon his *own* righteousness! For this *sandy* foundation cannot endure the *storms* of divine *wrath*, which shall be revealed from heaven against all unrighteousness of men ; nor secure the soul from being driven away, by the tempest of God's *anger*, and the floods of his *indignation*, into the abyss of eternal *misery*. The *house fell*, that was thus *built* upon the *sand*, and great was the *fall of it!* Oh, what a miserable disappointment will it be to that soul, that " goes down to the chambers " of *eternal* death, with this lie of his own righteous-" ness in his right hand ;" from which he had all along hoped for eternal life! when this *way that seemed right to him in his own eyes*, as if it would lead him to everlasting life, (by his *depending* thereon,) shall *end* in eternal *death!* *The hope of the hypocrite* (or of him that trusts in himself, that he is righteous, by his own external performances, when yet his heart is far from that conformity to God, which the law *requires*) *shall perish at the giving up of the ghost*. His *hope* (i. e. his *salvation* hoped for) *shall* then *be cut off*. *He shall lean upon his house*, (i. e. his own *righteousness*, which

which he had raised up, in his imagination, to *shelter* him from the *storm* of divine vengeance,) " but it shall " not stand ; he shall hold it fast, but it shall not en- " dure, *Job* viii. 13, 14, 15. No, this *house* of his shall be as soon destroyed, by the storm of God's indignation, as a *spider's web* is swept down, by the besom that comes against it ; and the miserable soul, that trusted herein, shall be driven away into eternal perdition. Thus an error in the *foundation* will prove *fatal* to the building ; and therefore the *knowledge* of *Christ*, as the alone way of a sinner's *justification*, and *life*, must need be of the highest *importance;* since no other *refuge* can stand the *storm*, but Christ, as THE LORD OUR RIGHTEOUSNESS, this glorious *hiding-place*, which God has prepared for poor sinners, whither they may *run*, and be for ever *safe*. And as for *those* who live and die in *ignorance* of, and *non-submission to* the righteousness of Christ, they will certainly *die in their sins*, and *perish* for ever. They will all be found *filthy*, at the day of judgment, that have not been enabled to *believe* in Christ's *blood*, for cleansing from all sin ; they will all be found *unjust*, at that awful day, that have not *believed* in the Redeemer's *righteousness*, for their justification before God ; and so must remain for *ever*. For concerning them, it will then be said, " He that is filthy, let him be filthy " still ; and he that is unjust, let him be unjust still ;" *i. e.* let him *abide* so, to an endless *eternity*. But,

4. Since there is but one *way* for a sinner to be *justified* before God, and that is by the *obedience* of Christ alone ; this informs us, what great *folly* those persons are guilty of, who *press* poor sinners to obey the *law*, to make themselves *righteous* in the sight of God, when there is no law given that can give life unto them ; and how *dangerous* it is for souls, to sit under such a ministry, that naturally *misleads* them ; since while " the blind leads the blind, both fall into the ditch. If " there had been a law given that could have given " life,"

"life," says the apostle, "verily righteousness should have been by the law," *Gal.* iii. 21. But as there is no law given that can give life to a sinner, it is a *vain, foolish* thing to *press* such a soul, to get a *righteousness* by his own *performances*, which was never appointed of God, nor can be *attained* by man: No; *the scripture hath concluded all under sin, that the promise* (of life) *by faith of Jesus Christ* (as a sinner's righteousness) *might be given to them that believe*, ver. 22. And those who receive it not in this *way*, shall never attain it in any *other*, but must go *without* it for ever. *The labour of the foolish*, says the wise man, *wearieth every one of them, because he knoweth not how to go to the city*, Eccles. x. 15. A man may labour all his *days*, to make himself *righteous* before God, by his own *performances*, and to make his *peace* with him, by his *legal* repentance, and humiliation for *sin;* and yet *lose* all his labour at *last*, and so weary himself in *vain*, being never able to reach that *city*, that eternal rest, which God has prepared for his people: because he *knoweth* not *Christ*, the only *way* that leads thither; and so *walks* not by faith, in him, as such. All men by nature are ignorant of Christ's *righteousness*, as it is God's *way* of *justifying* and *saving* a sinner; and it is *dangerous* for souls, to sit under such a ministry, that presseth *doing*, and persuades them their *safety* lies there, instead of *believing*. "For how shall they be-" lieve," saith the apostle, "in him of whom they" have not heard? And how shall they hear without "a preacher? And how shall they preach except they" be sent?" *Rom.* x. 14, 15. How shall poor souls *believe* in Christ for *justification*, when they have never *heard* of his *righteousness*, which is the proper *object* of faith? And how shall they *hear*, without a *preacher* of that gospel that declares it? And how shall they *preach* the gospel to others, who have never *seen* that salvation it reveals for sinners, by the *righteousness* of Christ, themselves? How shall they declare the glory and efficacy thereof to *others*, that have

never

never seen, nor experienced it *themselves?* And how does it appear, that they are *sent* by Christ, to preach the gospel, who neither *know,* nor *proclaim* his *righteousness,* for the *justification* of a sinner; which is such a main *doctrine* thereof? Have we not reason to fear, that many of those who are called *ministers* of the *gospel,* are rather *preachers* of *Moses,* than of *Christ?* and that their *ministry* rather tends to lead souls to the bondage and death of the *law,* than to the liberty and life of the *gospel?* But " how beautiful are the feet " of them that preach the gospel of peace, that bring " glad tidings of good things!" that publish that *peace* with God, which was made for sinners alone, by the *blood* of Christ's cross; and is possessed only by *faith,* in him! that proclaim the glad tidings of those good things, which God has prepared, to be enjoyed by *sinners,* through the justifying *righteousness* of his Son! And how great is the privilege of those souls, who sit under a *gospel-*ministry; since this is the *means* appointed of God, to work *faith* in them, and to bring *salvation* to them! Once more.

5. Since the *justification* of a sinner is by the *righteousness* of Christ, *imputed* to him, and received by *faith* alone; we may hence learn, how great the *obligation* of the *justified* ones is, to *live* to the *glory* of that *grace,* which has so freely and fully *justified* them, in and through Christ, unto eternal *life,* by him! When the apostle had asserted the justification and salvation of God's people, both *Jews* and *Gentiles,* to be wholly of his free *mercy,* in and through Christ, Rom. xi. 32. and admired the riches of his *wisdom,* which was so brightly displayed in the dispensations of his *mercy* towards him, ver. 33. he thus concludes his discourse, ver. 36. " For of him, and through him, " and to him are all things; to whom be glory for " ever," *Amen.* 'Tis as if he should say, Since all things, relating to the justification and salvation of God's people, are *of* him, and *through* him, it is meet
that

that the glory of all should, by them, be given *to* him. And therefore, when he applies this doctrine of God's free mercy in Christ, to them who had obtained it, he thus addresseth them, *chap*. xii. 1. " I beseech you " therefore, brethren, by the mercies of God, that ye " present your bodies a living sacrifice, holy, accept-" able unto God, which is your reasonable service." I beseech [*you,*] says he, *you* that have obtained *mercy*, [*therefore,*] or since it is God's design, to *glorify* his mercy, in the salvation of sinners, that you give him the *glory* of it; [*by the mercies of God,*] those mercies of God, which you are partakers of, in the *forgiveness* of all your *sins*, and in the *justification* of your *persons*, [*that ye present your bodies a living sacrifice, holy, acceptable unto God,*] that ye continually offer up yourselves, as a whole burnt-offering, in the flames of *love*, unto him that hath *loved* you, in all holy and acceptable *obedience*, to the *glory* of that God, who has thus had *mercy* upon you ; [*which is your reasonable service.*] For it is a most reasonable thing, or a thing for which there is the highest *reason*, that you should ever *serve* the Lord, to the *glory* of that *grace*, by which you are freely *justified*, and shall be eternally *glorified*. And thus, the apostle *Peter*, 1 *Pet.* ii. 9. " But ye are a chosen generation, a royal priesthood," (who are washed from all your sins in Christ's blood, and clothed with his righteousness,) " an holy nation, " a peculiar people ; that ye should shew forth the " praises of him who hath called you out of darkness, " into his marvellous light." *And*, " you know," says the apostle *Paul*, " how we exhorted and comforted, " and charged every one of you, (*i. e.* of you justi-" fied, saved ones,) that ye would walk worthy of God, " who hath called you unto his kingdom and glory." 1 *Thess.* ii. 11, 12. And in short, as it was God's design to get himself *glory* in the *justification* of sinners, by the *righteousness* of Jesus Christ; so the *display* thereof, throughout the whole gospel, lays *them* under the highest *obligation* to *live* to his *praise*. Does God the

Father

Father impute the *obedience* of his Son to poor sinners? did God the *Son* obey in *life* and in *death* for them? and does God the *Spirit reveal* and *apply* this *righteousness* to them; and enable them to *receive* the same, as a *free gift* of grace, unto their eternal *life* in glory? What thanks, what praise, is due to God, in each of his glorious persons, for this abundant grace! And let the language of the justified ones, in heart, lip, and life, in all kind of holy *obedience*, both now and always be, *Thanks be unto God, for the grace of* JUSTIFICATION! *for this his unspeakable* GIFT! 2 Cor. ix. 15. *Amen! Hallelujah!*

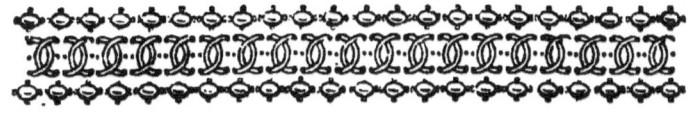

A DEFENCE

OF

THERON and *ASPASIO*,

AGAINST THE

Objections contained in a late Treatise, entitled, *Letters on Theron and Aspasio*.

TO WHICH IS PREFIXED,

A series of Letters from Mr HERVEY, to the Author, authenticating this Defence with his entire approbation, and manifesting it to be the only one that can be presented to the public with that authority.

PREFACE.

THE intention of prefixing Mr *Hervey*'s letters to this *reply*, is, in fact, to recommend it to the attention of the public, as such a farther explication and defence of *Theron* and *Aspasio*, as was quite agreeable to his own judgment; such as (in substance) would have appeared in the world, in his elegant and entertaining manner of address, had it pleased the Sovereign Disposer of all events to have continued him in life and such as the present situation of his writings require.

It has been already remarked in the public intimation of printing Mr *Hervey*'s letters, that " when writers of a distin-

"guished superiority have gained our admiration and applause, "we are fond of penetrating into their more retired apart"ments, and associating with them in the sequestered walks of "private life." A curiosity of this nature cannot be more *usefully* gratified; we cannot be ushered into Mr *Hervey*'s company to better purpose, than to hear him declare what he himself counted most valuable in all his writings; that which was his main design, and to which he would have his readers continually advert; those sentiments, which (as he expresses it in one of his letters) "I wish to have written on my heart; "such as I wish to speak and teach while I live; and in my "writings (if my writings survive me) to testify when I am "dead." More especially, if what he so esteemed is the doctrine of our Lord and his apostles, otherwise Mr *Hervey*'s esteem will be but of small account.

It seems the more necessary that he should thus be made to speak for himself, since some who have distinguished themselves as his peculiar friends, and as very angry with Mr *Sandeman* in his behalf, are at the same time very likely to be no friends to his defence. The reason is, whatever may be the motive for their professed regard, they have for many years past, and do unto this day, manifest great ignorance, if not great enmity, in respect of the principles which formed and influenced Mr *Hervey*'s faith and practice; and on which he ventured his eternal concerns; stigmatizing, or, I should rather say, honouring them, with the same kind of reproaches as the ancient opposers of Christianity cast upon our Lord and his disciples. Perhaps it may awaken the attention of some to inquire of the unerring oracles, *What is truth?* when they find, by these letters, that there is no dependence to be placed elsewhere; and that those in whom they have trusted as spiritual guides, applaud, or censure, with very little judgment, or with a worse design.

After all, I am not so sanguine in my expectation, as to think that by this, or any other method, the despised truth of the gospel will prevail with many, against the stream of the reputed devout and highly esteemed of this world. We must remember the treatment which our Lord and his disciples met with; and as the world is not better now than it was in those days, we have little reason to expect better success.

Mr *Hervey* began to find he had been in a mistake in this respect, and would have publicly acknowledged as much, had he lived but a few months longer. He began to be acquainted

with

with that true grace of God, which is contrary to the course of this world, in its devoutest form, for upwards of twelve years before our correspondence commenced. He was willing to recommend it to their consideration, and (if possible) make it appear lovely to their view. He dressed it up with all the beauties of eloquence, and all the winning arts of persuasion. He concealed whatever he thought might give his readers disgust and even intreated his friend to conceal their correspondence for the present, left the power of prejudice (raised by his professed friends) should prevent them from looking into his books: and all this in hopes to prevail, and give the despised gospel of Jesus a recommending appearance in their eyes. But alas! he died before he had accomplished this design; and perhaps, had he lived to the age of *Methuselah*, he would never have brought it to pass. So that we can only look upon this as his fervent desire, that the important truth, in which he had found all he wanted, should be as great a blessing to others as it had been to him. He gained a return of compliment for his favourable sentiments and kind behaviour, but it was in vain for him to expect to prevail any farther.

His notion was, as he himself expresses it, that " the taste " of the present age is somewhat like the humour of children, " their milk must be sugared, their wine spiced, and their ne- " cessary food garnished with flowers and enriched with sweet- " meats." His desire that what he called his *principal point* might be, if possible, made thus palatable, engaged him in several correspondencies, suited to the embellishment of his works; his superiority as a writer, caused many to covet an acquaintance and friendship with him; and his tender and complaisant behaviour, even to those who differed, gave some of them hopes of prevailing with him, or by him, to advance their own various and opposite sentiments. Filled with these hopes, their behaviour towards him was accordingly respectful; which, together with his retired situation in life, prevented him, in a great measure, from discerning their enmity to his principles. Taking it for granted they meant as they spake, he judged them aiming to promote the same important cause. Had this been fact, they would have still merited the regard he paid them; their professed zeal would have been commendable, had it been subservient to the *true grace of God* for which he pleaded; but bears as different an aspect when their enmity and opposition thereto is discovered; even as

Paul's

Paul's most hardened wickedness, was to the piety and zeal of his Pharisaic state.

No sooner was he dead than consultations were on foot, tending to bury his principles as well as him. His private letters were publicly advertised for, in order to be printed; which by the use made of them, seems not done with any design to establish the truths he contended for, but to pick out, if possible, something to their disadvantage; and, what is still more unworthy, to establish their own characters in such attempts on the encomiums he had at one time or other bestowed on them, for want of seeing them properly; for want of knowing that their ruling principle was a fixed enmity to that gospel which was his sole delight. Besides this, several reports were spread, detrimental to the important truth he had so contended for. And knowing that all and every one of them could be fully disproved by Mr *Hervey*'s own hand-writing, I counted it my duty to print the defence, and to publish the letters to the author to authenticate it with Mr *Hervey*'s approbation. Though I was apprehensive, at the same time, it might carry the appearance of ostentation, to such as did not know what was in hand, and so could not be sensible that the support of the important truth, which shines through all his works, depended, in some measure, on the publication of these letters.

Notwithstanding all this, the persons concerned in the publication of two volumes, under the title of *The letters of the late Rev. Mr James Hervey*, have exerted themselves, with uncommon boldness, in disfiguring his principles; and, at the same time, introduce their own. This is evidently manifest from several notes annexed to these letters *. In these volumes they have insinuated that the author of the defence of *Theron* and *Aspasio* was " on the *Antinomian* side of the question, and that " Mr *Hervey* by no means approved of his sentiments." Upon this there immediately appeared in the *Gazetteer, Aug.* 22. and *London Chronicle, Aug.* 26. a letter to the editor and publisher of these volumes, signifying the shocking appearance of slander and detraction in volumes under the name of a man so averse to such proceedings; and proving, from Mr *Hervey*'s own words, the most apparent falsehood in their assertions; there being no letter in the whole two volumes, so expressive of *sameness of sentiment*, as the letters to the author of the defence of *Theron* and *Aspasio*; and concluding with these words, " The secret stabs that are given to characters, by
" modern

---

* All these notes are thrown out of this edition of our author's works.

"modern pretenders to piety, would make a court of justice
"blush. And I am persuaded the real friends to Mr *Hervey's*
"memory, or writings, will not be pleased to find his name
"made subservient to such base purposes." The proceedings
are a little more open in the *Gentleman's Magazine* for *August;*
where we are told, that Mr *Hervey* himself " is by no means
"free of the charge of stretching the principles of *Calvin* in-
"to *Antinomianism,*" p. 379. It is very evident Mr *Hervey*
concerned himself with no *Calvinistical* or *Arminian* disputes.
In one of his letters, speaking of Mr *W——y's* conduct, he
says, " I am sometimes apprehensive that he would draw me
"into a dispute about particular redemption; I know he can
"say startling and horrid things on this subject; and this, per-
"haps, might be the most effectual method to prejudise peo-
"ple against my *principal point.*"

As to the charge of *Antinomianism,* unless the particular
errors are pointed out, (which may as well be done without
the assistance of reproachful names,) it is no more than a very
vague uncertain sound, made use of by some leaders in the
various classes of religious people as a political bugbear, where-
by they disguise and disfigure the party they intend to re-
proach *. It is a term not confined to any dictionary-inter-
pretation,

* When these religious politicians have raised an alarm, *Beware
of the Antinomians!* the ignorant multitude are upon the inquiry to
know, what this dreadful thing called *Antinomianism* is; they are
told a hundred bugbear tales of monsters in human shape; when
they inquire farther who are *Antinomians,* meaning who are the per-
sons so abandoned as to hold such dreadful opinions or practices,
they have nothing more to do, than to place the name upon whom
they please; and it follows of course, by this artful shift, that the
credulous and deceived multitude believe the persons, so pointed
out, to be guilty of whatever has been charged under that name.
Were it not for this piece of artifice, they might, perhaps be oblig-
ed, honestly and fairly, to point out the particular errors of those
they dislike and accuse; and, in so doing, might manifest, that
they themselves know not what they say, nor whereof they affirm.

Mr *Hervey* has very properly exhibited such vain declaimers in
the following note:

" This puts me in mind of what *Theodorus* replied to *Philocles;*
" who was often insinuating, that he preached *licentious* doctrine;
" because he enlarged, with peculiar assiduity, upon faith in J e-
" s u s C h r i s t; and frequently chose such texts as, *Believe in
" the Lord Jesus, and thou shalt be saved.*"

" I preach salvation by J e s u s C h r i s t; and give me leave
" to ask, whether you know what salvation by C h r i s t means?
Philocles

pretation, but admits of a variety of definitions, according to the various sentiments of the persons who use it, from the most professed preachers of Christ, down to the *Monthly Reviewers*, who esteem no better of any that concern themselves with the name of Jesus, farther than what becomes a decent complaisance to the profession of their country. These gentlemen can read the Bible as well as these volumes, " without " the least intellectual improvement" in the doctrine of Christ; and can also give a solid reason for it, *viz*. that they have no taste for this kind of reading; it is very disagreeable to them. They judge, " that one virtuous design promoted, one good " action done, or one bad habit subdued, is worth more than " all such trifling considerations" as the death and resurrection of Jesus. The scripture-language concerning salvation only by Christ must be *Antinomianism* in their esteem. They expect to be saved in doing well; and the scripture assures them, that *if they do well, they shall be accepted*. Our Saviour declares, he never came to interrupt such people in their good intentions; but to save the lost, and worthless, such as ought to perish, according to every rule of equity; and the real gospel of our Lord Jesus Christ will ever prove *foolishness*, *a stone of stumbling*, and *rock of offence*, to any but these sort of people.

Any one who has read the letters on *Theron* and *Aspasio*, or ever seen Mr *Hervey*'s sentiments of that author, will easily perceive that a reply to that performance was absolutely necessary, or else, as he observes in one of his letters, " what is " not confuted by argument, is confirmed by silence." It was
also

" *Philocles* paused; he began to blush; would have eluded the ques-
" tion, and declined an answer. No, said *Theodorus*, you must per-
" mit me to insist upon a reply. Because, if it be a *right* one, it
" will justify me and my conduct: if it be a *wrong* one, it will
" prove, that you blame you know not what; and have more rea-
" son to inform yourself, than to censure others.

" This disconcerted him still more. Upon which *Theodorus* pro-
" ceeded: Salvation by C H R I S T means, not only a deliverance
" from the *guilt*, but also from the *power* of sin. He gave himself
" for us, that he might redeem us from all iniquity; *redeem us from*
" *our vain conversation*, as well as deliver us from the wrath to
" come.—Go now, *Philocles*, and tell the world, that by teaching
" these doctrines, I promote the cause of licentiousness. And you
" will be just as *rational*, just as *candid*, just as *true*, as if you should
" affirm, that the firemen, by playing the engine, and pouring in
" water, burnt your house to the ground, and laid your furniture
" in ashes." *Note*, vol. II. dial. x. p. 357.

PREFACE.

also necessary, if possible, that this defence should be by himself, or by his approbation; and also that the public should be ascertained of this, that so it may be considered as a proper and necessary supplement to his volumes. As these particulars can be so plainly discovered by the letters prefixed, it is well that Mr *Hervey* was so open in his declarations.

As to our debate with Mr *Sandeman*, it seems to stand as follows:

The turning-point from despair to good hope, he observes, is the hinge of the controversy; and this point is with Mr *Sandeman* the finished work of Christ, as it is fully sufficient to vindicate the divine justice in saving the most guilty. All the hope he has by this, is represented by the hope of a man has from hearing of the plentiful importation of corn in the time of famine; while it yet remains a hazard whether he shall ever obtain any; and his expectation to obtain, is by labouring in painful desire and fear till crowned with enjoyment.

Aspasio's turning-point is the finished work of Christ, revealed in the gracious declarations of the gospel, not only as supporting the divine justice in saving the most guilty, but also as the sufficient object of the sinner's immediate trust and confidence, agreeable to the repeated divine assurances that such shall not be confounded or disappointed. And the works and labour of love *Aspasio* pleads for, are works of love to God thus manifested and trusted in.

Aspasio's former opponents have objected to this immediate trust of a sinner upon Christ alone for everlasting life by pleading for what they have conceived to be previously necessary, under the names of faith, repentance, sanctification begun, &c.

Mr *Sandeman* has undertook to prove, that all true sanctification, conversion, faith, &c. springs solely from the truth of Christ's sufficiency for the most guilty, without any addition whatever, as the central point of divine revelation, and that all other religion is not any part of Christianity; not any part of that doctrine which came from heaven; but only the vain efforts of the natural man to lower the divine character of the infinitely righteous and just God, and quiet his guilty conscience with a righteousness insufficient, or, in other words, a righteousness stained with sin; and that the names of conversion, faith, sanctification, applied to this kind of religion, are only fitted to deceive; and supposing our appropriation of trust to be a denial of this sufficiency of Christ alone, he opposes that also. This then is what we are concerned to defend.

To

To this purpose I have endeavoured to shew, that, in trusting to the sufficient righteousness of Christ alone for everlasting life, we keep clear of the charge of denying the sufficient righteousness, and of adding or mixing another righteousness with it. We may rather ask, How does it appear that any man believes it to be sufficient, when he dare not trust his soul upon it, but waits in painful desire and fear, to discover himself possessed of the distinguishing qualities of a believer? And as he carefully separates what he believes, from all foundation of hope or confidence therein for everlasting life, he appears to us involved in the absurdity of hoping for eternal life by Christ, because he discovers himself without any foundation of hope, either in himself, or in the gospel he believes.

He may say, "he trusts to be saved by what Christ has "done, if saved at all;" but that very *if* signifies, that he does not trust upon what Christ has done, but is waiting to discover something else as a more proper ground of his confidence. And what is that *something else*, but the difference he discovers betwixt himself and other sinners? So that after all our flourishes against self-dependence and Pharisaic doctrine, if we are not upon our guard, we shall be at last settled on no other foundation.

Mr *Sandeman*, in endeavouring to prove that his view of the gospel "quiets the guilty conscience of a man as soon as "he knows it," acknowledges with us, that the gospel is designed for that end; but fails in his attempt to make out, that the guilty conscience of that man is quieted who discovers no foundation in what he believes, to trust in Christ's righteousness for everlasting life. He supposes, that the uneasiness and dread of conscience arises only from the appearing impossibility of a just God being a Saviour; from whence he infers, that the revelation of a righteousness removing this seeming impossibility, brings the rest and peace the scripture speaks of; without revealing any ground for trust and confidence in that righteousness. But this supposition is not true; few or none are troubled with such apprehensions, nor does the scripture address men as though they were. It is self-evident, that the cause of our dread is an apprehension of *our want* of a righteousness acceptable to the divine purity; and what relieves must be *our having* such a righteousness either in ourselves, or by God's free gift. This Mr S———n himself seems to acknowledge, when he talks of "labouring in painful desire and fear," as the effect of his cramped view of the gospel. For why is this

the

PREFACE.

the effect? but because what he believes does not afford the proper satisfaction.

Mr Sandeman's jealousy is, lest we, by pleading thus for a sinner's trust and confidence on Christ, should lead man into a self-dependence on his doing something to relieve himself from his dreadful circumstances, instead of being supported only by what Christ has already done. But how easy is it to perceive, that no man is or can be supported by what Christ has already done, but he that discovers it the object of his trust and confidence for everlasting life; and that so to depend on Christ, and what he has done, is the very opposite of all self-dependence, and inconsistent with our depending on our doing any thing either present or future?

It is true, a man that is at an entire uncertainty without any dependence whatever, is as clear of self-dependence, as he is of dependence on what Christ has done. So a man that neither eats nor drinks, is as much out of danger of dying with gluttony and excess, as he is of being poisoned with unwholesome food. But how long can a man live thus? And how long can a man support without having some dependence or other for his soul? It is as natural for the mind of man to depend on something against the fears of hereafter, as it is for his body to gravitate or sink till it meets with a proper support. Hence we find, that those who depend not on the truth, depend on some falsehood or other which they suppose to be true; and when a man is beat off from one false dependence, he is sinking to despair till he finds another, or is relieved by the *real truth*. And that *truth* which relieves, must reveal a foundation of dependence for everlasting life; to attempt to rest short of this, is to attempt to build a castle in the air. The discovery, that " God may, if he pleases, have mercy upon me " as I at present stand," although it tends to remove the Pharisaic wish or want to know that I am distinguished from others, yet leaves me unsupported as to original and real dread of conscience arising from my personal deficiency. And as such slight the divine warrant for the sinner's trust and confidence in Christ's sufficient righteousness, they naturally sink to the hope of eternal life, not by what Christ has done, or what the gospel declares, but a hope that they are the sheep of Christ who hear his voice, which is in fact only a hope *in themselves.*

The generality of mankind are but little concerned about the truth of the foundation of their peace of conscience; so

they

they have got some hope, it is enough; they do not care to be disturbed from it with such a controversy as this; especially if they can but conceit themselves holy, or feel themselves happy: not considering, that if their hope is founded on falsehood, their whole religion is a deceit: But they who are taught of God, are not led by fond conjectures; they will not be satisfied with any other reason of their hope than the voice of that God who speaks in the conscience; and Christ the Saviour of the guilty given to be trusted in, is the only foundation that God has laid in *Zion*.

I have only to add, that the manner in which the subject is treated, that is, by short remarks on the passages we are concerned with, was the way in which the subject was treated for Mr *Hervey*'s view; and as I could think of no shorter method of defence, it is so presented to the public.

LETTERS

FROM

Mr HERVEY

TO

THE AUTHOR.

Dear Sir,

LAST night I received your kind letter *; and this morning I have but a moment's space, in which to acknowledge it. However, I cannot neglect the first opportunity.—Are you the author that has given us an abridgment of Mr *Marshall?* Truly, I think, you have well bestowed your labour, and well executed your work. I wish you had not given yourself the trouble of sending me the book, because I have it, and highly prize it.—The abridgment I mean.

I should be very glad if you would read the dialogue you mention with a critical attention, if you would point out the places where you think I am confused in my apprehensions, injudicious in method, or weak in argument. As you have so thoroughly

---

* When I perceived by his first edition of *Theron and Aspasio,* that he had so publicly espoused the truths for which I had incurred the displeasure of many of his professed friends and admirers, I wrote to him, signifying my fellowship with him in the despised truth.

thoroughly studied the point; and so often taught the doctrine you must easily see where the essay lies most open to objection, and where the point might receive additional strength.—You would much oblige me, if you would do this with the utmost impartiality and freedom; and, I hope, you would do service to the truth as it is in *JESUS*. Several persons, I find, are dissatisfied with my opinion on this head. Do, Sir, review dialogue xvi. and favour me with your free remarks, and friendly improvements. Whatever of this kind is done, I beg may be done speedily; because a new edition is in the press, and the printers will soon come to that part.—When I hear from you again, I will speak my sentiments with relation to your well-calculated design of an evangelical library *. At present I have leisure only to assure you, that I am,

Dear S I R,

Your affectionate friend in *JESUS CHRIST*,

Weston, Apr. 15.   JAMES HERVEY.

Dear S I R,

I Received your present by the coach; I thank you for it; and am much pleased with it—The doctrine † which you approve in my essay, and have clearly displayed and fully proved in your own writings, is not relished by every body; no, not by many pious people. I take the liberty to send you a couple of letters containing objections ‡. I wish you would be
                                                        so

---

* An intended collection of the most evangelical pieces from the beginning of the reformation down to the present day. And as nothing was designed but the marrow of each performance, so he judged it might be comprized in six volumes, and desired that an abridgment of *Theron and Aspasio* might have a place in one volume of it.

† This was a summary of doctrine, extracted from Theron and Aspasio, in Aspasio's own words.

‡ These objectors were adding no revealed truth to our minds, but on the contrary were only attempting to overthrow the solid foundation laid for the hope, confidence, and salvation of guilty sinners; that which makes the gospel glad tidings indeed to such. They allowed, that the free and unconditional nature of the divine declarations concerning Christ as an object of trust and confidence was
                                                        the

so kind as to confider them, and in your *concife* way, which I much admire, to make your remarks upon them.—One of the letters, in cafe it exactly co-incided with my fentiments, I fhould think too diffufe and prolix. I love to have the force and the only foundation upon which truft or confidence could be eftablifhed; but then they immediately contradicted this freenefs of the divine grant, by clogging it with the pre-requifites of feriouinefs, fenfibility of need, real defires, and in fhort every qualification that human pride could prefume upon the divine favour with, provided no Saviour had ever been revealed: Whereas, the man taught of God is made *fenfible*, that no qualification in him is to be a ftepping-ftone to the Redeemer's righteoufnefs. His real *defire* is daily to live by that righteoufnefs, not by his own; and he is *ferious* in this matter as being of the greateft importance, counting all things but lofs and dung, that he may win Chrift, and be found in him, not having on his own righteoufnefs which is of the law. They allowed the gofpel-declarations contained what might be compared " to a free welcome to an entertainment, by a friend's invitation ;" but denied that this gave them leave to believe that this entertainment was theirs; and only ferved as an inducement for them to do fomething, called reception, in order to found a title. They were anfwered, it was not theirs as a property in their difpofal to give away, or trifle with; but theirs to partake of, it certainly was, by virtue of the invitation. And this partaking of Chrift, and falvation in him, could be neither more nor lefs, than living by him in virtue of thefe declarations, inftead of feeking a title by inherent qualifications; which would be, in fact, living by our own righteoufnefs, and not by him. That if they allowed he was free for us to truft in, then the truft and confidence we pleaded for was vindicated as no prefumption, but rather an obedience to our divinely-gracious Benefactor. The difference between Mr *Hervey* and them, lay in their different fentiments about what was the truth of the gofpel: what *they* counted gofpel, left them to feek for a fomething in themfelves under the name of faith, on account of which they might conclude themfelves faved perfons. What Mr *Hervey* counted gofpel, was the revelation of the divine righteoufnefs to the moft guilty, warranting their immediate truft and confidence therein; affuring them fuch confidence fhould not be difappointed. It is eafy to perceive, that fuch confidence muft be effential to the real belief of fuch doctrine; as, on the other hand, no affurance or confidence can be effential to the belief of that doctrine which leaves me to feek for my ground of confidence in a fomething more than what Chrift has already done, and God has fo freely prefented to me. Mr *Hervey*'s view was not to eftablifh a ftandard for the hope of falvation of this kind, as depending upon our inherent qualifications, whether called convictions, faith, repentance, or by any other name;

and spirit of a subject contracted into a small compass, and exhibited to our minds in one clear and easy view. Long discourses, and protracted arguments, dissipate the attention and overwhelm the memory.—I think you are very happy in expressing yourself with a brevity that is striking, yet perspicuous.

I am not shaken in my own opinion by these attacks; but I should be glad to deliver it more clearly, and establish it more firmly in another edition. If you can spare a little time from your own labours, I hope you will gratify me in this request; and I trust HE, whom you serve, will make it a blessing to me and to others.

I would beg of you to return these letters, and (if the LORD should enable you) with free observations on the MOST MATERIAL points, as soon as POSSIBLE; because our new edition goes on apace, and will soon come to dialogue xvi. I have some thoughts of enlarging it a little, and dividing it into two dialogues. At present it is rather too long to be read at once.

I heartily wish you success in your projected work. *I assure you*, it is my opinion, that such a work, if well executed, will be one of the most valuable services to the present age. You will not, I hope, be too hasty. Mr *W*—— has huddled over his performance in a most precipitate, and therefore most imperfect, manner. One would think his aim was, not to select the best and noblest passages, but to reprint those which came first to hand.—If I live to see another edition of *Theron* and *Aspasio* published, I will desire your acceptance of a set; and I hope it will be improved and enriched with your observations: which will be a favour acknowledged by,

Dear SIR,
Your affectionate friend in JESUS CHRIST,
JAMES HERVEY.
P. S.

name; but rather to establish an important, comfortable, precious truth, concerning an open door of access to God by what Christ has done, and salvation in him, granted to the most guilty, on a supposition that every mouth is stopped, and all the world (in every pretension or plea unto righteousness) become perfectly on a level before him. This truth he apprehended was, when received, the conviction and faith of every true believer, and the foundation of immediate trust and confidence, and as such was necessary and essential to solid peace of conscience, and true holiness of heart and life; yet, at the same time, entirely opposite to the peace and holiness of men of the Pharisaic spirit. In short, we seemed to be only upon the old apostolic or reformation dispute still, *viz.* whether we are to be justified by faith in Christ without works? or whether we are first to find some righteousness in ourselves?

P. S. Pray don't spare my own performance; but freely animadvert upon *Aspasio*. I am sensible he sometimes speaks unguardedly, and sometimes seems inconsistent with himself.

Weston-Favell, Apr: 22. 1755.

Dear SIR,

I Received your last valuable letter, and sincerely thank you for the judicious observations it contained—Your other letter also, which conveyed an answer to ——, came safe to hand.—How is it, dear Sir, that godly * people are so averse to this doctrine †?

I have another letter from ——, containing remarks upon, and objections to, Mr *Marshall*, I would transmit it to you by this conveyance, but I remember you have already work upon your hands. In my next it shall wait upon you. My only aim, I trust, is to find out the truth as it is in *JESUS*; which, at present, I am convinced is with you. There is so much clearness and simplicity in your doctrine, it is so suitable to the goodness of GOD, and so eminently conducive to the comfort, recovery, and happiness of a sinner, that I cannot be persuaded to relinquish it.—I should be glad to maintain it in a convincing, yet the most inoffensive manner. I propose
to

---

* Mr *Hervey* here uses the word *godly* in the common signification of it, as distinguishing the religious from those who profess no religion; but, in the scripture-sense of the word, it is confined to those whose religion is formed by the belief and love of that truth which came from God for the hope of the guilty.

† These godly people he mentions mistook him continually, by apprehending all he said in the light of the properly-qualified faith; whereas his apprehension was totally in the light of free salvation to the guilty, as the ground of immediate confidence: and as they could make no hesitation about confiding in the Lord, if (as they termed it) *their evidences were clear;* so he made no hesitation about confiding in the Lord as a guilty sinner; the divine declarations to the guilty answering to him as the foundation of his confidence, as their evidences would to them if they could conceive them to be clear; and as his confidence only arose from the truth he believed, it stood in so near a connection with it, that he accounted it essential to it: as, on the other hand, their confidence depending upon what they found in themselves, as distinguishing characteristics of God's children, could only have existence when and while they could thus conceive of themselves.

to allot two dialogues for this very important subject. How, in what form and order would you advise me to proceed? Pray don't scruple to express yourself with all possible freedom. Direct and correct, as a friend and fellow-labourer *, &c.

Dear SIR,

LAST night I received the favour of your two packets; and, I assure you, a real favour I esteem them. Your answers are so clear, so consistent, so comfortable; they very much tend to establish my mind.—I find by your experience, the " account I mean of GOD's dealings with your soul," that you have incurred (but surely without any just cause) the displeasure of many. Now, as this is the case, my dear Sir, let us act prudently; be wise as serpents. Don't you think, I beg of you, that I am ashamed of your friendship. GOD forbid! But as I have some concern, and you have a greater zeal for these precious doctrines, let us use the most probable means to spread them. You know the power of prejudice is great; is almost incredible. Many people, were they to know, that you and I have been laying our counsels together, perhaps would never look into my book. We seem now to have a favourable opportunity of diffusing these sacred and delightful truths †. My books have been well spoken of in three of the *London* ‡ Magazines successively; and there is printing a new edition. The LORD JESUS, the WONDERFUL COUNSELLOR, direct us in this truly-important affair. —I will now, relying on his unerring SPIRIT, set about preparing the xvith dialogue for the press; and I should be very desirous to have it pass under your examination before it is launched into the world. You will give me leave to expect

---

* The remainder of this letter is lost.

†. How evidently does Mr *Sandeman* appear to be mistaken, in calling this the popular doctrine, or in judging that Mr *Hervey* had gained a public esteem on the account of it?

‡ Some of these recommendations were not to the advantage of the truth, which it was his main design to communicate: of this Mr *Sandeman* has not failed to take notice; and it must be acknowledged, that a resentment of the offices of such a friend might not have been improper. But the same reasons which he had for desiring the silence of one friend for the present, may be justly supposed the reason he shewed no resentment to the officiousness of the other.

pect an answer; and let me know from time to time, where a letter may find you, sent by,

Dear Sir,

Your obliged and affectionate brother in CHRIST JESUS,

Weston, May 8.   J. HERVEY.

Dear Sir,

I Have been so poorly in my health, and so much engaged in company, that I could not possibly get the inclosed ready before this time; which is the cause, the only cause, of my deferring my thanks for your last favour.

As to the doctrine under consideration, I have given a favourable and attentive ear to all that is said against it; and yet the more it is attacked, the more I am convinced of its truth. The LORD JESUS enable me to deliver and testify, with clearness of sentiment, and meekness of temper, what I am persuaded in my own conscience, is the true gospel of grace!— The inclosed paper contains some of the alterations which I propose to make. Another sheet will comprise the remainder. Let me desire you, dear Sir, to examine them, and remark upon them, as freely and impartially as you have done upon other papers. Pray treat me with a kind severity. Whatever sentence or expression appears wrong, I beg of you, animadvert, correct, spare it not. I assure you, I can bear to be told, (by your friendly pen at least,) this is not evangelical; here you contradict yourself; this is redundant, and that ambiguous.—Please to make little marks of reference in the MS. and pen down your observations on a separate paper.

I think to drop my first design of dividing the essay into two dialogues, and answering the various objections. *This* I intend to postpone for the present; and would print no more than is needful to explain, establish, and guard the tenet.—I think to add in a note, a friendly invitation to any serious and ingenuous person on the other side of the question, to debate and sift this very important point; professing, that if it can be proved erroneous, I will retract and renounce it, not only without reluctance, but with pleasure and thankfulness. Truth, the truth of the gospel, is my pearl; where-ever I find it, thither (without respect to names or persons) would I resort, and there would I abide. May that gracious promise be fulfilled to us in our searches, "The LORD shall guide thee continually!"—I hope to send you, very soon, the residue, and am,

Dear SIR,

Your obliged and affectionate friend in CHRIST JESUS,
Weston, May 31. 1755. J. HERVEY.

Dear SIR,

LAST night I was favoured with your second letter, and sincerely thank you for the freedom you have used, and the corrections you have made.—Herewith I send the remainder of dialogue xvi. those parts, I mean, that are to undergo some alteration. I wish you could borrow the larger edition; to that the numeral references are made, as from that the new edition is printing.—I hope you will be so kind as to examine this MS. also with a friendly severity. Spare no sentiment or expression, I beseech you, that so much as seems contrary to the sound words of our LORD JESUS CHRIST. If you see any thing that may conveniently be omitted, I wish you would inclose it in a parenthesis; for, I fear, the dialogue will be too long, and overwhelm the attention.

I am sorry that I am so straitened in time, and can say no more; my servant waits, and if I delay him any longer, will be too late to dispatch some necessary business for the family.— Be pleased to favour me with your observations as soon as possible, because the printers will, if they are delayed much longer, be tempted to impatience. I should be glad if you would make *Weston* in your way, when you return from *Norwich*. May the *LORD JESUS* strengthen your judgment, make you of quick understanding, and enable you to detect every thing, in my poor essay, that is not agreeable to his word!—I am in doubt whether this letter should be directed to you at *London*, or *Norwich*.—A mistake in this particular may cause a longer delay in the affair. The all-seeing GOD guide me in every thing! I chuse *London*, and hope it will come to your hand before you set out. I am,

Dear SIR,

Your obliged and truly affectionate friend in CHRIST JESUS,
Weston, June 12. J. HERVEY.

Dear Sir,

I Should be very glad, and much obliged, if you could give me your company in your return from *Norwich*, that we may thoroughly canvass, and carefully examine the important subject of our correspondence. I have ordered the printers to keep their types, composed for this part of my work, standing; and to proceed with the remainder, before this is worked off. So that I hope to have the whole, in proof-sheets, to lay before you in one view, provided you could favour me with your company pretty soon.

A celebrated divine from abroad writes thus, in a private letter to his friend; in which he speaks the very sentiments of my heart, and I apprehend, of yours also.

" I apprehend, Mr *Hervey*'s definition of faith will expose
" him most to the generality of divines, both of the church
" of *England* and dissenters; though it is a very good one,
" when well explained. The persuasion or assurance which is
" in the very nature of faith, must be carefully distinguished
" from that which has, in a manner, appropriated the name
" of assurance to itself; I mean that exercise of spiritual sense
" following upon saving faith, whereby a believer sees, and,
" upon good grounds, concludes himself to be in a state of
" grace and salvation, and that he has an actual interest in
" *CHRIST*, and his whole purchase, even eternal life.
" The foundation of this assurance of sense, is the believer's
" experience and feeling of what the HOLY GHOST has al-
" ready wrought in his soul, and it runs into this conclusion;
" I find the fruits of the SPIRIT planted in my soul; I am a
" new creature; I love the *LORD JESUS* in sincerity *;
" and it is one of the greatest burdens of my life, that I have
" no love suited to so glorious a one †. From all which, I
" am sure, GOD has given me *CHRIST*, pardoned my
" sins,

---

* It must be remembered, that they who love the Lord Jesus, love him that came to save, not the righteous, but the guilty; not the qualified, but the lost.

† This manner of expression, which this friend never learned from the scriptures, but catched (as I suppose) thro' common custom, favours too much of the leaven of the Pharisees. The Christian, conscious to himself that he is guilty, makes no account of the degrees of imperfect love, but lives solely and entirely by the righteousness revealed for the hope of the guilty: and what he lives by, he loves; not as a task proportioned by the worthiness of the object, but as an affection arising from the truth believed.

" fins, I am in a state of grace, and must go to glory. But
" the ground and foundation of that particular persuasion and
" assurance, which is in the nature of saving faith, is the glo-
" rious authority and faithfulness of GOD in the gospel re-
" cord, promise, and offer; and it rises no higher than this,
" that GOD offers, and thereby, as he is true and faithful,
" gives *CHRIST*, with all his fulness, to me, to be believed
" on, and trusted in, for life and eternal salvation *. So that
" I not only safely and warrantably may, but am obliged † to
" receive, apply, and make use of *JESUS CHRIST* as
" my own Saviour, by resting on him, and trusting to him as
" such. JEHOVAH's great gift, offer, and promise, gives
" every sinner a sufficient warrant to do this, and are a strong
" immoveable foundation for this persuasion or assurance of
" faith Nor can any other solid satisfying answer be given to
" a broken-hearted humbled creature ‡, who puts away from
" himself the gracious promises and offers of the gospel upon
" this ill-grounded imagination, that they do not belong to
" him. To whom it always may, and ought to be answered,
" that they do belong to him, in the sense I have mentioned ||."

This

* This is well expressed, and evidently distinguishes his meaning of the word *offer*, from the *offer* of a bargain to any who will come up to the terms. He evidently means the *real grant* of the blessings, as when money, food, and cloathing, are offered to the poor, famished, or naked.

† They who hear and understand this gospel-grace, find it their bounden duty, as well as their happy privilege, and heart's inclination, no more to seek to live by their own, but to live entirely by the divine righteousness.

‡ If this gentleman, by *a broken-hearted humbled creature*, means some that were hereby more qualified for mercy than the rest, he would differ from us widely; but if (as I apprehend) he only means those whose criminal remorse renders them absolutely destitute of every other hope than by Christ alone, we are of one mind.

|| One of the most evangelical-appearing objections against this grant of Christ to be believed on, is, " That, according to this
" doctrine, the free gift does not secure their reigning in life on
" whom it is bestowed; because they may rise to damnation for all
" that abundance of the gift." To which it may be answered, That gift, though to sinners indefinitely, that they may live by it, yet is a nonentity to every one till he hears it, and no conveyance of righteousness to any man that does not believe it, according to that which is spoken. And on the other hand, where a man does really believe it, he undoubtedly lives by it; and there *grace reigns thro' righteousness to eternal life*, over all who are thus begotten again,

This extract is, I think, the precise explanation of our doctrine. If you find any expression, not exactly suited to your opinion, please to observe it. I am,

Dear SIR,

Your affectionate and obliged brother in CHRIST,

Weston, July 6. 1755.   J. HERVEY.

Dear Mr CUDWORTH,

LAST night I received your favour, and according to your request, have written to my excellent friend, without delaying a single post. The LORD JESUS accompany my conciliatory offices with his heavenly blessing!

I hope you had a good journey, and are well in health, and joyful through faith.—We shall all be glad to hear, that ―― bore his journey comfortably, and is returned home more and more established in the love of his blessed LORD.

I hope you do not forget me and my family, my people, and my work at the press.—May the good LORD prosper you, and your labours of love!

I am much straitened for time, and can add no more at present, but that

I am yours, most cordially,

Aug. 4.   J. HERVEY.

Dear Mr CUDWORTH,

MR W――d has been with me, and went away last week. We had much talk concerning you. I told him what I thought of your conversation and doctrine. What I could urge seemed to make no impression. I assure you, my esteem for you is not diminished. I am more and more persuaded, that your method of stating that grand and precious doctrine —the doctrine of faith in CHRIST—is the truth of the gospel. Your company, whenever you come this way, will be truly acceptable to all my family.

I wish you would inform me of the mistakes which you apprehend to be in Dr *Crisp's* sermons. I have the new edition; intend

intend to read them very attentively; and should be glad of your cautionary hints.

Pray let me hear from you soon; and believe me to be,

Dear Sir,

Your cordial and faithful friend,

Weston, Sept. 9.
J. HERVEY.

Dear Mr CUDWORTH,

I Received your welcome letter from *London*. I should have answered it much sooner, but I had quite forgot where to direct. The direction was given in the first letter you ever wrote to me, which, consisting only of kind and friendly expressions, I suffered to perish, as I do all letters of that kind. Your other epistolary favours I carefully preserve.—I have waited and waited one day after another, in hopes of seeing you at *Weston*, in your return to *Norwich*; and have been uneasy in myself, least you should think I neglect your correspondence. Indeed I do not. Neither do I forget my promise. I have a set of the new edition, reserved on purpose for you; to be delivered into your own hand, if you call upon me. Or I will order a set to be left for you in *London*, where-ever you shall appoint.

I sincerely thank you for the copy of your letter. The sentiments are such as I wish to have written on my heart; such as I wish to speak and teach, while I live; and in my writings (if my writings survive me) to testify when I am dead. May the good LORD bear witness to such doctrine, by making it healing to the conscience, and fruitful in the conversation.

Your treatise of *marks and evidences* I will attentively read. If any thing occurs, which seems to need explication or alteration, I will most freely communicate it.

Pray let me hear from you soon. Inform me how you go on with Mr ———. Depend upon it, I will do you all the service that lies in my power. Not merely because you are a friend, whom I esteem, but also because I am persuaded, you work the work of the *LORD JESUS*.—To whose tender love I commend yourself and your labours; and am,

Dear Sir,

Your truly-affectionate friend,

Weston, Oct. 9.
J. HERVEY.

TO MR CUDWORTH.

My dear friend,

YOUR welcome letter is now in my hand. I thank you for the remarks it contains. The LORD make us of quick understanding in the fear of the LORD!

I have read the treatise concerning *marks and evidences.* I am going, as soon as I have dispatched this letter, to read it again. If to do the heart good be a sign of its value, I can very confidently bear this testimony to its worth. It refreshes my spirit and comforts my soul. I hope, when re-published, it will be attended with this blessed effect to multitudes of readers *.—I believe it would be adviseable to send it abroad without a name, and commit it wholly to the disposal of Him, who is head over all things to the church.

Did you ever see a little treatise written by one Mr *Beart,* formerly pastor of a church in the place where you now reside? It is styled *A vindication of the eternal law and everlasting gospel?* It is but very lately that it came to my hands. It appears to me a truly valuable piece.—I forgot to desire, that you would present my most cordial salutations to Mr ———. It is not for want of esteem that I do not write to him, but from want of health, and a multiplicity of engagements. I should be very glad, if he would communicate with all freedom, any remarks that he himself has made, or has heard from others, relating to *Theron* and *Aspasio.*

Mr ——— called upon me, about ten days ago, in his return to *London.* He staid only to make a hasty breakfast, so that I had very little conversation with him. I hope the GOD of power, and the GOD of peace, will unite our hearts in the love of the spirit, and unite our hands in the work of the LORD.

There is no stage goes from *Northampton* to *Suffolk.* I believe I may convey a parcel by the *Cambridge* carrier. I will inquire of him, when he comes this way; and if it is a practical thing, you shall have the books by his next return.

We shall be all glad to entertain you at *Weston,* and my best prayers will always accompany your labours in the LORD.
—I

* This treatise, so useful to my worthy friend, was one of the most offensive pieces to my opponents; which very plainly manifests, that whatever compliments and pretensions of regard might be paid to Mr *Hervey,* they differed exceedingly in taste and judgment of spiritual things.

—I send a frank, lest your stock should be exhausted.—Write to me soon, and pray for me ever, who am,

Dear Sir,

Your affectionate brother in CHRIST,

Weston, Nov. 8. 1755.   J. HERVEY.

My dear friend,

I Sent, last week, by the *Cambridge* carrier, a set of my books. He promised me to deliver them to the *Bury* carrier; and, I hope, by this time, they have reached your hands.—Whenever you peep upon them, pray be so kind as to note down any expressions or sentiments that are not THOROUGHLY evangelical. I shall be pleased with them, and thankful for them, even though I should not have, through the want of a new edition, an opportunity of inserting them in my volumes.

I have been thinking of your proposal to re-publish your treatise on *marks and evidences*. Suppose you transmit it, detached from any other piece, under a frank to me. Suppose I send it to an understanding and sagacious friend; and learn his sentiments, and get his critical observations on it. By this means, you will see what is likely to give offence, or meet with objection; and may, perhaps, be enabled so to form your arguments, so to draw up your forces, as to prevent or baffle any attack. If you approve of this scheme, send me a copy of the piece; tear off the title-page, and I will immediately convey it to a friend, who lives at a great distance from *London*, who knows nothing of the author, and will give me his opinion, without favour or disaffection.

Lest you should not be furnished with a frank, I send the inclosed.—My sister is gone from home; my mother is in health, and will always be glad of such conversation as yours; which will be equally agreeable to,

Dear Sir,

Your affectionate friend and brother in CHRIST JESUS,

Weston, Nov. 25. 1755.   J. HERVEY.

My dear friend,

I Received, with pleasure and gratitude, your letter and its contents. Would have made my acknowledgments immediately; but waited a post or two, in hopes of transmitting to you some remarks on your treatise. But my friend has not sent them. As soon as they come, they shall be forwarded to you.

I am very much pleased with your explanation of, *In the* LORD *have I righteousness.* " *I* a sinner, not I a new or " sanctified creature." This is encouraging; this is delightful; it is like a door opened in the ark for me, even for me to enter. Blessed be GOD for such truths! Such truths make the gospel glad tidings indeed to my soul. They are the very thing which I want; and the only thing which can give me comfort, or do me good *.

When

---

* If Mr *Hervey* may be believed, nothing was more offensive to him, than those encomiums on his piety, which only serve to render his confession of himself hypocritical, and his doctrine false. In all his thoughts, in all his practice, he found himself a sinner; and in nothing more so, than in entertaining any good conceit of himself, or his own state, by comparison with other men. God had taught him he had no rule to measure by, but the perfect law, or will of heaven; and every single deviation served to render his plea of righteousness vain, to class him among the rest of mankind-sinners, and subject him to eternal vengeance. In the view of these circumstances, mercy revealed in Christ Jesus to the guilty, was a precious joyful sound, which he heard and lived by. Had he heard any one describe the holy, heavenly, pious Mr *Hervey*, he would have replied, You have described a man that will never enter heaven; but in the guilty Mr *Hervey*, living only by the divine righteousness, you find the man that is taught of God.

To love the divine righteousness provided for the guilty as such; to love God thus characterized as just, and the justifier of the ungodly by the righteousness of his Son; to love them that are of this truth, for the truth's sake dwelling in them, is, according to scripture-account, the distinguishing *holiness of truth*, whereby the children of God are manifested from the children of the devil; and the works of love to this righteousness, are the only works that will be openly rewarded and acknowledged in the great day. It is also evident, from scripture and experience, that men may compass sea and land to make a proselyte, may give all their goods to feed the poor, and even their bodies to be burned, yet want this charity; they may do all this, and at the same time manifest themselves to be the children of them who crucified Jesus, by their conduct towards his real gospel, and the disciples of it.

When people inquire, whether sanctification is an evidence of justification? I suppose, by sanctification, they mean what St *Paul* calls the fruits of the SPIRIT; love of GOD, charity to man, meekness, temperance *, &c. Now, may we not allow these to be proper evidences of faith, but maintain that the appropriating faith, or the faith of persuasion †, is the appointed means of producing them! *The life which I live in the flesh,* the life of holiness, usefulness, and comfort, *I live by the faith of the SON of GOD.* What this faith is, he explains in the next sentence; by viewing the SON of GOD, *as loving me, and giving himself for me.*—Pray favour me with your opinion of 1 *John* iii. 19. This seems one of the texts, least reconcileable with our doctrine ‡.

I have a long letter from a new hand, wrote very fair, and drawn up in an elaborate manner, in opposition to my account of faith, and to several parts of *dialogue* xvi. It consists of five sheets, wrote on every side; too large I apprehend to come under a frank, otherwise I would transmit it to you for your

---

* /They should mean so; and the fruit of love, &c. which is evidently from this operation of the divine truth we plead for, is undoubtedly a confirming evidence of its having become our faith, and of its divine efficacy in working by love.

† By *appropriating faith*, he means the confidence arising from the belief of the truth, of righteousness and salvation freely presented to the guilty in Christ Jesus, as their immediate ground of confidence; which he also styles the *faith of persuasion*, to distinguish it from that which is described, not by what we are persuaded of, but as a hidden, holy principle, discoverable only by the good qualifications which distinguish us from others.

‡ *Hereby we* (the children of the truth, by loving one another for the truth's sake alone, not in word and in tongue, but in deed and in truth) *hereby we know* (or have an additional confirming knowledge,) *that we are of the truth* we profess, *and shall assure our hearts before him,* saying with Peter, *Lord, thou knowest all things, thou knowest that we love thee:* For *if our hearts condemn us,* that we love not those who are of this truth, or that our love to them is not for this truth's sake, whatever pretensions we may make to the faith, and of comfort, joy, holiness, &c. yet *God is greater than our heart, and knoweth all things;* therefore cannot be deceived by our pretended regard to him and his truth, while we love not them who are of this truth. But, *beloved, if our hearts condemn us not,* (if the law of the New Testament, *Jer.* xxxi. 33. to believe on Christ, or live by his righteousness, and love one another for this truth's sake, is written on our hearts,) *then have we confidence towards God.*

your perusal. And I hope to see you ere long; then we may examine it together.

I am glad to hear that you are acquainted with Mr ———, and that he is so well acquainted with the truth as it is in *JESUS*. The LORD enable him, and raise up many more ministers, to spread abroad the joyful sound.—When you give me your company, do not forget to bring with you the evangelical piece on the work of the SPIRIT in bringing a soul to *CHRIST*.

There is one passage in *dialogue* xvi. which, I think, is very injudiciously inserted, and is really a mistake. The *note*, p. 303. I observed it a good while ago, and expunged it from my copy; and my new opposer has not spared to animadvert upon it. What need have we to pray for that divine GUIDE, *who leads into all truth!* May this divine GUIDE dwell in us, and walk in us, be our counsellor and comforter even unto death!—Dear Mr *Cudworth*, I hope, will not forget in his prayers the weakest of ministers, and the weakest of believers, —but his

Affectionate brother in CHRIST,

Weston, Jan. 26. 1756.   J. HERVEY.

My dear friend,

I Received your valuable remarks, and sincerely thank you for them. May our divine MASTER enable us, both to discern and to display the truth as it is in *JESUS*.

I am much pleased, and thoroughly satisfied, with your explanation of *Acts* ii. 39 *. The proposals seem to me clear, pertinent,

---

* *Acts* ii. 39. The persons mentioned, were pricked in their hearts, at hearing that God had made that same Jesus, whom they had crucified, both Lord and Christ, and said, *Men and brethren, what shall we do?* We don't find that *Peter* had been preaching to them any such doctrine as that, " if they were much affected with their " sins, and wounded at heart with a godly sorrow for them, they " had an interest in the promise of life and salvation." This would have been only introducing the *Pharisaic* distinction, which our Saviour constantly opposed. On the contrary, when *Peter* declared, that God had made *that same Jesus*, who opposed such distinctions in the *Pharisees*, and was rejected on that account, that God had made him *both Lord and Christ,* they were confounded. All their pretensions to righteousness, and acceptance with God, forsook them.

They

pertinent, and weighty. If I am able to make any flight correction in the ftyle, it fhall be tranfmitted in my next.—I would now only afk, how far you have proceeded in the work? I think you fhould by all means get the greater part (the whole, I would rather fay) completed, before you begin to publifh. If this is not done, many unforefeen accidents may arife, which will probably ftraiten you in point of time, and oblige you to be precipitate in your preparations for the prefs. And I am inclined to query, whether it is not a piece of juftice we owe to the public, not to engage them in purchafing a piece, till it is put beyond the power of common cafualties to render it imperfect.—Pray, therefore, let me know what progrefs you have made. I could wifh to have it judicioufly executed, and not performed in that confufed, inaccurate, flovenly manner, which muft be a continual difcredit to Mr *W*——'s *Chriftian library*.

I rejoice to find, that the gofpel of our falvation is fpreading. May it have a free courfe and an extenfive circuit! till the fountain becomes a river, and the river widens into a fea!

The inclofed came a little while ago.—My friend is very fevere. It will give you an opportunity of exercifing forbearance and gentlenefs. He knows nothing at all of the author.

When They were pricked in their hearts at thefe tidings, and cried out, *Men and brethren what fhall we do?* If Jefus is Lord and Chrift, what will become of us? Then *Peter* exhorted to the affurance we plead for, in thefe words, *Repent, and be baptized in the name of Jefus, for the remiffion of fins;* (for the words thus circumftanced bear evidently this fenfe): "Your cafe is undoubtedly defperate; you have been to this moment God's enemies; even fo far have you carried your oppofition, as *with wicked hands to crucify and flay the Lord's* Chrift, fent for your deliverance. Neverthelefs, *in this man's name is preached unto you remiffion of fins:* therefore *repent* of your wickednefs in oppofing him; fubmit to him as your free given righteoufnefs and falvation; be baptized in his name *for the remiffion of your fins,* and live free from henceforth by him, as your proper righteoufnefs: affuring yourfelves of *remiffion of fins* by him alone; and you fhall receive the promifed gift of the *Holy Ghoft* as it has come upon us: *For the promife is to you and to your children.*" And *with many other words did he exhort them, faying,* (by flying to this fame Jefus as your proper refuge,) *Save yourfelves from this untoward generation. Then they that gladly received his word,* out of the mixed multitude, *were baptized; and the fame day were added about three thoufand fouls.*—From the whole thus confidered, there is nothing to contradict the call and promife of God directed to finners as fuch; but, on the contrary, a foundation for calling upon the moft guilty to live immediately by the Redeemer's righteoufnefs.

When your other affairs will allow leisure, please to return the letter with your observations; which will oblige, and, I trust, edify,

Dear Sir,

Your affectionate friend,

Weston, Apr. 21. 1756.   J. HERVEY.

Dear Mr CUDWORTH,

I Have only time to beg of you, if you have the letter of remarks on Mr *Marshall*'s book, to return it to me as soon as you can. If there are any observations that are just, and such as animadvert upon passages *truly exceptionable*, be so kind as to give me your opinion on them. The reason of my desiring this, is a prospect of a new edition of *Marshall*.—A bookseller is inclined to print one, and sell it at half a crown price; I believe encouraged thereto by my recommendation of it. The recommendation has been printed in our *Northampton* news-paper, and immediately there was a demand for twenty-three of your abridgements. But the printer could not procure enough to supply the demands. Mr K—— desires you will send a fresh supply to him.

In the greatest haste, but with great sincerity and affection,

Yours,

May 27.   JAMES HERVEY.

My Dear Friend,

THis comes to inform you, that Mr —— has begun an edition of *Marshall*; in much the same size, and exactly the same letter, as *Theron* and *Aspasio*. If you have any thing to observe, pray let me have it with as much speed as you can make. If you have Mr ——'s objections, examine them attentively; and, I hope, you will be enabled to obviate what is material. I should be glad if you could, after you have digested your notes, give me your company, that we might talk them over. Now is the time, in all probability, to make *Marshall* a well-known spreading book.— I hope the LORD will enlighten your understanding; fructify your invention;

vention; strengthen your judgment; and enable you to write
" found words, such as cannot be condemned."—I am,

Very affectionately yours,

Weston, June 17. J. HERVEY.

My dear friend,

YEsterday I received your letter, and am much obliged to you for it. Pray do not mention Mr ———'s name, nor shew his letter. I hope to adhere to the truths of the gospel; but yet I would endeavour to live in harmony, of affection and friendly intercourse at least, with those who differ.—I cannot think, that Mr ——— could have any knowledge of the author of the discourse *against marks and evidences*.—I will read your treatise over again, with my best attention. For, I assure you, it always does me good. I will also compare it with your remarks on Mr ———; which, in my opinion, are solid and satisfactory; I am sure they are encouraging and comfortable.

When *Marshall* was advertised in our news-paper, the gentleman that inserted my recommendation, added this note to explain one sentence.—" By uncommon road, 'tis presumed, the recommender means the very evangelical nature, and remarkably-instructive method of the directions laid down by Mr *Marshall* (than whom no man, perhaps, was ever better acquainted with the human heart) for the effectual practice of holiness, as likewise somewhat of obscurity which is confessedly in his 3d and 4th direction."

I apprehend, the obscurity of chapter 3. and 4. arises, not from any improper manner of treating the subjects, but from the mysterious * nature of the subjects themselves.—I will write to the bookseller to suspend his procedure of the prefs till he hears farther. But let this *hasten* you, my dear friend, in communicating what you have to observe. I should be glad to have our common favourite, as clear and unexceptionable as possible, &c. &c. †

My dear friend,

THE cause of my writing is this, Mr ——— is upon the point of publishing a new edition of *Marshall*. I have

given

* Mysterious, because contrary to our natural notions, the *natural man not receiving the things of the Spirit of God.*
† The remainder of this letter is lost.

given him the inclosed letter, to introduce it into the world; but was defirous to have you peruse it and correct it, before it goes to the prefs. Be fo kind, therefore, as to examine it ſtrictly; and where-ever you think it ſhould be altered, ufe with it the freedom of a friend. The more rigour, the more kindnefs.

I fend a Frank to be the vehicle of your obfervations, together with the printed half-ſheet.

As foon as I have finiſhed what you mention, it ſhall be tranfmitted. Though I would fain fee one of the books completely abridged, before any propofals or advertifements appear. It is a matter of great importance, pray let it be executed with care and correctnefs. May the Keeper of *Iſrael* protect you in your journeys, and the Light of the world guide you in your work!

Affectionately yours,

Wefton, Oct. 6. 1756.   J. HERVEY.

My dear friend,

MR —— told Mr W——d that I *offered* to write a *preface* to your remarks on his fermons. I told Mr W——d the whole of the affair. That you informed me of your defign, and what I anfwered. That I defire it might be conducted in a tender and refpectful manner. That the title ſhould be more friendly and benign. That you read what you propofed to fay concerning my mentioning of *Marſhall*; which I obferved was inexpreſſive. If you faid any thing, I thought it ſhould be more weighty and fignificant. This was all the concern I had in the affair.

—That I had promifed, not offered (for I don't remember I ever did fuch a thing in my life) to write a recommendatory introduction to the work, which you have in hand. That it was at your requeſt, but with the real approbation of my judgment; for I apprehended that your defign, when well executed, would be a valuable prefent to the world.

This comes by a gentleman who knows you. Let me hear what Mr —— fays about the affair. And remember to give me a direction where to write to you. You date from *Margaret-ſtreet*; but this I fuppofe is not particular enough. I can

can add no more, leaft the bearer fhould be gone. Only I wifh you much fuccefs in preaching *CHRIST*.

Yours affectionately,

Wefton, Dec. 24. 1756.   J. HERVEY.

My dear friend,

I Received your parcel containing feveral copies of *The Friendly Attempt*, &c. * My thanks fhould have been returned fooner; but I have been under that indifpofition and languor of fpirit, which renders me unfit for every thing.

I think there is rather too much afperity in the clofe; and I wifh that expreffion "refined idolatry" had been a little foftened. This I mention only to yourfelf, and to give you a fpecimen of that opennefs and freedom, which I would have take place in all our perfonal and epiftolary intercourfes.

I have read your manufcript again and again, with my beft attention, and with much delight †. I have made here and there a fmall alteration with regard to the language, only to render the fenfe fomewhat more perfpicuous, not to vary the peculiar caft of your diction.—I heartily concur in receiving and embracing thefe doctrines. I think them to be truths of very great importance, and fhall be truly glad to fee them in print, that they may be fpread and be univerfally known.

IF I fhould be enabled to finifh a fourth volume of dialogues, I propofe to have one conference on the affurance of faith ‡; to ftate it more clearly, and to eftablifh it more ftrongly. In this, I fhall be glad to borrow feveral of your thoughts, and will make my acknowledgments accordingly; declaring, at the fame time, my opinion of the piece, which lends me fuch valuable affiftance.

Prefent my moft affectionate falutations to ——— ———. I received

---

* A friendly attempt to remove fome fundamental miftakes in the Rev. Mr *W———d's* fermons.

† *Aphorifms on the affurance of faith.* The fubftance of them originally was what Mr *Hervey* takes notice of in his letter, dated Oct. 9. 1755 Afterward Mr *Hervey* defired me to draw up the fubftance of the whole, that had been canvaffed, in as concife a manner as poffible, for his own ufe. This, fome time after, I propofed for printing, and is the manufcript here mentioned.

‡ Or in other words, the confidence that is founded on the truth we believe concerning Chrift given to be *believed on*, or confided in.

received his obliging letter; I most sincerely wish him success, in displaying the unsearchable riches of grace, and the infinitely-glorious righteousness of *CHRIST*. I hope he will not be displeased with my silence. It proceeds from no disrespect, but from a multiplicity of engagements, and a poor pittance of strength, utterly insufficient to fulfil them.—Please to thank —— for his very encouraging and comfortable letter. I wish, when he is at leisure, he would favour me with another on this subject, how holiness springs from faith, or a view of sanctification as the effect of justification. When shall I see you?—If —— writes to me on the subject you mention, he shall have a speedy answer.—You need not send me the twelve queries, because they have been transmitted me from *Scotland*. But cease not to send up your prayers and supplications in behalf of your truly-affectionate friend,

J. HERVEY.

My dear friend,

I Have, with attention and delight, read over your pamphlet. A slight alteration or two, relating to the language, I have made. But I desire you will follow the determination of your own judgment.—As soon as they are printed, send me a quarter of a hundred; not as a present, but as a purchase.

The LORD has lately visited me with a dangerous fever; which confined me to my room many days, and excluded me from the pulpit several *Sundays.* I am still extremely weak in body. Pray that I may be strong in the faith of our *LORD JESUS CHRIST.*—In his most precious and everlasting righteousness, I remain,

Affectionately yours,

J. HERVEY.

P. S. Send me a dozen of your *Aphorisms*, when they are published.

Mr dear friend,

ONE principal cause of my long silence, I do assure you, was my ignorance of the place of your residence in *London.* I knew not, till Mr ——, yesterday, gave me a direction where to write to you.

I thank you for your last packet. But you must give me leave to insist upon paying for the contents, when I have the pleasure of your company, which I want much. Can't you make *Weston* in your way, and contrive to spend a couple of days with me? I cannot be satisfied with a shorter stay.——I have much to say to you; but as I will hope to see you, and converse face to face, I shall not attempt to communicate my thoughts by ink and pen.

I have just published three sermons. If you will call upon Mr R——'s in St *Paul's* church-yard, or send a messenger with the note subjoined to this letter, he will deliver two of my pieces. Let me beg of you to peruse them, with your pen in your hand; and to transmit whatever observations may occur.— I have some remarks upon your *Aphorisms*, which you shall see, when you give me your company.—Have you seen a couple of volumes, lately published, and entitled, *Letters on Theron and Aspasio?* You come in for a share of chastisement. What is your opinion in general of this performance? As to particular passages, we will postpone the examination of them, till GOD's providence grants us a personal interview *. Do you know who is, or who is supposed to be the author of this piece?

May the work of the LORD JESUS prosper in your heart, your tongue, your pen, and in those of your truly

affectionate friend,

Weston, Sept. 8. 1757. J. HERVEY.

Dear Mr CUDWORTH,

I Received your letter, and return you my very sincere thanks for your remarks †. I only wish that there had been more of them.

I hope it will not be long, before you give me your company at *Weston*. Then we will examine the three dialogues, as they appear in their new form; and will consider, and determine, concerning their publication ‡; or rather will beseech the only

* The result of this consideration, and of my after-correspondence with Mr *Sandeman*, at Mr *Hervey's* request, see in the defence of *Theron* and *Aspasio*.

† Remarks on *Theron* and *Aspasio* considered with regard to the objections raised by the author of the letters.

‡ The publication of the 15th, 16th, and 17th dialogues corrected with regard to the objections of Mr *Sandeman*.

only wife GOD our SAVIOUR, to over-rule and guide our determination. Contrive to stay some time with me.

Try if you can get me *Taylor's* book; or any of those which you shewed me. *Neonomianism unmasked*, if you can light on, purchase for me —I wish you growing consolation in CHRIST, deliverance from all your troubles, and abundant success in spreading abroad the favour of our REDEEMER's name, In whom I am,

Dear SIR,
Your true and affectionate friend and brother,

Weston, Feb. 22. 1758.   J. HERVEY.

Dear Mr CUDWORTH,

YEsterday your favour came to hand. I hope to see you at *Weston* ere long, and then I will deliver the letters * into your own hand.—I have sent you a couple of franks. If you want more, when I see you, I will endeavour to supply you.—I am glad you are debating the important point with Mr *Sandeman*. He seems to be an acute person; and if there is a flaw in our cause, he will be likely to discover it. But, as far as I can judge, he has found no such thing hitherto.

May the GOD of truth and grace be with you; and enable you to understand and defend the first; to experience and abundantly enjoy the last.

Please to present my very affectionate respects to your worthy kinsman Mr ——, and recommend to his prayer, and remember in your own,

Dear SIR,
Your brother in CHRIST,

Weston, Mar. 1. 1758.   J. HERVEY.

Dear Mr CUDWORTH,

THIS comes to desire you will inform me how I may direct a large letter to you; which I will send, as soon as your answer is received. It is a manuscript †, which wants your examination,

* Letters of correspondence between me and Mr *Sandeman*.
† This was an answer to Mr *John Wesley's* objections against *Theron* and *Aspasio*, and is so valuable a defence of imputed righteousness, that its publication is much to be desired.— It has been since published by Mr Hervey's brother, and may be seen in the preceding part of this volume.

examination, and it is of some importance. Therefore I am somewhat solicitous, that it may not miscarry.

        Yours affectionately,
Weston, July 15. 1758.   J. HERVEY.

P. S. You may direct your letter, to stop at *Northampton*. Don't use any of your franks. You will have greater occasion for them. Or, if your stock is spent, let me know.

Dear Mr CUDWORTH,

THIS day I received your letter, with the two *MS.* sheets inclosed. Accept my thanks for your remarks, and let me beg of you to examine the two sheets, which are now sent. I will take your advice with regard to Mr B——; and follow your hint, concerning your own work.——I apprehend there will be about *ten* such sheets; and that the piece will make a two-shilling pamphlet. I must intreat you to get time for the revisal of all; which shall be sent you, as you shall be able to dispatch the work. I am,
     Dear SIR,
       Most cordially yours,
July 27. 1758.   J. HERVEY.

My dear friend,

LAST week I sent you two sheets of the manuscript, now I send two more for your revisal. If you see a fair opportunity of contracting, please to make use of it: for, I fear, the piece will be too long. Inclose what you think may be omitted in a parenthesis, by a pencil.——Pray examine rigorously, by which you will very much oblige
     Your truly affectionate
Weston, Aug. 2. 1758.   J. HERVEY.

My dear friend,

HERE I inclose two sheets more. They are very long. But I hope you will get time to revise them. Your last packet I received, and am much obliged for your remarks.——I apprehend, the piece will make a two-shilling pamphlet. If
            you

you could suggest or insert any thing to make it *edifying* and useful, I should be glad. Would it not be proper to print Mr *W———y*'s letter, and prefix it to my answer?——Have you left your own two books for me at my brother's? If you have not, please to leave them at Mr *J. R.*——'s in St *Paul*'s church-yard. I am,
  Dear S i r,
   Cordially yours in CHRIST JESUS,
Weston, Aug. 9. 1758.   J. HERVEY.

P. S. I suppose about three sheets more will finish the work.

My dear Friend,

HERE are two more sheets. The last I received, with your valuable remarks. Pray bestow the same attention on these. Two more, or less, will finish the essay; then I will discontinue writing, and employ myself in reading, especially in reading *Luther*'s comment*. Can't you procure for me *Taylor*'s book? I am,
  Dear S i r,
   Affectionately yours,
Aug. 16.   J. HERVEY.

My dear Friend,

I Received in due time your last letter. Should have sent the conclusion of my manuscript, but it has been lent out, and is not yet returned.

I shall be glad to see your correspondence with Mr *Sandeman*.—The inclosed is a copy of a letter, which I sent some years ago, to two malefactors under sentence of death.—It is got into a good many hands. Some would have me print it. I wish you would be so kind as to revise it, and give me your opinion.—People say, there is not enough said concerning the spiritual change, or the new heart.

My next shall bring you a little piece of mine, which, without my knowledge, has passed the press.—I have lately been in great want of franks. But now I have got a recruit.

I have been very ill this week, but had strength enough to
             read

* As abridged and designed for the Evangelical Library.

read in your book. I was much edified by Mr *Simpson's* sermons. Pray, are his whole works to be procured? and are they of the same spirit with the sermons which you have given us? If so, I should desire to see, to possess them all.

I am

Very affectionately, yours,

Weston, Sept. 23. 1758.   J. HERVEY.

My dear Friend,

EXcuse me for keeping your *MS.* * so long; I have been extremely ill. This morning I have been up for four hours, and in all that time not able to look into a book, or hold up my head.

I fully assent to your opinion. Think you have proved the warrant for a sinner's application of CHRIST very satisfactorily.—If I live, I should much desire a copy of this your correspondence, when you have revised and finished it. Or do you intend to print it?

Have you got some complete sets of all your works? If you have, I wish you would lodge about four of them at Mr R———n's. Let them be only in sheets. And when you have given me notice, that they are deposited with him, I will order him to pay you a guinea for them. I promised a worthy clergyman a set, some days ago.

Yours affectionately,

Weston, Dec. 2.   J. HERVEY.

Dear Mr CUDWORTH,

I AM so weak, I am scarcely able to write my name †.

Dec. 15, 1758.   J. HERVEY.

A

---

* The remaining part of my correspondence with Mr *Sandeman.*

† Hearing how dangerously ill Mr *Hervey* was, I wrote to remind him of leaving something under his hand in regard to his writings, as he knew the situation of them *now* required it; and this was all the answer he could give me.

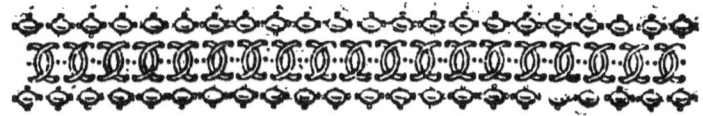

A DEFENCE

OF

THERON and *ASPASIO*,

AGAINST THE

Objections contained in a late Treatise, entitled, *Letters on Theron and Aspasio.*

THE sum and substance of the doctrine pleaded for by *Aspasio*, is, " That God hath so given " eternal life in his Son, to guilty sinners, as that " they are fully warranted to receive Christ, or assure " themselves of salvation by him alone, without wait- " ing for any inward motions, feelings, or desires, " as any way requisite in order to such a reception or " assurance."

This doctrine has been hitherto opposed under the notion, (1.) That some inward motions, feelings, or desires, were some way requisite in order thereto. That these inward motions, feelings, or desires, were the faith or reception of Christ spoken of in the scripture; or at least the indications of it; and must be discerned in us, in that light, before there can be any well-grounded assurance of salvation by him. (2.) That if we are called directly to live by Christ, or appropriate him, he is ours and we are safe, whether we appropriate him or no. (3.) That it is assuring ourselves of what, for ought we know, is absolutely false. (4.) That the wicked, the presumptuous, and the hypocrites, may, and do often, thus assure themselves. (5.) That there is nothing in faith, thus understood or exerted, which is a proper spring and cause of good works, by which it is in itself different from a false faith. (6.) That it is contrary to all self-examination, and assurance thereby. And, (7.) That such doctrine is a great discouragement to weak souls.

In answer to all this, we have asserted, (1.) That the divine revelation concerning Jesus is addressed to sinners, the world, the lost, and that without being directed to wait for any inward motions, feelings, or desires: remission of sins and eternal life in Christ, are said to be presented or given to them, and they are immediately called to believe on him as so granted. That the inward motions, feelings, or desires, correspondent to these gospel-declarations, are motions, desires, &c. to live by Christ alone, immediately, without waiting for any thing previous thereto. And that this voice of God, in these declarations of the gospel, was a sufficient authority for the whole we plead for, without waiting for any inward motions or excellencies in us to add thereto. (2.) That it is very absurd, to infer, that Christ being given for us to feed upon, or live by, that there is therefore no need to live by him. Nor is it (3.) assuring ourselves of what may be false; the divine declaration having secured this, that they which believe on him shall not be confounded; nor does any man thus live by Christ alone, but he who is chosen to salvation by the belief of the truth. Notwithstanding many deceive themselves, professing great confidence, but it is in some undue mixture or addition of their own to what God hath spoken. And, (4.) that it is here the presumptuous and the hypocrite do err and destroy themselves, and not in believing according to that which is spoken. (5.) That good works are works of love to God, thus manifested, and therefore it is the only principle of good works on this account. *We love him, because he first loved us.* So that it differs from a false faith, as
the

the belief of a truth differs from the belief of a falsehood; and as an apprehension of the divine favour begets love and obedience rather than an apprehension of wrath. (6.) That a proper self-examination is therefore, whether we thus live by Christ alone, or whether we are waiting for something more? And, (7.) that it is far from discouraging the chiefest sinners, to let them know, that God hath given to them eternal life in his Son, altho' it very possibly may, and ought to discourage every one from seeking relief in themselves, while the divine declarations point us so plainly to the salvation given in Christ Jesus to the guilty.

We have now to engage with another kind of an opponent, one that tells us, " That on account of our thus pleading for assurance of salvation, by receiving or appropriating Christ as given to us, we are also to be classed with the popular preachers, in as much as we also lead the guilty as they do, to seek after some inward motions, feelings, or desires, as some way requisite, in order to acceptance with God, not understanding how God can appear just to an unrighteous person, in justifying him as he at present stands, without some motion in his will, &c. That the whole doctrine of the popular preachers is devised for producing, animating, and directing this motion, that so the anxious hearer may find, about himself, some distinguishing reason why the Deity may regard him more than others. That the work finished by Jesus Christ in his death, proved by his resurrection, is all-sufficient to justify the guilty. That the whole benefit of this event, is conveyed to men, only, by the apostolic report concerning it.—And that this whole benefit is no more than a possibility of salvation, depending upon the divine sovereignty. That every one who understands this report to be true, or is persuaded that the event actually happened, as testified by the apostles, is justified, and finds relief to his guilty conscience, *i. e.*

the relief of the above-mentioned poſſibility. That ſuch are relieved, not by finding any favourable ſymptoms about their own heart, but by finding their report to be true. That all the divine power which operates on the minds of men, either to give the firſt relief to their conſciences, or to influence them in every part of their obedience, is perſuaſive power, or the forcible conviction of truth. That our primary notion of the divine character, can give no comfort to the guilty, but, on the contrary, make them miſerable by a ſenſe of fear and ſhame. That when a man knows how God may be juſt, in juſtifying him as he at preſent ſtands, he finds relief from the aforementioned diſquieting fear."

To this we reply in general, That we agree to the greater part, to almoſt all theſe aſſertions, as moſt valuable truths, and ſtand corrected by ſome of them, particularly, where-ever we have too charitably ſuppoſed or admitted a belief of the report, contrary to the ſcripture-declaration, *They that know thy name will put their truſt in thee* *; and thereby have been ſometimes † led to fall in with the multitude, who make light of the belief of the report, as a common thing; whereas, to know the real truth of the goſpel, in diſtinction from every corrupting and contradictory falſehood, is the peculiar teaching of God ; and every one that has ſo *heard and learned of the Father, comes to CHRIST.* We agree, that " our primary " notion of the divine character makes the guilty mi" ſerable, by a ſenſe of fear and ſhame." But we deny, that relief from this fear is obtained without being as certain that we have righteouſneſs, as we are
that

---

* Mr *Hervey* had begun a correction of his three laſt dialogues in this view, as mentioned in the letter, p. 324.

† *Sometimes*, for the force of truth frequently prevailed againſt this miſtake, before Mr *Sandeman*'s performance appeared.

that we have guilt. The divine declaration of Chrift, given to be believed on, affords a foundation for this certainty; and contains, therefore, more than fuch a poffibility as is above mentioned. We alfo deny the charge, that we lead the guilty, as the popular preachers do, to feek after fome inward motions, feelings, or defires, as fome way requifite, in order to acceptance with God. For notwithftanding the righteoufnefs appropriated relates to acceptance with God, the appropriation we plead for, relates only to the confcioufnefs, knowledge, and enjoyment of that righteoufnefs whereby the guilty are juftified. And we affirm, that to receive a gift, is no pre-requifite or condition, as fuch receiving has no exiftence without the thing received; and to be fo enriched, is not to be enriched by our act of receiving, or what we do, but only by what we receive. But as Mr *Sandeman*'s attack well deferves a more particular defence, we confider it as follows:

"Has our favourite author then at leaft fo far loft "fight of the imputed righteoufnefs, as to mix ano-"ther with it? Has he fo embarraffed, or rather fhut "up our accefs to the divine righteoufnefs, as to hold "forth a preliminary human one, as fome way ex-"pedient, or rather neceffary, to our enjoying the "comforts and benefits of it?" *Letters on Theron and Afpafio*, p. 4. *

No, far from it; but as the pinching point in the confcience is not, that there is no fuch righteoufnefs in being as pleafeth God; but that WE have no fuch righteoufnefs; fo, we underftand the comfort and benefit of Chrift's righteoufnefs to be, that it is a fufficient righteoufnefs in OUR behalf. And we who plead for the divine grant of this righteoufnefs to finners, as fuch, very evidently maintain, that there is no preliminary righteoufnefs neceffary to fuch a conclufion.

"I

---

* *N. B.* Mr *Sandeman*'s words are included with the commas, the other paragraphs are the reply.

"I speak of those teachers, who, having largely insisted on the corruption of human nature, concluded the whole world guilty before God, eloquently set forth the necessity of an atonement, zealously maintained the scripture-doctrine concerning the person and work of Christ; yet, after all, leave us as much in the dark as to our comfort, as if Jesus Christ had never appeared; and mark out as insuperable a task for us, as if he had not finished his work." p. 8, 9.

This charge may be very properly exhibited against those teachers who leave us as much in the dark as they found us, unless we can find out something within ourselves to distinguish us from other sinners. But *Aspasio's* doctrine brings Christ near to guilty sinners, as such, for their immediate enjoyment. Take and have, receive and possess, relates only to personal enjoyment, is no task, no entitling condition; the appropriation being fully warranted by the truth believed, and effected by the belief of it.

"While, with great assiduity and earnestness, they are busied in describing to us, animating us with various encouragements, and furnishing us with manifold instructions, how to perform that strange something which is to make out our connection with Christ, and bring his righteousness home to us." p. 9.

We say, Christ's righteousness is "brought home to us," in the gospel-declaration; without the necessity of any intervening righteousness to warrant us to call it ours. We only receive what is freely given; that is all the strange something we have pleaded for; and that not for our acceptance with God in virtue of our act, but only to know and enjoy that righteousness as ours, on account of which alone we are accepted.

"Setting them to work to do something, under
"whatever

"whatever name, to make up their peace with God."
Ibid.

Not so with us, who receive and live by Christ's righteousness, with which God hath declared himself already well pleased.

"Every doctrine which teaches us to do or endeavour any thing toward our acceptance with God, stands opposed to the doctrine of the apostles." p. 11.

But the doctrine we plead for, teaches us to live by what Christ has already done, as being given to us for that purpose. To say that I must do, or endeavour any thing that I may be accepted, is a contradiction to that believing on Christ we plead for; which is, in fact, neither more nor less, than living upon him as our whole, only, and complete salvation; and will, on that account, bear the test of the apostle's word, *To him that worketh not, but believeth on him that justifieth the ungodly,* &c. As this faith cannot be separated from the truth believed, nor the truth believed from Christ the subject of that truth, so to be justified by faith, by Christ, or by his blood, is the same thing. Nor can any doing for acceptance be charged upon this believing on Christ, while its native language is, *In the Lord have I righteousness.*

* Palæmon's main argument is, "If the work finished by Jesus Christ is alone sufficient to justification, then no appropriation or reception is necessary thereto." We reply, that that alone is sufficient; therefore reception or appropriation belongs to our conscious possession and enjoyment of the justifying righteousness, to the manifestation of our justification by it, and to the influence of it in our lives and conversations.

Palæmon thinks he does not deny the sufficiency of
Christ,

* The name the author of the letters has chosen for himself, as Mr *Hervey* is to be understood by *Aspasio.*

Christ, when he connects faith and salvation together, and maintains, that all who believe this sufficiency will be saved, and all who believe it not, will perish.

He admits, that a work of God is necessary in the justified, that is to beget faith, to beget in them a persuasion of the sufficiency of the justifying righteousness.

He judges this cannot be a contradiction to the one thing needful alone, because it is wholly a persuasion of the sufficiency of that alone, without more. In what light then are we to consider this farther work of God, in persuading us of the sufficiency of this righteousness? Not as an addition to the sufficient righteousness, but only as relative to the knowledge of it. He is justified by believing only as he is justified by what he believes.

Neither does he think he denies the sufficient righteousness, when he maintains faith, love, and self-denied obedience, as necessary to demonstrate his portion in this righteousness, or that he is a justified person. Because in these acts, or in this obedience, he is not doing something to be justified, but proceeding in the way " *of painful desire and fear,*" in order to *know* himself to be justified.

Hence it is apparent, that he must be obliged to allow, that altho' the work finished by Christ on the cross, is the *sole requisite* to justification; yet, in this view, *something more* is necessary to the *knowledge* of his interest in this righteousness, or of his justification by it. And that to maintain this, is no contradiction to the *sole requisite*, but a procedure upon it. What he is obliged to plead for himself, he must also allow to us; and the difference between us is not in regard of the *sole requisite*, but our present *enjoyment* of it, or the *knowledge* of our justification by this alone. He says, with the multitude, " in the way of painful desire and fear," till we come to the knowledge of the difference God has made between us and others; we say, by the free grant of the gospel, to the absolutely guilty without difference. The

" The doctrine of the apostles, instead of directing
" us what to do, sets before us all that the most dis-
" quieted conscience can require, in order to accept-
" ance with God, as already done and finished by
" Jesus Christ." p. 11.

A disquieted conscience requires a righteousness pleasing to God in *its own* behalf. No righteousness will quiet my conscience, unless I consider it as a righteousness *for me*. The righteousness which pleaseth God, is already done and finished by Jesus Christ. *Palæmon* considers this righteousness as respecting himself, only as far as he discovers his own faith, love, and self-denied obedience. We consider it as given to the absolutely guilty, warranting such to live by it, as so given to them for that purpose.

Palæmon's notion, that God hath appointed no way, but by our works, to be assured of salvation by Christ alone, renders his doing, endeavouring, striving, &c. scarcely different in any thing from doing that we may live. There are few so weak as to think they can alter God's mind or purpose by their performances. But not knowing what he has purposed, they do, that they may obtain satisfaction in their minds about their salvation; and *Palæmon*'s doing seems to be wholly of this sort, that is, in fact, *for* peace with God, and not *from* it.

" What Christ has done, is that which pleaseth
" God; what he hath done, is that which quiets the
" guilty conscience of man as soon as he knows it."
Ibid.

As soon as he knows it respects him a guilty sinner. If the fear of the guilty conscience, consisted only in an uncertainty of their being any righteousness which pleaseth God in the behalf of the elect, or the qualified, then the guilty conscience would be quieted as soon as it is evident there is such a righteousness. But this is not the case; the fear of the guilty conscience is a dread of God, because I have no such righteousness; because I have no righteousness, upon which I can be assured he is pleased with me. And this guilty conscience cannot be quieted, unless I discover the righteousness which pleaseth God in my own behalf.

As we conceive the report of the gospel of sufficient righteousness, freely given in Jesus, suits the guilty conscience thus understood; so we agree, that whenever we hear of this provision of divine grace, we have no occasion for any other question but this, "Is it true or not? If we find it true, we are happy;" and it is *Palæmon*, and not we, that stands in need of another righteousness to quiet the guilty conscience.

Palæmon considers "the work of Christ as a suf-
"ficient foundation whereon to rest the whole weight
"of our acceptance with God," p. 12. while at the same time he asserts, that his own part or lot in this righteousness "is not so easily settled;" p. 13. but that he must wait, and work for it in the way of "painful desire and fear, till he is at the last crowned "with enjoyment," in a clear discovery of his having faith, love, and self-denied obedience, p. 419. We judge ourselves not left to this uncertainty; and that, without the discovery of any such difference betwixt us and other men, we are allowed to receive, enjoy, and live upon Jesus Christ, as freely given to sinners in the gospel. Even as those who are invited to an entertainment, are freely allowed to partake of what is set before them. *Palæmon*'s view of the gospel-report, sets him at a distance from enjoyment, or leaves him in uncertainty, till his obedience manifests a difference betwixt him and others. Our view is of the sufficient righteousness, brought quite home, so that our first act is to live by it, that in the strength thereof we may be influenced by love to him that first loved us.

It is true, the scripture "no where ascertains that "Christ died for me in particular." But it allows, invites, and commands me a guilty sinner, without
more,

more, to believe on him, live by him, &c, phrases evidently expressive of the appropriation, trust, or confidence we plead for.

Our author says, " That Christ died, that he gave " his life a ransom for many, is, indeed, a truth fully " ascertained in the scriptures,—for the relief of the " shipwrecked and desperate." But can it relieve any farther than it respects ourselves? And if the gospel-declaration concerning this righteousness doth not respect us any farther than as we apprehend we may be of the elect, or that we have their qualifications, how does it relieve the shipwrecked and the desperate? It rather relieves the elect and the qualified. This point seems to be Mr *Sandeman*'s mystery, and he guards the inquiry with something like, Hence ye profane! " The " world (says he) will always be objecting thus." A plain acknowledgment, I think, that *that* is the question to be answered, or the guilty conscience cannot be believed; and a vindication of our view of the gospel-report, as furnishing us with the gracious answer.

" The scripture often affirms the final perdition of " many, not merely hearers of the gospel, but who " have heard and received it with joy." *Ibid.*

This is an objection against depending on any thing I at present feel, but not against complying with the divine invitation to live by the sufficient righteousness of the Son of God; an objection against the certainty which arises from inherent qualifications; but not against that which proceeds solely on the divine invitation and faithfulness.

" Many shall seek to enter in, and shall not be able." *Ibid.*

Because they seek not by faith (by the *truth* of the gospel,) but as it were by the works of the law.

" Notwithstanding their great confidence about " their acquaintance with Christ, and their interest in " him, and their experience of his presence with them; " he will at last say unto them, *I never knew you, de-* " *part from me.*" *Ibid.*

The confidence of those condemned, is evidently, not a confidence built upon the finished work of Christ, given to them, or the divine faithfulness pledged to sinners in the gospel report; but a confidence on their own attainments and experience, wherein they judged themselves peculiarly entitled to the heavenly admission.

Let who will be condemned, it is allowed by Mr *Sandeman*, that every believer of the sufficiency of the work of Christ, to justify the ungodly, is justified. And it is very evident, that whoever lives by that, as sufficient for him, believes that sufficiency, and is really saved by what he believes, though ten thousand professors perish.

" When they are condemned then as hypocrites
" and unbelievers, they are not condemned for want
" of *Aspasio*'s faith; and that for these two reasons;
" the first is, it was never true that Christ died for
" them; the second is, they were not faulty in this
" respect, for the sacred text describes them as rather
" too confident about their interest in Christ." p. 14.

As to the first, it is not *Aspasio*'s faith that Christ died for them, whether they believe it or no; and as to the second, they may be condemned for neglecting or rejecting the gospel-grant of a Saviour to the guilty; which is the truth *Aspasio* pleads for, and, at the same time, too confident upon their imagined attainments on which they found their hopes.

" The gospel proposes nothing to be believed by
" us, but what is infallibly true, whether we believe
" it or not." *Ibid.*

But it proposes something to be immediately received and enjoyed by us, without performing any entitling condition whatever. We plead for such a persuasion as is the reception of a gift; and what we thus receive, or assure ourselves of, depends for its truth (or infallible certainty) on the veracity and faithfulness of God, who has promised such shall not be confounded.

founded. We agree, that a perfuafion of a propofition, true in itfelf, muft be grounded on the evidence of that truth. But this is not the cafe, when we are commanded to believe on, or truft in the Lord.

"The gofpel, which foretells the final perdition of "fo many of its hearers, fo many ferioufly and zea-"loufly exercifed about it, can never warrant us, to "perfuade every one who hears it, that Chrift died "for him." *Ibid.*

The gofpel, which foretells the final perdition of fo many of its hearers, at the fame time warrants every hearer to live by the righteoufnefs it reveals; and affures them of eternal falvation who thus believe on the Lord Jefus Chrift, or live by his righteoufnefs alone, without more.

"Unlefs we fhall fay, that Chrift died for every "individual of mankind, and confequently, that none "of mankind owe their falvation wholly to his death." *Ibid.*

They owe their falvation, and afcribe their falvation, wholly to his death, who live, and found all their hopes on that alone. Befides, our appropriation relates only to our confcious poffeffion or enjoyment of that which juftifies, and therefore is no more liable to the above-mentioned objection, than *Palæmon's* working to the fame end, in a way of painful defire and fear, till he is crowned with enjoyment. If a man receives 10,000 *l.* as a gift, does the act exift without the gift? And is it the act that enriches him, or the riches he receives? We on both fides plead for the confcious enjoyment of the divine righteoufnefs. He, that we enjoy from our confcioufnefs of our acts of obedience, &c. We, by a difcovery of the fufficient righteoufnefs granted indefinitely to the guilty, in fuch a manner, as warrants each one's particular application. Who ftands freeft from the doctrine of felf-dependence, I leave others to judge.

In the fecond letter, our author wifhes *Afpafio's* faith

faith had been "equally precious with the apostolic." p. 18. As the difference between his faith and ours is, that we believe the righteousness which pleaseth God, is given to us guilty sinners immediately, to live by as our own, which he does not; his faith does not in that respect appear to be more precious, or more apostolic.

It is true, "the apostles never taught men to make "one step of advance towards God, on the prospect "that God would condescend and come down the "rest of the infinite distance to meet them." p. 23.

And this may be a suitable argument against those who spend their time in offering Christ upon certain terms or conditions to be performed by the sinner. But this is far from being the case in what we plead for. Christ or his righteousness, does not meet our believing application, but is the object of it, the thing applied. It is Christ, and his righteousness, that is immediately received, applied, or accounted ours, as being freely given or granted in the gospel-report. So that our appropriation terminates in its object, and can no more exist without Christ, than eating can without food. Is it proper to say, that in eating, a man makes only a step of advance towards his food, on the prospect that the food shall meet him? Just as improper to apply such representations to the appropriation pleaded for.

The apostles called men to believe on the Lord Jesus Christ, in such a manner of address, as is inconsistent with intending thereby only such convictions as are purely passive; only such as force themselves upon the mind by the evidence of their truth. The apostolic language is, *Repent and be baptized every one of you, in the name of Jesus Christ, for the remission of sins*, Acts ii. 38. *And with many other words did he testify and exhort, saying, Save yourselves from this untoward generation*, 40. And again, *Repent ye therefore, and be converted*, chap. iii. 19. And again, *To him gave all the prophets witness, that thro' his name, whoso-*

ever

ever believeth in him, shall receive remission of sins, chap. x. 43. And again, *Be it known unto you, therefore, men and brethren, that through this man is preached unto you the forgiveness of sin. And by him all that believe are justified,* chap. xiii. 38, 39. And again, *Believe on the Lord Jesus Christ, and thou shalt be saved,* &c. chap. xvi. 31. In all these instances, there is something exhorted to, called believing on, or in Christ; being baptized in his name for remission of sins; repenting, and being converted; something more than passive conviction, and, at the same time, something consistent with the alone sufficiency of Christ's righteousness, which can be neither more nor less, than the appropriation, trust, or confidence we plead for.

That " the promises of the gospel are made only to " believers," will never invalidate our plea for appropriation, while it remains true, that the grant of Christ, and the salvation in him, is made to sinners; and in receiving the grant, they evidently commence those to whom the promises are made; that is, those who believe on Christ according to the apostolic exhortation. And to sinners, thus immediately believing on Christ, the promises are made; first, to encourage such to draw near and live with confidence on the sufficient righteousness; secondly, to give them a certainty dependent upon the divine faithfulness, and animating thereby to the most ready and willing obedience.

To say no one must account the righteousness of Christ as belonging to him, in any sense, until he discovers himself a true believer, as it excludes the application we plead for, so, in its room, it introduces all the pernicious consequences this author professes to avoid in his accusation of *Aspasio, viz.* " holding forth " a preliminary human righteousness as some way ex- " pedient, or rather necessary, to our enjoying the " comfort and benefit of Christ's." Unless *Palæmon* can make it manifest that we enjoy the comfort and
benefit

benefit of Chrift's righteoufnefs, while we are, according to him, " working in the way of painful de-
" fire and fear, till we come to that enjoyment ;"
common experience teacheth us, that righteoufnefs
can only relieve or comfort us, as far as it refpects us.
That he is able to fave his elect, is no comfort to me,
further than I conceive myfelf to be one of them;
and in this cafe I am comforted, either by a conjectural hope, or by a hope founded on the difference
there is betwixt me and others.

" And to obviate the difficulty, how fhall I know
" that the promife is to me! they addrefs their bre-
" thren in this manner: In the name of the great
" God we declare, that the promife is to thee, and
" thee, O man, woman, whofoever thou art." p. 23.

The promife of falvation, to whofoever believes on
Chrift, is evidently to the finner, as his encouragement to come to the fure enjoyment of the righteoufnefs and falvation given in him, by receiving, appropriating, and trufting confidently on him as fo given.

" In his name, we call you this moment to ftretch
" forth the withered hand, and the withered heart,
" and take hold of Chrift, faying, *He is mine, and I*
" *am his.*" Ibid.

That may be underftood thus; " We fpeak not in
our own name, as fignifying our own importance, but
inform you of the glad tidings, that it is God's command, and your duty, not to wait to feel fome power
or alteration in yourfelf, as a ground for your confidence, but juft as you are, in obedience to the divine
command, receive or appropriate Chrift, faying, *He
is mine, and I am his.*"

The withered hand and the withered heart, are expreffions ufed to fignify a powerlefs, helplefs condition, which, confifting in the prevalence of our naturally-evil difpofitions, ferves to denominate us finners,
and fpoils our hopes of living by our own performances; yet it is no objection againft living by his
obedience

obedience who hath become the righteousness of the guilty. For it must be remembered, we are not justified by our acts, but by the righteousness we appropriate; and our appropriation only serves to give us the divinely-authentic enjoyment by the word, of that justification of the ungodly, and without strength, whereby we are saved. Hence we are called not to wait for strength to do something for the enjoyment of this justification, but stretch forth the withered hand, or just as we are, to live by Christ's righteousness, when we feel nothing but what marks us out for eternal destruction. When *Lazarus* was made to hear, he came forth, according to the command he heard, or in obedience to the voice that quickened him; and when we are made to hear the divine invitation and command to live by this righteousness, we appropriate it in obedience to him that makes us hear his voice. The righteousness itself, is that by which we are accepted; the appropriation respects our possession and enjoyment. In the latter we may be weaker or stronger; in the former, is the invariable ground of our confidence.

That God has given to us eternal life in his Son, is the apostolic style, and the very record which is pointed out for our peculiar attention; and when the word *offer* has been made use of, and understood to convey nothing more than this important truth, the believer of the record has become the receiver of the gift, or the enjoyer of the blessing.

" Hence we see, that *This is mine*, or *this was done*
" *for me*, is a truth, whose evidence takes its rise from
" the pains I take to believe it." p. 26.

Its evidence depends on the veracity and faithfulness of him who spake the world into being, has provided the sufficient righteousness, and has commanded us to give him this honour of depending on his word, in our enjoyment of this salvation.

It is not in this case the language of the belief of a

truth, but of the reception or appropriation of a free gift; the belief of the truth of the sufficiency of Jesus Christ, and of his being freely given, goes before, and is that knowledge of the name of the Lord which emboldens us to put our trust in him. What we thus assure ourselves of, in compliance with the divine invitation, &c. as it is a certain truth in the divine mind, so it appears a truth by the divine word, when it is evident I am begotten to this Christian faith, hope, and charity. The difference here between us is, that, with *Palæmon*, *This is mine, this was done for me*, is a truth, whose evidence takes its rise only from a discovery, that I am distinguished from other sinners by my faith, love, and self-denied obedience. With us it is the language of a reception, appropriation, trust, or confidence, grounded upon the divine declarations to sinners for that purpose.

"This, I must say, is indeed a very strange and " uncommon way of finding truth." *Ibid.*

But such a way of dependence on the divine veracity and faithfulness as becomes us, and gives glory to God.—It is the reception of a gift by a persuasion of the mind.—It is trusting to the faithfulness of God to make out, in this particular case, a blessing indefinitely promised; not assuring myself of a proposition being true, but of eternal salvation, by a Saviour, given to me.

To receive a gift, or to partake of any thing upon invitation, is nothing strange or uncommon. In this case, when the gift is given in divine declarations, and the reception of it purely mental, an answerable persuasion of the mind, or (in dependence on the divine veracity and faithfulness) an assuring ourselves of the blessing granted; what we are persuaded of is in a way *peculiar* to itself, and very consistent before him, who said, *Whatsoever things ye desire when you pray, believe that you receive them, and ye have them*. *Palæmon* will allow, that Christ's death is an uncommon affair, as is also imputing righteousness without works, &c. Why then should the *peculiarity* of thus enjoying righteousness without works, be so much the subject of sneer, because accounted *strange* and *uncommon?*—May it not rather be accounted such a way of dependence on the divine veracity and faithfulness, as renders him his proper glory?

"If he (namely Christ) died for them that perish, then the happiness of them who are saved, must be owing to something else beside his death." *Ibid.*

Aspasio is no farther concerned here, than as he maintains, that Christ is given for the guilty to appropriate and live by. And in this regard, may it not be said, with as much propriety, If an entertainment, provided in common, is refused by some, that then the nourishment of those who partake of it, is owing to something else besides the food? this coming pretty near to our Lord's representation, *John* vi. 53. A fallacy or impropriety charged upon the former, is also a reflection upon the latter.

If we understand, by the happiness of them who are saved, their redemption from the wrath to come, and title to future glory; this is owing strictly to his perfect righteousness. If we mean their present happiness in a conscious possession, knowledge, or enjoyment of this redemption; this we may say is owing to his death, given to be received. *Palæmon* says, to a discovery of our faith, love, and self-denied obedience.

It is a very just observation, That "in speaking of the redemption that is in Jesus Christ, we had need keep clear of all human systems, and hold close by the scriptures." p. 30.

And it is in strict conformity to this we assert, that although God has given eternal life in his Son, even unto them, who, by disbelieving it, make God a liar; yet no man has that life, but he that has the Son. God gives being to that which he commands, authorifes, and thereby enables us to receive, appropriate, or be perfuaded of. And if we admit of his character as a juſt God and a Saviour, in juſtifying the ungodly, why ſhould we object thus giving him the glory of his power and faithfulneſs ? Thus *S A R A H received ſtrength to conceive ſeed,—becauſe ſhe judged him* (not only able, but) *faithful that had promiſed.*— And thus our Lord ſpeaks, Mark xi. 22, 23, 24. Shall it be diſputed, whether God can give an exiſtence to things that yet are not, and make out that to be true, which we, according to his word, depend upon him for ? This confidence is due to God only, and is giving him glory. On the other hand, to ſuppoſe this cannot be, and, on this account, to ſet aſide this manner of *believing* or *truſting* in him, is to rob him of his proper glory.

This perſuaſion may properly be called T R U S T I N G in the Lord, becauſe it proceeds neither on pre-evidence, nor inward qualifications, but on God's bare word of invitation, promiſe, &c. taking that as a ſufficient authority and ſecurity. By this a proper dependence of the creature on the Creator is preſerved and kept up. And unleſs it can, without miſrepreſentation, be ſhewn inconſiſtent and antiſcriptural ; all other objections raiſed againſt it are but of ſmall account; and labour to form it into a propoſition, true in itſelf, whether we believe it or no, is the labour of diffidence and unbelief. For it is plain, they cannot truſt to God's invitations, commands, and declarations ; and are ſeeking a reaſon of hope more agreeable to themſelves.

" *Aſpaſio* maintains, that none have the proper ſcrip-" tural faith, but thoſe who are taught by the en-" lightening Spirit to draw the concluſion." p. 34.

Aſpaſio maintains, that " when the divine Spirit opens our eyes, &c. we diſcover and make uſe of the fame right or warrant as is the privilege of the vileſt miſcreant ; a right founded, not on our awakened deſires, fires, but purely, solely, entirely on the free grant of a Saviour." *Dialogues*, vol. ii. p. 361.

" They maintain, that reprobates have as fair a re-
" vealed warrant, to draw the conclusion, as the elect
" have." *Ibid.*

That is, that no man need to wait to see his election, or, in other words, any difference between himself and other men, to warrant his confidence in Christ. The general indefinite expressions, contained in the declarations of the gospel, such as *whosoever, any man, he that believeth on him, &c.* fully authorising or warranting *he, any man, whosoever* he be, to *believe,* or *trust confidently on Christ alone* for everlasting life. Being taught of God this truth, he lives by Christ as the Saviour of the lost, even as being taught the sufficiency of Christ he lives by that alone.

In the third letter, our author mistakes the real question between us. It is not, " Whether or not
" did Christ finish upon the cross, all that God re-
" quires, every requisite, without exception, to pro-
" cure acceptance for, and give relief unto the guilty
" conscience of the most profane wretch that lives?"
p. 41. 42.

This is not disputed by us, but maintained more properly on our side than by our author. The question. between us, is, Whether the guilty conscience can be relieved from the sentence of condemnation, by the consideration of a sufficient righteousness for the elect and the qualified ? Or, Whether God hath not provided for the relief of the guilty conscience, by giving his only begotten Son that we might live through him ? giving him not only to die, but giving him in the divine declarations to be believed on ?

" It must be the very same thing which placates
" divine justice, or which fully expresses the neces-
" sary opposition of infinite goodness to evil or sin,
" that relieves the sinner from the sentence of con-
" demnation,

"demnation, which is no other than the voice of "God naturally residing in the conscience." *Ibid.*

As it would be very absurd to suppose it placates the divine justice, without being considered by that justice in the behalf of the transgressor; so it seems to be equally absurd, that it can "relieve the guilty "conscience from the sentence of condemnation," without being appropriated by that conscience.

The sentence of condemnation, naturally residing in the conscience, requires a revelation of righteousness, that I may as really impute to myself, as the sin that condemns me, or the condemnation still remains untouched. A possibility, that I may be an elect person, cannot give relief, because it may be ten to one it is not true. My hope is only in proportion, as I apprehend many, or few, to be elected; and, after all, it is not, in fact, Christ's righteousness that relieves me, but my conjectural or fond hope of being one of elect.

Christ did finish upon the cross that righteousness "which placates the divine justice, or which fully "expresses the necessary opposition of infinite good-"ness to evil, or sin." That righteousness which alone can relieve the sinner from eternal death, entitle him to eternal life, and bring peace and hope of everlasting life to the most guilty conscience. At the same time, it would be absurd to say, Christ finished on the cross every requisite or commandment relative to this righteousness as preached or declared in the world. For instance; *He hath commanded all men every where to repent.* Which I understand a repentance respective of this righteousness, and the same with the *commandment, that we should believe on the name of his Son Jesus Christ*. Again, the voice from heaven, *This is my beloved Son in whom I am well pleased,* was attended with a commandment to *hear him*, agreeable to *Is.* li. 1,—5. If it is again inquired, of what avail are these commandments? It may be answered, as

the

the commandment to preach the gospel to every creature, availed to be the favour of life unto life in them that are saved, and of death unto death in them that perish; so the commandment to believe on the name of his Son Jesus Christ, avails to encourage and warrant the sinner, as such, to trust, believe in, or appropriate and enjoy that righteousness. I am persuaded *Palæmon* will not say, that Christ finished upon the cross any of the commmandments above mentioned. As it may be affirmed on the other hand, that the obedience to these commands is no part of that *righteousness* which procures acceptance for, or gives relief unto the conscience of the most profane wretch that lives. But *Palæmon's* reply is, That all obedience to these commands, supposes the belief of the gospel-report. Be it so, the commandment speaks to them, not as to believers, or to the distinguished among mankind, but as to sinners or children of wrath, even as others; and is the divine method of grace in giving us a conscious possession or enjoyment. Which *Palæmon* seeks totally by works.

" What is the *turning-point* from despair to good
" hope?" *Ibid.*

The finished work of Christ alone. How is that our hope? As it is given for that purpose to be the hope of the guilty.

" *Aspasio's* faith rests, one foot on the work of
" Christ, and the other on human efforts, or the mo-
" tions of man's heart." *Ibid.*

Quite a mistake. *Aspasio's* faith is, that the work of Christ is given to him; on this he rests, and on no motions of his heart whatever.

" What gives right to eternal life? The imputed
" righteousness. What gives right to that? The
" work of faith. Who have a right to act faith?
" Those who feel an aversion to sin," &c. p. 44.

This is also far from being *Aspasio's* view of the matter: he should be represented thus; What gives right to eternal life? The imputed righteousness. What gives right to that? The declarations of the gospel, giving it freely to sinners as such. Who have a right to act faith, or appropriate this righteousness? All the ends of the earth; as many as can be included in the word *whosoever*. To any of all the ends of the earth were the apostles commissioned to say, *Believe on the Lord Jesus Christ, and thou shalt be saved*. To exhort thus to a passive involuntary conviction, would be very absurd.

Aspasio's observation is, the " grant is made to sin-
" ners; in receiving the grant we commence belie-
" vers," according to the above-mentioned apostolic exhortation.

" But *Aspasio* will still insist, that these qualifica-
" tions are by no means the *ground* of their right.
" Let us see then, where the ground of their right
" lies?" p. 46.

In the divine declarations to sinners as such.

" I think the obvious meaning of *Aspasio*'s words is
" this: these persons, so qualified, have the right ex-
" clusive of unqualified sinners. *Ibid*.

It is very obvious this is not his meaning.

" Where then can the ground of this right lie, but
" in the distinguished qualifications? It cannot lie in
" any thing common to both; for, in that case, the
" unqualified would have as good a right as the qua-
" lified." *Ibid*.

They have so. These are *Aspasio*'s real sentiments; whatever qualifications make a difference between one man and another, they confer no right to the kingdom of God, they confer no right to the imputed righteousness. For as *all have sinned, and come short of the glory of God*, they who are justified, are *justified freely by his grace, thro' the redemption which is in Jesus Christ*.

" They have nothing in the heaven above, nor in
" the earth below, to keep their hearts from sinking
into

" into utter defpair, but the bare propitiation. This,
" and this alone, encourages them to make their ad-
" drefs to God." 'p. 48.

Can this encourage further than they fee their intereft in it, or right to draw near to God thereby, in virtue of his gracious declarations? And how are they to addrefs God? As their friend and father, on account of this righteoufnefs? Then they, in fact, appropriate it, and our debate is at an end; we are agreed. Or, do they addrefs God only as the friend of fome who are to be known in time by fuitable qualifications? If this is our author's meaning, then it is he, and not *Afpafio*, that, in drawing near to God, feeks for inherent qualifications, inftead of the imputed righteoufnefs.

" By this, and this alone, God conveys the firft
" tafte of his favour and peace into their hearts." *Ibid*.

Unlefs we conceive of the imputed righteoufnefs as gracioufly granted unto us in this deftitute condition; where is the connection? What tafte of favour and peace can be admitted barely by the confideration of fufficiency for the elect? Sufficient for me a guilty finner, without any other confideration, is evangelical. To wait for *fomething more* before we are allowed to call him friend or father, on account of this righteoufnefs, is not at all adapted to bring us nigh to God by *the bare propitiation*.

" And it pleafes me to find, *Afpafio* had not courage
" to clofe this period, without bringing forth the plain
" truth at laft. For pointing to the poor, indigent,
" and guilty finners, he concludes, For fuch the Sa-
" viour is provided; to fuch his benefits are propofed;
" and on fuch his grace will be magnified." p. 48. 49.

If it is allowed, that his benefits are propofed to fuch, the debate is ended. We mean no more. It is undoubtedly warrantable to receive and appropriate what is provided for the enjoyment of *any*, or *whofoever* among the guilty; and propofed to our truft and confidence under that name. If any other confideration muft intervene, then it is plain, the benefits are not provided for and propofed to fuch, but only for, and to thofe who have the additional confideration.

"As for the bare work finifhed on the crofs, or the bare report about it, however true we think it, fo far have we miftaken it, that, fetting afide *our active operations about it, we do not fee what comfort or benefit can be derived from it.*" p. 85.

This proceeds on a total miftake and mifreprefentation of *Afpafio;* he is not putting the leaft flight on the report or perfuafion of the fufficiency of the finifhed work of Jefus Chrift, to juftify the moft guilty without more; he is here oppofing a qualified perfuafion, or rather mere profeffion, artfully fubftituted in the room of the fufficient righteoufnefs, and the finner's living by that alone—A perfuafion, "that the fhelter of the fummer-houfe is free for our ufe, accompanied with a high efteem of its accommodation, an earneft defire after its protection, or an habitual tendency towards it." *Afpafio* afks not whether a perfuafion of the fufficiency of Chrift, but "a perfuafion that the fummer-houfe is free for our ufe," whether this, tho' accompanied with efteem, defire, or tendency, unlefs "carried into actual entrance and poffeffion," would anfwer the end and defign of fuch a truth, "would be a proper fafe-guard, or indeed any manner of advantage as to our perfons," that is, in refpect of poffeffion, enjoyment and advantage from that enjoyment. Thefe are his very words, 16th dialogue, p. 398. And let any one impartially judge, whether *Afpafio* is here objecting againft the finifhed work of Jefus? or rather, is he not fetting afide a fruitlefs perfuafion, or rather profeffion, that the fhelter is free for our ufe, with dependence on our fuppofed efteems, defires, tendencies, &c. that the foul may reft purely and entirely on Jefus Chrift alone? Whom in the fame page he defcribes from the prophet *Ifaiah*, as "a place
"of

" of refuge, as a covert from the storm and from
" rain." *Aspasio* asks, if a persuasion that Christ is
such a place of refuge and covert free for our use, ac-
companied with any esteems, desires, and tendencies,
will answer to such a representation? Which is, in
fact, whether we may trust in such a persuasion, e-
steem, desire, and tendency, instead of that righteous-
ness which is our appointed refuge? It is plain, all the
active operations pleaded for, is to live by this alone,
in distinction from any other dependence. And the
advantage arising from these active operations, is the
enjoyment, comfort, and influence of this sufficient
righteousness.

If the objector had been pleading for the entire suf-
ficency of the works of Jesus, *Aspasio* would readily
agree to that, and have recommended living by that
alone. But after he had so far co-incided with *Aspasio*,
as to allow, " that all this grace, and each of these
" benefits, are free, perfectly free, for you, for me,
" for others;" might not *Aspasio* ask, would this bare
persuasion answer the end and design of such a truth,
unless I was induced thereby to really use it as a shel-
ter? that is, to oppose Christ's righteousness, thus
freely given unto me, to every sense of guilt and con-
demnation, and assure myself of salvation by that alone.
As I suppose Mr *Sandeman* in his view of things, will
allow the believer of the gospel-report to oppose the
truth of Christ's sufficiency to every declaration or
conviction of guilt tending to despair, and this may
as properly be called *reducing* that truth *to practice*.
This is what *Aspasio* calls *reducing to practice*, the
truth of Christ being given for us to receive and live
by him as such a gift, as a refuge from all curses of
the law, and danger of damnation, unto the end of
peace, assurance, and holiness. We do not consider
the gospel as barely furnishing us with good and ex-
cellent materials *to work upon*, but with blessings *to
enjoy and possess* as our own ; and our whole comfort,

or any part of it, does not arife from the *fuccefs of our labour*, but wholly from the bleffings fo freely prefented to us to take comfort in them, and is very far from making them fit to comfort us.

"Now, it does not fignify much by what name "we call the mean of efcape, whether we call it the "law or the gofpel; for the great concern we have "with either of thefe, is to obtain righteoufnefs or "a title to life." p. 92, 93.

However true this may be of thofe who feek by works in a way of "painful defire and fear till they "are crowned with enjoyment:" *Afpafio* is not chargeable, whofe doctrine allows an immediate enjoyment, without the intervention of any righteoufnefs or work whatever.

"For—it is not the bare knowledge of the law or "gofpel that can do us any fervice, but *the ufe we* "*make of them.*" p. 93.

This is but mere found; for our author pleads for the above-mentioned ufe to be made of the report, previous to the enjoyment of the privilege. The ufe we make of the gofpel-report, is immediately to live by the righteoufnefs it reveals: whereas the ufe of the law is to do that we may live. Is not here a manifeft? yea, is not here a fufficient difference?

"So each one reafons thus: *Seeing many fhall pe-* "*rifh, and feeing the gofpel fays nothing to me, but* "*what it fays to every one, what comfort can I reap* "*from it, unlefs I can find about myfelf, at leaft one* "*grain of odds, cafting the balance in my favour, in* "*comparifon with others, or in comparifon with what* "*I myfelf have hitherto been?*" p. 94.

But this is not *Afpafio's* language, which may rather be reprefented, *Seeing the gofpel authorifes me and every finner to live by the righteoufnefs it reveals, why fhould I not make this ufe of it? Since the door into the kingdom of God is thus open for finners, why fhould I any longer hefitate?*

"But

"But what signifies all this, says the proud devo-
"tee, unless I can find some reason about myself,
"why the Deity should distinguish me as his favourite
"beyond other men? And thus he treats the bare
"truth of the gospel with scorn and contempt."
Note, p. 97.

Aspasio waits for no such reason, therefore this re-
presentation does not affect him.

"In vain shall he (any sinner) expect to hear one
"syllable more from God, to encourage him to draw
"nigh to him, than that *he is well pleased in his be-*
"*loved Son;* that JEHOVAH *is well pleased for his*
"*righteousness."* p. 115.

Hath not God already said, *He that believeth on him
shall not be ashamed?* that *he that cometh to him shall
in no wise be cast out?* &c. Hath he not given him as
bread from heaven, that *whosoever eateth him should
live by him?* Has he not given *eternal life to us in
him?* even so given to us, that *whosoever* of us *believe
not this record* that he hath given of his Son, *makes
him a liar?* Are we to set aside these declarations as no
encouragement to us to appropriate or to draw nigh to
God, lest we should not sufficiently submit ourselves
to the divine sovereignty? Or are we not rather to
look upon them, as the declarations of sovereign grace;
which has found out a way consistent with the highest
justice thus to shew favour to the guilty, and for the
encouragement of such to believe on him, or draw
nigh with confidence through the faith of him?

"The apostle *John* says, *This is his commandment,*
"*that we should believe on the name of his Son;* not
"that we should do any thing to obtain life, but that
"we should live by what he hath done. It is a command-
"ment not requiring any thing of us, but bestowing
"life by the knowledge which it conveys." p. 126.

If I live by what he hath done, I account what he
hath done, given me for that purpose. And this is
also the use I make of it; and this commandment, so
understood,

understood, requireth nothing of us, but bestows life by the knowledge it conveys. So that what our author has here said, expresses our whole mind, and may end the dispute.

"*Paul*, in the deepest of all his distresses, was relieved by that very faith, which we modern Christians, in the height of our complaisance, chuse only to call, of the enfeebled and infantile kind." p. 128.

A mistake this; *Paul* was relieved by a view of the sufficiency of grace for himself in particular, *My grace is sufficient for* THEE. He waited for no other righteousness to certify him, that this sufficient grace belonged to him.

"If we hearken to them, the great point about which our faith is principally concerned, is a matter which turns out to be true; no book nor man can tell how." p. 168.

It turns out to be true in God's faithfulness, answering to his gracious declarations. Our assurance or appropriation is founded and exercised upon God's faithfulness to answer to what he has revealed as the ground of our confidence. That *he has given to us eternal life in his Son;* that *in this man's name is preached to us remission of sins;* and that *whosoever believeth on him shall not perish, but have everlasting life.* So that, in the very nature of the thing, the appropriating language is only the language of trust and confidence, and will turn out to be truth if God may be depended on, as he most surely may.

"In the gospel-offer, we are told, is presented to the poor bankrupt, a bond, or bill indorsed to him, to relieve him from his poverty.—It is not his as yet." *Ibid.*

It is freely given to him, it is his in right to possess and enjoy, as any thing we are invited to partake of. It is therefore his to live upon, though not his in present enjoyment. It is not presented to him, but in common with others who perish, rejecting it as insufficient;

ficient; yet it is so really presented to him, that he is welcome to live by it, or avail himself of it as his own, without performing one act, or obtaining one qualification to entitle him to it. The difficulty lies in a man's being thoroughly persuaded that this is true; which, when a man really is, he immediately lives by this revealed righteousness without more.

"He at last lays hold of it,—so it becomes his." *Ibid.*

It becomes his by that same grace which has convinced him of its truth, and influenced him thereby to appropriate and enjoy it. It becomes his in possession and enjoyment. Not that God imputes it on account of our appropriation; that only serves the use of peace of conscience by it, and a warrantable enjoyment by the divine word, and to demonstrate we are those to whom it is imputed.

Mr *Marshall*, Mr *Boston*, and Mess. *Erskines*, maintain, that, according to the law, "man is bound to believe whatever God declares, and do whatever he commands; that the duty of believing to be true what God has reported, and receiving what he has commanded us to receive, or take to ourselves, belongs to the law; which fastens the new duty upon us, the moment the gospel reveals the new object." And if this is not true, how will the hearers of the gospel be condemned for despising or neglecting this great salvation? And if this is true, why may not gospel-ministers declare against the rejectors of this grace, what will be matter of their just condemnation? Or, in other words, what proves, that they that perish, perish justly, and of their own will and choice, vindicating the righteous judgment of God.

And is it not to be maintained consistent with this, that the gospel is purely and entirely a revelation of a sufficient righteousness for the most guilty, that where it takes place in the heart, it is by the sovereign grace of him who provided the righteousness it treats of? That in receiving it for true, and living by it, they
are

are fulfilling the command of the new covenant; they are performing of duty; and, at the same time, the subjects of the New-testament promise, in having that obedience, or law written on their heart by the Spirit of the living God, as a Spirit of grace and truth?

"I hope *Satan* does not chain you to your houses, nor stake you down to your fields on the Lord's day." p. 267.

This is rather to be considered as a convicting them of their sinful negligence and willing ignorance, than giving any directions what we must do to be saved. In that case we allow the answer is, Either keep the law yourself, or live by what Christ has already done.

"We may now turn our eyes more particularly to those who are most successful in propagating a perverted gospel.—These men do indeed press very hard upon the conscience to awaken fear: but when they have driven the serious hearer almost to despair, by an awful description of his miserable condition, and by representing him as utterly unable in every respect to contribute any thing toward his own deliverance, they at last condescend, with no small art and address, to make some comfortable exceptions from the foregoing awful doctrine.—Now is described, in a variety of particulars, a convenient resource, where the pride of the serious hearer may exercise itself with great hopes of success." p. 279.

The pride of the serious hearer, is the conceit of his being able to do or obtain something to deliver himself, as proceeding from his propensity to live by something he is to do, whereby he becomes self-dependent. The truth is, the gift of the divine righteousness depends on no doing or difference in man. The being quickened by the truth of the gospel to hear the voice of God therein, depends on the sovereign good pleasure of heaven. A man hearing this voice of God, not to the qualified, but to the absolutely guilty

guilty and loſt, is made obedient to the commands and exhortations to believe on the Lord Jeſus Chriſt, or to live by his righteouſneſs, without waiting for any other; and the obedience that anſwers as an echo to that divine voice, command, invitation, &c. is, and can be no other, than truſting, depending, and aſſuring ourſelves of ſalvation by Chriſt alone, in obedience to the divine declaration; as *Lazarus* came forth in obedience to the voice that quickened him. When we bid ſinners believe on Chriſt, we would be underſtood as exhibiting a quickening truth, as well as a divine command; that is, there is a ſufficient Saviour who may ſafely be depended on. And in obedience to this voice we are not doing that we may live, but we are living by Chriſt alone, in obedience to him who makes the dead to hear his voice. The pride of the ſerious hearer may be as much excited by being told to do that they may know their ſalvation, as to do to be ſaved.

"The preacher finds it neceſſary to warn his hear-
" ers to avoid all thoughts of this doctrine of election
" at preſent." *Ibid.*

That is, when election is objected againſt the divine declarations, encouraging the guilty under that character, and without any evidence of election, to live immediately by Chriſt's righteouſneſs. For the jailor to have objected election againſt *Paul*, when he bid him believe on the Lord Jeſus Chriſt, would have been from the enemy.

"Becauſe (ſays he) there is in this doctrine no vi-
" ſible ground for faith to reſt upon,—no viſible re-
" ſource for the pride of any man." p. 280.

No viſible ground for a ſinner's *confidence* or *truſt in Chriſt alone*, which is not the pride of man, but eſſential to the faith of God's elect.

"Sometimes they take great pains to ſhew us how
" little we do when we put forth an act of faith."
p. 281.

The act we plead for, is to live alone by what Chrift has done, whether we call it believing on Chrift, receiving, appropriating, trufting, or whatever name we give it; this is what we mean. Our opponents on this head, are thofe who are for having fome good thing to be wrought in us, or done by us, before we are to be allowed to live by what Jefus has done; which is, in fact, a denial of its being wrought for the guilty. When they have been driven out of every fubterfuge, they at laft plead, that we tell people to believe on Chrift; whereas it is the Spirit's work, and they muft wait for this working of the Spirit before they are able to believe. We do not pretend to deny, that for a man to believe on the Son of God is the Spirit's work; but at the fame time are affured, that when a man is taught of God to believe Chrift's righteoufnefs a provifion for the guilty, he is not taught to affume any other character as his title to it. Nor is he taught of God to confider himfelf in any other light than as guilty, and juftly condemned. And therefore we farther infift upon it, that a man, without waiting for any thing more than what Chrift has already done, is to live by *that*, as fufficient for him, and given to him in the indefinite grant of the gofpel. And this he is to do, that is, live by Chrift's righteoufnefs in obedience to the divine command and invitation, when he feels nothing good in him, to embolden him thereto; and to depend upon it, that *that* righteoufnefs will not fail him. And thus far we proceed fcripturally, according to the anfwer given to the *Philippian* jailor.

We have alfo afferted, that a man may afk the queftion, What fhall I do to be faved? and yet be but upon nature's bottom. The direction to that man, is not to wait for to do fomething, or to get fomething done in him, but to believe on the Lord Jefus Chrift. When it has been objected to this, that nature cannot believe on Chrift, and therefore fuch are not to be told so; we have answered, he that gives the command is able to overcome this difficulty by divine conviction of the truth, writing his laws in our hearts and minds. And while we, thus taught of God, in obedience to the word, are endeavouring to believe or trust on the Lord Jesus Christ, to obtain our certainty, and rest satisfied with this righteousness, the Spirit of grace and truth may further dissipate every distrustful suggestion, and make us fully so. And here, by believing on Christ, we mean such a trusting, confiding on him, as we allow follows a divine passive conviction of the truth, that kind of activity which is intimated in the scripture-phrases, *Acts* xvi. 31. *John* vi. 35. and *John* iii. 23.

We cannot believe through our own natural averseness to live by the righteousness of another, or our proneness to establish our own. But, at the same time, he that is taught of God, when he acknowledges he can do nothing, he rejoices that nothing is left for him to do, but on the contrary that he is called to live by what Christ has already done. And they who will not distinguish this life from an endeavour to live by our own righteousness, cannot be farther talked with.

As conviction of the truth of the sufficiency of Christ, and his being freely given to the guilty and lost, is the only conviction of truth that is free from self-righteousness; so to live by this sufficient righteousness as so given, is the only activity that most immediately answers to the above-mentioned truths.

Palæmon cannot deny, but *coming to Christ* has the promise of *being in no wise cast out;* but he judges it to be an obedience in consequence of faith, or the belief of the truth. This, on the other hand, is not denied him. And it may be also affirmed, that the promise is an encouragement of certainty of success to every one that comes to him, and a divine declaration which ascertains the sufficient righteousness to be imputed

puted to every particular person answering that character. *Coming to Christ* is allowed to be more than a passive conviction; it is allowed to be something active in consequence of such a conviction; and as it cannot be any such activity or coming as contradicts the alone sufficiency of Christ's finished work, what answers to the scripture-descriptions or names given to this activity, more properly than living by that sufficient righteousness, instead of doing or seeking to do any thing to add thereto?

And as far as *Aspasio*, *Marshall*, &c. plead for, or encourage, to an activity of this kind, they cannot be accused justly of setting up another righteousness.— This activity terminates in its object, and resolves itself entirely therein. The business to be accomplished by this activity, is only to come under such a certainty of salvation by Christ alone, as is implied in the words *trust* and *confidence;* and the nature of it is as opposite to setting up another righteousness, as the persuasion of Christ's sufficiency. *Palæmon* pleads for activity in coming at the certainty of our interest in Christ's sufficient work, and we plead for no more. Which therefore removes our plea beyond the reach of his objections.

To plead for appropriation as something to be added to entitle to acceptance, is liable to *Palæmon*'s objections. To plead for it, so as to make the sufficient righteousness depend on that act for its acceptance with God in our behalf, may also be accused as a doctrine of self-dependence; but to appropriate as an effect of the report believed, as a means of ascertaining to ourselves eternal life by that righteousness revealed, and as an animating principle of obedience evidencing our special interest therein, is not at all liable to such objections.

" If faith must be called an instrument, and if it
" be at the same time maintained, that justification
" comes by faith only; then I am at full liberty to
" affirm,

" affirm, that he who is poſſeſſed of the inſtrument,
" hand, or mouth, is already juſtified, without regard
" to his uſing the inſtrument," &c. p. 285.

Quite a miſtaken view; becauſe faith, or appropriation of Chriſt, has no exiſtence in itſelf without its object, as material inſtruments have.

" We ſhall ſeldom find them ſpeaking any thing
" like the language of the goſpel, without cautioning,
" mincing, or clogging it with ſome exceptive, but,"
&c. Ibid.

The apoſtle ſays, To him that worketh not, *but* believeth, &c. There is a believing that ſtands oppoſed to working; and if our *but* is the *but* of the apoſtle, and only reſpects our receiving the record, and appropriating the revealed righteouſneſs accordingly, it is free from this exception.

" 'Though *Theron* is diveſted of all *righteouſneſs of*
" *his own*, of every *qualification* and every *recommen-*
" *dation*, he muſt yet be well provided with *requiſites*,
" even ſuch as may embolden him to make the ap-
" propriation." p. 287.

A wide miſtake; *Aſpaſio*'s ſcope and deſign throughout, is to ſhew, that nothing emboldens to appropriation, but the divine grant to ſinners, as ſuch.

" He (*Theron*) is very willing to believe that he is
" a gracious perſon." p. 288.

How evident does it appear from the paſſage here quoted, that the *faith* or *truth* recommended was, " *that all was his;*" that is, by way of the divine grant of heaven to the guilty?—Quite different from believing about himſelf that *he is a gracious perſon*.

" And while *Theron* cannot be brought to believe,
" *Aſpaſio* beholds his title perfectly clear." p. 289.

Aſpaſio beheld his title or warrant to appropriate from the divine grant made to ſinners; not from the pre-requiſites of *Theron*.

" I muſt frankly own,—that I ſee no more differ-
" ence betwixt a careleſs and convicted ſinner, than
" is

"is betwixt a felon ranging his round at large, and
one newly apprehended by the officers of justice:
and for my part, I think it would look liker an im-
pertinent sarcasm, than any thing else, to tell either
of these last, that he was now in a very hopeful
way." p. 293.

As faith comes by hearing, we hope for another when we can prevail with him only to hear. This does not imply, that there is a foundation of hope in them. We hope when we see people concerned about their everlasting state, that this concern will terminate in listening to the remedy that is graciously provided.

"As if one could reap any spiritual benefit from
studying the divine law, or know how pure, how
extensive, how sublimely-perfect it is, before he
knows Christ the end thereof for righteousness; as
if such a one could judge of his spiritual state im-
partially." p. 295.

Palæmon seems to forget, that in page 51. he has intimated, that " it was for want of comparing themselves with the divine law, that the Pharisees made their mistake." He that measures himself by others instead of this sublimely-perfect standard, must at last stand self-condemned *. He that measures him-self hereby, will know his state to be desperate, unless relieved by the finished work of Christ.

"*Aspasio*, then, hath found out a path, by walk-
ing wherein the guilty may confidently hope to ar-
rive at righteousness at last." p. 296.

Not so, but *Aspasio* hath found himself guilty by
comparing

---

* If, as the scripture affirms, *the thoughts and imaginations of man's heart are evil, and that continually;* if this compound of evils is only in some measure restrained and covered in the brightest characters amongst men; if these restraints are only from the various workings of *pride, fear,* and *shame,* in all who are not influenced by the saving truth: how wretchedly are they mistaken, who found their hope on self-excellencies arising from so poor and shameful an original?

comparing himself with the divine law;—he hath found the difference so great, as to lead him to despair of himself;—he hath found Christ the end of the law for righteousness, and the principle of new evangelical obedience.—He testifies of this with confidence, as a subject wherewith he is really acquainted, and testifies of what he has experienced to be true.

"The doubtsome faith he (*E. E.*) complains of, is that which admits of a doubt concerning one's own state. Now, a man may have some doubts about this, who is very firmly persuaded of the truth of the gospel." p. 334.

The doubtsome faith we complain of, is the want of that confidence answerable to the gracious declarations of salvation in Christ to the absolutely guilty; and not a man's doubting about himself, or what he at present is. On the contrary, we maintain, that this persuasion of a new state in Christ, implies our natural state to be quite bad, and past recovery; and the particular application we plead for, is flying from a bad state in our natural situation, to a good state in the person, righteousness, and blessings of Christ.

As existence, and consciousness of existence, bear such a relation to each other in the human mind, that the former is only enjoyed by the latter; so is justification, and the consciousness of it. If I perceive not my justification, it is to me as if I was not justified. If I apprehend it is so from a false foundation, it will prove to me as a dream which vanishes when wide awake. If a man, by some kind of argument, was to persuade me that I existed a thousand years ago, though I am not now conscious of it, it would be the same delusion, as if he was to persuade me that I am now King *George*, or the King of *Prussia*. For a hundred such existences is, in fact, a hundred men, every man's own consciousness ascertaining himself to himself in distinction from any other. In like manner, if a man was to use arguments, to persuade
me

me that I was juſtified long ago, when I was not conſcious of it, he could propoſe no other end, his labour could no otherwiſe terminate, than in perſuading me that I am now juſtified. And that which is brought to prove, that I am one of thoſe who were juſtified long ago, when I was not conſcious of it, may as well give me a conſciouſneſs of my preſent juſtification, without all that round-about labour. Unleſs it is, that while we are conſidering theſe pre-exiſting juſtifications, we are apt to ſlip ourſelves in for a ſhare, upon a foundation that will not bear a preſent ſcrutiny. The ſcripture, therefore, does not thus metaphyſically ſubtilize, it does not thus ſeparate our juſtification from the conſciouſneſs of it. He that is juſtified, by the finiſhed work of Chriſt, without any conſciouſneſs of a difference between himſelf and others, is juſtified as ungodly; has peace with God by that which juſtifies him; and is juſtified by his faith, that is, not by what he does, but by what he believes: and the additional confirmation, by the fruits of faith, or conſciouſneſs of our not being deceived in our juſtification by faith, is called by the apoſtle *James*, juſtification by works, without bearing any contradiction to the alone righteouſneſs by which we are juſtified. If my juſtification ariſes to me from the difference there is betwixt me and others, I may be ſaid to be juſtified, or enjoy juſtification by that difference. If the ſpring of my hope ariſes to my view from the report making me welcome to the finiſhed work of Chriſt, as the righteouſneſs provided for the guilty to live by, then I am juſtified, or enjoy juſtification by Chriſt's righteouſneſs given to me, in oppoſition to any thing done by me, or performed in me. If my perſonal juſtification, and the conſciouſneſs of it, ſtand ſo nearly related, it is not at all improper that the ground of our acceptance with God, and the ground of our conſciouſneſs of that acceptance, ſhould be of the ſame kind. So that if I am accepted with God by the work of Chrift alone, given to me, I am to know my acceptance with God juft upon the fame, and no other foundation. If it were not fo, the favourite fomething might be fet up, and the pride of man as fully gratified under the name of marks and evidences, as it is under the name of entitling conditions; and we are as effectually taught to draw near, with a *God I thank thee, I am not as other men.* The fufficient righteoufnefs juftifies a man, or gives him a confcioufnefs of his acceptance with God, when he knows it is gracioufly given to him, fo that he is made welcome to draw near to God on that account. He that believes to the peace of his confcience, believes this, and does not reft in an uncertain conjectural hope. Says *Palæmon*, a hope grounded on the fovereignty of God;—fay we, not unlefs that fovereignty has declared a ground of hope for us; otherwife we reft in bare conjecture. But hearing that Jefus has fulfilled all righteoufnefs for the juftification of thofe guilty ones who believe in his name, from a conviction that the doctrine is true, we affure ourfelves, in dependence on the divine veracity and faithfulnefs, that the privileges are our own; or that we fhall not be confounded in fo trufting to Jefus.

"*Paul* calls upon fome whom he himfelf looked
"upon as believers, to examine themfelves whether
"they were in the faith; and he exhorts others, about
"whom he obferved the fureft tokens of their being
"true Chriftians, to give all diligence to remove e-
"very doubt concerning their ftate." p. 334.

When *Paul* bid the *Corinthians examine themfelves,* &c. he plainly intimates their being in the faith a felf-evident matter; and that to be in the faith, and to have Chrift in them, as the peace of their confciences, and hope of glory, is the fame thing; and this was the fureft evidence that he had been a minifter of Chrift unto them. He is not here calling them to remove the doubts concerning their own ftate, by a difcovery of their faith, love, and self-denied obedience. It is also very improbable, that the apostle should (as *Palæmon* says) have the surest tokens of their being Christians, and yet call them to doubt of it.

"I am sorry to see *Aspasio* so much carried away "with their (*i. e.* the popular preachers) dissimula-"tion." He points out to *Theron* his danger and remedy in the following manner : " *If you fail in one* " *point, or in any degree, you are guilty of all. If your* " *conformity be not persevering as well as perfect, you* " *incur the penalty, and are abandoned to the curse,*" unless you find mercy by what Christ has already done. No; but " unless, renouncing all your personal per-" formances, you place all your affiance on a *Saviour's* " atonement and a *Saviour's* righteousness." p. 334.

They who endeavour to renounce their personal performances, as an entitling performance required of them, act inconsistently ; but they who evidently renounce their own, from a gospel-discovery of the Redeemer's righteousness, and live alone by that, in virtue of the divine declarations, are taught of God, and find mercy by what Christ has already done.

" This good conduct of ours, by which we are " said to escape the curse." Note, p. 334.

So we are, according to *Palæmon*, to take care that we have no affiance or confidence in Christ's atonement, or righteousness, because that is escaping the curse by some good conduct of our own!

" *Were* (says Aspasio) *that firm and joyful reliance* " *on Christ Jesus, in any degree proportioned to his in-* " *finite merits and inviolable promises?* And if (says " *Palæmon*) I cannot find acceptance with God, but in " being conscious of perfect conformity to this new " law, then I am in as great danger as before." p. 325.

Aspasio moves this very question, not to obtain a prerequisite, but to manifest the necessity of a better righteousness than our reliance, considered as a performance or work of ours, that we may rely upon the suffi-
cient

cient work of Christ, without recurring to any other. The gospel-declarations are not to be separated from our Saviour, his atonement, or righteousness. Nor can our affiance, knowledge, or enjoyment through that report, be separated from either. Is Christ's righteousness presented to me as a security from the curse of the law? My affiance therein, or knowledge thereof, is Christ, my security, enjoyed by me, and manifested to me. The apostle was not so curious as to distinguish and divide with our author, when he said, *I count all things but loss*, not for the excellency of Christ, in distinction from the knowledge of him, but *for the excellency of the knowledge of Christ Jesus my Lord;* and this he styles, *not having on his own righteousness.*

" My expectations were greatly raised by the
" beautiful and affecting description of the *royal stag*
" *chace* in *dial.* 9. till I saw the sinner's relief descri-
" bed as coming to him by means of such conflicts
" and struggles, *&c.*" p. 337.

Aspasio does not mean struggling to believe the report, but struggling for that *rest*, which comes at last in a way they thought not of; that is, by the report. The reasons of the soul-struggles described, are ignorance and self-righteousness, seeking other methods of relief than by the declaration of eternal life given in Christ ; and it frequently proves, that after many useless struggles in divers ways, the soul thus finds rest.

" They knew their interest in Christ's death, by the
" effect that his death had upon them." p. 339.

Christ's death hath its effect upon us when we draw near to God thereby ; which is, in fact, when we appropriate it. .

" They imagine, that something besides the bare
" truth may contribute more or less toward their e-
" scape." p. 339.

They are clear of this charge, who escape by what that truth declares.

"The gospel leads a man to the greatest reverence for, and submission to the divine sovereignty, without having any claim upon God whatsoever, or finding any reason why God should regard him more than those that perish." p. 345.

Palæmon maintains, that all who acknowledge the truth of Christ's sufficiency have the promise of salvation. He does not imagine a dependence on this promise opposes the most absolute submission to the divine sovereignty; but is rather a dependence on the promises of sovereign grace. And if we are persuaded of a grant of this sufficient righteousness to the guilty, why may not this be admitted as fully consistent with the same submission to the divine sovereignty?

"The divine sovereignty appearing, that grace might be shewn to the worthless; and the divine justice appearing in justifying the ungodly," it is very readily acknowledged, leaves a man entirely at the mercy of God for his salvation. Here no man's pride is flattered; "no man can find any ground to presume, that the Deity regards him more than others. And the relief a man finds by this discovery, is, that God can be just, and justify him as he at present stands without more, or while he finds nothing about himself in the way of wish, desire, or otherwise, but what renders him obnoxious to the divine displeasure." p. 346. The question that remains is, Whether God has not intended a farther relief for such guilty helpless ones, even to assure them of their particular salvation in believing, trusting, and confiding, in this sufficient righteousness, as given freely to them to be thus depended upon? Whether there is not a word, promise, call, or testimony, to this purpose? and whether Christian obedience is not influenced by an assurance thus obtained? At the same time we can also readily agree, that "no man can warrantably be assured that he is already a Chris-
"tian,

" tian, a believer in Chrift, or that he is an object of
" the peculiar favour of God, but by being alfo con-
" fcious, on good grounds, that his practice, in obe-
" dience to the peculiar precepts of Chriftianity, is
" influenced by that fame truth, which influenced the
" lives of the apoftles."

Now, if there is fuch a *word, promife, call,* or *tefti-mony,* as above-mentioned, it is very diftinct from, though not contrary to the declarations concerning the *purpofe* and *election* of God ; and affords a vifible ground for our confident dependence on that righteoufnefs, as finners, without finding any reafon about ourfelves, why God fhould regard us more than others : whereas the doctrine of election, in the nature of it, is not of itfelf capable of affording us this relief.

It is true, " this *word, promife, call,* or *teftimony,*
" leaves it as much a fecret what particular perfon
" fhall be faved, as the doctrine of the divine *purpofe,*
or *election* does." p. 348. but does not leave the finner fo much without a warrant to appropriate. Notwithftanding the doctrine of election, *Palæmon* will allow, that *by him, all that believe are juftified.* So alfo it is faid, *He that* cometh to him *fhall in no wife be caft out; He that* believeth on him *fhall never be confounded.*

In this view of things, we are fully warranted " to
" reprefent the Deity, as keeping fecret his gracious
" intentions" to beget this or that particular perfon, by the word of truth ; and, at the fame time, " re-
" vealing his gracious intentions" to fave all thofe, or any, whofoever they be, that, without feeing any difference at all between themfelves and others, fhall, upon the bare invitation and divine promife to the guilty, live, truft, or depend on his Son and his righteoufnefs, gracioufly provided as a refuge unto fuch. And while we " are bufy in prompting our hearers to
" live thus by Chrift alone, as given freely and inde-
" finitely to the guilty ; we have reafon to fhew no
" fmall

"small concern, left Satan tempt them" to think, that because God's people are chosen to salvation, they are not allowed to feed upon the bread of life, till they know themselves to be distinguished from other sinners as God's chosen. Hereby salvation, to the absolutely guilty, is denied; and the people are taught to hope for eternal life, only by that which distinguishes them from the rest of mankind. This is building wood, hay, and stubble, on the precious foundation, Christ the Saviour of the lost.

"They tell us, *that God hath made a grant, or deed*
"*of gift of Christ, and all his benefits, to sinners of*
"*mankind.* But when we inquire into this again, we
" find it turns out to be a gift of benefits to multi-
" tudes who are never benefited thereby." p. 350.

And what of all that? Could there be no such thing as manna given to, or rained daily around the camp of *Israel*, because some despised it, and longed for the flesh-pots of *Egypt?* Must it follow that there is no such gift, because multitudes neglect and slight it? or because, like *Palæmon*, they will not be persuaded there is such a gift? Shall our unbelief make the gift, the faith, or faithfulness of God, of none effect? It remaineth nevertheless a truth, that whosoever believeth on him, or receiveth the gift, shall not perish, but have eternal life. And why may not they miss of the benefit of this gift who thus reject it, as the word preached never profited, not being mixed with faith in them that heard it?

" It might, with equal propriety, be said, that
" there is a grant of life made in the law, and that
" the divine willingness to bless men is therein ex-
" pressed; Keep the commandments, and thou shalt
" live." p. 351.

It might so; the difference lies here. The grant of life in the law, requires conditions to be previously performed, before we may presume to account the blessing ours. The gospel bestows life in Christ without

out any condition, or as a free gift, to be immediately enjoyed.

In page 352. several instances of the faith of those who were healed by Christ; are reduced to evidence, that they only believed Christ's ability to cure them. To this I answer, that in those instances they waited for a proper ground, or declaration to proceed upon, in believing that he would; and for that purpose they made application to him. And where they had ground for concluding the event, they were as certain of *that*, as of his ability. And faith in those cases includes *that* certainty. 1 *Cor.* xiii. 2. *If I had all faith, so that I could remove mountains*, comp. with *Matth.* xvii. 20. *When he saw he had faith to be healed*, Acts xiv. 9. and in *Luke* v. 19, 29. they neither doubted his ability, or willingness. In our case, the grant of a Saviour to the guilty is declared, as well as the sufficiency of his righteousness; hence we make God a liar, if we do not proceed on the truth of both.

" The leper, like the two blind men, was fully
" persuaded that Christ was able to relieve him. Yet,
" as he had no claim upon him, he referred his re-
" quest entirely to his sovereign pleasure. In the full
" assurance of faith he was at Christ's mercy, who
" was nowise obliged to apply his healing power to
" him." p. 352.

But this is no argument against that appropriation, which proceeds entirely upon the gracious declaration, and grant of that sovereign good pleasure. If the sovereign good pleasure has declared the guilty as such, so welcome to what is already done, that *whosoever believeth on him shall have eternal life;* he hath no other application to make, or to wait for. We may be without any claim upon God to do for us any thing that he has not already done, or to give us any right unto what is already done; but as far as he is pleased to declare himself, it is our business assuredly to believe, trust in him, or hope in his mercy. And that
appropriation,

appropriation which proceeds wholly upon his gracious declaration, is confiſtent with the utmoſt ſubmiſſion to ſovereign grace.

"Sovereign grace interpoſed, providing a righte"ouſneſs for the guilty world." p. 353.

Palæmon ſhould ſay, to aſcertain his meaning, "providing a righteouſneſs for ſome of the guilty "world."

"When once the gift of righteouſneſs is made "known to a man." p. 353.

Can the gift properly be ſaid to be made known to a man, unleſs he knows to whom it is given? A gift to nobody, is no gift. A gift to the elect, or to the qualified, is not a gift to the guilty world, but to them that are choſen out of it, and diſtinguiſhed from it.

"He that believeth on the Son of God, hath the "record in himſelf,—the record that God gave of "his Son." *Ibid.*

Palæmon ſlips over the record here treated of, *viz. That God hath given to us eternal life, and this life is in his Son.* This the apoſtle points unto, as what is to be particularly regarded, *And this is the record,* &c. Nor ſhould the teſtimony, that he is well pleaſed in him, be underſtood in any ſenſe excluſive of it.

"In like manner, all his children in the faith be"lieve the divine word for righteouſneſs, without "perceiving any ſhadow or ſymptom of it about "themſelves, without feeling or being conſcious of "any thing about themſelves, to concur with the "divine word, to make out their righteouſneſs." *Ibid.*

This deſcription ſuits *Aſpaſio* much better than *Palæmon*, who waits for a diſcovery of his faith, love, and ſelf-denied obedience.

"If we look into the ſcripture, muſt we not ſay, "that all the good works which ſhall be recompenſed "at the reſurrection of the juſt, are produced by the "influence

"influence of the divine Spirit dwelling in the hearts
"of thofe who believe? Yet fuch is the connection
"betwixt every good work and its reward, that, ac-
"cording to the fcripture, the juftice of God, not
"to fay his grace, is concerned to make it good:
"*Heb.* vi. 10. *God is not unrighteous to forget your*
"*work and labour of love.—Whofoever fhall give you a*
"*cup of water to drink in my name,—verily I fay un-*
"*to you, he fhall not lofe his reward.* Juftice, as well
"as grace, will appear in the laft judgment; then due
"regard will be had to every man's works. But in
"the juftification of finners, God has no refpect to
"any man, as better than another. He confiders men,
"when he commends his love to them, as ungodly,
"and without ftrength, that is, without any will to
"be better. And all who find mercy, are brought
"to view themfelves in that fame point of light,
"wherein God beheld men when he gave his Son to
"die for them. They do not find themfelves pre-
"pared, or made fitter than others for mercy, by
"any work of the divine Spirit upon their minds;
"but they find their firft tafte of comfort by hearing
"of him, *who through the eternal Spirit offered him-*
"*felf without fpot to God.*" p. 257.

Then they find their firft tafte of comfort indepen-
dent of any previous difcovery or difcernment of their
faith, love, or felf-denied obedience. And their firft
tafte of comfort is, not that there is a fufficient righ-
teoufnefs provided for the elect, or the qualified, but
that there is a fufficient righteoufnefs provided for the
guilty to live by, without waiting for any farther dif-
covery.

"The popular doctrine fuppofes, that unbelievers
"may be ferioufly engaged in praying for the Holy
"Spirit to help them to faith, and exhorts them ac-
"cordingly; which is as abfurd as to fuppofe, that a
"man may be defirous of being influenced by the Spi-
"rit of a truth, which, at prefent, he neither be-
"lieves

"lieves nor loves. For I reckon it muſt be granted, that no man loves the goſpel before he believes it." p. 360.

If we only underſtood by the goſpel that we were welcome to do ſomething, or to wait and pray for ſomething to denominate us Chriſt's people, then we might be complaining for want of this power, praying for it, and perhaps falſely comforted with the ſuppoſed will for the deed; and all the while there is no willingneſs to live entirely by what Chriſt has done. But this is not the caſe: when *Aſpaſio* conſidered appropriation as eſſential to faith, and preſſed it accordingly, he underſtood by appropriation, a living entirely by Chriſt's righteouſneſs alone, without waiting for any other.

"When our ſyſtems deſcribe faith to us, as a ſaving grace beſtowed on us, by which we make uſe of Chriſt for ſalvation; are we not led to think of ſome grace neceſſary to our ſalvation, beſide what appeared when Chriſt, by the grace of God, taſted death for the ſins of men?" p. 361.

But in as much as *Aſpaſio*'s whole plea is to live immediately by that grace alone, without waiting for any other; he ſtands clear of this miſtake.

"They ſeem to forget, that Chriſt is in heaven, and we on the earth;—that the only way wherein we can receive benefit from Chriſt, is by the report concerning him conveyed to our ears." p. 363.

If the report, in this particular caſe, invites and authoriſes us to live by him, and the righteouſneſs which he performed, who is gone to heaven; we may, notwithſtanding he is gone to heaven, receive the report for true, and alſo lay hold of, or live by the righteouſneſs it thus reveals and conveys to us.

"When he comes to know that he may be juſtified, he finds immediately a covert from the ſtorm." p. 364.

But according to *Palemon*, he does not find this to be a covert *for him*, till he diſcovers diſtinguiſhing qualifications;

qualifications; whereas *Aspasio* finds a covert for the guilty sinner, without any such distinction.

"If now we understand by the *storm*, the wrath
"that is to come, the believer, knowing that Christ
"hath done enough to deliver from it, loves him,
"takes hold of him, or flies to him."

How?

"In obeying his commands, and frequenting every
"mean of correspondence with him." *Ibid.*

He that loves him, takes hold of him, or flies to him, obeys his commands; and is inclined to frequent every means of correspondence with him; but to give us this as the meaning and import of those scriptural phrases and representations, more becomes Mr *Locke*, or Archbishop *Tillotson*, than the evangelical *Palæmon*. He may be assured, if he abides by this doctrine, the offence of the cross will soon cease. The primitive Christians were taught to obey, because *Jesus had delivered them from the wrath to come*, 1 Thess. i. 10. They fled to him as the righteousness provided for the guilty and destitute; and by the enjoyment of him, under this character, they were disposed to all other obedience.

"Accordingly we find *Barnabas* exhorted those at
"*Antioch*, in whom he saw the grace of God, that
"with purpose of heart they would *cleave unto the*
"*Lord*. The consequence of which was, they assem-
"bled together in the appointed church-order, and
"denied themselves in sending relief to their brethren
"in *Judea*." p. 365.

Did they not assemble as members of Christ, and partakers of his righteousness? Did they not cleave to him as the Lord their righteousness? Or did they only fall into the appointed church-order, in order to escape the wrath to come? If so, what is now become of the sufficient righteousness? or, in short, of all the apostolic exhortations, which constantly proceed upon the certainty of salvation by Christ, as the principle of all the obedience they call for.

"See what effect the knowledge of Christ had on "*Paul*, and what was his steady purpose: *Yea doubt-* "*less, and I count all things but loss, for the excellency* "*of the knowledge of Christ Jesus my Lord.*" Ibid.-

Paul says, *My Lord*, the thing we plead for, and counts himself *apprehended of Christ Jesus*. So that it is plain, he *ran not as uncertainly, he fought not as one that beateth the air*. And as his assurance did not allow him, or lead him to trifle, or slacken his diligence in pressing forward to the desired end; so, on the other hand, his pressing forward was far from being the result of his uncertainty; far from being animated with a view to know by his performances, whether the divine sovereignty had interposed in his behalf.

Palæmon does not approve of *Aspasio* saying, "You "must endeavour, diligently endeavour, to believe." *Ibid*. But we may plead, in his excuse, that *Aspasio* is not here pressing to receive a report as true without evidence, but to appropriate and live by the revealed righteousness; to obtain and maintain thereby that certainty of acceptance with God, which was necessary to animate and incline to all evangelical obedience, and is included in every apostolic exportation. *Wherefore as ye have always obeyed—As ye have received Christ Jesus the Lord, so walk in him.—Work out your own salvation—Fight the good fight of faith, lay hold on eternal life*, &c. And thus understood, we may allow, with *Palæmon*, that " by such arguments God "worketh in them that believe, both to will and to "do, not any thing in order to justification, but all "those things wherein their salvation is evidenced." p. 367.

" If a friend of mine should see me chearful, on " hearing something new, and I should tell him, I was " comforted by an act of faith; would he not say I " trifled with him, and readily ask what good news I
" had

" had heard, that he might partake in my satisfaction?" p. 369.

But this reprefentation does not reach thofe who plead for an immediate and conftant living upon the complete and perfect righteoufnefs of Jefus Chrift. They are comforted by *his* acts, and their own has no other concern in it,

"Faith, with its effects, is in fcripture often figni-
"fied by one expreffion, and accordingly connected
"with falvation, as when it is faid, *Whofoever fhall
"call on the name of the Lord fhall be faved.* Now,
"though we cannot fay that a believer is faved on
"account of his prayers; yet we may fay, that he is
"faved on account of what he believes, and by which
"he is encouraged to pray. It is eafy to fee love and
"hope expreffed in all the prayers of faith recorded
"in the fcripture; yet it would be abfurd to infer
"from thence, that prayer, love, and faith, are re-
"quifites in order to juftification: for, if we agree
"with the apoftles, we muft ftill maintain, that juf-
"tification comes by faith, and not by works, not
"by any thing we do in obedience to any law what-
"foever." p. 370.

And at the fame time it muft be acknowledged, that faith is duty and obedience to the divine law, and in this fenfe a work: for, as our author has obferved, p. 354. "Will not that law which Chrift came to
"fulfil, the law which requires love to God with all
"the heart, condemn all who by their unbelief make
"God a liar? Does not the Spirit of God convince
"all whom he brings to the knowledge of the truth,
"of fin, becaufe they believe not on Chrift? In
"fine, is there any thing contrary to the gofpel
"of the glory of the bleffed God, not condemned
"by the divine law?" How can thefe be reconciled, unlefs we admit that faith is fo far a work, duty, or obedience, as has been above mentioned. Yet, as *Palæmon* maintains, we are juftified
only

only by *what we believe.* We are juſtified by faith as we are pleaſed with a ſight, that is, with *what we ſee.* And God juſtifies us by faith when he gives us this ſight or faith, whereby we are thus juſtified. And thus to be juſtified by Chriſt's blood, and to be juſtified by faith, is the ſame thing.

If *Palæmon* will abide by what he ſays, p. 371. that " the ſcriptures point forth the freedom of divine " grace to the ſetting aſide all human diſtinctions, in " ſuch language as this, *If any man will come after* " *me;—Let him that heareth ſay come; and whoſoever* " *will, let him take of the water of life freely,*" p. 371. we are then agreed, this is the foundation of all we plead for, that ſinners, as ſuch, are made welcome to take of the water of life freely.

" If the ſcriptures deſcribe believers as pilgrims, " and ſtrangers on earth, as running the Chriſtian " race, denying themſelves for the ſake of the hea- " venly inheritance, and accordingly *flying for refuge,* " *to lay hold upon the hope ſet before them;* our " preachers, ever mindful of their acts of faith, are " ready to exhort us to put forth the acts of *flying to* " *Chriſt, and laying hold on him.*" p. 372.

The paſſage alluded to is *Heb.* vi. 18, 19. *That by two immutable things, in which it was impoſſible for God to lie, we might have a ſtrong conſolation, who have fled for refuge, to lay hold upon the hope ſet before us. Which* hope *we have as an anchor of the ſoul, both ſure and ſtedfaſt,* &c. Who have fled is an act paſſed, and bears a manifeſt reference to flying from the revenger of blood to the cities of refuge, *Numb.* xxxv. 27. to which city the man-ſlayer being fled, was, while there, ſecure; not in his act, but in the privilege of the city wherein he now dwelt; and waited unto the death of the high prieſt, as the hope ſet before him. The hope ſet before us, the apoſtle tells us we yet ſee not, *but with patience wait for it,* Rom. viii. 25. But how can we with patience wait for it, if it is not at preſent the

anchor

anchor of the foul, both fure and ftedfaft? Or, as the apoftle fays in another place, *I fo run, not as uncertainly.* Yet as his fecurity lay in that righteoufnefs of Chrift alone, he kept *his body* (all his temporal concerns) *under fubjection* thereto, even as the man-flayer abode in the city of refuge, knowing there was no fafety for him elfewhere. When a man performs his acts of obedience, that he may thereby gain himfelf a confcious title, poffeffion, or enjoyment, of the favour of God, it is but of little moment whether he ftyles it the favour of God by Chrift, or by any other name. His way to come at it is ftill the fame, by his own obedience. Nor can this be flying for refuge to Chrift, but rather chufing my own performances as my fecurity, and betaking myfelf to them.

" If *Barnabas* exhorts thofe in whom he faw the
" grace of God, with purpofe of heart to *cleave unto*
" *the Lord*, after the example of the believers who
" were faid to be added unto the Lord, when they
" were added to the fociety of the difciples, keep-
" ing his commands, then we are told that juftifying
" faith is a *cleaving to Chrift.*" Ibid.

It will anfwer our purpofe, and convey our whole meaning, to fay, The faith which juftifies cleaves to Chrift; and in exhorting to cleave to Chrift, we exhort to continue in the faith. The phrafe, *Believers were the more added to the Lord*, is, very evidently, neither more nor lefs, than that many more were begotten to the faith. As to what relation thefe phrafes may alfo bear to fellowfhip in the gofpel, fee the anfwer to p. 365. in p. 379.

" But *Afpafio* tells us, in this page, that it is the
" office of faith, *to take and ufe the ineftimable gift*. If
" in this, or any other part of the *New Teftament*,
" more be meant by *receiving Chrift*, than knowing
" him, or believing on him, then I am ready to fhew,
" that more than *faith* is meant, namely, faith with
" its fruits and effects." p. 373.

By

By *receiving Chrift* more may be meant than *knowing him*, but not more than *believing on him*. We may be faid to *know* a thing when its evidence forces itfelf upon the mind; but to *believe on Chrift*, is, in the fcripture-fenfe, the fubject of exhortation. If *Palæmon* will confine himfelf to mean by faith, no more than a paffive conviction of truth, it fhall be allowed him, that by *believing on Chrift* more than he means by faith is intended. The fame may be faid of the phrafes *laying hold, leaning*, &c, more is allowed to be meant by thefe expreffions than *Palæmon* means by faith. At the fame time it may be affirmed, that thefe expreffions of activity " do not contribute their quota" to our juftification, fince we are juftified by the righteoufnefs received, trufted, or leaned upon, and not by our act. We are juftified by *what we receive*, even as *Palæmon* will allow we are juftified by *what we believe*.

"The faith of the gofpel is indeed the bafis of "truft." p. 374.

If fo, we are agreed again, for this *truft* we call *believing on Chrift*. If the faith of the gofpel is *the bafis of truft*, it is of appropriation; for how can I truft in that wherein I am not allowed to take any fhare? If we are not allowed to truft in the Redeemer's righteoufnefs when abfolutely guilty, the faith of the gofpel is not the bafis of truft. In *Palæmon*'s view, the gofpel only fhews us the poffibility of the falvation of the elect, and cannot therefore be the bafis of truft to a finner, but the difcovery of his obedience, as giving him hopes that he is one of the elect, is, in fact, the matter wherein his *truft* is founded.

" If one approaching to a frozen lake or river, over
" which he has occafion to pafs, tells me, that he has
" been affured, by good information, that the ice was
" fufficiently ftrong to fupport him; and yet, after all,
" proves timorous, and averfe to make the trial, *by*
" *venturing his perfon freely upon it;* I plainly perceive
" he

"he has no faith in the report he heard; becaufe he does not *truft in it;* or, which is the fame thing, he cannot truft, rely, confide in, or venture himfelf upon the ice." *Ibid.*

There cannot be a more apt illuftration of what we plead for. And he that ventures his eternal concerns on the all-fufficient righteoufnefs of Chrift, with the fame confidence that he that believes the ice will bear him ventures his body upon that, will not be averfe to run the rifk of his intereft and reputation alfo for the fake of it. We can therefore have no objection to *Palæmon,* when he fays,

"If one tells me, that he believes the gofpel, and yet proves averfe to rifk his intereft or reputation in the world for the fake of it; I immediately perceive, that whatever he fpeaks with his mouth, he does not in his heart believe the gofpel, becaufe he puts no truft in it." p. 375.

"Perhaps it will now be inquired, Are no rules to be obferved, no means to be ufed, no works to be exerted by the human mind or body, in order to juftification? The anfwer is ready: Yes, very many. And they may be thus fhortly fummed up: Be perfect, keep the commandments, and thou fhalt live. The obligation of the law is eternal, and cannot be loofed.—But, perhaps, another ftate of the queftion will be demanded, and that faith fhould be more directly refpected therein: Well then, let it ftand thus: Ought not a man to be at pains to attain the perfuafion, that all the pains he takes are good for nothing, except to enhance his guilt? Here, methinks, we are landed at downright abfurdity. For who will labour in hopes of being convinced, that all his labour is to no purpofe, unlefs to his hurt?" p. 387. 388.

This we may allow to be very well ftated, with refpect to the perfons whom it concerns. But the queftion between our author and *Afpafio,* really ftands thus:

thus: Are no rules to be obſerved, no means to be uſed, no acts to be exerted by the human mind or body, to arrive at the certainty of our own particular juſtification? *Palæmon* ſays, Yes, a great many; as many as will ſerve to demonſtrate that we are elected. *Aſpaſio* ſays, only thankfully to receive or accept the bleſſings as freely given: and all the direction given by *Aſpaſio*, reſpects this queſtion, and not the ſufficiency of the finiſhed work of Chriſt to juſtify the moſt guilty.

"The deſign of the paſſage (*Rom*. x. 19, 20, 21.) "is plainly to ſhew, that faith comes not by any hu- "man endeavours, or the uſe of any means, even "under the greateſt advantages that men can enjoy, "but of that ſame ſovereign good pleaſure which "provided the grand thing believed." p. 390.

Here is then, notwithſtanding all *Palæmon*'s exactneſs, a *ſomething more* than the finiſhed work of Chriſt, a ſomething called faith, which he tells us comes "of "that ſame ſovereign good pleaſure which provided "the grand thing believed." *Palæmon* will reply, he means no more than believing that which is provided is ſufficient; nor do we mean any more by appropriation, than *receiving* that which is ſufficient, as believing it to be freely given to us for that purpoſe.

"I would here ſubjoin, by way of poſtſcript to "this, ſome reflections on the *aſſurance* or *appropria-* "*tion* ſaid to be eſſential to ſaving faith.

"While various terms and diſtinctions are coined "by popular preachers on this ſubject, great neglect "is ſhewn to a very plain and obvious diſtinction, "which *Paul* makes betwixt the aſſurance of faith, "and the aſſurance of hope." p. 393.

Upon a review of the ſcriptures to ſee what foundation there was for this remark, I gathered the following:

1. In regard to faith. *Being juſtified by faith, we have peace with God, through our Lord Jeſus Chriſt*, Rom.

Rom. v. i. *All joy and peace in believing*, Rom. xv. 13. and not by what *Palæmon* styles assurance of hope gathered from a discovery of our faith, love, and self-denied obedience.

The language of faith is not barely concerning others, the elect, &c. But WE *believe, that, through the grace of our Lord Jesus Christ,* WE *shall be saved,* Acts xv. 11.

Faith is described, *Heb.* xi. 25, 26. to be so far the assurance of eternal life by Christ, as to be on that very account, *the victory that overcomes the world.*

They that died in faith, *not having received the promises, but having seen them afar off, and were persuaded of and embraced them,* and (therefore) *confessed they were strangers and pilgrims on the earth,* Heb. xi. 23. did they not appropriate these promises? or, did they only consider them as belonging to the elect, and themselves uncertain whether they were of the number, till they could discover it by the discovery of their faith, love, and self-denied obedience?

The assurance of faith proceeds upon *having boldness to enter into the holiest by the blood of Jesus,—by a way consecrated for us,—and having a high priest over the house of God,* Heb. x. 19, 22. And can all this be in a fixed uncertainty, or without appropriation? Can I draw near, as having a way consecrated, or as having a high priest over the house of God; and, at the same time, don't know whether I have or no?

If we are condemned for asking doubtingly, *James* i. 6, 7. and for little faith in providence, *Matth.* vi. 30. does not the opposite character imply a certainty of divine favour and regard by sovereign grace, independent of a discovery of our previous obedience?

Rom. xiv. 23. *Whatsoever is not of faith,* (i. e. whatsoever action is not of confidence of acceptance with God,) *is sin.* Does not this scripture make confidence essential to faith?

Rom. iv. 5. *To him that worketh not, but believeth on him that justifieth the ungodly,* &c. Is not this inconsistent with waiting to be godly, before I dare put my trust in him?

We cannot *call on him in whom we have not believed,* Rom. x. 14. that is, we cannot *call in faith, nothing doubting,* as above, *Jam.* i. 6.

It is the divine commandment to *believe in his name,* 1 *John* iii. 23. and it is the strength of faith *against hope,* of what we see or feel, *to believe in hope* of what God has freely given and promised.

Eph. iii. 12. *In whom we have boldness and access with confidence by the* FAITH *of him.* Can this be where there is no appropriation?

Gal. v. 5. *We, thro' the Spirit, wait for the hope of righteousness by* FAITH. Can this be said in uncertainty? or in a conditional certainty depending on our performance?

Can the dead live by *believing on him,* according to *John* xi. 25. if they are to wait till they feel life first?

2. In regard to hope, we are told, that not our performances, but God's promise and oath are the *strong consolation* of them *who have fled for refuge to lay hold of the* HOPE *set before them; which hope we have as an anchor of the soul, both* SURE *and* STEDFAST, *and which entereth into that within the vail.* Heb. vi. 18, 19.

We are told to *hold fast the beginning of our confidence---the confidence and rejoicing of the hope, firm unto the end.* Heb. iii. 6.

As we *have not seen and yet have believed,* so we are said to *hope for that we see not,* and *patiently wait for it,* Rom. viii. 25. *We are saved through faith,* Eph. ii. 8. *We are saved by hope,* Rom. viii. 23. *We are said to purify ourselves by this hope,* 1 John iii. 3. *To have our hearts purified by faith,* Acts xv. 9. *To purify our souls in obeying the truth through the Spirit, unto the unfeigned love of the brethren,* 1 Pet. i. 22. *We are said to be all the children of God by faith in Jesus Christ,*

Chrift, Gal. iii. 29. to be *begotten again to a lively hope*, not through a difcovery of our obedience, *but by the refurrection of Chrift from the dead*, 1 Pet. i. 3. And *the God of hope* fills us with *all joy and peace in believing*, Rom. xv. 13. *And being juftified by faith, we rejoice in the hope of the glory of God*, Rom. v. 2. When we are exhorted, 1 Pet. iii. 15. to *be ready always to give an anfwer to every man that afketh us a reafon of the hope that is in us*, I apprehend our faith, or that truth we believe, is that reafon, and not our own righteoufnefs or qualifications. Upon this review of thefe fcriptures, it appears to me, that *Palæmon's* refinement upon the fcripture-phrafes, to the excluding appropriation or certainty of falvation from faith, and afcribing it wholly to a difcovery of our inherent qualifications, under the name of affurance of hope, is not fo fcripturally founded as he has imagined.

" The affurance of hope, is enjoyed only by thofe
" who give all diligence to obtain it." p. 393.
That they are exhorted to fhew *the fame diligence to the full affurance of hope unto the end*, is true. We are alfo to *hold faft the beginning of our* confidence *ftedfaft unto the end.*

" The firft of thefe (the affurance of faith) was
" called for in a man's firft profeffion of the faith,
" upon his firft hearing the gofpel, in order to his be-
" ing acknowledged for a Chriftian." *Ibid.*

Hope is alfo called the *hope of our calling by the gofpel*, Eph. i. 18. not the hope of our obedience, or hope arifing from our qualifications. And upon a man's firft hearing the gofpel, when he was firft begotten again by the word of truth, he is faid to be *begotten again unto a lively hope, by the refurrection of Chrift from the dead*, 1 Pet. i. 3. Chrift is faid to *dwell in our hearts by* FAITH, Eph. iii. 17. and *Col.* i. 27. as our HOPE *of glory.* And if he is not thus in us, we are faid to be not young profeffors, or young Chriftians, but *reprobates.*

" The

"The assurance of faith is likewise necessary to the drawing near to God in his worship." p. 394.

We are likewise said to *draw near to God by the better hope*, Heb. vii. 19., *which hope we have as an anchor of the soul both* SURE *and* STEDFAST.

"The assurance of hope again, is an enjoyment proposed to them who believed." *Ibid.*

A stedfast continuance, full assurance, and increase in the faith is proposed to them also.

"The assurance of hope, then, holds pace, first and last, with the work and labour of love." *Ibid.*

The apostolic *hope* held pace, first and last, with the apostolic faith; and love or charity followed both. The apostles do not teach the order to be *faith, love*, and *hope*, because I love; but *faith*, in the revealed righteousness, is the spring of *hope;* and *love* flowing from both. *Now abideth faith, hope, and charity; these three* as the root, and not the fruit of our obedience.

"There was no Christian, however eminent, in the days of the apostles, but needed the exhortation, to give all diligence for maintaining and confirming the assurance of hope." *Ibid.*

Nor was any Christian so far advanced, but he might be exhorted to be *strong in the grace which is in Christ Jesus, and continue in the faith grounded and settled.*

"They often called on men to examine themselves." *Ibid.*

They declared remission of sin immediately in Christ's name, as the truth whereby we pass *from death to life*. They did not teach people to find remission of sin by the way of their inherent dispositions, or works; but when the apostle *Paul* was called upon for a proof of Christ speaking in him, he bid the *Corinthians examine themselves* for that proof; for if they had not received Christ, they were *reprobates;* and if they had, they were his *epistle of commendation*, agreeable to what he had said, chap. iii.—xiii. 5.

"No

" No man, then, can be charged with the sin of
" disbelieving the gospel, for doubting, if he be a
" good Christian." *Ibid.*

But he may, for doubting whether Christ is given
to him in the divine declarations to sinners; or, whether he may trust to those declarations; or, for doubting whether he may venture his eternal concerns upon Jesus Christ alone, without, and before any discovery of his excellency above other men.

" Yea, we find the apostles ready to quash the con-
" fidence of those who were ready to conclude their
" state was changed; by such awful sentences as this:
" *He that saith I know him, and keepeth not his command-*
" *ments, is a liar, and the truth is not in him.*" p. 395.

They who professed the faith and hope of Christians, and were evidently not influenced by the Christian love, to observe the commandments of him in whom they professed to believe, were undoubtedly the subjects of this censure; which may well be admitted without any contradiction to the *hope* of a guilty sinner *by Christ alone.*

" The apostles frequently declare their assurance of
" faith and of hope in the same passage. While they
" express their faith in Christ, they are at the same
" time confident of their interest in him." *Ibid.*

This proves, that either the apostles Christian *hope*, stood in a nearer connection with their *faith*, and sprung more immediately from their doctrine, than *Palemon* will admit of; or else that he is more accurate than they in describing it.

" This joint assurance they sometimes express in
" fellowship with all that follow their footsteps, and
" often, in language plainly, distinguishing the apostles
" themselves from other professors of the faith." *Ibid.*

The 1 *John* v. 11. is not of this sort: *This is the record, which he that believeth, hath in himself; he that believeth it not, maketh God a liar, because he believeth not the record which he gave of his Son.* And THIS IS

THE RECORD that God hath given, not to us apostles, exclusive of others; not to us who can say, God, I thank thee, I am not as other men; but to us, guilty, sinners, lost, &c.; to us, as numbered with them, who, in not believing it, make God a liar. *God hath given to us eternal life, and this life is in his Son.* So given him, that *he that hath the Son hath life, and he that hath not the Son of God, hath not life;* it being only to be received, possessed, or enjoyed in receiving, possessing, and enjoying of him.

" The same Spirit, acting as the Comforter, is given
" only to those who are already the friends of Christ.
" —To this purpose, *Paul* says, *Gal.* iv. 6. *And because*
" *ye are sons, God hath sent forth the Spirit of his Son*
" *into your hearts, crying, Abba, Father.*" p. 397.

That is, and because ye, while enemies, have received, through the gospel, *the adoption of children by Jesus Christ*, Eph. i. 5. Because, also, according to the fulness of time, ye are sons; the church being come out of her nonage. As a proof of this, it is evident, God hath not given you *the spirit of bondage again to fear*, but *he hath sent forth the Spirit of his Son into your hearts*, whereby ye obtain such a discovery of salvation to the guilty, as enables you to cry, *Abba, Father*.

" The Holy Spirit then acts a twofold part, as he
" breathes in the gospel. He reconciles enemies, and
" he comforts friends. *Ibid.*

He reconciles and comforts enemies in the same instant, and by the same truth; so the distinction is not properly founded. Besides, the consolation we have by Christ to the end, is of the same nature with the beginning; the grace that is manifest in Christ Jesus to the guilty. Not but that we have also the additional consolation of those sayings which relate to our witnessing and suffering for the truth.

" What then shall we say of those pretenders to
" the apostolic consolation, whose very profession of
" Christianity, instead of being any loss to them,
" spreads

" spreads their reputation for piety, and procures
" them esteem and reverence from the world?"
p. 398.

We will say, their consolation is not apostolic, that the offence of the cross has ceased with them, or that they are of the world. But it is very plain, *Aspasio*'s appropriation, or that trust where in he is comforted, has not had this effect; however he may have been honoured on other accounts.

" In latter times, not a few have, from the hand
" of church-authority, supported by secular power,
" endured the same sufferings which the apostles met
" with from the *Jews* and *Romans*, and accordingly
" enjoyed the same consolation. It was very natural
" for such of them as were writers, to commend the
" faith which thus wrought by love." *Ibid*.

They suffered as maintaining the certainty of salvation by Christ alone; and did not ground their certainty upon their sufferings; although they were far from being discouraged thereby, but endured them with additional consolation. Their assurance gave the offence, and caused their sufferings.

" Shall we say, that these friends of Christ would
" have approved of that assurance of an interest in
" him, which men now pretend to acquire by some
" *heart-work*, in a full consistency with their worldly
" ease and reputation?" p. 399.

Nor does *Aspasio* plead for such an assurance; what he pleads for is founded only upon the divine declarations to guilty sinners; and is far from having the approbation of the devout and honourable of the world, however they may profess to esteem his writings on account of the elegancy of the style, or some particulars foreign to his main intention in them.

" The modern assurance—proceeds on the principle,
" that the simple truth believed, affords no joy nor
" comfort." p. 402.

This cannot be our case who plead for the joy and comfort

comfort of the sufficient righteousness, as given freely to the guilty in those evangelical declarations. See remark on p. 85. in p. 354.

"Will the news of a plentiful importation of corn, in the time of famine, give joy to many ready to perish, and revive even the poorest with the hope that they may be fed?" *Ibid.*

Will the joy and comfort of this news be set aside, by understanding that the corn is freely given for us to live upon without money or price? Will not this rather enhance the joy? Does not the poorest receive comfort from such tidings, because they expect either to be able to buy some, or to have some given them? See remark on p. 429.

"Yet no man knows certainly, but his present day may be his last."

But the joy created by the news above mentioned, proceeds on a contrary supposition, *viz.* That he shall live and be sustained by it. Besides, the bread of life concerns a day that will never have an end, therefore this uncertainty is foreign to the purpose.

"And however diffident the convert" (that is, the convert of *Aspasio's* stamp) "be, he is still supposed to be possessed of some degree of assurance, provided he blame himself for the want of it." p. 403.

He is supposed to live by Christ alone, as his sufficient righteousness, who condemns every word, work, or thought, to the contrary, or who fights this fight of faith against all oppositions and trials, inward or outward. But though we may make such an allowance, this is not our point. The question is not so much about whether I believe, let that make itself evident. The proper question to be always considered and rested in, is this: Does God give to guilty me eternal life in his Son? Is this the spring of my hope, and the source of my love and obedience? Do I live, not by my notion that I am a believer, but do I live by this?

"They

"They (the devils) believe, they hate, and yet they tremble at that truth which Chrift's people believe, love, and find falvation in. With them are ranked all thofe of mankind, who know as much of the truth as inclines them to hate and pervert it." p. 405.

Yet it cannot be faid of the devils, they have the fame confidence. It cannot be faid of the devils, that they receive or appropriate the divine righteoufnefs as freely given to them, or that they fee any foundation for it.

"In this view the fame truth is the favour of life unto life unto fome, and of death unto death unto others. In this view, the fame truth is the object of contempt and chagrin to fome, and of love and joy to others. *Ibid.*

True it is fo, but not by both believing it alike for themfelves.

LETTER VI.

"We are now then to confider faith as a principle of life and action." p. 406.

Palæmon is here obliged to admit of a different confideration of faith. If he confidered it in juftification as a principle of life and action, he would have been involved in the miftakes he has been oppofing. If on the other hand he denied faith to be a principle of life and action, he would overthrow the principle of the Chriftian obedience he pleads for. Now, fince he is thus obliged to take up this diftinction for himfelf, why fhould he not allow it to *Afpafio*? Why fhould he not allow that appropriation, although it is an act, or work exerted by the human mind, in confequence of the belief of the gofpel, and as a principle of all other Chriftian obedience; yet we are not juftified by our appropriating perfuafion, but by the righteoufnefs we appropriate, even as *Palæmon* fays, we are juftified by what we believe, and not by faith, as a principle of life and action. See obf. on p. 483.

"And here we must carefully distinguish betwixt all works by which men would pretend to acquire faith, and those which faith produces: for if we will contend that justification comes by faith without works, and that there is no acceptable working but what follows upon this, and yet maintain that faith is acquired by works, we undoubtedly reason in a circle.—And however seriously and devoutly we may be occupied in this kind of reasoning, it is evident we are employed in nothing else but solemn trick and dissimulation; unless it may be pled in our behalf, that we are imposing on ourselves by the same means by which we impose upon others.

"Men are justified by the knowledge of a righteousness finished in the days of *Tiberius;* and this knowledge operates upon them, and leads them to work righteousness. *If ye know*, says the apostle *John, that he is righteous, ye know that every one that doth righteousness is born of him.* Faith is not acquired, but is obtained, as *Peter* says, (τοῖς λαχοῦσι) *To them who have* OBTAINED BY LOT *like precious faith with us.* Of two criminals justly condemned to die, if one escapes by a favourable throw of the dice, and the other dies for his crime, we see mercy in the deliverance of the former, and no injustice in the death of the latter. Two men may be employed with equal diligence in studying the scripture, and with equal seriousness in praying for divine assistance; the one may come to know the truth, and the other may grope in the dark all his lifetime. He who comes to know it, plainly perceives that he has found what he was not seeking after: He plainly sees, that his most serious devotion was pointed in direct opposition to what now comforts him." p. 406, 407.

Nevertheless, the truth being declared, they may, like the noble *Bereans*, search the scriptures, *whether these things are so?*

"Thus

"Thus the word of life is held forth in the world—
"serving as a mean of divine appointment to lead
"some to the faith, and render others inexcusable."
p. 408.

This is a proper reply to *Palæmon*'s own objection, p. 350. "That the grant of the gospel is a gift of be-
"nefits to multitudes who are never benefited there-
"by." It serves as a means of divine appointment to lead some to faith, and leave others inexcusable.

"The change made upon a man by the belief of
"the gospel, may be thus illustrated: When *Lazarus*
"was revived to the enjoyment of this mortal life,
"neither his will, nor his power were concerned in
"the obtaining of life. Yet his life could no other-
"wise be continued and enjoyed, but in his voluntary
"exercise of it. As soon as he revived, the principle
"of self-preservation, with all its hopes and fears,
"behoved immediately to be set in motion. No soon-
"er was he possessed of life, than the active love of it
"behoved to take place. Accordingly no sooner does
"a man begin to know the grace of God in truth,
"than love to it takes place in his heart. Love is
"the activity of that life which a man obtains by
"faith, for faith worketh by love." *Ibid.*

But what is all this to the doctrine of working in painful desire and fear, till we come to the enjoyment of life, or the knowledge that we have life? *Lazarus* had no principle of self-preservation before he was conscious he had a self to preserve, nor had he any love of life before he enjoyed it. In like manner, we can have no love to that grace of God we know not, nor desire to preserve that life we never enjoyed.

"If a man of low condition, is by a royal patent
"ennobled, and entitled to a place in the politest as-
"semblies, he cannot enjoy the pleasures of his pro-
"motion, but in as far as he loves and studies to learn
"the manners suitable to his rank and company."
p. 409.

And

And his motive to this improvement of thefe manners is, that he is promoted to a ſtation he deſires to enjoy more perfectly. So we being called to the adoption of children by Jeſus Chriſt, toil no more in the way of painful deſire and fear, to attain to a conſciouſneſs of the privilege, but as partakers of it, are influenced thereby.

"The apoſtle *John*, fpeaking of obedience to the "new commandment of love, ſays, *Beloved, if our* "*hearts condemn us not, then have we confidence to-* "*wards God;* that is, if, notwithſtanding our natural "bias againſt the gofpel, with its remaining effects, "giving us daily difquiet, our heart condemn us not "as deſtitute of love to that truth which the world "hates, then we have confidence towards God; even "as much confidence as the teſtimony of our own "confcience can give us." p. 414.

This is plainly not the confidence which the truth itſelf affords a guilty ſinner, but confidence " that " we are not deſtitute of love to that truth the world " hates." The former is our life, the latter is only an additional corroborating comfort.

"Yet this is but one witneſs, and needs to be ſup- "ported. For in this cafe one may be liable to doubts, "left even his own confcience fhould be partial in his "favour."

If we have confidence in Chriſt by the truth itſelf as we are guilty ſinners; if I am confcious that the truth, or, which is the fame thing, my faith, and confidence in it, works by love; if our hearts condemn us not in this matter, then have we confidence towards God. Firſt, becauſe we are confcious we proceed on divine authority. Secondly, we prove the bleſſed effect of the truth. Theſe then are two witneſſes infeparably united. The firſt a divine truth, the teſtimony of the divine Spirit, than which there cannot be a greater ground of certainty; the latter is the confciouſneſs of the effect of that truth.

"Here

" Here then the Spirit of truth, who never fails to
" bear witnefs to the genuine effects thereof, gives
" his teftimony as a fecond witnefs fupporting the
" former. Thus *Paul*, after he had faid, *As many as
" are led by the Spirit of God, they are the fons of God;*
" adds, *The Spirit itfelf beareth witnefs with our fpirit,
" that we are the children of God.*" p. 417.

The apoftle *Paul*, after he had faid, *As many as are led by the Spirit of God, they are the fons of God;* adds, *For ye have not received the fpirit of bondage again to fear; but ye have received* (i. e. by the gofpel-truth) *the Spirit of adoption, whereby we cry, Abba, Father;* and then follow the words, *The Spirit itfelf* (which ye received in the hearing of the gofpel, emboldening us guilty finners to cry, *Abba, Father*, through the divine righteoufnefs freely given to us; this Spirit received in the gofpel) *beareth witnefs with our fpirit, that we are the children of God*, and not of them who deceive themfelves with vain thoughts.

It is already granted, p. 397. that " the Spirit of
" truth never fpeaks one word or fentence to any
" perfon beyond what is written in the fcripture."
And what is written in the fcripture is either the declarations of free falvation to finners in Jefus Chrift, or divine affurances of no difappointment to them that believe on Chrift, or an account of the genuine effects of faith. In the firft we are taught to apply what is faid to ourfelves as finners: In the fecond we are encouraged to believe on the Lord Jefus Chrift, in affurance of falvation by him without difappointment: In the laft we are informed of the genuine effects of this truth, or faith, correfponding to what we find and feel to be true, when we believe according to that which is written,

" And this he (i. e. the Spirit) does by fhedding
" abroad in the heart fuch an abundant fenfe of the
" divine love, as leaves no room for, fo cafts out,

"the anxious fear of coming short of life everlast-
"ing." *Ibid.*

The love shed abroad in the heart, is that manifested in Christ dying for the ungodly when enemies and without strength. Not love manifested to the qualified. For *if when we were enemies we were reconciled to God by the death of his Son* (given freely unto us,) *much more being reconciled*, as is apparent to us in what we believe, and in its genuine effects, we have a hope (that maketh not ashamed) that *we shall be saved by his life;* that he who gave us righteousness while enemies, will save us for ever who are thus reconciled to him.

"Thus that love to the truth, which formerly
"wrought in a way of painful desire, attended with
"many fears, is perfected by being crowned with
"the highest enjoyment it is capable of in this mor-
"tal state." *Ibid.*

I do not read in the scripture of any love to the truth of the gospel so described. *Herein is love, not that we loved God*, and he crowned us with enjoyment, *but that he loved us, and sent his Son, his only begotten Son, into the world, that we might live through him;* sent his Son *to be a propitiation for our sins. If we who are of this truth love one another, his love is* already *perfected in us. And we have known and believed the love that God hath to us. Herein is our love made perfect.* *He that feareth*, and is not emboldened by the truth to venture his everlasting concerns upon Jesus Christ alone, *is not made perfect in love. We love him because he first loved us, purifying our souls by obeying the truth through the Spirit; unto the unfeigned love of the brethren*, as its proper and genuine effect.

"Jesus Christ, who loved his Father with a perfect
"heart, even while sorrowful unto death, received
"the highest proof of his being the beloved Son of
"God, when being exalted at the Father's right hand,
"and being made most blessed with a sense of his
"love,

"love, he experienced fulness of joy in his presence." *Ibid.*

But he knew he was the Son of God before he had this highest proof; he, though sorrowful unto death, had none of the anxious fear of coming short of his glory, but was animated by that glory. *For the joy that was set before him, he endured the cross, despising the shame.* He received the word in its accomplishment, as the highest confirmation of the veracity of what his Father had spoken. But surely he shewed himself entirely satisfied with the bare testimony, when he answered the tempter, *Man shall not live by bread alone, but by every word that proceedeth out of the mouth of God.*

"The report of this draws them who believe it to love him, and suffer for his sake. To such Jesus Christ promised fellowship with him in the fulness of joy." *Ibid.*

That *fulness of joy* must be in the life to come, according to *Psal.* xvi. 11. For in this life we walk by faith and not by sight, and hope which is seen is not hope. And it is also acknowledged, that Jesus himself did not enter into this joy till he ceased from this world.

John xv. 10, 11. "*If ye keep my commandments, ye shall abide in my love, even as I have kept my Father's commandments, and abide in his love. These things have I spoken unto you, that my joy might remain in you, and that your joy might be full.*" Ibid.

The commandments here spoken of are to believe, and love for the truth's sake. The love and joy is that which is manifested by the word in this life; and which neither *life, nor death, nor angels, principalities, nor powers*, nor any kind of suffering nor affliction, shall be able to separate us from. Nevertheless, we yet but hope for the fulness of joy that Jesus is now arrived at, with hope that maketh not ashamed, but animates us to be followers of Jesus, *enduring the cross, despising the shame.*

"When

"When the saving truth first shines into the hearts of men, the effect is suitable to the divine promise, *Jer.* xxxii. 40. *I will put my fear in their hearts, that they shall not depart from me.* This fear dwelling in their hearts, checks and recalls them when ready to be utterly led away by their former evil inclinations. They are preserved from falling away, by the fear of falling away." p. 419, 420.

This is no more than a fear of caution, consistent with the utmost confidence of the sufficiency of Christ, and the veracity and faithfulness of God. Consistent with a firm persuasion, that nothing shall *be able to separate us from the love of God which is in Christ Jesus our Lord.* The slavish fear which ariseth from uncertainty, and is seeking after a differencing something to remove our torment, is so far from preserving us from falling, that it is rather a proof we are not satisfied with the sufficient righteousness, with the sufficient ground of faith and hope, and have at present no part or lot in the matter.

"It is evident, that to have the Holy Spirit as the comforter and earnest of the heavenly inheritance, is an attainment far beyond any influences of the Spirit that are common to those who believe for a time, and those who believe to the saving of the soul. Yea, beyond the regenerating work of the Spirit, by which men are at first brought to the knowledge of the truth, and taught to love it." p. 420.

"*To find by experience* (in the effects of the report on our minds) *the truth of what they formerly believed on testimony,*" (which is what *Palæmon* declares himself to mean, p. 416.), is certainly an attainment of another kind than the joy and comfort of the truth itself. But that a conscious certainty, that " *I depend on the promise of Christ, and run all hazards for his sake,*" is what the scripture means by the *comforter* and *earnest* of the heavenly inheritance, does not so evidently appear:

pear: becaufe, 1. This is not taking of things of Chrift, but taking of our things, and fhewing them to us. 2. It is not the Spirit's bearing witnefs itfelf with our fpirits, but bearing witnefs by the medium of our obedience. 3. It would be fpeaking more to us than what is written in the fcripture. 4. This confcioufnefs, and the joy accompanying it, was an attainment of the people of God before the refurrection of Chrift, as really as it has been fince; whereas the Comforter promifed was to be the confequence of Chrift's afcenfion to his Father, and was firft performed on the day of Pentecoft, *Acts* ii. 33. Laftly, To wait for an attainment far beyond the knowledge of the truth, or, which is the fame thing, of the power of Chrift's refurrection, ferves, in fact, to fet afide that refurrection as infufficient, fo to deny the one thing needful. More efpecially as, according to *Palæmon*,

" *It* (this fuppofed attainment) *muft be diftinguifhed*
" *from any joy or fpiritual delight which neceffarily at-*
" *tend the obtaining of faith, or its beginning to work by*
" *love*." And " *that it is vain and abfurd to call men*
" *to be affured of their being children of God, when they*
" *are not enjoying it.—That it cannot further appear that*
" *any man has known the grace of God in truth, than he*
" *gives all diligence to the end, in order to obtain it*."
p. 420. Now the grand arcanum in *Palæmon*'s doctrine is, how a man can live entirely by the *one thing needful*, and yet be fo diligently employed in labouring for fo important a *fomething more?*

" It is alfo plain, that the promife of the Spirit as
" the Comforter is common to all thofe who follow
" the faith and practice of the apoftles." *Ibid.*

It is plain, they were comforted by the Spirit of God, in the joy of the truth concerning Jefus the Saviour of finners, and had alfo the additional comfort of thofe confirming declarations concerning the children of God and their bleffings, which are recorded for that purpofe. But that we are taught to wait for any other attainment, under the name of the Spirit, as the Comforter, does not appear.

"Their (the *Jews*) appropriation was the great spring of all their pride, of all their disaffection to the true gospel, and all their ruin." p. 424.

The *Jews* appropriation was upon the ground of the difference between themselves and others; which we readily agree has this effect, that "*the more men excelled in this way, they proved the more hardened enemies to the true God, and the eternal happiness of mankind.*" p. 422. But what is this for an objection to that appropriation which proceeds entirely on the free grant of heaven to the guilty, excluding all such difference? *Aspasio* is still left to affirm of his appropriation, that "*nothing will be so powerful to produce holy love, and willing obedience, to exalt our desires, and enable us to overcome the world.*"

Who stands nighest to the *Jewish* appropriation, *Aspasio* or *Palæmon? Aspasio*, who in *dial.* 16. vol. iii. compares "*those who advise us to prove our title to comfort by genuine marks of conversion, and teach us on this column to fix the capital of assurance, unto those who would fix the dome of a cathedral upon the stalk of a tulip,*" or *Palæmon*, who judges this "*talking profanely.*" p. 425. Neither do I see how this is talking profanely, until it is first proved, that the marks whereby we suppose ourselves entitled to comfort rather than others, are the Deity in which we are to put our trust. *Aspasio* rightly judges, that this is placing a most weighty affair upon that most flight and uncertain foundation, what we feel, or do, instead of the Rock Christ, given to guilty sinners. Does not the Holy Ghost prove a comforter, by manifesting to us, guilty sinners, *the things that are freely given of God; taking of the things of Christ, and shewing them to us?* And must not every genuine mark of conversion have its foundation here?

"*He that heareth my word, and believeth on him that "sent*

" *sent me, hath everlasting life, and shall not come into*
" *condemnation, but is passed from death to life*, John
" v. 24. *Here we see how men pass from death to life."*
.p. 426.

The word that Jesus hath spoken, and the declaration the Father hath made, is the first and surest ground of undeceivable certainty. The dependence hereon proceeds entirely on the *truth* and *faithfulness* of God; and that dependence is the assurance we have pleaded for; and they who thus depend, our Lord declares *have everlasting life*, are already *passed from death to life*.

" Here we see how men pass from death to life.
" John declares how they come to know this; while,
" plainly pointing at the words of Jesus, he says, *We*
" *know that we are passed from death to life, because*
" *we love the brethren*." Ibid.

There is no foundation for the distinction here made by *Palæmon*, viz. *That our Lord only declares how men pass from death to life*, and *John only declares how they come to know this*. It is plain, that our Lord's declaration runs in the same strain with that of his disciple; our Lord says, He that heareth my word—*is passed from death unto life*. *John* says, He that loveth the brethren, *is passed from death unto life;* where is the difference? Both are declarations of who are passed from death to life, therefore both alike in that respect. Our Lord intimates, the life-giving *word* the matter believed by all who are passed from death to life; his disciple intimates, the proper and genuine *effect* of that word on all who believe. " *We know* (says *John*, we have an additional proof, that the word of Jesus is true) *that we are passed from death unto life, because we love the brethren*. It is plain, that they abide still in death who abide in the hating murdering spirit of the world; and more especially, who cannot love them who are of the *truth* for the *truth's sake*. On the other hand, the uniting life-giving tendency of the

truth,

truth, appears to us who are of it, since it causeth us thus to love one another for *the truth's sake*, and proves what Jesus said, that *he that heareth his word, and believeth on him that sent him, is passed from death to life.*

Jesus faith, He is passed from death to life *that heareth my word, and believeth on him that sent me.* John faith, *We know he has passed from death to life who loves the brethren.* The only difference is, Jesus declares the privilege by that whereby we enjoy it; John gives proof in the love of the brethren, as a demonstrative effect, that Jesus's words are true.

" By this proof, men come to know, that the joy " they had upon their first believing, was not the joy " of the hypocrite." *Ibid.*

The joy true believers have on their first believing, is the joy of the truth. If that we rejoice in is found to be true, our joy is proved genuine.

" And so their joy is made full." *Ibid.*

Our *joy* is not made full by a discovery of itself, but by farther confirmations of that truth which begat and supports it. The believer gives an account of his *faith and joy* when he gives an account of what he believes and rejoices in. And it is made full by a farther supply or confirmation, of the truth and faithfulness of God on which he depends.

" By this they come to know it was the genuine " truth of God, and not any human counterfeit and " corruption of it, which they at first believed." *Ibid.*

The genuine truth of God makes itself manifest to be such at our first believing, 1 *Thess.* ii. 13.—1 *John* i. 10. and thereby begets faith, joy, and every other effect. He that waits for such effect, to know whether he has the genuine truth or no, may finish his inquiry, by reminding himself that he is in this inquiry very evidently but upon the search, and therefore has not found truth as yet. He may also be convinced his search is wrong and preposterous, as if a man that

should

should make an inquiry after what was proper food, should, instead thereof, be waiting to know by certain effects, whether he had eat any or no. The noble *Bereans* inquired after truth, by searching the scripture to see whether *those things were so; therefore* (it is added) *many of them believed.* The truth was made manifest unto them as the truth of God. And when this was the case, they did not wait for the joy of it with its effects, to know whether it was so or no.

" Thus they receive an additional knowledge and
" certainty about the truth, in the way of experience,
" by perceiving that it works effectually in them, pro-
" ducing its genuine effects."

If the experience of the effects of the genuine gospel, produces only an additional knowledge and certainty from experience, as the first knowledge and certainty came by divine evidence of the truth itself; this is all we plead for, then we are again agreed.

" As often as the apostles speak of their interest in
" Christ, and life eternal, or use any language to that
" effect, we shall find that they either speak of them-
" selves separately, or in conjunction with those only
" who are possessed of the same unfeigned faith and
" love with them." *Ibid.*

That the apostles wrote their epistles to professed believers, may be very readily admitted. As on the other hand, that the apostles did not live by Christ alone, under the notion and view of themselves as guilty sinners, but only through a medium or discovery of their own faith, love, &c. will be very difficult to be proved, however confidently asserted.

" *Hereby we,* who love the brethren, *perceive the*
" *love of God, because he laid down his life for us.* We
" who are conscious of the effects, and enjoy the fruits
" of the atonement, know that God first loved us,
" and had a peculiar regard to us in providing the
" atonement." p. 428.

The effects and fruits of the atonement, are sinners
peace

peace with God; their *access to the holiest of all* thereby; if it is allowed that we enjoy and are conscious of these, we are again agreed. But if *Palæmon* means only being conscious of "working in the way of "painful desire and fear, till we are crowned with "enjoyment," there cannot be a plainer deviation from the intent of the apostle. The apostle says, Hereby perceive we the love of God, *because he laid down his life for us*. *Palæmon* says, Hereby perceive we the love of God, because we are conscious of the effects, and enjoy the fruits of the atonement. The apostles lead us to think he laid down his life for us who were justly doomed to eternal death. *Palæmon* leads us to think he laid down his life for us, who can say, God, I thank thee, I am not as other men; "*who can find* "*some reason about themselves, why all the great things* "*spoken and done by Jesus, should bear its peculiar di-* "*rection towards them*."

Besides, how does it appear we love the brethren, when those we call so, are seeking the reason of their hope, certainty, and assurance of eternal life, wholly in their own love and obedience? consequently are not in this respect the *despised few*, but of the same mind and judgment with every natural man.

" He who perceiving the divine love to sinners of
" all sorts without distinction, manifested in the a-
" tonement, is thereby led to love the atonement,
" and the divine character appearing there; and so to
" enjoy the promised comfort resulting thence to the
" obedient." p. 428.

If the promised comfort is suspended for want of obedience, or depends on obedience as its condition, the divine love is far from being manifested to sinners of all sorts without distinction.

" And thus by happily experiencing the truth of
" the gospel." *Ibid.*

He does not experience the truth of the gospel, but only the effect of that doctrine that tells him, if he is

willing

willing and obedient, he shall eat the good of the land. Whereas, the truth of the gospel, relieving the guilty without condition, animates thereby to all the obedience it calls for.

"So he labours neither first nor last to acquire any "requisite to justification; but all his labour proceeds "on the persuasion that the atonement itself is the "sole and sufficient requisite to justification." *Ibid.*

All his labour proceeds on the persuasion, that however sufficient the atonement may be for the elect, yet he is not allowed to account it of any use to him a sinner, or to trust or depend upon it, but to be at an entire uncertainty about it, until he discovers his works of obedience to such a degree, as to conceive himself to be an elect person.

"So he knows, that all his holiness, as well as all "his happiness, comes entirely of that grace which "provided the atonement." p. 439.

Far from it; all his holiness, as well as all his happiness, according to *Palæmon*'s representation, comes entirely of the painful desire and fear, lest he should have no part in that grace which provided the atonement.

"The merchant who, being encouraged by some "credible intelligence Providence has favoured him "with, from an unexpected quarter, sets out all ha-"zards on some new branch of traffic, will be great-"ly animated to proceed, when he finds his labours "crowned with success." *Ibid.*

But our obtaining salvation is not like a trading merchant setting out at all hazards on a new branch of traffic; this is salvation by works indeed! *Matth.* xiii. 45. describes the merchant as finding one pearl of great price, which puts an end to all future merchandizing.

"He who so knows the bare report thereof, as to "love it, and to run all risks upon it, shall in no wise "lose his reward." *Ibid.*

True, but *Palæmon*'s Christian rather runs all risks in order to know his part in the atonement, than on the account of the bare report of salvation to the guilty.

"The passages in the dialogues which appear to
"me to deserve the greatest censure, are those two,
"which in a very confident manner deny; the one,
"the comfort attending the simple report of the gos-
"pel; and the other, the additional comfort attend-
"ing the self-denied obedience to it." *Ibid.*

These passages have been considered, and it appears that neither are denied, but confirmed by *Aspasio*'s doctrine. We proceed on the report in appropriation, so it is the very basis of our comfort. We are confirmed by the effect of the enjoyment, that our enjoyment, or the foundation of it, is not a fancy.

"And all this is done, in order to rest, I cannot
"say our comfort, but a good opinion of our state,
"on what is neither faith nor obedience." *Ibid.*

Not so, but to rest our souls on Christ alone, and neither on our faith, obedience, nor good opinion of our state.

"For, according to the popular doctrine, men li-
"ving for a course of years together in unbelief, con-
"sequently neither loving the gospel nor enjoying the
"comfort of it, are allowed to consider themselves
"all the while as regenerate, provided they have once
"in their lifetime exerted a certain act." p. 330.

It may be so according to the *popular* doctrine; but according to the *unpopular doctrine*, which *Palæmon* excepts against, we depend upon no acts but the perfect obedience of Christ.

"I shall now take some notice of a treatise highly
"esteemed by the votaries of the popular doctrine:
"I mean, *The gospel-mystery of sanctification.*" Ibid.

This book was so far from being highly esteemed by the votaries of the popular doctrine in *England*, it was hardly known till *Aspasio* recommended it, and

and since that disapproved of by many devout people: Because, 1. It proves that the most earnest desires and endeavours after obedience to the law, may be in the natural state of man. 2. That the new life, new state, or new creation, is inseparably in Christ; so that we have no such privilege, but in enjoying Christ himself through the report of the gospel. 3. That there is no furniture for the obedience of love, but in partaking of this reconciliation, or new state in Christ. 4. That no conditions or performances are to be placed between the sinner and the Saviour, but the first step of practical religion is to trust on Christ alone, as given to us for the sure enjoyment of himself and his salvation.

"This author supposes his unconverted reader, when beginning to be concerned about religion, to propose for this end such an obedience to the divine law, as may be acceptable to God."

He rightly supposes, that men who are yet in their natural state, may attain with great zeal to great heights of legal obedience, and, as *Paul* and others, be very earnest after it, counting it their truest gain; and like *Paul*, at the same time, totally unacquainted with, yea enemies unto real Christianity, and the obedience of love to the truth, and to God manifested thereby.

"According to this author, then, Christ is not the end of the law for righteousness, but the best means one can make use of for enabling him to perform that righteousness which is the end of the law." *Ibid.*

He (as the apostle does) directs unto that love which is the fulfilling of the law, by the enjoyment of that righteousness which is the end of it, by enjoying that new state of peace and reconciliation with God which is inseparably in Christ; or, in fact, his view is, to recommend the gospel of our Lord Jesus, as a principle of obedience, in opposition to that preliminary

grace, which, as *Palæmon* well says, p. 445. " how-
" ever much it has been christianized, is at bottom the
" same thing with that divine AFFLATUS, influence,
" or energy, by which it was supposed philosophers and
" heroes of old became good and great men."
" Accordingly the well-disposed reader is led for-
" ward to his desired end, in consequence of the same
" good dispositions that led him to use the means."
p. 431.

Not so, however fair the directions may seem to promise at first to him that is naturally desirous to keep the law that he may live; yet no man is made a disciple to these directions, but by being converted from this false hope, to the hope of the gospel. No man is disposed to use the means of reconciliation with God by Christ, alone as a principle of obedience; but he that is converted from the false hope of obtaining life by any obedience he can render, to live alone by what Christ hath already done, as the spring of his hope, and the source of his future obedience.

" But why all this round-about course? Why
" should we seek to repress any man's impetuosity to
" fulfil the law? Why should we retard his course,
" by entangling him in a labyrinth about the use of
" means?" *Ibid.*

Men, naturally desirous to keep the law, that they may live, may, and do, as Mr *Marshall* observes, "*rush
" blindly upon immediate practice, making more haste than
" good speed, crying with* Israel *of old, All that the
" Lord saith we will do. At the same time there is no
" such heart in them.*" But through a natural propensity to those things which are contrary to the divine law, they continually fail in the obedience they have so strongly purposed. "*And some of these, when they
" have misspent many years in striving against the stream
" of their lusts, without any success, do at last fall mi-
" serably into despair, and turn to wallow in the mire
" of their lusts, or are fearfully swallowed up with hor-*
" ror

"*ror of conscience.*" As all their religion, or impetuosity to fulfil the law, is founded on a miserable mistaken hope, to live by their own obedience; so Mr *Marshall's* aim is to throw down that *false hope*, by proving that there can be no obedience acceptable to God, till we are first made *accepted in the Beloved;* or, in other words, till we first live by Christ's obedience alone, and are influenced thereby. His hope to live by his own obedience is criminal; it is therefore no matter how soon we repress his impetuosity, and retard his course; and when he understands his reconciliation with God by Christ alone, to be the principle, or means of gospel-obedience, he will not be entangled in a labyrinth, but made free by the Son of God.

" As for the gospel, it was only intended to relieve
" those ill-disposed people who despair of ever doing
" any thing to render them acceptable to God, by any
" assistance whatsoever." *Ibid.*

And Mr *Marshall's* design is to shew, that those *well-disposed* people who hope to live by their own obedience, are, in fact, at the same time, those *ill-disposed* people, who will never be really obedient till they despair of ever doing any thing to render them acceptable to God, by any assistance whatsoever; and, in that despair of themselves, live alone by what Christ has already done.

" It (the gospel) was never intended to be an auxi-
" liary to those good people who are desirous to give
" acceptable obedience to the divine law." p. 431.

But it was intended to remove their mistake, that they may be obedient from a more divine principle; that is, reconciliation with God by Christ alone. And this, it is evident, is the main design of Mr *Marshall*.

" All such (who are desirous to give acceptable o-
" bedience to the divine law) wheresoever they are,
" shall undoubtedly be happy, without having any
" occasion to trouble their heads about the gospel."
p. 431. 432.

All

All such who are of this character uniformly, and without contradiction. But it must be allowed, that there are many, even every natural man has a propensity to live by his own obedience, or to do, that he may live. At the same time, he is desirous of those things which are contrary to that obedience, whereby he forfeits the character, and becomes guilty before God.

" Let us now observe the use of means to which " our author directs, *direct.* 11. p. 208. Endeavour " *diligently* to perform the great work of *believing* on " Christ." p. 432.

That is, in Mr *Marshall's* sense, endeavour diligently to live by Christ alone, to be satisfied with him, to assure your soul of salvation by him, by what he has done and suffered; that you may, in this way, have a personal conscious enjoyment of him and his fulness, in which fulness we enjoy reconciliation with God, and every blessing tending to the obedience of love. Was *Palæmon* to direct to personal conscious enjoyment of Christ, he would tell us about working diligently, working in the way of painful desire and fear, till we were crowned with enjoyment, in a conviction that we were distinguished from others, by having faith, love, and self-denied obedience. Where lies the difference between the two, but that the latter says, Do that you may live; that you may be crowned with enjoyment? the other says, Live by Christ, that you may do? Enjoy as sinners, that you may live as saints.

" It is necessary that we should endeavour it, (*i. e.* " to believe on Christ,) and that before we can find " the Spirit of God working faith effectually in us, or " giving strength to believe." *Ibid.*

Mr *Marshall* here considers faith as a duty required by the law, which *Palæmon* also asserts, p. 354. At the same time, he so explains himself, as it is evident faith neither justifies nor sanctifies as a duty; but by
Christ

Chrift alone believed on. And it is alfo evident, he means not the divine paffive conviction, but an obedience to the apoftolic exhortation; a " trufting on " a Saviour as difcovered by a teftimony, which (as " he fays) is properly *believing on him*."

He oppofes, at the fame time, the popular notion, that we muft wait for God to give us fomething called faith, before we are to attempt to believe, or live by his righteoufnefs; whereas, in whomfoever faith is wrought, they immediately live by Chrift alone; they wait for nothing, they fee nothing to be waited for, but they fee Chrift's fufficient work, and the grant of it to the guilty, a fufficient ground for immediate truft and confidence.

" Only (fays Mr *Marfhall*) I fhall prove, that we " are bound, by the command of God, thus to af-" fure ourfelves; and the fcripture doth fufficiently " warrant us, that we fhall not deceive ourfelves in " believing a lie; but according to our faith fo fhall " it be to us, *Matth.* ix. 29.—Here (fays *Palæmon*) " is the great whirlpool of the popular doctrine." p. 433.

A very great miftake to call this the popular doctrine; whereas Mr *W———d*, Mr *W———y*, and numbers more, fuch as have been named, are full as great adverfaries to it as himfelf. Nor is any point more univerfally oppofed, than that of affuring ourfelves of falvation, only from the grant of a fufficient righteoufnefs in Jefus Chrift to the guilty.

" When we have thus, according to our author, " wrought ourfelves into a new ftate." *Ibid.*

This reprefentation is not juft; would it be proper, when a man receives a prefent, or gift, to fay that he works himfelf into it? It is true, he may meet with fome oppofition in the enjoyment of that which is freely given him. And in this cafe, the fcripture prevents *Palæmon*'s reflection, by exhorting us to work out our own falvation, *&c.*

" According

"According to him, there is no practice of holi-
"nefs, but what proceeds from the perfuafion of our
"ftate being changed." *Ibid.*

Rather from our perfuafion of our reconciliation with God by Chrift alone, arifing not from the conceit of our being better than others, or having done fomething towards it; but as given freely in Chrift Jefus.

"This perfuafion (of his ftate being changed) is
"his faith." *Ibid.*

No fuch matter. Mr *Marfhall*'s doctrine, or the truth believed in, his faith is, that there is a new ftate prepared in Chrift for the guilty, which we are divinely authorifed to enter into and enjoy without any works at all. As, on the other hand, *Palæmon*'s doctrine leaves him working in painful defire and fear, till he be crowned with enjoyment.

"If we hearken to this author, we muft fet out in
"the fervice of God, from the confidence of our be-
"ing in a better ftate than other men." p. 434.

Is it not highly confiftent that we fhould fet out in the fervice of God, with the furniture God hath provided us? If God hath given to us eternal life in his Son, is not our firft obedience to receive and enjoy the eternal life that is in him? This does not confift in any perfuafion that we are better than other people, that there is any new ftate in Chrift for us rather than for others; but it confifts purely in what is infeparably in Chrift Jefus, given to us in him, and only to be enjoyed in enjoying him. So that the whole is, we muft fet out as followers of our Lord, from the confidence of the eternal life given freely to us in Chrift Jefus.

"He makes no account of the grand things tefti-
"fied of Chrift, as any way fufficient to lead us to
"holinefs, without a good opinion of our own ftate."
p. 435.

Palæmon fhould fay, if he would give a juft repre-
fentation,

fentation, that Mr *Marſhall* makes no account of all that holineſs which is not influenced by the reception and enjoyment of that new ſtate, and eternal life, which is freely given to the guilty, in Chriſt Jeſus. Mean-while, the opinion we have of our own ſtate, is, that it is ſtark naught, and cannot be mended. This is far from having a good opinion of it.

" Thus the ancient goſpel, which, from the begin-
" ning, turned many from idols to ſerve the living
" God, is now ſet aſide." *Ibid.*

The ancient goſpel held forth the new ſtate, and eternal life given in Chriſt, which we plead for.

I have nothing to ſay in defence of myſelf from the charge in p. 448. of patronizing my creed by the names of fallible men. I acknowledge my fault. If I have not the doctrine of the apoſtles, what ſignifies having all the world on my ſide ? and if I have them to keep me in countenance, it ought to be little concern, though the whole world are againſt me *.

" The

---

* Methinks this author diſcovers too much complaiſance, when he compliments Mr Sandeman ſo far as to make an apology for his conduct in profeſſing an agreement, in ſome fundamental articles of the Chriſtian faith, which the late Meſſ. Erſkines and the Seceding miniſters in Scotland, according to ſcripture, and the judgment of all ſound Proteſtant divines, and in quoting a few paſſages from a ſermon of Mr Ebenezer Erſkine; as if he had thus made Meſſ. Erſkines, and the Seceding miniſters, with other Proteſtant divines, the vouchers of his creed, and given a manifeſt proof of his yielding implicit faith to their dictates and ſentiments. Is it culpable, then, to yield obedience to our Lord's command in going forth by the footſteps of the flock, Cant. i. 8. or *to remember them who have ſpoken to us the word of God, whoſe faith* we are exhorted to *follow, conſidering the end of their converſation !* Heb. xiii. 7. Muſt an endeavour to keep the unity of the faith in the bond of peace be reputed a fault ? and a ſovereign contempt of the doctrine and principles of Chriſtian teachers uninſpired, however conſonant to the word of God theſe may be found, accounted eſſential to the character

"The use these people (*i. e.* the people in fellowship with *W. C.*) have for Christ is, to give them strength to do something toward their justification." p. 449.

Our appropriation stands in no opposition to free justification by Christ alone, but rather to *Palæmon's* coming to the knowledge of it only, in a way of painful desire and fear.

But *Palæmon's* main objection to this reception, or appropriation of Christ, and eternal life in him, is, that "*this is doing something toward our justification.*" To what has been already said, I would only add the following illustration: A man has a large estate fallen to him by inheritance or legacy; he is now informed that he need do nothing toward his maintenance at all, for he has a sufficiency to live upon, and that it would dishonour his benefactor, and be a disgrace to him to think of it. The man believes this, and accordingly sits down to a plentiful table provided, under a notion that all things being ready, he has nothing to do but to EAT or ENJOY. Upon this, a virtuoso in criticism, like *Palæmon*, informs him, that to eat, is to do something towards his maintenance, that the victuals, and in short every thing, is his, without any act of his at all. So that if he imagines himself under any necessity of eating, he dishonours his benefactor, and denies the estate his benefactor has given to him, as though it was not in itself enough to maintain him without doing something towards his own maintenance. What answer would this person in all likelihood return? Very probably he would say, You speak extremely absurd; for if I eat not, all my

character of a true believer and apostolic Christian? What pity is it, that men should suffer themselves thus to be bantered, by the scornful and senseless reflections of one of the most trifling, though one of the most arrogant writers that this, or perhaps any age, has produced? *Wilson's Palæmon's creed reviewed and examined;* pref. p. lii. note.

my right and title to it will be of no service to me; I starve, I die in the midst of plenty; besides, I love to eat *. The case is as parallel as possible; our Lord says, he is *the bread of God come down from heaven to give life to the world; and that except we eat the flesh of the Son of man, and drink his blood, we have no life in us.*

This objection of *Palemon*'s is such a fine-spun cobweb of criticism, that he seems to have catched himself in it while he was endeavouring to entangle us. "Is it possible (says he) after what we have seen, for "any one to maintain, that these people *look for* ac-"ceptance with God only through the sacrifice of "Christ, once offered for the sins of many?" p. 450.

Now to *look for* acceptance with God only through the sacrifice of Christ, is the very thing we plead for, and he has been opposing. His argument has been, "The sacrifice of Christ is sufficient of itself. To ap-"propriate, or to *look for* acceptance with God on "that

---

* If any object, that this representation relates only to personal enjoyment, and manifestation to our own consciences, it may be granted; and it may be also affirmed, that the whole of God's revelation bears this design. The scriptures were never designed to inform God about our justification, but to inform us. And whenever any, who dislike the scripture-account, endeavour to scheme out another, what is their design, to inform God, or to inform man? If one tells me, I am justified (according to his scheme) whether I am persuaded of it or no, is not his design at the same time very evidently to persuade me that I am justified, or to manifest my justification according to his scheme? Shall I not rather let God be my instructor? And when I ask the question, *Wherewith shall God be pleased?* he answers, *I am pleased in my Son.* When I inquire further, How I shall know my own interest herein? he tells me, *he gives me eternal life in him;* and so makes me welcome to call it my own without more. Is it not the height of disaffection to this, to say, I will call it my own upon some other account; but not because he either bids me, or gives it to me?

"that account, is evidently to do something towards
"our justification; this is to set up in its stead
"another sacrifice of their own preparing and offer-
"ing.

"He who maintains that we are justified only by
"faith, and at the same time affirms with *Aspasio*,
"that faith is a work exerted by the human mind,"
"undoubtedly maintains, if he has any meaning to his
"words, that we are justified by a work exerted by
"the human mind." p. 483.

May not *Aspasio* as readily retort, He who maintains that we are justified only by faith, and at the same time affirms with *Palæmon*, "That faith is a "principle of life and action," undoubtedly maintains, if he has any meaning to his words, that we are justified by a principle of life and action? The answer that retrieves him out of this difficulty, will also serve us. See remark on p. 406, p. 395.

I have now considered all that I apprehend we are concerned with in Mr *Sandeman*'s performance, not with a design to manifest his blemishes, or to defend *Aspasio*'s; but to preserve the important truth he contended for, from the objections arising through evident mistakes and misrepresentations. Not pleading for a *manner* of believing, either *active* or *passive;* but pleading against the private interpretation of those divine declarations, which are the sinner's only ground of immediate trust and confidence in that sufficient righteousness. It is no pleasure to me to find a people to whom my heart inclines on account of their appearing attachment to this sufficiency of Christ, at the same time so inclined to explain away those divine declarations, and tell us, that "God may, if "he pleases, have mercy upon me," is all the conclusion that the guilty and destitute can draw from what God has revealed. Now, in this case, are we not to take heed, lest, under the notion of purer faith, *we depart from trusting in the living God* (to a labouring in
painful

painful defire and fear) *through an evil heart of unbelief?* And as there is a natural propenfity in man to felf-dependence, is there not a proportionate averfenefs in him to truft on the bare declarations of the divine word? And may not this be the fource of thofe Pharifaic attempts Mr *Sandeman* has fo juftly detected, of the objections that ftand between us ; and alfo of thofe laboured inventions of others, to make out that men are faved by Chrift in a way of natural neceffary connection ; hereby, at once, fetting afide the divine fovereignty, declarations, promifes or truft therein. I fhall only add, that if what we have pleaded for, is (without mifreprefentation) proved a contradiction to the fufficiency of the finifhed work of Chrift, then, and not till then, I fhall fee a neceffity for underftanding the fcriptures on this fubject in another light than I do at prefent, and fhall make my public acknowledgment accordingly.

DIRECTIONS

To the Readers of *Theron* and *Afpafio*, with refpect to the Amendments which were intended by Mr Hervey, had he furvived another edition.
—Taken from Mr CUDWORTH's Defence.

VOL. III. p. 8. l. 20. read, " This, he fays, as it was wrought in the name and ftead of the guilty, enemies and rebellious, was wrought out in my name, and in my ftead ; that is, in a name and character that undoubtedly belongs to me, and, according to the declarations of divine grace, fufficiently authorifes me to draw near to God thereby."

P. 318. l. 4. " Not one among all the numberlefs productions which tread the ground, or ftand rooted to the foil, wants any convenience that is proper for its refpective ftate. And the fame heavenly FATHER has

has provided for the moſt guilty, the righteouſneſs which is abſolutely neceſſary to his preſent comfort, and his final happineſs."

P. 319. l. 5. "Conſider thoſe ſtately *poppies,* &c. obſerve the *young ravens,* &c. He accommodates the former, though incapable of aſking; he attends to the latter, though inſenſible of their Benefactor. He alſo *regards* our preſſing wants; he has alſo ſuperſeded our earneſt petitions by ſuch free and unmerited gifts, as it is both his delight and his honour to beſtow."

P. 320. l. 23. "So that nothing is required, in order to our participation of CHRIST and his benefits. We receive them as the freeſt gifts; as matter of mere grace."

P. 322. l. 3. "The man without the wedding-garment, *&c.* Your former miſtakes, and preſent objections, tend to place you in the ſtate of this unhappy creature. The returning prodigal came with no recommendation either of dreſs, of perſon, or of character. None but his nakedneſs and miſery; his acknowledgment was vileneſs, which had every aggravating, not one extenuating circumſtance."

P. 323. l. 19. "If there be any qualification, I think, it is our extreme indigence; and this, I preſume, you are not without."

P. 324. l. 14. "Sanctification, heavenly-mindedneſs, and a victory over our luſts, are not the qualities he *requires,* but the bleſſings which he *confers.*"

P. 326. l. 30. "The greateſt *unworthineſs* is no objection in Chriſt's account; it is as much diſavowed by the goſpel, as *equivocal* generation is exploded by the diſcoveries of our improved philoſophy."

P. 329. l. 24. "From the King, *whoſe name is the* LORD *of hoſts,* let us expect (if he vouchſafes to ſhew us any mercy) not barely what correſponds with our low models of generoſity,—much leſs what we ſuppoſe proportioned to our fancied deſerts,—but what is imitable to the unknown magnificence of his name,

and

and the unbounded benevolence of his heart. Then we shall no longer be afraid, assuredly to trust to the gracious declaration, *that* CHRIST JESUS *is made of* GOD *to us wisdom, and righteousness, and sanctification, and redemption*: That HE hath *given* himself for us, hath *given* himself to us, with all the blessings of his purchase, of his SPIRIT, and of eternal life."

P. 331. l. 11. " That we all deserve this misery, is beyond dispute. We are also told, that the LORD JESUS has satisfied divine justice."

P. 332. l. 15. " You are *still corrupt;* does this exclude you from being the *very person* for whom the Saviour's righteousness is intended, and to whom it is promised ?"

P. 333. l. 3. " And sure it cannot be a fanciful persuasion of our health which renders us proper objects of his recovering grace."

P. 335. l. 3. " I behold it (*Theron*'s title) perfectly clear, not because you long or pray for it; but because the all-sufficient righteousness is granted to you *a sinner* in the record of the gospel."

P. 335. l. 22. " *If any man*, however unworthy his person, or obnoxious his character, *thirst;* thirst for something to make him happy ; let him not seek to that which satisfieth not, but *let him come to me* the fountain of living waters, *and drink* his fill.

" The clergyman," &c.

P. 336. l. 31. " They are to be enjoyed by *every one*. No exception is made."

P. 337. l. 18. " To us, says the prophet, a child is born."

P. 338. l. 19. " Since the LORD JEHOVAH *has given* us his SON and all his unutterable merits ; and also seals this grant unto us in every sacramental ordinance ; why should we not confide in it, as firmer than the firmest deed ? and far more inviolable, than any royal patent?"

" *Ther.* My servant never," &c.

P.

P. 350. l. 21, "It seems to be quite out of my reach."

Asp. "That is, because you still imagine something is to be done by you, to entitle to this immaculate and perfect righteousness; you give no credit to those declarations of heaven, which brings it near to your view and home to your condition. Remember rather the words of our LORD, *Come unto me, all ye that are weary, and heavy laden, and I will give you rest.*"

P. 351. l. 14. "Nothing short of these mercies, can afford any satisfaction to the guilty conscience, or *true* satisfaction to the restless soul.

"Say not then, my dear friend, that Christ, and the blessings of his purchase, *are beyond* your reach. They are now, even now, at your door.

P. 352. l. 34. "If you heard his voice, you would believe on him agreeable thereto. You then open the door, and *he sups with you*, makes his abode with you, manifests his salvation, and communicates his blessings. If you believed his promising word, you would no longer hesitate to believe on him accordingly. You then *sup with him*. This will be refreshing to your distressed soul, as the most sumptuous banquet to the famished stomach and craving appetite. *Expunge all from here to the words,*

Ther. "This I believe—That I am a lost sinner;" &c.

P. 353. l. 31. "He that believeth on the *Son* hath a chimerical? far from it; a real substantial happiness; even everlasting life.

"Can you doubt of his willingness to save the chief of sinners? or his sincerity in his declarations? Then go to mount *Calvary.*"

P. 354. l. 26. "What a stranger was I then, to the blindness of my understanding, and the hardness of my heart; to my bondage under unbelief, and my natural averseness to the way of salvation by grace through faith!"

Asp.

Asp. "Are you sure this is not now your case? This sentiment, though ever so just, will not palliate your present infidelity. Since the Great Jehovah has declared the grant of his Son to you a sinner; since he has thus given you eternal life in him; since he has warranted your immediate reception and enjoyment by his commands, invitations, and promises, you make him a liar in all; you reject his word as not to be depended on, every moment you thus unbelievingly hesitate." *Expunge from here to*

Ther. "But is not faith the work of God's Spirit? how, or in what manner, &c."

P. 356. l. 4. "I very much question, whether I shall ever be able to attain it."

Asp. "The true belief, *Theron*, has no existence without its proper object Christ, and is never to be considered in the light you speak of, that is, as a most refined and exalted virtue. When, upon the divine grant in the word, you behold Christ, as your given righteousness and strength, then you truly believe; you believe God's truth which can never deceive, you receive the gift which enriches you with grace and glory. But permit me to ask," &c.

P. 376. l. 19. "If you rely on the all-sufficiency of his gracious declarations as the foundation of immediate trust or confidence, as well as the all-sufficiency of his power."

l. 25. "Let the most wretched sinner, and most afflicted soul, *trust in the name of the Lord.*"

In note, p. 385. l. 5. "We only affirm, that an appropriating persuasion of salvation by Christ alone, is that confidence which properly answers to the divine report, and grant of a Saviour to be believed on for everlasting life."

P. 394. l. 27. *Asp.* "The *If* is what I greatly question; but of this I am certain, that you are still inclined to spare *Agag.*"

P. 395. l. 12. "You ask, whether the state of these

persons is *safe* and their faith *real?* I answer, What evidence is there of their *safety* or their *faith*, while Christ the only security is neglected, and the free grant of him to sinners thus disbelieved? Besides, why should, &c."

P. 396. l. 11. " GOD has freely loved me so as to give his Son unto me; CHRIST has graciously died for me, to take share in his death as my own; and the HOLY GHOST sanctifies me in the belief and appropriating confidence, arising from these precious truths."

P. 398. l. 30. " When the divine SPIRIT, speaking in the gracious declarations of the gospel, manifests the grant of Christ to me a sinner, then am I enabled to receive and appropriate his death as the desert of my sins, and his obedience as the matter of my justification."

P. 399. l. 3. " May I firmly believe on Christ for everlasting life? may I firmly believe, that in this infinitely-meritorious Redeemer I have granted unto me pardon and acceptance, &c."

P. 402. l. 21. " I do more than pardon my dear *Theron*. I feel for him, and I sympathize with him; not because he has not sufficient evidence from God's word, for trusting in Christ for everlasting life; but because I have also felt that perverse tendency in my own heart, to mistrust the infallible word of my God, as tho' he was less to be depended on than fallible man."

In like manner, p. 243, 244, 284, 285, 295. were to be corrected, and all other passages in his writings which might be understood, as making thirstings, awakenings, earnest prayers, sorrows, tears, good desires, or sense of unworthiness, as the encouragement for confidence. This Mr *Hervey* acknowledged was inconsistent with his main design, which was to come to God by him only, who was able to save to the uttermost; but he had been drawn sometimes into this way of expressing himself by too great a regard for the current customs; and not considering,

that

that till the divine relieving truth appear in view, the wishes and desires of the distressed are as much pointed against the salvation of the guilty, as the carelessness of the profane. He was sensible, that " the gospel-history gives us no instance of an unbeliever diligent to obtain faith;" and therefore intended to expunge every thing that tended to encourage such mistakes.

When he took notice of " a speculative assent to all the principles of religion," he intended by it such agreeing with the current opinions as will stand consistent with sentiments quite subversive of the saving truth. Not such a knowledge of the truth as the apostle speaks of, when he says, *Ye know the truth, and that no lie is of the truth.* He well knew, that there was no man, but he that is taught of God, could be satisfied with the apostolic account of salvation; and would have informed *Theron*, had he had another opportunity, " that if he attempted to do any thing easy, or difficult, under the notion of an act of believing, or any other act, in order to his acceptance with God, he only thereby heaped up more wrath against himself."

He was also sensible, that a man may be very useful and amiable amongst men, and at the same time an utter enemy to the grace of God's kingdom:—That he had been too forward in commendations of those, who were no friends to apostolic Christianity. His design was only to commend what was amiable in every one, passing over their blemishes.—In this design he acknowledged, he was carried to an extreme. When he says of *Erasmus* and *Locke*, that they sat at the feet of Jesus, he only meant to express in an elegant way, that they betook themselves to the reading of the scriptures, and not to vindicate their notions.

And he counted it an observation well worthy regard, that " it may be maintained by some, that conversion is carried on by grace assisting nature; and by others, that this matter is wholly conducted by irresistible grace; and yet both sides may be equally disaffected to that doctrine, which maintains the work finished by Christ on the cross, to be the only requisite to justification.—And that while many Christian teachers maintain, that no man can be eminently virtuous without divine energy, they say no more than Heathen philosophers have said before them."

These remarks and observations may be sufficient to direct the intelligent reader of *Theron* and *Aspasio*, to avoid needless objections, and also to improve that performance more agreeably to the scriptures and the author's own mind.

It appears by the Letters *prefixed to this* Defence, *that an improvement of Mr* Marshall's *book was intended, to obviate as much as possible all objections; which, through the pressing importunities of the printer, and Mr* Hervey's *hopes of accomplishing a fourth volume of* THERON *and* ASPASIO, *was not executed. The following is a plan of such improvement, where, by changing the fourteen* directions *into the form of* assertions *or* propositions, *the strongest objections are enervated.*

ASSERTION I.

THAT practice and manner of life, which the scripture calls holiness, righteousness, or godliness, obedience, true religion, is not attained by our most resolved endeavours, but is given through the knowledge of him that has called us to glory and virtue.

ASSERT. II.

No man can love God, till he knows him, nor till he knows him to be his everlasting friend. Therefore the spring of true holiness, is a well-grounded persuasion of our reconciliation with God, and of our future enjoyment of the everlasting heavenly happiness, and of sufficient strength given in him for all that he calls us unto.

ASSERT. III.

These endowments, so necessary to the obedience of love, are continued in the fulness of Christ, and are enjoyed only by union and fellowship with him.

Assert. IV.

The means or instruments whereby the Spirit of God accomplisheth our union with Christ, and our fellowship with him in all holiness, are the gospel, whereby Christ entereth into our hearts, begetting us to the faith whereby we actually receive Christ himself, with all his fulness, unto the hope of eternal life by him. And thus, by the influence of the Spirit of truth, we unfeignedly believe the gospel, and also believe on Christ, as he is revealed and freely promised to us therein, for all his salvation.

Assert. V.

The practice of true holiness is not attained by any endeavours of our natural state, but is a blessing of that new state given in Jesus Christ, and partook of by union and fellowship with Christ through faith.

Assert. VI.

Those that endeavour to perform sincere obedience to all the commands of Christ, as the condition whereby they are to procure for themselves a right and title to salvation, and a good ground to trust on him for the same, do seek their salvation by the works of the law, and not by the faith of Christ, as he is revealed in the gospel: and they shall never be able to perform sincerely any true holy obedience by all such endeavours.

Assert. VII.

We are not to imagine, that our hearts and lives must be changed from sin to holiness, in any measure, before we may safely venture to trust on Christ for the sure enjoyment of himself and his salvation.

Assert. VIII.

True holiness of heart and life, hath its due order where God hath placed it, that is, after union with Christ, justification, and the gift of the Holy Ghost. It is not therefore to be expected, but in that order, as what accompanies salvation.

Assert. IX.

It is only by the comforts of the gospel revealing a just God and a Saviour, that God works in us to will and to do of his good pleasure.

Assert. X.

The comforts of the gospel, necessary to Christian obedience, contain sufficient grounds of assurance of our salvation, not because we believe, but in a way of immediate trust and confidence. Therefore, instead of seeking other methods of peace and holiness, we must endeavour to believe or trust on Christ confidently; persuading and assuring ourselves, according to the divine declarations, that God freely gives to us an interest in Christ and his salvation, according to his gracious promise.

Assert. XI.

It is therefore belonging to the practical part of the Christian life, to maintain the same immediate trust and confidence in dependence on the divine faithfulness, not to suffer us to be confounded, that so our enjoyment of Christ, union and fellowship with him, and all holiness by him, may be continued and increased in us.

Assert. XII.

The scripture calls upon Christians to walk no longer according to the principles or means of practice that belong unto the natural or original state of man, but only according to that new state given in Christ, which we receive by faith, and the principles and means of practice, that properly belong thereunto; and to strive to continue and increase in such a manner of practice.

Assert. XIII.

All ordinances of divine appointment, for the establishment and increase of our faith and love, are to be considered only in this way of believing in Christ, and walking in him according to this new state given in him.

Assert. XIV.

That we may be confirmed in holiness only by believing in Christ, and walking in him by faith, according to the former assertions, we may take encouragement from the great advantages of this way, and excellent properties of it.

A Recommendatory Letter

FROM

Mr HERVEY

TO THE

Publisher of a new Edition of MARSHALL on Sanctification.

SIR,

IT gives me no small pleasure to hear, that you are going to republish Mr MARSHALL's *Gospel-mystery of sanctification* *. The instruction, consolation, and spiritual improvement, which I myself have received from that solid and judicious treatise, excite in me a pleasing hope, that it may be equally instructive and advantageous to others.

The recommendation of it in *Theron* and *Aspasio*, with which you propose to introduce the new edition, is at your service. To this proposal I consent the more readily, because Mr MARSHALL's book may be looked upon as no improper *supplement* to those dialogues and letters. The author of which intended to have closed his plan with a dissertation on practical holiness, or evangelical obedience. But this design was dropped; partly on account of his very declining

---

* It is said, by the very best judge of propriety in sacred writing, *Great is the mystery of godliness*, 1 Tim. iii. 16. This passage, I presume, Mr MARSHALL had in his view, when he pitched upon a *title* for his book. And this passage will render it superior to all censure; unexceptionably just and proper.

ning health; partly, because the work swelled, under his hands, far beyond his expectation.

He has been advised, once more, to resume the pen; and treat that grand subject with some degree of copiousness and particularity. If he should be enabled to execute, what he acknowledges to be expedient, the doctrines already discussed, and the privileges already displayed, will furnish the principal materials for his essay. Justification, *free justification*, thro' the righteousness of JESUS CHRIST, is the sacred fleece from which he would spin his thread, and weave his garment; agreeably to that important text, *Ye are bought with a price; therefore glorify GOD* *.—If Providence, in all things wise, and in all things gracious, should see fit to with-hold either time or ability for the accomplishment of my purpose, I do, by these presents, nominate and depute Mr MARSHALL *to supply my lack of service.*

Mr MARSHALL expresses my thoughts; he prosecutes my scheme; and not only pursues the same end, but proceeds in the same way. I shall therefore rejoice in the prospect of having the *Gospel-mystery of sanctification* stand as a fourth volume to *Theron and Aspasio*. Might I be allowed, without the charge of irreverence, to use the beautiful images of an inspired writer, I could with great satisfaction say, *If* this *be a wall, that will build upon it a palace of ivory; if* this *be a door, that will inclose it with boards of cedar* †.

Mr MARSHALL represents *true holiness* as consisting in the love of GOD, and the love of man;—that unforced, unfeigned, and most rational love of GOD, which arises from a discovery of his unspeakable mercy and infinite kindness to us; that cordial, disinterested, and universal love of man, which flows from the possession of a satisfactory and delightful portion in the LORD JEHOVAH. These duties, of love

---

* 1 Cor. vi. 20. † Cant. viii. 9.

love to our Creator and our fellow-creatures, are regarded as the sum and substance of the *moral* law; as the root from which all other branches of pure and undefiled religion spring.—Holiness, thus stated, is considered, not as the means, but as a part, a distinguished part of our salvation; or, rather, as the very central point, in which all the means of grace, and all the ordinances of religion, terminate.

Man, in a natural state, is absolutely incapable of practising this holiness, or enjoying this happiness.—If you ask, What is meant by *a natural state*? it is that state, in which we are under the guilt of sin, and the curse of the law; are subject to the power of Satan, and influenced by evil propensities.—From this state none are released, but by being united to CHRIST; or, as the apostle speaks, by *CHRIST dwelling in the heart through faith* *.

Faith, according to Mr MARSHALL, is a *real persuasion*, that GOD is pleased to give CHRIST and his salvation; to give him freely without any recommending qualifications, or preparatory conditions; to give him, not to some sinners only, but to *me* a sinner in particular.—It is likewise an *actual receiving* of CHRIST, with all the benefits, privileges, and promises of the gospel; in pursuance of the divine gift, and on no other warrant than the divine grant.—This last office is particularly insisted on, as an *essential* part, or as the *principal* act of faith. To perform which, there is no rational, no possible way; unless, as our author declares, we do, in some measure, persuade and assure ourselves †, that CHRIST and his salvation are ours.

As

* Eph. iii. 17.
† It is not, by this expression, affirmed, or insinuated, that we are able to produce faith in ourselves, by any power of our own. This self-sufficiency the author has professedly and frequently disclaimed; asserting, That " the SPIRIT of " GOD habitually disposes and inclines our hearts to a right " performance of this most important act."—This manner of

As faith is such a persuasion of the heart, and such a reception of CHRIST, it assures the soul of salvation by *its own* act; antecedent to all reflection on its fruits or effects, on marks or evidences.—It assures the soul of acquittance from guilt, and reconciliation to GOD; of a title to the everlasting inheritance, and of grace sufficient for every case of need.—By the exercise of this faith, and the enjoyment of these blessings, we are *sanctified;* conscience is pacified, and the heart purified; we are delivered from the dominion of sin, disposed to holy tempers, and furnished for an holy practice.

Here, I apprehend, our author will appear singular, this is the place in which he seems to go *quite out of the common road.* The generality of serious people look upon these unspeakable blessings as the reward of holiness; to be received, after we have sincerely practised universal holiness; not as necessary, previously necessary to perform any act of true holiness. This is the stumbling-block, which our legal minds, dim with prejudice, and swollen with pride, will hardly get over.—However, these endowments of our new state are, in our author's opinion, the effectual, and the only effectual expedient, to produce sanctification. They are the very method which the eternal SPIRIT has ordained, for our bringing forth those *fruits of righteousness, which are by JESUS CHRIST unto the glory and praise of GOD**.—Whereas, if there be any appearances of virtue, or any efforts of obedience, which

---

speaking is used, I imagine, for two reasons: To point out the first and chief work, which we are to be doing, incessantly and assiduously, till our LORD come: To remind us, that we must not expect to have faith wrought in us, by some fatality of supernatural operation, without any application or endeavour of our own; but that we must make it our diligent endeavour, and our daily business, to believe in CHRIST. We must *labour to enter into this rest,* and *shew all diligence to the full assurance of hope.* * Philip. i. 11.

which spring not from these motives and means of practice, Mr MARSHALL treats them as " reprobate " silver." He cannot allow them the character of *gospel-holiness.*

This is the plan, and these are the leading sentiments, of the ensuing treatise. To establish or defend them, is not my aim. This is attempted, and, I think, executed, in the work itself. My aim is, only to exhibit the most distinguishing principles, in one short sketch, and clear point of view; that the reader may the more easily remember them, and, by this key, enter the more perfectly into the writer's meaning.—Let him that is *spiritual* * judge ; and reject or admit, as each tenet shall appear to correspond or disagree with the infallible word. Only let candour, not rigour, fill the chair; and interpret an unguarded expression, or a seemingly inconsistent-sentence, by the general tenor of the discourse.

We are not to expect much pathos of address, or any delicacy of composition. Here the gospel-diamond is set, not in gold, but in steel; not where it may display the most sprightly beam, or pour a flood of brilliancy; but where it may do the most signal service, and afford a fund of usefulness.—Neither is this book so particularly calculated for careless insensible sinners, as for those who are awakened into a solicitous attention to their everlasting interests ; who are earnestly inquiring, with the Philippian jailor, *What shall I do to be saved* †? or passionately crying, in the language of the apostle, *O wretched man that I am! who shall deliver me from the body of this death* ‡? If there be any such, as no doubt there are many, in the Christian world, I would say, with regard to them, as the *Israelitish* captive said concerning her illustrious but afflicted master, *Would GOD my master were with the prophet that is in Samaria; for he would recover him*

of

---

* 1 Cor. ii, 15. † Acts xvi. 30. ‡ Rom. vii. 24.

of his leprosy *. O that such persons were acquainted with the doctrines, and influenced by the directions contained in this treatise! they would, under the divine blessing, recover them from their distress, and restore them to tranquillity; they would *comfort their hearts, and* thereby *establish them in every good word and work* †.

But I am going to anticipate what the following extract ‡ speaks. I shall therefore only add my hearty wishes, that you may meet with encouragement and success in the publication of this truly-valuable piece. Since there is, in this instance, an evident connection between your private interest and the general good; I think you may promise yourself the approbation and acceptance of the public; as you will assuredly have all the support and assistance that can be given, by,

SIR,

Your humble servant,

*Weston-Favell, near
Northampton,*   JAMES HERVEY.
Nov. 5. 1756.

---

* 2 Kings v. 3.   † 2 Thess. ii. 17.
‡ This extract, or the recommendation given of this excellent book, entitled, *The gospel-mystery of sanctification*, is to be found in our author's works, vol. iii. p. 389. note.

End of the FOURTH VOLUME.

www.ingramcontent.com/pod-product-compliance
Lightning Source LLC
Chambersburg PA
CBHW020532300426
44111CB00008B/639